Families As We Are

Publication of *Families As We Are* has been supported by

The United Nations Children's Fund (UNICEF)
The United Nations Development Programme (UNDP)
The United Nations Environment Programme (UNEP)
The United Nations Fund for Women (UNIFEM)
The United Nations Population Fund (UNFPA)
The Secretariat for the International Year of the Family—1994

The John D. and Catherine T. MacArthur Foundation
The Ms. Foundation for Women
The Summit Foundation
The Wallace Global Fund

Families As We Are

Conversations from Around the World

Perdita Huston

Foreword by Richard C. Holbrooke

THE FEMINIST PRESS
AT THE CITY UNIVERSITY OF NEW YORK
NEW YORK

Published by The Feminist Press at The City University of New York
The Graduate Center, 365 Fifth Avenue, Suite 5406, New York, NY 10016
www.feministpress.org

First edition, 2001

Photo credits: Perdita Huston, pages 34, 73, 79, 82, 94, 104, 144, 148, 152, 154,
158, 161, 168, 173, 175, 179, 185, 191, 196, 198, 203, 213, 235, 238, 245, 247,
252, 253, 275, 290, 293, 296, 310, 312, 321, 323, and 327; Stanley Staniski, pages
36, 41, 55, 58, 64, 68, 111, 113, 129, 134, 136, 215, 250, 257, 259, 265, 284, 317,
and 318; Ed Vinson, page 44; Kiyimba family, page 103; Barros family, page 122;
Egan/Brooks family, page 206.

Library of Congress Cataloging-in-Publication Data

Huston, Perdita, 1936–
    Families as we are : conversations from around the world / Perdita Huston;
    foreword by Richard C. Holbrooke.—1st ed.
        p.   cm.
    ISBN 1-55861-250-5 (hardcover : alk. paper)
    1. Family—Cross-cultural studies.   2. Interviews.   I. Title.

HQ518 .H85 2001
306.85—dc21

                                                                    2001025861

The Feminist Press would like to thank Mariam K. Chamberlain, Florence Howe,
Joanne Markell, and Genevieve Vaughan for their generosity in supporting this book.

Text design and typesetting by Dayna Navaro
Printed on acid-free paper by Transcontinental Printing
Printed in Canada

09 08 07 06 05 04 03 02 01   5 4 3 2 1

For the families of those who are recorded here

For my family, extended, kin and non-kin, and grandchildren
Gabriel, Elie, Eliza Marion, and Adrien

And in memory of Shirley Smith Anderson, Jonas Salk, and
Thomas P. Wilson, whose intellect and friendship enriched so many

Contents

Foreword

Perdita Huston wants me to write about her book in this foreword, and I shall, in a moment. To begin, however, I must insist, in total disregard of her wishes, on discussing Perdita herself. Characteristically, Perdita wishes to remain virtually invisible, letting the story of the modern family emerge through the voices of her subjects themselves. But first a word about the author.

Perdita is an American original, born and raised in what she calls the "charmed security" of a traditional family in Maine. After college in Colorado and Paris, she married a French doctor who was drafted and sent to Algeria during the Algerian war for independence. Living in a tiny village in the most dangerous area of Algeria, the Constantinois, Perdita turned herself into a medical social worker, doing everything from food distribution to helping deliver babies to serving as a local scribe for the illiterate. This experience began a permanent identification by this tall, striking, and brilliant woman with those who, in her words, "have little voice, about whom the educated tend to pontificate without knowing of what they speak."

Many people try to help the disenfranchised, the uneducated, the poor, the voiceless. Their intentions are good, but all too often they bring theories with them that do not stand up to reality. Then, if their programs or ideals fail, they blame the very people they are trying to help.

Perdita, of course, is different. She *listens*. From the beginning, she asked questions, and did not offer untested advice. She set out to *learn* from the the disenfranchised, the uneducated, the poor, the voiceless. And then she gave them a voice. She published her first book in 1977, called *Message from the Village*. Few listened at first, but Perdita persevered.

Her second book made a tremendous impact on me. It was called, quite simply, *Third World Women Speak Out*. Published by the Overseas

Development Council with Praeger Publishers in 1978, it was, as far as I can tell, the first book that documented—in women's own words—the unexpected *negative* consequences that even a good development process had on Third World women. Having lived in Southeast Asia and Morocco, and worked on development programs, I thought I understood something about the development process. But Perdita's book was an absolute revelation, showing, among other things, that foreign aid in a developing economy often increased the inequality between men and women, especially in the agricultural sector. New agricultural methods and technologies would be controlled by the men; leisure time would be enjoyed by them; education programs were not offered to women; and so on. Development, wrongly applied, could actually disadvantage women. It was a profound and prophetic book. Even today, many people do not realize how pernicious the problem has been, but exposing it was essential.

Perdita alternated between writing and action. We worked together in the Peace Corps, where both of us served in one of the most rewarding of all public sector jobs, Peace Corps country director (she in Mali and Bulgaria, I in Morocco).

Now this extraordinary woman has turned her attention to the changing nature of the family, from Missouri to Bangladesh. She still believes in the centrality of family, but her interviews suggest that the nature and definition of family has evolved in many ways that are not yet fully understood. Deeply traditional in her attachment to the idea of family, Perdita is characteristically open to examining the different forms it takes in the modern world. Some of her interviews will perhaps distress some people, but she wants us to see things as they really are, and come to terms with the many different types of "families" that now exist, in order to help preserve what matters at the core. The "mythical, harmonious past," she says, should not obscure to us the fact that "families of the past were no different from those of today: some were kind and nurturing, others exploitative and cruel." Literature, she reminds us, is "full of examples."

As always, Perdita is a listener. She is, in her way, still the scribe of the Constantinois, writing down the words and thoughts of the voiceless, helping give them shape and, above all, giving them to us.

Richard C. Holbrooke
New York City
March 2001

Acknowledgments

That five specialized agencies of the United Nations system chose to support this consultation with families demonstrates that each agency, urged on by the International Year of the Family, saw in this effort a vehicle to better understand their unique missions. The John D. and Catherine T. MacArthur Foundation, the Ms. Foundation for Women, the Summit Foundation, and the Wallace Global Fund believed that the voices of families should contribute to public policy debates and generously supported this work. In addition, the Centre for Development and Population Activities (CEDPA) offered administrative support; Population Action International (PAI) provided an office space for research interns; the Japanese Organization for International Cooperation in Family Planning (JOICFP) provided travel assistance; to all three, I am most grateful. These organizations and foundations and the UN agencies are to be credited with this publication, although they are in no way responsible for its content.

It is with considerable respect that I express gratitude to the patient individuals who transcribed hundreds of hours of recorded interviews. Appreciation is also due to the dozens of interpreters, both volunteer and professional, who assisted me. Their skills and sensitivity were essential to enhancing trust and candor in the interviews. I am also indebted to the many UN drivers whose skill and courteous patience contributed to this project.

I would also like to mention several people in specific countries. In Bangladesh: at Naripokkho, Shireen Huq, Mahbooba (Leena) Mahmood, Rokya Buli; Raisul Awal Mahmood (BIDS); Begum Masuda Begum Shefali (Nari Uddug Kendra). In Brazil: Thais Corral (REDEH); Binka Le Breton, Ana de Filgeiras, Meuma Anguiar (DAWN); Ceres Fiacmo de Almeida, Ana Cristina de Almeida Carvalmo (SOS Crianca); Maria Barcelos (Cacoal). In China: Mme. Zhung Zhiming, Professor Liu Qilin (Soong Ching Ling Foundation);

Zhang Yexing, Lu Xuehu, Mme Liu Guiha, Yu Ming Quan (Ningxia); Susan Holcombe (UNICEF). In Egypt: Heydayat Abdel Nabi (UNIC); Fatma Khafagy (UNICEF); Azziza Hussein, Aida Gindy; Barbara Ibrahim (Population Council); Dr. Marlene Konawati (Center for Development Services); Ingy Rouchdy; Mahfouz El Ansari; Marlene Tadros; Khadra Salah Ibrahim; Salha Awad. In El Salvador: Nora Staben (UNFPA); Anders Kompass (UNDP); Patricia Weiss-Fagan, Ana Kelly (UNHCR); First Lady Margarita de Cristiani; Umberto Pacas; Isabel Borja; Dr. Jorge Antonio Giammettei; Oscar Morales Velado; Zoila de Innocenti; Dr. Simon Isidro Rivera Argueta; Anita Calderon de Buitrago; Ana Virginia de Huezo; Maria Teresa Delgado de Mejia. In Mali: Alain Everett, Miriam Traore Kanakomo (UNICEF); Abdoulaye Allassane Maiga, Aminata Dramane Traore, Jacquline Urbain; Tieman Diarra (ISH), Sy Sokona Diabate; Mme. Traore Nene Dolo; Mamadou K Konate (CERPOD). In Japan: Aiko Iijima, Yuriko Ashino, Yasuro Kon (JOICFP); Anwarul Karim Chowdhury (UNICEF); Akiko Kato; Ms. Myoshi Ohba, Hilary Salmon, Kuniko Funabashi. In Jordan: Hassan Shawareb (UNICEF); Sri Nasser, Helmi Sari, Amal Sabbagh, In'am. In Thailand: Suteera Thomson (GDRI); Khunying Kanitha Wichiencharoen (Association for the Promotion of the Status of Women); Keith R. Emrich, Marcia M. Brewster (ESCAP); Juree Vichit-Vadakan (NIDA); Rotjana Phraesrithong (Duang Prateep Foundation); Amara Pongsapich (SRI) Chulalongkorn University; Ornan Chanlerfa, Jintana Kamphet. In Uganda: Lars Sylvan (UNDP); Carol Jaenson (UNICEF); Joyce Mungherea (YMCA); Hon. Speciosa Wandira Kazibwe, then Minister of Women in Development Culture and Youth; Rev. Kefa Sempangi (African Foundation); Joan Harriet Babara; Gertrude Bajenja; Alice Turyahikayo, Noreen Kareeba, Anne Kaddumukasa (TASO). In the United States of America: volunteer interns Alissa Strauss, Janeen M. Shaffer, Fahnya S Bean; research assistant Jennifer Wisnewski Kaczor; Adrienne Fitch-Frankel, Kelly Rozewicz, Shayna Steinger; translators/transcribers Francoise Gayet, Kassem Tfayli, Alexandra Martinovic, and Sylvia Carts.

I am also grateful for personal support from Margaret Snyder, Robin Morgan, Susan Goodwillie Stedman, Sally Epstein and Donald Collins, Peggy Curlin, Sharon Camp, Catherine Cameron, Vicki Sant, Gloria Steinem, Page Wilson, Lael and Ron Stegall, Anne Zill, Nancy Leindenfrost, Catherine Mumaw, Joan Martin Brown, Valeriana Kallab, Jennifer Froistad, Nancy Graham, Joan Fox-Przeworski, and, tirelessly, Karen and Fritz Mulhauser.

Having tried for many months to interest a publisher in a book on global family trends, I found few willing to take on the project. The Feminist Press at the City University of New York was the exception, believing that we must listen to the smallest unit of society in this era of globalization. To

Florence Howe, Jean Casella, Lisa London, and all their colleagues I express gratitude for their generous personal and professional support.

Lastly, I am grateful to all of the family members who candidly and courageously shared their stories. Time has moved on since I begn this consultation with families; people's lives have changed, ended, or begun. Women of these families have given birth to more children; some of the elders and a youthful husband have been taken from their families. In Uganda, Benedict Kiyimba passed away from heart failure three months after being interviewed. In Washington, D.C., Marina Meija's husband died in a traffic accident two days before he was to be interviewed. Alvin Bowman of Bishop, California, and Leslie Young of Keokuk, Iowa, have also passed on. I feel privileged to have known them.

There are others, to be sure. The family cycle continues, in grief and in joy.

Perdita Huston
Washington, D.C.
March 2001

Introduction | Listening to Others, Hearing Ourselves

We have to know where we come from to understand where we go.
—Zulu song, "Give to the Tortoise"

The view from the hilltop was of a vast expanse of rolling green hills, reaching all the way to the horizon. The cool afternoon breeze moved among us as we sat in handmade wooden chairs placed in front of the modest home. I was visiting the home of Azaliya and Kengeye Rwabulinbale, an elderly farming couple in western Uganda, a nation the size of Oregon snuggled in the heart of East Africa. A legend contends that if you drop a seed in Ugandan earth it will sprout forthwith. It may well be true: lush fields and rich soils abound, village markets overflow with fruits and vegetables.

Eighty-two-year-old Azaliya is a small man in both height and frame, and the oversized jacket he wore made him appear even smaller. When he settled in his present home in 1947, he was alone, he said, amid thick forests and wild animals. In the intervening years a multitude of settlers, a school, several churches, and furniture had entered his life. The animals went away. So, too, did his children. "I grew coffee to pay the children's school fees and provide for them. Now they don't come back to help me. Their heads are elsewhere."

His wife Kengeye, a tall, lanky woman of seventy, joined in. "We thought that by giving our children education we were doing something good. The end result is they're useless. They dress smartly, go to discos, and drink. Instead of devoting themselves to our country, our children push it back. And they don't listen." Kengeye covered her ears to make us laugh at the young's foolish ways, adding, "Madame, you are discovering many things in your travels. Could you give us a plan for our children so they calm down?"

There was a relaxed moment of laughter before Azaliya spoke again. With a swooping gesture of his arm, he pointed toward the distant hills and asked, "Madame, tell us. Do you meet any families that live in harmony?"

Azaliya's question is not unusual. In this era of economic and cultural globalization, people everywhere are puzzled by the transformations they witness.

In the lifetime of our living elders, technological innovations have pro-pelled us from horse and buggy to space and cyberspace. We have jettisoned traditions that had sustained social order for centuries. World population has quadrupled, political and economic structures have been transformed, and the context in which we live was recast at a fearsome pace.

It is this pace of change that sets us apart from generations past. It demands immediate adjustment, obliging us to define our lives almost as we go along. This is not an occurrence taking place in one society or another, but a worldwide phenomenon. Whether we like it or not, there are a host of trends—some positive, others not—that circle the world to influence our lives and permeate our thinking. The global village is here, and it is us. We come to understand we are members of a global family when we hear others speak of the same forces. We find we are not alone, and can learn from one another how best to adapt to that we cannot control.

We must not let ourselves be caught up in a fruitless debate among change-resistant leaders who would convince us that any modification in family struc-ture is disastrous. Throughout human experience, families have met the challenge of change. Indeed, there are two constants: change and family. In the following chapters we will listen to families in diverse cultures explain how these constants converge.

Today's families are the result of this ongoing process and their infinite variety demonstrates our creativity in caring for one another in a rapidly changing world. It is the intent of this book to learn how families in vast-ly different settings describe global trends and explore ways of adapting to them. By interviewing three or more generations in each family, we gain per-spective on the transformations in family structure and relationships that took place in the past century and continue today.

The twentieth century was indeed a transforming century. Family elders tell us that in the early 1900s and well into the post–World War II era, food was neither as abundant nor as well distributed as it is today. Living conditions, yet to be eased by modern technologies and medicines, were harsh and dan-gerous. Maternal death was common and the average life span for men at mid-century remained only in the forties.[1] The elders interviewed for this book reported that, for the most part, women had few opportunities for education or inde-pendence; respect and status were gained by hard work in family production, well-raised children, neat homes, and kitchen skills. Women also cared for the sick and the elderly within the home. Responsibility for the family's safety and well-being resided in its males, whose authority was rarely questioned. Guided by their elders, boys learned the skills needed to carry on the fami-ly's livelihood; girls learned to manage homes and provide labor for family production in agriculture, cottage industries, or child care.

No nation, in 1900, had universal suffrage, whereas nearly all do at the beginning of the twenty-first century. Indeed, one of the most dynamic influences on family life and society in the last century was the extension of concepts of individual worth and human rights. Following the adoption of the Universal Declaration of Human Rights in 1948, the rights agenda continued to evolve, and now includes a host of international instruments covering cultural, environmental, and economic rights of individuals and groups. As these ideas became better known and widespread, public and private behavior was altered. Colonized and oppressed peoples organized and reached for democratic expression. As colonies became independent in the 1960s, and as citizens became better educated and informed, the notion of individual worth took flight and challenged both political systems and age-old customs. As sons and daughters sought to define their own lives, strict patriarchal family structures began to be viewed as antithetical to individual rights and democracy. The foundations of society and family were shaken, and reshaped.

Gradually, wrote environmental activist Thomas W. Wilson, "people were laying claim to their value as distinct individuals, not cogs in a family wheel."[2] Hierarchical structures, mostly male and patriarchal, from religious communities to institutions of learning, parliaments, businesses, and families, were recast by emerging democratic values. Family roles and relationships were refashioned among the old and the young, women and men, parents and children. When the century ended, injustice in many forms still remained, but the gain in individual rights was manifest.

A second factor shaping the course of family life in the twentieth century was the search for security in times of economic transformation. No society remained untouched. As more and more people were employed outside the home—and often far from that home—the number of extended families shrank, and even nuclear families were sometimes broken apart. This remains an ongoing process in many areas of the world, as is the move of families to urban areas. In 1900, barely 13.6 percent of the world's population was urban-based. By 2005, the UN estimates that urban dwellers will reach 50 percent. Twenty years later, it will reach 60 percent.[3] This wholesale urbanization and the rural exodus on which it feeds holds profound consequences for family life and relationships.

Those who speak most eloquently of these trends are, of course, our elders. They praise the changes that have brought improved health and nutrition, education, and diverse employment opportunities. At the same time, they claim the pace of change in the contemporary world often outstrips their ability to adjust to new technologies and lifestyles. Feelings of alienation and vulnerability often result. The young, they say, are more interested in television, pop music, and imported youth culture than in learning about family history from their elders.

In nearly every society, economic imperatives thrust women into the monetized economy. In subsistence agricultural communities, in which women have supplied over half the agricultural labor, the burden was particularly harsh when the family turned to producing cash crops. Women's labor was doubled by the need to work both on family food crops and cash crops. In highly industrialized regions, women entered the workforce at all levels and in increasing numbers. The International Labor Organization (ILO) reported that the percentage of women in the global labor force had reached 60.7 percent by 2000.[4] Economic pressure also resulted in the wide-scale emigration for wage employment. Cross-border labor migrants number 40 million per year and, when counting their dependents, the total reaches between 80 and 97 million people.[5] This massive movement of people—the majority of them men—has profound consequences for family relationships and stability.

Households headed by women are increasing everywhere, due to migration, divorce, widowhood, political conflict, or simply abandonment. In some nations, the percentage of women-headed households reached 30.4 percent in urban areas and 30 percent in rural regions. In Africa, the percentage climbs to 60 percent in some rural areas.[6]

Meanwhile, access to education, broadened legal rights, and a worldwide feminist movement expanded women's knowledge of the wider world, of one another, and of their own individual potentials. The radical notion that women could aspire to rights and opportunities hitherto available only to men was finding its way to women everywhere. Domestic violence—long considered "women's lot" to be borne in silence—was exposed and condemned as a violation of the most basic human rights.[7] Although the problem persists, the silence surrounding it has been broken, along with the silence around such widespread problems as rape, sexual abuse, and workplace harassment and discrimination.

At mid-century, medically approved and reliable contraceptive methods became available in many industrialized societies and, in the ensuing years, to less developed nations as well. For the first time, many couples had the opportunity to choose when, and if, to have children and to plan for an optimum family size. For women, the physical and psychological consequences were far-reaching. Planned pregnancies freed millions of women from ill health and fear—though for social and economic reasons, millions more still await free and safe access to contraception.[8]

There has been much discussion about the changing roles of women in contemporary society, but the debate has often ignored what is happening in men's lives. Conversations herein reveal that men of all ages are confused by the changes in our societies that result in a shifting of their roles and responsibilities. Such confusion is understandable, given the fact that for the greater part of recorded history being born male has been a guarantee of privilege and authority. But patriarchal power was associated with the capacity to provide for one's family; in today's world, economic and demographic realities often thwart men's ability to do so. A father's or grandfather's skills prove useless in a rapidly evolving technological era. Livelihoods must be sought in constantly shifting, increasingly competitive, often faraway settings.

The fact that one quarter of the world's households are headed by women raises the question of how well men are adjusting to the new times—how well they assume the responsibilities of son, husband, father, and provider (or co-provider) in times of social transformation. Divorce rates have risen to over 50 percent of all once-married couples in some regions.[9] In the United States 40 percent of divorced fathers pay no child support; in Japan, the figure reaches 75 percent.[10] The term dead-beat dad has entered common parlance.

The youth of this new century are faced with the most rapidly changing economic and technological society ever known. Access to education and to information technologies offers exposure to a world that was unknown in their parents' time. Generally better educated and more self-confident, the young are less willing to accept parental control or exploitative partners. Where in many societies parents once arranged their children's marriages, the tendency toward mutual choice, the "love match," built on "partnership," has gained credence and is becoming a common goal of young people around the world. The problem lies now in the fact that in many nations, millions of young people are unable to marry and start a family due to a lack of employment opportunities.

The physical place, or environment, in which families reside can have a dramatic effect on family living arrangements, health, prosperity, and safety. Small dwelling size, for example, dramatically reduces the possibility of living in extended family groups. By 2000, nearly half the world's people lived in urban settings, where millions of people are crowded into unsanitary slums.[11] In addition, families are the first to suffer the consequences of environmental degradation and poor management of communities. Soils, pasture lands, forests, seas, and rivers are the foundation on which millions of families build their livelihoods, yet these natural systems have become seriously degraded in the past century. A May 2000 report, for example, found that soil degradation has reduced food production on about 16 percent of the world's cropland.[12] Air pollution clouds cities and foul slum quarters menace public health. Such worldwide phenomena as toxic waste, acid rain, and climate change threaten all regions.

The twentieth century was one of continuous conflict. Warfare escalated from a clash of opposing armies to wholesale killing of civilians through high-tech bombings and gruesomely low-tech genocides. Sadly, such new terms as *ethnic cleansing* and *post-traumatic stress disorder* had to be added to our vocabulary.

To the political, economic, and ecological turmoil of past decades must be added the specter of a new health crisis that threatens the survival of millions of individuals and leaves millions of orphans in its wake, the human immunodeficiency virus (HIV). According to the 2000 UNAIDS report, over 58 million people have been infected with HIV since the onset of the epidemic fifteen years before.[13] The long-term consequences of the HIV pandemic, be they social, financial, or emotional, are yet another burden families and nations must bear.

Taken together, these changes have undermined our sense of continuity and security. In public and private spheres, issues of family well-being are widely discussed. In the United States, the debate has largely focussed on "family values"—or, more precisely, a fear of their loss. The media depict family discord. The clergy exhort parishioners to maintain stable families. Politicians blame every social ill on the decline of "family values" and promise to restore, defend, and promote them. And the United Sates is not alone in facing this quandary; on all continents, one encounters people who say that the family is somehow in decline.

When I first spoke of writing a book on the contemporary family, I was often greeted with the remark, "Oh, don't do that! The family is too controversial." That's just the point. The changing family has become hostage to all sorts of political and emotional manipulations. Rather than acknowledge that today's families are besieged by change more profound than at any time in history, conservative ideologues, fundamentalists of all stripes, and far too many politicians persist in making pronouncements ad nauseam on the failing family. From pulpits and parliamentary seats, they condemn families who strive for more egalitarian and democratic relationships. Harking back to some mythical, harmonious past, they condemn the transformations underway, ignoring the fact that families of the past were no different from families of today—some kind and nurturing, some cruel and exploitative. (Lest we forget, literature is full of examples.) As an ultimate act of hubris, they cast the beleaguered family as villain for all that ails contemporary society. Such strategies not only serve a conservative social agenda, but also allow governments to evade the responsibility—and cost—of social programs that would support vulnerable families—families of all kinds—through a difficult era of transformation.

The very word *family* is charged with emotion. It reaches deep into our sense of self, conjuring up feelings about our core identity and ancestry. Each of us belongs to at least one family, and the desire to belong to a family unit seems to be one of our deepest human instincts: if we are deprived of a family, we form another through alliance or living arrangements. Family structures are never cast in stone. Throughout history, family forms have evolved to meet the changing demands of society. Change is inherent and inevitable, and in any change there are positive and negative elements. The challenge comes in how we respond to those elements, as individuals, as family members, and as a society.

Perhaps it was a defensive response to those who claim that family values have been irretrievably weakened. Or perhaps it was something more personal—the charmed security of my childhood in Maine, the stability offered by generations of family rooted there. Whatever the reason, I believed that conversations *with* families *about* families would help clarify the forces shaping family life and expose stereotypes upon which our idealization of the family flounders. I was particularly troubled by those who tend to blame "family disintegration" on the advancement in the status of women. On the contrary, women are the first to be victimized by family breakdown, for it is they who must shoulder the responsibilities discarded by others: educating the children, caring for elders, and earning the family's keep, no matter how difficult, or disagreeable, the tasks.

My professional experiences as a journalist and a representative of several international organizations had given me the opportunity to observe some of the challenges today's families face—and to observe, as well, how seldom the voices of families themselves are included in the public debate. My personal experiences as a girl child, daughter, adolescent, woman, wife-partner, mother, wage earner, divorcée, single parent, mother-in-law, and grandmother had aroused my curiosity about how others undergo similar transformation in rapidly changing societies. Were others as disquieted as I, watching relatives leave the circle of family to find work or security elsewhere? Were others as far away from their loved ones as I? Were they wondering, as I did, if this was a malady of my immediate society or truly a global phenomenon? This journey to families was a way to find out.

It was a long journey. Over a period of three years—1992 to 1995—I traveled to a variety of continents, climates, and cultures. Commencing in Japan, I went on to Thailand, Bangladesh, China, Mali, Uganda, Egypt, Jordan, Brazil, El Salvador, and, finally, to the United States of America. These travels resulted in hundreds of hours of taped conversations with scores of families. Their stories and opinions reveal commonality as well as uniqueness, transcending degrees of development, education, and wealth. In Mali there were stories of drought; in Bangladesh and the American Midwest, tales of floods. In China there were complaints of too few children; in Jordan, protests of too many. In homes built of mud, brick, wood, or carved stone, I watched families go about their daily tasks while elders told of dreams past and the young spoke of those yet to come.

The process was simple: having first selected countries where the major global trends of our time—economic transformation, galloping urbanization, labor migration, women-headed households, environmental stress—are found, I then wrote to sociologists and activists in each nation. Explaining my task, I asked their counsel on whom to meet and what issues to explore. Based on their advice, I met with those most knowledgeable about social and economic trends, those who could introduce me to families coping with these trends. Being introduced to each family by someone well known to them assured a level of trust that would have been impossible to create on my own.

Usually I spoke with three or more generations of each family, believing that through the prism of the generations, change could be more readily discerned. I pursued contrasts in family situations within and among countries. There were rural and urban dwellers; farmers, merchants, miners, office workers and professionals; affluent families as well as families subsisting in a daily search. There were families living in multigenerational groups; nuclear families and single-parent families. There were closely knit families and families separated by geography or education. There were polygamous, patriarchal, and matriarchal families, and same-sex couples who were raising children in strong family units. There were families where violence and abuse are daily events, and others ignorant that such horrors even exist. There were families of prostitutes who live together to support and protect their children, and families of children who live by their wits on city streets.

In each setting, we met first in a large family group. I explained my objective of giving voice to families, and began our conversations by describing my own. I told of my grandparents, of how their children were dispersed by World War II and never returned to the family home, of how each generation became more educated and more mobile. The exchange of family stories was thus begun, and during the ensuing hours, we shared laughter, food, tales of the past, and hopes for the future.

When it came time to record the interviews, I suggested that they be conducted individually to ensure that each person would feel at ease, free to speak her or his mind openly. Based on past experience, I knew that when others are present, the individual being interviewed hesitates to speak freely, fearing others might disagree, correct facts, or tease.

Each conversation was recorded regardless of where it took place. The tape recorder's remarkable sensitivity added multiple background noises to the dialogue; donkeys, roosters, children, and passing trains are all part of it. The patient individuals who transcribed the recorded words despite braying, crowing, and babies' cries deserve my gratitude. Appreciation is also due to the dozens of interpreters, both volunteer and professional, who assisted me. Their skills and sensitivity were essential to enhancing trust and candor in the interviews. Together we gathered insights from three generations of eight to ten families in each country, resulting in hundreds of pages of transcripts.

I traveled by all modes of transportation and on all conditions of road and path. In Egypt, a rowboat deposited me on an island in the Nile to meet a farming family. In Brazil I rode horseback to reach the farm of an admired patriarch. As could be expected, capital cities were each different, some clean and safe, others polluted by toxic air and human folly. Learning about them, how to maneuver within their bureaucracies and in their streets, was a first step in reaching families.

I was often alone and usually illiterate in the local language, and the travels were not always easy. There were many times that I stood waiting for early morning transportation, unsure if I was waiting in the right place, on the right train platform, or in the proper ticket queue. There were days when discouragement set in, when attempts to arrange interviews failed. Then a breakthrough would occur, and I was off again, to another place and another warm welcome from people eager to tell of their lives. Some admitted that they had never had the opportunity to talk about their lives and were grateful for the occasion, the only people with whom they might converse were family and community members who might not take kindly to their opinions.

The interviews that make up this book have been edited for clarity and for reasons of space. I believe, however, that I have respected the intent and meaning of the interviewee in all cases. I have inserted basic facts and statistics in the text where they seemed necessary for context and comparison. The photographs are, admittedly, of varying quality. Some were taken by the author for the purpose of sending them to the families interviewed. Others were provided by families themselves and still others are the work of professional photographer Stanley Staniski, who was able to visit five of the countries where interviews took place.

The reader will note that each of the first two chapters is devoted to extensive interviews of three families, as a way of hearing about the trends faced by families in a range of settings. Each of the subsequent chapters quotes many families, as a means of focusing on a particular concern voiced by families elsewhere.

The following brief descriptions of the countries where families were interviewed are not meant to be all encompassing; their purpose is to orient the reader and provide some general context for the interviews that are to follow.

JAPAN

From an agrarian, near-feudal society at the turn of the twentieth century, Japan became, successively, a militaristic colonial power; a defeated, wounded nation; and an industrial giant—all in three generations. A visual reminder of this extraordinary transformation is often seen on Tokyo's streets: a small, kimono-clad elder shuffles slowly in her *zori* sandals amid a crowd of fashionable young office workers wearing Gucci or Yves St. Laurent apparel. Neither generation bothers the other; their worlds have little in common.

Population: 127.1 million
Density: 336 per square km.
Urban: 78%/Rural: 22%
Life expectancy: 81.5 years
Population under age 15: 14.7%
GNP per capita: $23,257
Adult literacy: 99%
Female parliamentarians: 5% [14]

Shintoism and Buddhism are the dominant religions although the traditional Japanese family was influenced by Confucian teachings and took the form of the patriarchal stem family, in which the eldest son replaces the family patriarch at his death, inherits most of the property, and is charged with the care of elders and siblings. Families lived in multigenerational groups; marriages were arranged by parents, and total obedience was expected of a daughter-in-law, who, by tradition, went to live with, and serve, her husband's family. According to the elders interviewed here, these customs began to erode following World War II. The terms of Japan's surrender included adoption of democratic institutions and practices. Japan became a parliamentary democracy in which the emperor is (only) a symbol of the state and the unity of the people. The new ways had formidable consequences on social organization and on families.

In 1945 more than 8,000 farming villages dotted the Japanese archipelago; by 1993, according to the *New York Times*, there were fewer than 700. [15] Salaried factory or office work is preferred to field labor, and food can be imported, as can a host of luxuries from afar. Families, however, are struggling with the by-products of affluence: long work days, hours of commuting, competition, stress, an influx of foreign values and customs, and a weakening of family bonds. Members of the younger generation want to choose their marriage partners and most women hope to continue their working careers. As a result, the Japanese birthrate has declined. Some add that cramped urban living quarters are another incentive to limit family size; living in large family units is out of the question, and "nuclear" arrangements become the only sane options.

The drastic decline in birth rates in the past two decades has dramatically altered the age structure of Japanese society. Children under age fifteen make up barely 15 percent of the Japanese population (less than half of what they make up in Bangladesh). Elders represent 17 percent of the total population. [16] Japan has the world's highest longevity: seventy-seven for males, eighty-four for females. By 2015, the over-sixty-five age group will double to 25 percent. [17] Each Japanese retiree is supported by three workers today; by 2020, that number will decrease to two. In an aging and long-lived society, the elders' need for good physical and emotional health, economic stability, and a meaningful old age becomes a major concern of public policy and of families.

Japanese families are rarely free of an all-encompassing work ethic. From early childhood, Japanese children are taught to serve the good of the group and to compete among themselves. Before they enter the first grade, most children have spent a year or two in serious study. Leisure disappears and is replaced by the pressure of doing well enough to enter one of the top universities, once a guarantee of lifetime employment. Their fathers, and increasingly their mothers, have tiring work schedules. A ride on public transportation in Japan's large cities, at any time of the day, reveals the consequences of this lifestyle: fashionably dressed women and men of all ages sit side by side, sound asleep. The Japanese work ethic may have built a robust economy, but it has had a less positive impact on family life. Fathers have little time to spend with their children. Women who don't work outside the home are becoming more readily dissatisfied with this way of life; divorce is on the rise, particularly among retired people. It would seem that after all the years of living separate lives, husband and wife discover they have little in common. "Elderly couples are reaching retirement age without ever once having had a real conversation," said Noburo Kurokawa, a doctor who specializes in marriage-related stress. "Spending time together becomes a huge burden." A recent initiative of the Ministry of Education offers training programs to company men on why and how they should become more involved in family life.

Japanese women are marrying far later than their mothers, and 46 percent of them are in the labor force.[18] Young rural women prefer to work in factories rather than marry farmers' sons as their mothers did. Male farmers sometimes turn to mail-order brides from the Philippines and Korea in the search for a wife willing to work the land. Foreign women are a source of much discussion in Japan. I heard about "little Bangkoks," towns where there is a well-developed sex industry that depends on young girls from Thailand, the Philippines, and Korea. Recruited with a promise of work in restaurants or the entertainment business, they find themselves prisoners of the sex industry, controlled by *yakuza*, the organized crime underworld, from which it is difficult—and dangerous—to attempt escape.[19]

Coping with an aging society, strains among the generations, the overpowering work ethic, and the rising independence of young women were major concerns of the families I met. In Nagano Prefecture, on the island of Fukuoka, and in the Tokyo area, the sense of vast transformations in Japanese behavior and values was ever-present.

PEOPLE'S REPUBLIC OF BANGLADESH

Once a part of British India, then of independent Pakistan, Bangladesh became an independent nation in 1971 following war with Pakistan.

Bangladesh is the most densely populated country on earth. Roughly the size of Wisconsin, which has a population of 4 million, Bangladesh counts 137 million. Seventy-eight percent of its population lives in absolute pover-

Population: 137.4 million

Density: 1,026 per square km.

Urban: 22%/Rural: 78%

Life expectancy: 60.7 years

Population under age 15: 38.7%

GNP per capita: $1,361

Adult literacy: 40.1%

Female parliamentarians: 9%

ty. Life expectancy is twenty years less than that of Japan.

The predominantly Muslim nation sits astride a vast tropical flood plain of the Ganges, Brammaputra, and Meghna rivers. Their combined outflow is the third highest in the world, after the Amazon and Congo systems, and their cyclical floods are the heart of Bangladesh's river culture. Flood waters replenish soils and provide spawning waters for the hundreds of species of fish essential to the Bengali diet. But the great rivers, like the nation's people, have undergone significant change. Population increases in the lands to the north and northeast, in Nepal and India, led to the deforestation of hillsides, which could thus be planted with crops. When the monsoon rains come, powerful and persistent, the hillside farming terraces give way; tons of earth and water rush into the valleys below and, further on, into the rivers of Bangladesh. Filled with this soil, the rivers leave their beds and meander through the flatlands, seeking a route to the sea. (The Jamuna River alone is estimated to carry 900 million tons of silt each year.) Riverbanks change; land disappears, and new land emerges elsewhere. Millions of people lose property, and some lose their lives. Cyclones formed in the Bay of Bengal are yet another recurrent tragedy befalling Bangladesh, which has a coast barely a meter or two above sea level.

But the struggle with nature is not the only burden Bangladesh bears. A lack of natural resources, a large, poorly educated population, and customs that hinder the participation of women in public life are equally troublesome. Nearly 40 percent of the population is under fifteen years of age. The creation of sufficient employment for this vast, expanding labor pool is virtually impossible in a nation where the per capita income is but $370 per year.[20] Earning strategies include, of course, rural-to-urban migration. In most cases, that means the capital, Dhaka; now with 12.3 million inhabitants in its metropolitan area, the city has grown by 80 percent in the past twenty-five years and is teetering on the brink of service and infrastructure collapse.

Temporary emigration, thus, is the only means of wage earning for thousands of men and women who seek jobs in wealthy Asian nations or the Gulf states. The consequences for families left behind are particularly harsh on women. A dramatic rise in women-headed households through divorce, abandonment, and migration has marked the last decades. Women's vulnerability to these trends is a growing concern in Bangladeshi society. Few women are seen on the streets of the capital; those who do go out in public are from opposite poles of the social structure: either malnourished beggars or wealthy, educated matrons in chauffeur-driven cars. Although the dowry system has been outlawed, in practice dowries are still required if a daughter is to have a husband—and, of course, the bigger the dowry, the "better" the husband, at least in earning capacity. Bound by the isolating customs of purdah, the great majority of Bengali women have rarely emerged from their homes to go beyond a few years of primary school or to work in the public arena—but this is changing. The first generation of women wage earners are employed in the expanding garment industry; many among them are rural migrants. Masuda Begum Sofali, a woman activist who created Nari Uddug Kendra (Center for Women's Initiative), an organization to assist women, noted, "Traditionally, rural girls had usually been married off by the age of fourteen. The fact that girls age ten to fourteen are coming from rural areas to find jobs in the cities implies that there has been a social change in attitude toward marriage. Instead of getting a daughter married, parents are sending daughters to make their own livelihood. Thus there is one mouth less to feed and the family can get some remittances from these workers."

Earning wages has transformed women's sense of self-worth. A new perception of women's role in society is taking root. Unfortunately, so is opposition to these changes—the backlash. Attacks on women, and on schools or organizations that work with women, have increased significantly. According to Fazel Hasan Abed, of the Bangladesh Rural Advancement Committee (BRAC), "The village cleric doesn't like the fact that women are coming out of their homes and asserting themselves by earning a living in our programs."

In a country that will again double its population by 2050, the impact of these factors—the dearth of livelihoods for the young, emigration, ecological vulnerability, and women's emergent role—raises unsettling questions about family formation and the potential of national development in the years to come.

KINGDOM OF THAILAND

Bangkok is a jumble of cars, jitneys, water taxis, cycles, and an opaque, stifling haze that causes pedestrians to clutch at their noses. (Most traffic police wear nose masks.) Construction sites are everywhere: highways, overpasses, glass-walled high-rises, conference halls, bridges, and shopping malls are being built en masse. But Bangkok, the city, has little to do with Thailand, the country. With merely 15 percent of the total population, Bangkok accounts for over half of the nation's GNP. It is an entity apart, where wealth, modernization, and the nation's social ills are concentrated.

The first census taken in Thailand was in 1911; the kingdom then counted 8 million people. In 1952, a publication of the International Planned Parenthood Federation noted that Thailand had barely 18 million inhabitants and naively concluded, "In this little country over-population is no problem."[21] Twenty years later, a national family-planning effort was begun in response to overly rapid growth. Even so, in 1998, Thais numbered 61 million, more than a sevenfold increase in eighty-seven years. That the nation was able to provide education and health care to such a rapidly expanding population is a measure of its success.

Population: 62.8 million

Density: 123 per square km.

Urban: 20%/Rural: 80%

Life expectancy: 70.8 years

Population under age 15: 26.7%

GNP per capita: $5,456

Adult literacy: 95%

Female parliamentarians: 6%

Ethnic Chinese represent 14 percent of the population and Buddhism is the spiritual framework of 95 percent of Thais. Its practice guides attitudes, codes of behavior, and the Thai way of life. Today even Buddhism is under pressure from socioeconomic change that widens the gap between beliefs and daily reality.

Traditionally an agrarian-based economy, Thailand is considered an NIC: a newly industrializing country. Since the 1970s, the manufacturing and service sector has expanded tremendously. In the late 1980s, the economy was growing at more than 10 percent a year. Rice and textiles are the most important exports, and tourism is the single largest earner of foreign exchange, a $4 billion industry, attracting millions of tourists from Japan, Europe, the United States, and Taiwan. In came the 1997 Asian financial crisis, however, Thailand's economy faltered dramatically.

Rapid development—as well as the sudden stalling of that development—are not without its social costs. The success of Thailand's has industrialization relied significantly on women's labor. Women represent 45 percent of the manufacturing workforce. Only 30 percent work in factories that pay the minimum wage, the other 70 percent are being exploited by small and medium-sized factories.

Child-rearing practices have been transformed both by women's employment and the nuclearization of the family. According to Thai sociologist Amara Pongsapich, who writes about changing family patterns, most families do not have a grandparent or other relative to care for children, who are increasingly raised by baby-sitters or neighbors.[22] Despite the economic imperative to work, working women are often criticized for "abandoning" their children or because their success unsettles their menfolk. There is a prevalence of second wives, or mistresses, which undermines family cohesion and has resulted in a sharp increase in divorce, particularly in the cities.

According to the Thai National Institute of Development Administration, the highest rate of divorce is in Bangkok, where in 1986 one out of four marriages ended in divorce.[23]

Although occupied by the Japanese in World War II, Thailand is proud of the fact that it was never colonized and is now a stable constitutional monarchy. Its history, however, was profoundly influenced by the turmoil of colonial, ethnic, and super-power conflicts. The Vietnam war did more than devastate Vietnam and Cambodia; it reached into neighboring Thailand, where U.S. bases housed 50,000 troops, and where 6,000 war-weary soldiers arrived each week for "rest and recreation." At the time, this presence brought profits and wealth to many, but it is now deplored as the commencement of the "industrial phase" of the Thai sex trade. It is a trade that goes beyond the Thai borders: the Coalition Against Trafficking of Women (CATW) estimates that nearly one million women from Burma, South China, Laos, and Vietnam have been abducted and smuggled into Thailand.[24] With the rising fear of HIV/AIDS, sex clients seek younger and younger prostitutes who, they believe, might not yet be infected. UNAIDS estimates that 755,00 Thai adults and children are infected with the HIV, and 75,000 children have been orphaned by the disease.[25] Child prostitution—of both girls and boys, some as young as seven or eight—is rife, organized by crime syndicates and individual "brokers."[26] Rapid economic growth has brought affluence to some; many more have been left behind.

PEOPLE'S REPUBLIC OF CHINA

Nothing in China is small or average. In comparison with most countries, both problems and solutions appear gigantic in size and scope due to the dimension and diversity of its territory, the number of its people, and the growth rate of its economy.

With 1.28 billion people, China has 21 percent of the world's population, which must provide for itself on barely 8 percent of the world's arable land.[27] In the 1980s and 1990s, millions of rural workers left the land to seek their livelihoods in China's growing cities.[28] The rapid, and largely unregulated, expansion of the economy is creating a widening gap between rural and urban incomes and a host of social problems due to insufficient housing and services.

Population: 1.275 billion

Density: 133 per square km.

Urban: 30%/Rural: 70%

Life expectancy: 71.2 years

Population under age 15: 24.8%

GNP per capita: $3,105

Adult literacy: 82.8%

Female parliamentarians: 22%

Prerevolutionary China, the country remembered by today's elders, was a land of feudal fealty in which men, women, and children were readily bought and sold to supply sweatshop labor, brothels, or the desire for concubines.

Famine was a cyclical reality feared by millions. Confucianism dominated the social order as well as family structure.

From that not-so-distant past has emerged, albeit rather painfully, an immense modernizing nation-state. To improved the quality of life of a billion people in a mere fifty years was no simple task. The cost, in terms of human rights, was—and remains—high. At the same time, the gains were many. Since the 1940s, China has passed through a trouble metamorphosis via which class hierarchy was for the most part abolished and individual security became dependent upon one's willingness to serve the state. Cadres were trained and health care provided; hunger was kept at bay. Workers and peasants were valued as a prime resource and women, once bound of foot and mind, became salaried workers and, as such, most say, gained dignity and self-confidence.

For elders who knew life as disinherited, hungry peasants, the new China is a miracle of Mao Zedong's leadership. For the young, who watch Hong Kong television, the miracle has yet to happen. Today's China is in an all-pervasive rush toward freemarket consumerism; foreign influences abound. Once again, it is the pace of change that risks becoming the destabilizing factor.

The demographics of China confound anyone attempting to predict the nation's future. Even with the modest annual population growth rate of 0.7 percent, China will have to provide for an additional 195 million people by 2025. As the first nation to undertake a long-term, concerted effort to limit fertility by adopting the "One Child" policy, China now finds itself heading toward a perplexing age structure. By 2025, 20 percent of China's total population will be over sixty.[29] This increasing proportion of elderly, coupled with a decreasing number of young and a tendency toward nuclear family living arrangements, foreshadows a dramatic crisis in elderly care.

That said, if it weren't for grandparents, most particularly grandmothers, who care for children, working parents would carry yet another burden. At the same time, however, multigenerational living is on the decline in both rural and urban areas, and the incidence of divorce is rising. Long a nation of arranged marriages, China is seeing the "love match" become far more common. According to a researcher at Beijing's Child Development Center of China, 60 to 70 percent of divorces are initiated by women, who speak of disagreement about children's schooling, family finances, or "no love."

Chinese environmental scientists spoke about the lack of regulations to curtail industrial pollution and waste. Village-level industries were created without close monitoring, and scientists predict increasing pressure on China's natural resources as a result. Coastal waters are polluted, fisheries depleted; future drinking water needs pose a frightening dilemma. Population Action International notes that in 2000, renewable water sources per capita were at 2,215 cubic meters (compared with 8,902 in the United States), and that figure is bound to decrease with population growth in the coming decades years.[30] Air pollution is also on the rise due to dependence on coal-fueled factories.

The information revolution has also shaken China. Foreign images received by television or, increasingly, the Internet, are said to contribute to the growing communication gap among the generations. Longtime resident and scholar of China Israel Epstein, whom I interviewed in his Beijing home, noted, "Parents and elders think vertically—from where they have come from and how good it is to have what is. The young think horizontally—out, to other countries and influences." Then, with a smile he added, "Even if the government gave out 100 million passports for travel abroad, there would still be more than a billion Chinese."

REPUBLIC OF MALI

Mali straddles the heart of the African Sahel. Landlocked and made up largely of desert and savanna, its greatest blessing is the Niger River, which flows through its center. It is a land of nomads and pastoralists, farmers, fishermen, and traders.

In the thirteenth and fourteenth centuries, people from North Africa, Arabia, and the kingdoms of West Africa gathered in its ancient capital, Djenne, and in Timbuktu, a center of enlightenment, to listen to sages and poets who found a haven there. The origin of Mali's former wealth was the now-defunct trans-Saharan camel caravan trade.

Population: 11.4 million

Density: 9 per square km.

Urban: 27%/Rural: 73%

Life expectancy: 52.1 years

Population under age 15: 46.1%

GNP per capita: $681

Adult literacy: 38.2%

Female parliamentarians: 12%

Today, Mali's 11.4 million people are among the poorest in the world. In the great Sahelian drought of 1984–85, Mali suffered widespread famine, and between 40 percent and 80 percent of its livestock, the country's single greatest resource, was lost. The precariousness of depending on the vagaries of nature haunts Malian farmers and pastoralists alike.

Coupled with its lack of resources, Mali faces the geographic isolation of a landlocked Sahelian nation, a factor which has forestalled development and, thus, the provision of essential services to its people. Mali has only one medical doctor for every 25,000 people (compared with one for 334 people in Sweden).[31] It also has one of the highest rates of maternal and infant mortality in the world. For every 100,000 births, 1,200 Malian mothers die (compared with 7 per 100,000 in Sweden).[32] Early marriage and pregnancy are complicating factors.

Provision of universal education is out of the question despite Mali's tradition of, and respect for, learning. Nearly half—46 percent—of Mali's population is under fifteen, and with only livestock and cotton for significant export earnings, Mali's government is hard-pressed to educate and train teachers or to provide schools for its scattered school-aged population. Those who are educated find few employment opportunities in their native land. They, like their uneducated rural cousins, are often obliged to export themselves, in an effort to repay families that "went without" to educate them.

For centuries the seasonal migration of rural youth to the coast of West Africa was a sort of rite of passage. Today it is far more than a seasonal adventure for young men; it is an economic necessity. Some migrants spend years away from family and community. As elsewhere, this has also resulted in a more vulnerable status for women and children; women-headed households now constitute 8 percent of all Malian households.[33]

The economic crises that followed the droughts in the 1970s and 1980s radically changed family structure and relationships by undermining the ability of traditional patriarchs to provide for their families. Traditional management of family affairs and resources has been called into question by new economic realities.

Mali is rich in diverse ethnic groups—Mande, Peul, Voltaic, Sonhrai, Tuareg, and Moor—which share and honor one another's historic, cultural, and religious traditions. The market language, Bambara, is spoken by nearly 80 percent of the total population. Traditionally, each ethnic group was tied to a specific occupation; the groups complemented and depended upon one another. Mali may be a nation under economic and environmental stress, but it is certainly blessed by the resilience and creativity of its people, who ridded themselves of a long dictatorship in 1992 and established a true parliamentary democracy which sets an example among African states.

REPUBLIC OF UGANDA

Nestled on the banks of Lake Victoria, Uganda is roughly the size of the state of Oregon and counts over 21 million people. It is blessed with abundant water sources and fertile lands, and inhabited by a hardworking people determined to make the most of its resources.

Population: 23.3 million
Density: 98 per square km.
Urban: 13%/Rural: 87%
Life expectancy: 46 years
Population under age 15: 49.2%
GNP per capita: $1,074
Adult literacy: 65%
Female parliamentarians: 18%

When Arab traders reached the interior of Uganda in the 1830s they discovered several African kingdoms with centuries-old political institutions. In the late 1800s, Uganda was colonized by Great Britain; by the time the British protectorate ended in 1961, Uganda had a significant educated elite, a renowned university, and a substantial road system. Five years later, Uganda began its descent into chaos. Rival dictators Milton Obote and Idi Amin Dada alternated their grasp of power, sacking the country and abusing its people. Not until 1985 were Ugandans finally freed by the National Resistance Army, led by Yoweri Museveni, Uganda's current president. Eight years later, as I stood on a hilltop in Western Uganda with a preacher of the Church of Uganda, I marveled at the serene beauty of the land. The reverend turned to me saying, "Yes, it is truly beautiful. But you know, even a country can die—and our Uganda died for a while."

Indeed, the end of civil war was not the end of Uganda's anguish. The nation was barely beginning to regain hope when the dying began again. Uganda has been at the epicenter of "the killing disease"—the HIV/AIDS pandemic. Life expectancy for Ugandans has plummeted to forty-six years. An estimated 2 million children have been orphaned by AIDS.[34] A grandmother in western Uganda explained that she had lost seven of her nine children and their spouses to AIDS. I met thirteen of the sixteen grandchildren for whom she cares. Since many in the childbearing generation are ill, dying, or dead, it is the elderly who provide care for children and orphans.

Agriculture accounts for 46 percent of GDP and over 95 percent of merchandise exports (mainly coffee). Women provide 80 percent of the agricultural labor force; they produce 90 percent of Uganda's food crops and 60 percent of the cash crops.[35] Uganda's vice president, Speciosa Wandira Kazibwe, was minister of Women, Youth and Culture when we discussed Uganda's families. She said, "The extended family that was part and parcel of our society is now disrupted. The economy has uprooted people from villages, and if you get a job you have to support the extended family as well. The burden is being carried more and more by women. It's the women who are doing the farming because the children are in school and the men have gone off to the cities. Now we have the HIV death rate of women between twenty-five and thirty-five years. That means they were infected eight to ten years earlier, at fifteen or sixteen. They die as young mothers."

In addition, economic conditions and civil unrest have resulted in a flight of intellectuals, causing a sharp decline in the quality of local education and a lack of technical training institutions. Then, too, Uganda's involvement in regional power struggles continues to drain resources away from investment in long-term development.

Uganda's misfortunes would be overwhelming to a country less well endowed by nature. For the time being, the country's potential is overshadowed by the need to maintain the peace, rebuild its infrastructure, fight its epidemic, and educate its young.

ARAB REPUBLIC OF EGYPT

When I first visited Egypt twenty-five years ago, the total population of Egypt was nearing 45 million. It now stands at close to 70 million and will most likely reach 95 million by 2025. This inexorable population expansion dominates Egypt's reality: half a million people enter the workforce each year.

There is no possibility that job creation, housing, and basic services can keep pace with this galloping growth in human numbers. Egypt relies on foreign donors for both food imports and infrastructure development. One of the Middle East's most powerful nations, a country that has endured as a unified state for more than five thousand years, is in danger of outgrowing its capacity to feed and fend for itself.

Population: 67.9 million

Density: 67 per square km.

Urban: 44%/Rural: 56%

Life expectancy: 68.3 years

Population under age 15: 35.4%

GNP per capita: $3,041

Adult literacy: male 65%, female 53.7%

Female parliamentarians: 2%

The shortage of lower-income housing is of crisis proportion. Three-quarters of Cairo's districts are "randomly constructed" shanty towns or squatter-built settlements. Overcrowding combined with poor municipal services creates serious public health risks. Garbage is dumped anywhere, everywhere; one sees people throwing waste into canals where women are washing clothes and dishes. On the city limits, cement and chemical factories belch a foul-smelling smog so thick as to obscure the other side of the Nile and challenge the sun to break through its darkness.

Mahfouz El Ansari, editor of the newspaper *El Goumeria*, explained that Egypt's cities have grown so rapidly that they have been "villagized"—overwhelmed by rural values and customs. Migrants who have returned from aboard bring still other values and aspirations. An estimated 2.5 million Egyptians—one in every seven people of working age—leave Egypt each year to seek work abroad.[36] Professionals and technicians—teachers, doctors—were the first to go. Later, unskilled workers also emigrated. This, according to Mahfouz el Ansari, weakened Egyptian families because couples were separated and women and children were left behind.

Egypt's women leaders speak often of the consequences of migration on women and of how Egyptian family law continues to keep women at a disadvantage. Economic decline also undermines women's status. The famous woman journalist Ingy Rouchdy lamented, "Women are the last hired, first fired. In parliament there was debate where many said that women should leave their places to men. This trend was picked up by fundamentalists, saying there is lack of transportation, day-care, house care. 'Women should stay home to take care of husband and family. No ship can have two captains.' Many women succumb to these pressures; the clerics say, 'Put on the veil, stay at home and we'll subsidize you.' Also, the high percentage of illiteracy affects family life by depriving both women and men of the knowledge to resist false religious teachings. We are headed for a fight—an ideological fight."

The ideological fight of which Rouchdy speaks concerns the condemnation of Egypt's multicultural origins, its internationally respected literature, music, and film, as "un-Egyptian" by religious extremists. And nearly all those I met wanted to discuss the role of television in Egyptian life and how pornography via satellite plays into hands of fundamentalists Islamics.

A place of contrasts between rural and urban, rich and very poor, educated and illiterate, Egypt finds itself faced with fearsome challenges to provide economic growth and development, in a nation where 35 percent of the population is under fifteen years of age.

HASHEMITE KINGDOM OF JORDAN

The ancient land of Jordan is an arid region of rolling plains, rocky deserts, and starkly denuded mountains that dominate the Dead Sea. Its history reads like the story of civilization itself, for it has been visited by all the great peoples of the Middle East, Asia Minor, and Europe, including the Nabataeans, who built their remarkable carved city, Petra, centuries before the birth of Jesus.

Population: 4.9 million

Density: 50 per square km.

Urban: 71%/Rural 29%

Life expectancy: 70 years

Population under age 15: 40%

GNP per capita: $3,347

Adult literacy: 88.6%

Female parliamentarians: 0%

Sandwiched between its oil-rich Arab neighbors and Israel, Jordan has few natural resources; barely 4 percent of its territory is suitable for agriculture. At the turn of the last century its people were seminomadic herders, dependent on subsistence agriculture and their animals. In 1950, when the Hashemite Kingdom was proclaimed, its population numbered 600,000 people; today, it has swollen to well over six million. This growth is a direct result of the conflict between the Palestinian people and the State of Israel, and Jordan's ancestral hospitality: 1.1 million of its residents are classified as refugees; many thousands more reside in Jordan temporarily. The "temporary" dates back to 1948 for hundreds of thousands of families whose lives were transformed by decisions made thousands of miles away.

In barely a generation, Jordan has become a nation of contrasts between a large, educated, urban population and the nomads and farmers who pursue their traditional livelihoods. Due to considerable investments in health services and education, Jordan has dramatically increased the life span of its citizens: in 1965, Jordanians lived an average of 48.2 years; today it is 70.1 years. Increased longevity and a high birthrate combine to add to Jordan's dilemma for, with a annual population growth rate of 2.85 percent, it faces a doubling of its population by 2040. With 40 percent of Jordan's population under fifteen, the problem of employment creation is reaching crisis proportions.[37]

Jordan has long been a source of skilled labor for other Arab countries. Up until the Iraqi invasion of Kuwait in 1990 and the subsequent Gulf War of 1991, the remittances of expatriate workers accounted for 14 percent of GNP, a significant contribution to the national economy. That ended abruptly with the Gulf War, with disastrous repercussions on the Jordanian economy. Nearly 400,000 Jordanian nationals who worked in the Gulf returned to Jordan. Unemployment skyrocketed to over 25 percent.[38]

In the capital, Amman, and in remote mountains farms and refugee camps, one hears a refrain deploring the disruptive speed of change. With 91 percent of households equipped with a television, modern ideas and new aspirations have captured the imaginations of the young. Elders worry about the shift to nuclear families and wonder if their children will support them. Women's roles have evolved considerably, and women now make up at least 15 percent of the Jordanian workforce.

The most formidable challenge for Jordan's government may well be the management of the nation's precious water resources. Rainfall is low and unreliable and groundwater is expensive and nonrenewable. By one estimate, per capita renewable water resources in 2000 stood at barely 132 cubic meters (compared with 8,902 in the United States).[39] A 1998 World Bank study noted that of the nation's agricultural land, only 5 percent is irrigated yet this irrigated land consumes 76 percent of all water used in the country.[40] With population expansion continuing, household consumption is expected to triple in thirty years. As a result, water allocated to agriculture may actually have to decline. These three elements—population growth, water scarcity, and employment—are the all-consuming concerns of a society which is also in the fulcrum of one of the most intractable political conflicts of the last sixty years.

EL SALVADOR

The story of El Salvador is one of wealth for the few and poverty for the many. It is also the story of how war ravages people, land, and institutions. When

Population: 6.3 million

Density: 298 per square km.

Urban: 45%/Rural 55%

Life expectancy: 70.3 years

Population under age 15: 35.6%

GNP per capita: $4,036

Adult literacy: 77.8%

Female parliamentarians: 17%

twelve years of civil war ended in 1992, 75,000 Salvadorans had been killed, thousands had escaped to refugee camps in neighboring countries, and still others, over a million people, had left the area altogether out of fear or economic need. One quarter of the country's land had been severely damaged by the war. Of its 6.3 million people, over half live in absolute poverty while a few wealthy families have second homes in Miami, Paris, or New York. The capital, San Salvador, had swollen from a half a million people in 1970 to over 1.5 million at the end of the century.

The National Secretariat for the Family, an agency created by Margarita de Christiani, wife of El Salvaor's first postwar president, attempted to document the social consequences of the war and propose legislation and programs to protect and serve the most vulnerable. "During the war many were killed, yes—but more damage was done to the living," explained Julio Villa-Alta, a young social worker who manages a home for street children. "It's not just social disintegration, it is the effective death of the family. Delinquent fathers multiplied during the war. Nearly 45 percent of households are now headed by women. Children are disoriented and dysfunctional. During the war they were taught to lie to save themselves, now they can't tell the truth. Very few families were spared separation, death, or displacement."

Pushed by poverty and unemployment, hundreds of thousands of men and women have left the country. By the end of the civil war, in some rural areas up to 40 percent of the population had emigrated to the United States to find work, many of them sending money to families left behind.[41] Most migrants leave their children with relatives or friends; the children often suffer psychological distress: feelings of inadequacy, sleep dysfunction, anxiety, fear of abandonment.[42]

According to several women's groups, socialization in a highly patriarchal culture has wide-ranging consequences for a nation attempting to rebuild and embrace democratic institutions. Many women believe they are inferior to men; as one midwife laughingly observed, "For midwife services, you pay a higher price for the delivery of a boy than for that of a girl." Violence toward the weakest and poorest family member is pervasive. Teenage pregnancy is on the rise and 75 percent of infants are born to unmarried women.

Approximately ten thousand youngsters live on their own at least part of the time in El Salvador's cities. Over half of them are between ten and twelve years old. Most have never been to school or have gone only for a year or so. Forty percent are addicted to glue or paint thinner, and more powerful drugs are also prevalent in El Salvador.[41] The tiny country sits in the path of the drug trafficking routes from South America to clients in the north; both drug trafficking and drug use are attractive to those traumatized by a decade of war. Leaders of Alcoholics Anonymous in San Salvador recognize that alcohol use is a prelude to drug use and deplore the fact that there is no minimum age for drinking alcohol. In the capital alone there are 450 AA groups; nationwide there are 1,500.

The role of the United Nations in negotiating a peace settlement and in managing the peace in El Salvador in the postwar, democracy-building phase is one of the successes of UN peacekeeping. Early on, UN officials recognized that illiteracy and ignorance of legal rights and status were barriers to social

reform and participation in public processes. A series of training programs were undertaken to teach Salvadorans about their rights, the reforms
underway, and their responsibilities as citizens. Over a period of weeks I
met dozens of men and women who had benefitted from these human
rights initiatives.

As we traveled throughout the country, evidence of the ravages of war on
the land and the nation's infrastructure was visible to the naked eye.
According to local environmentalists, 50 percent of the arable land is
eroded; barely 1 percent of the forests remain, and they are now under pressure for firewood and settlements. In addition, El Salvador has the largest
list of endangered species in Central America. Its coastal fisheries, mangroves,
and swamps are damaged by toxic pesticides, herbicides, and fertilizers. El
Salvador offers a case study in how war ravages the natural and the social
fabric of a nation, and how families go on to rebuild their lives.

BRAZIL

Ultra modern chic and desperate backwardness are the confusing twins of Brazil.
A few dozen kilometers from São Paulo, one of the world's most populated
and modern cities, peasants on donkey carts carry produce to market over unpaved
roads. Of the 170 million Brazilians, 1
percent possesses vast wealth and, says
UNICEF, 10 million children live in
poverty on city streets.[43]

Population: 170.4 million
Density: 20 per square km.
Urban: 78%, rural 22%
Life expectancy: 68.3 years
Population under age 15: 28.8%
GNP per capita: $6,625
Adult literacy: 84.5%
Female parliamentarians: 6%

The fifth largest country in the
world, stretching over half of the South
American continent, Brazil possesses
immense natural wealth that has attracted explorers and settlers since it was first
claimed by Portugal in 1500. The
Brazilian political experience has ranged from colony to empire, republic, military dictatorship, and parliamentary democracy. Throughout these changes,
its vast territory and riches have been a constant cause of violent power struggles that continue today. To its native peoples were added Portuguese settlers; African slaves; diverse European, Middle Eastern, and Asian immigrants;
and a host of religious missionaries. These peoples succeeded by 1999 in building the world's ninth largest economy, but one in which disparities in education, health care, and employment opportunities testify to the nation's troubled
governance. According to UN data, there are stark variations between the more
prosperous south and the impoverished northeast, where life expectancy is
five years lower, and where adult literacy and average income are 33 percent and 40 percent lower, respectively.[44]

In recent years, the biological and mineral resources of the 2.7 million-square-mile Amazon Basin and its vast rain forest have come under international scrutiny. Gold miners, rubber tappers, nomadic Indians, loggers, and farmers, not to mention vast commercial interests, are competing for a foothold, or simply survival, in the world's largest remaining forest region. Traveling by bus across the state of Rondonia, from PortoVelho to Cacaol, one can only guess at what the region was like two or three decades ago. In an effort to attract poor farmers to settle the region, the government built a two-lane highway into the Amazon forest with feeder roads to the right and left. Giant buses carried thousands of families and their meager belongings to administrative outposts along the way. Their efforts to clear the forest were successful, but their attempts to make a decent living from crops or cattle were less so. Yet buses continue to bring settlers north. (On one such bus, my seat mate was a weather-beaten, gun-toting miner who was heading into the forest's complex river system on yet another search for gold and diamonds.)

Despite the great expanse of Brazil's territory, three-quarters of all Brazilians live in urban centers. Of those city dwellers, nearly 40 percent live in miserable *favelas*, or slums. With 82 percent of the rural population living in poverty, Brazil's cities continue to attract rural migrants, and the *favelas* expand. By 2015, Brazil's population is expected to be 87% urban.[45]

Brazil is the largest Roman Catholic nation in the world, yet family planning programs have been highly successful in lowering the birth rates. But because half of all Brazilians are under age twenty-five and are in, or will soon enter, their reproductive years, Brazil's population will reach almost 219 million by 2025, and nearly an additional 50 million people will need education, social services, employment, and homes.[46]

UNITED STATES OF AMERICA

From a rural-based population of 92 million at the beginning of the twentieth century, the United States has been transformed into a land of 283 million people, of whom more than three-quarters reside in urban areas.[47] Blessed with vast natural resources, a range of climates, and water resources ranging from ground sources to complex river systems and coasts both east and west, the United States has developed its industries and expanded its economy to become the world's leading economic power.

Population: 283 million
Density: 29 per square km.
Urban: 77%/Rural 23%
Life expectancy: 76.7 years
Population under age 15: 22%
GNP per capita: $31,059
Adult literacy: 99%
Female parliamentarians: 12.5%

Since the mid-1800s, mobility of the workforce has been essential for this building of industry and business. Attracted by employment opportunities, families moved from the nation's small communities to large, anonymous cities. This vast migration included large numbers of formerly enslaved African Americans, leaving the South for the industrial North. The population has also been swelled by successive waves of immigrants from western and northern Europe, then southern and eastern Europe, and most recently from Africa, Asia, and Latin America and the Caribbean. (Meanwhile, the majority of those Native Americans who survived the genocide of European settlement were forced to assimilate or live on reservations.)

Both cities and families were transformed by these migrations and immigrations. During the industrial boom that followed World War II, the American family was to a large degree "nuclearized" by the need to follow the job market. Couples fended for themselves far from family support groups. In 1900, 18.3 percent of American women worked outside the home; by 1997 that figure had reached 46.2 percent according to the AFL-CIO.[48]

The bounty of the U.S. economy is increasingly out of reach to the least advantaged. In 2000, the Urban Insititute estimated that 2.3 million Americans are homeless and the U.S. Census Bureau estimated that 16.9 million American children lived in poverty.[49] Of America's 67.2 million families with children, 22 percent are headed by a single parent. In Washington, D.C., and Detroit, that percentage rises to 53 percent and 55 percent, respectively.[50] Nationwide, domestic violence is the leading cause of injury to adult women; nine out of ten female homicides are committed by men, half of them by the woman's partner. According to the U.S. Department of Justice, a woman is sexually assaulted every two minutes.[51] Violence has reached even the young, as evidenced by a series of shootings in public schools, as well as by the less widely reported shootings that are a daily occurrence on many city streets.

The United States has the highest number of its citizens in prison of any nation in the world, though on a per capita basis it is surpassed, barely, by Russia.[52] A study in 1994 revealed that four in ten Americans said that drugs and drug-related violence forced them to change the way they lived by making their homes more secure, staying inside at night, and avoiding certain areas.[53]

The land of opportunity. The country of individual freedom. Yes, but the United States is also engaged in a cycle of poverty, violence, and drug addiction. And the gap in income between the wealthy and the poor increases with every passing year.

Studies and statistics may document changing family circumstances, but it is the personal dimension—peoples' own individual and family stories, their ideas and opinions, and their fears and hopes—that reveals the depth of change in their lives. In the following chapters families in eleven nations share their lives and their thoughts. Their words reveal commonalities across countries and cultures, just as they confirm vast differences. Spanning different degrees of development, education, and wealth, these family stories tell of the forces confronted by a range families in a period of rapid transformation. They describe the realities of family life at the threshold of the twenty-first century.

This book is a listening tool. Its purpose is to offer readers the opportunity to hear a range of personal testimony on families of the past and families of the present. My hope is that, if w

e listen carefully, we may gain insights into how we might strengthen our own families, communities, and societies to meet the formidable challenges of our common future.

Part One

Families and Change

One | Families As We Were

It's a learning process to grow up in a multigenerational family. This was certainly true in my case. But at the same time, I lost my uniqueness, my individuality, because everyone has opinions and we often settle on the compromise. If I was to be a good boy, I had to compromise, to give up my personal opinion.
                    —Masanao Nakasawa, Susaka City, Japan

Years ago, while producing a film in the Sahel of West Africa, I spent several days with a family of Bororo nomads. The family had lost their cattle and camels—and thus their livelihood—in the great drought of 1984. They nearly lost their lives as well. Emaciated and exhausted, they were taken to a relief campsite for food and assistance. It was there that we met, eight months later, during the hot, dry summer. At the height of the afternoon heat, work was out of the question. We took refuge from the desert wind in a straw hut woven specifically for that purpose.

In the sanctuary of that makeshift shelter, I experienced a sense of family different from any I had ever known. Twenty or so men, women, and children rested together, intertwined—sleeping, singing, braiding each other's hair, telling stories, and teasing one another. There was no male-female separateness, no fear of elders or discernible hierarchy. Camaraderie, caring, and laughter dominated.

As I watched my hosts, I reflected on how our Western industrialized societies have become addicted to private space, technology, and mobility; how individuals occupy separate rooms, fixated on a screen or plugged to an earphone, or drive madly about in search of companionship; how rarely we are slumped in a group, one against another, in laughter. In the company of the Bororo, I felt I was experiencing another time—a time when families were bound together as units of survival, production, and reproduction; a time when the notion of change was not yet a constant concern.

Families of the early twentieth century, as described by those interviewed for this book, shared many characteristics across cultures. Most were large and multigenerational. When not actually dwelling under the same roof, relatives tended to live near one another. Older men made most decisions in an essentially patriarchal system. Marriages were often arranged by parents—

directly, through negotiations between families, or indirectly, through religious or community gatherings. Most couples had four or more children—and sometimes as many as eight or ten—all of whom bore significant responsibilities as working members of the family. Individual roles and behavior were well-defined; few digressions were permitted, and punishments were harsh. Children followed, generation after generation, in their parents' footsteps.

In 1900, the world population stood at 1.55 billion, one fourth of what it is today,[1] and land was not yet scarce nor soils depleted. Most families lived quiet lives in rural areas, undisturbed by communications technologies or international commerce. Immediate neighbors, the local community, and religious institutions offered the few distractions or leisure activities. The wider world was far away, only occasionally experienced by young men in times of war.

In the last half of the twentieth century, information, goods, and people all began to move within and across national borders. In 2000, rare was the village that did not have at least a radio or television set, or the family that had not watched images from afar, emanating from places they will never visit and cultures they do not fully comprehend. The ascendence of a global economy means that people make things for—and consume things made by—others thousands of miles away. Urbanization and the search for employment have led many to leave their homes and resettle across the country or across the globe.

The families quoted here, from Japan, the United States, and Mali, are the products of these trends in vastly different cultures. Within its distinct social setting, each is adjusting to a rapidly changing world. The common trait among them is that each family lives in a close-knit, multigenerational group, as was the case when their elders were children. Yet each is poised on the cusp of change: one generation dwells in the past, another attempts to adjust to continuously changing realities, and still another grasps for an uncertain future.

SUSAKA CITY, JAPAN

Once a small, backward village, bustling Susaka City is now but a half-hour ride by commuter train from Nagano, the city of 100,000 inhabitants that hosted the 1998 Winter Olympics. Susaka is surrounded by forested mountains that overlook valleys of apple orchards famous throughout Japan. It is a town that has prospered in recent years and boasts a smart rail station, an art museum, and a small zoo.

Susaka's metamorphosis is the story of contemporary Japan. Hundreds of villages have merged into urban centers where former farmers work for Japan's immense business and industrial interests. Recalling the quiet—and very poor—village of their youth, Susaka's older residents now complain of its crowded streets and an almost urban rhythm to its life.

Four generations of the Nakasawa family live in a large traditional-style farmhouse. Its huge roof envelops the dwelling, almost hiding its walls from view. Generations back, in this very same home, the family experienced extreme poverty. Now prosperous table grape growers, they have refurbished the home and created a formal garden to one side. The home's outer walls surround it completely; the entrance is found down a side lane and opens onto its lovely garden.

Setsu Nakasawa, 86
Ichiro Nakasawa, 67
Toshiko Nakasawa, 64
Mansanao Nakasawa, 40
Shigeko Nakasawa, 38

The entire family was waiting to greet us: great-grandmother, grandparents, parents and two of the three great-grandchildren. The third, a twelve year old, was off playing baseball with his school chums. The ever-present row of shoes and slippers was neatly arranged inside the entrance. Shuffling into the first room, I was urged on; we would hold our conversations in the furthest room, where all windows faced the garden, creating a sense of tranquil spaciousness. We gathered around a low, carved wooden table, about six feet square. Sitting cross-legged on floor pillows, I marveled at the agility of the eighty-six-year-old great-grandmother, Setsu, who, throughout the following hours of conversation, sat without moving or making allowances for age or stiff limbs. A portrait of her deceased husband, the family patriarch, hung on the wall beside me, watching over everyone. His death two years before had done little to lessen his influence on the way the family conducted its business or its relationships with one another.

SETSU   Not quite five feet tall, Setsu appeared even smaller due to her rounded back. Many farm wives of her generation are bent into a stoop by childhood malnourishment, fieldwork, and childbearing. She wore a gray kimono and round gold-framed glasses. Poor eyesight caused her to lean forward, looking at us closely, as if to compensate for her equally poor hearing. As is the custom of her generation, Setsu hesitated at first to talk about herself. "I feel uncomfortable," she told us, "because I'm not well-educated and I want to say the right thing." I assured her that there was no right or wrong thing to say—only whatever stories she wanted to tell about her life, or thoughts she wanted to share. Once she began her story, the qualms disappeared.

"I grew up in a family of nine people, including the grandparents. We were five children; I had three older sisters and one older brother. When I was just five, my brother left for the army and two sisters left to work in a factory. My mother was a second wife. The first had died of typhus.

"My father had invested in silkworms and done well, but suddenly all the silkworms died and we went bankrupt. We had to sell everything. My par-

ents went off to find work in Susaka City. I was then seven years old and
the only person living with the grandparents. We were so poor, we mixed the
wheat we grew with rice and sometimes a few vegetables. Only when there
was a festival did we have meat.

"When I was eleven my grandmother died, and soon after my grandfather became blind. One of my sisters came home to care for him. I attended school for six years, and when I turned eighteen I was sent to Tokyo to
work as a maid. Once, when I came
back for a visit, I learned that my
relatives had arranged my marriage with a man in Tokyo. Since I
had lived there, they thought it
appropriate. I lived in Tokyo for a
while, but I didn't get along with my
husband, so I returned to my family. But my husband's relatives
thought I was a very good wife;
they wanted me back. I returned for
a while and gave birth to a daughter, but I still couldn't stay.

"It was because of the beatings.
When his work didn't go well, my
husband beat me. I always thought
I shouldn't resist, so I didn't do
anything against him. I just got
beaten. I left and we were later
divorced. As was the custom in

The Nakasawa family: (*front*) Ichiro, Setsu,
Toshiko, (*back*) Masanao, Yoshiaki, Yumiko,
Shigeko

Japan, my daughter had to remain in his family. That's not right. I think
it's best if children stay with the mother. Luckily the person who took care
of my daughter let me see her from time to time. She had a weak heart and
died in her early forties."

At this point, Setsu paused and looked at me shyly, "You know, there is
seldom an occasion to talk about all this." She continued, "A year after the
divorce I married my second husband, the grandfather of this family. He,
too, was divorced. We met by photographs. His younger sister had married
a policeman who was working in our town. This fellow came to the house
and mentioned that his wife's elder brother couldn't find a wife. My relatives immediately recommended me, so our photographs were exchanged.
He was really good-looking in his military uniform. I decided, yes, I would
marry him. I didn't see him until I came to this house. There were six people living here: my husband, his parents, his younger sister, and his two children from the first marriage. Together we had four more children, three sons

and one daughter. Like everyone else, I worked in the field. I got along with everyone; they said I was a good worker. When I first arrived they teased my husband, asking why he took such a ridiculously small wife. But I gained their respect by my work."

Suddenly, leaning over to whisper in confidence as if afraid someone in the family might hear, Setsu confided, "One month before my husband died, he told me, 'It was so good to have you as my wife. Even though you are my second wife, it was good being with you.' He must have known he was dying."

Setsu was obviously proud that years of toil and service had finally received recognition: the approval of a dying husband. When I asked about the changes she had witnessed in women's lives, she shook her head and said, "Things are better economically, to be sure, and the environment is cleaner. But women's lives haven't changed that much. They work off the farm now but they still come home after dark and have to prepare dinner. That's not much different from when they worked on the farm. The greatest change I've seen is with children. In my childhood we obeyed adults without a word. We didn't speak unless spoken to, or complain. That has changed completely."◆

ICHIRO Setsu's sixty-seven-year-old stepson, Ichiro, is a slightly built man with a graceful, almost elegant demeanor. He is the nominal head of the Nakasawa family and looks unabashedly at those with whom he speaks, suggesting trust and attention to the subject at hand. We sat in the sunlit parlor as the afternoon shadows began to invade the room. Ichiro's youngest grandson, Hiroyuki, a boy of five, had arrived home from school and, as he does every day, came to spend time with his grandfather. The child sought the elder's attention, putting his arms around Ichiro's neck, jumping on his back, pulling at his clothes. The grandfather talked calmly, without outward expression of annoyance or authority. Ichiro didn't push the child away, or scold; he simply concentrated more closely on the questions asked.

"When I was a boy this entire region was devoted to the silk industry. We raised silkworms and the mulberry trees on which they feed. The United States was our greatest market, but when the Great Depression overtook the U.S. economy, the silk industry collapsed. This community went through very bad times. At one point a government official pronounced Susaka the poorest village in the region. I was about ten years old. We were so poor that the only thing we had to eat was gruel: half rice, half wheat. Now it's like paradise, all this food we have—meat, fish, fruit, vegetables, even food that comes from abroad.

"In 1938 government policy changed: we were told to grow fruit trees. When the war began and the young men were sent off, the trees were still not bearing fruit. It was a very difficult period for the women left behind. I didn't go into the army until I turned nineteen, in 1944. I was sent to northern Japan to work in a Chinese prisoner of war camp. I supervised their work. We were trained to strap bombs to our waists and throw ourselves on enemy tanks in case Japan was invaded."

Pointing to the elderly Setsu, who sat on the far side of the room, out of earshot, he added, "That mother sitting there is not my real mother; she's my father's second wife. He was a very strict person, as was his father, my grandfather, who dominated and taught us everything. My mother couldn't adapt, so my parents divorced. I think I still behave somewhat like my grandfather—but it doesn't fit today's times. I try to be more easygoing, but in reality I follow my grandfather's disciplined ways. You see, the old education was based on the rules, 'Respect the emperor and live for the country.' Do anything for the emperor and feel proud of it. But after World War II,

Eighty-six-year-old Setsu Nakasawa

since we were defeated, democratization became the norm. The education system changed completely. That's why people changed. If we behave like my grandfather's generation did, and say 'I'm an older person so you must do as I say'—if we do that, there's going to be trouble, because the trend is toward democratization. Children are more independent now.

"I had only two children. During World War II we Japanese were asked to have lots of children, but after the war the policy changed and we were told to make 'few, high-quality children.' That policy has been really good for Japan. We have prospered, and relations between people have changed. But the trend toward urbanization is strong, and agriculture will be the loser. People prefer to work for a company, to earn a salary. Big companies are taking over the land; they farm it like an industry. Land should remain in families, who care for it properly. Perhaps it's because I'm older that I fear these changes. My son doesn't agree with me; he thinks it's a good thing— it's progress.

"I work at least ten hours a day on the farm. My wife and daughter-in-law help me, but once I get too old, their labor will not suffice. My son will probably sell the land or rent it out. He hasn't said he doesn't want to farm, but since he has a job in the municipal administration, I think he wants to work there until he retires. And besides, he can't farm alone.

"These days, everyone thinks of themselves first. 'Me-ism' is the new way of thinking. That's why when people marry they live apart from their parents. When you work for a company, you can earn enough to get a house by yourself. Wages bring this independence. We used to expect children to remain at home and help with the farm, but now they work elsewhere for salaries. The generations are living together less and less. Individualism is the greatest influence for change. Maybe it's a good thing. But we must realize that life is not always as easy as it seems now. We have to teach the children about hard times—how to put up with, and manage, hard times. If you do something, do your best. That's what I'm trying to teach my grandchildren."

As Ichiro was expressing his concern for the younger generation, five-year-old Hiroyuki pulled at his sweater, obviously seeking his grandfather's attention. Ichiro seemed to notice him for the first time in a long while, and looked at him absently. Softly, he added, "I don't know whether they want to listen or not."◆

TOSHIKO Ichiro's wife had come in and out of the room while we talked, checking to see if our tea was hot enough, bringing sliced fruit and different cakes each time. The cakes had been specially prepared for our visit: hard nut cakes, round jelly-like cakes with sliced apples and pears, accompanied, of course, by piles of homegrown grapes. The parade of trays continued, even as Toshiko took her turn to tell us of her life. She is a tall woman, at least five foot nine, and, at sixty-four, slightly slow in her movements. She rarely smiled during the next hours' conversation; I suspect she was worried about what was going on in the kitchen, about who would bring the next serving of delicacies. She began by describing her childhood.

"I grew up in a small village which has become part of Nagano. We were eleven in the family: my parents, a grandmother, three sisters, four brothers, and myself. The grandmother was the second wife of my paternal grandfather. She was paralyzed and bedridden. All of us worked on the farm. My parents expected us to help with the farm work and with household chores. That was part of our responsibilities as children. There was not much difference in boys' and girls' duties, really. It was more a question of age. The girls helped in the kitchen as well as in the fields.

"I married at twenty-three. My husband's aunt was trying to find a wife for him. She asked friends in Nagano if they knew anyone, and I was recommended. When I came here we numbered eight: my parents-in-law, my husband and me, my husband's three brothers and one sister—all in this house. My husband is the eldest son.

"In past generations, family members could not disagree with the grand-father. But now, in such a large family as ours, decision making has several levels. For example, because my son gets a salary from the municipality, he is independent of the larger family. If he wants to send his children to private school or do something that regards his immediate family, he and his wife make the decision. But if it is a larger issue, concerning the entire family, then we all debate it until my husband, who controls the family money, reaches a decision. There's rarely a disagreement. It's because each of us always thinks about the others and we don't compete with one another. If there is a disagreement, we decide by simple majority.

"I must admit, there are lots of things we don't understand about the new society. For example, the elders mustn't say anything to their grandchildren because they are living in an entirely different society than that of our generation. Today's children have so much because the society has become rich. That makes it difficult for the elders to teach them. We teach manners to the children and, I think, they behave in a polite way outside the home. But here, they feel free to do anything they want. When my grandchildren leave their toys all over the room, I say, 'Let's clean the room, organize toys, pick them up.' But they don't listen. Sometimes they clean up immediately, but most of the time they make excuses, 'It's not me, it's not mine.' It's difficult to make them behave. Why? They are spoiled. They watch TV all they want. Maybe my grandchildren are still too small to obey, but it's difficult for grandparents to be really strict. Parents aren't teaching discipline. These days anybody can say anything to anybody!

"In Japanese families, the grandfather is really strict, especially with the daughter-in-law. In my generation, a woman could do nothing without the husband or the father-in-law's permission. We couldn't even go out of the house without it. In farmers' families everyone was so busy, they needed the woman's labor. But now the work has been cut in half, so it's much better for wives. These days I can go anywhere I want, do almost anything I want to do. This is a tremendous change.

"My daughter is another example. She worked before she married but quit her job to help her husband in his architectural business. Now she has two small children; she still helps her husband but spends most of her time raising the children. They live nearby in a nuclear family. She often asks me to take care of the children. So I assume there are lots of inconveniences to a nuclear family. Sometimes I feel the small family might be better, but I don't really know. In big families there are lots of hassles and arguments, but if I get sick or old, I will need the support of family members—so I think the big family is best for the elders and the sick. Since my husband is the first son of his family, it is his responsibility to care for his mother. My mother-in-law will live with us until she dies, unless, of course, she gets seriously ill and has to go to the hospital. But old people much prefer to die at home."◆

MASANAO   Forty-year-old Masanao is Toshiko's only son. He is a university graduate who works for the Susaka City municipality. He is taller and much bigger than his father, but his manner is similar—thoughtful, almost gentle. His voice, unusually deep, adds a tone of sincerity to his words.

"My parents were the greatest influence of my youth, especially my father. Both of them worked on the farm, so I followed them around. My grandfather was a municipal leader and was rarely at home, so he didn't influence me much. Before I left for university I helped my father on the farm, especially on weekends. I try to do so even now. As for my son, I don't know if he'll want to be a farmer. It's possible that he may get a job far from here. In that case we could rent the land to other people. Only ten out of one hundred residents in this area are now farmers; the others are employees of the municipality or of businesses. Japan's economic success has influenced everything—attitudes, lifestyles, everything. People measure everything by money, which has come to signify power and status. Money has created a self-centered way of thinking.

"When we first married I thought it might be good for us to live by ourselves, just the two of us. It's more intimate, for sure. But after the children were born, I realized I had much to gain from a large family group. There's so much support and stability around us. We can ask advice of each other. When a problem arises in this family, it can be discussed and solved. Everyone feels, 'I'm not alone'; there's a sense of security in being part of the unit. But living together has become more a question of occupation, of jobs. People have to live where they have jobs. Also, if you live in a nuclear family it is nearly impossible to maintain the land. If you are farmers, it's natural to live with the grandparents, all together. I strongly believe it is to the children's advantage to live this way because they can see and hear all different views from different adults. It's a learning process to grow up in a multigenerational family. This was certainly true in my case. But I must admit, at the same time, I lost my uniqueness, my individuality, because everyone has opinions and we often settle on the compromise, the average opinion. So if I was to be a good boy, I had to compromise, to give up my personal opinion.

"I want my children to be free to choose whatever job they want. But I also want them to respect others, to think about others as much as they can. People are so self-centered now. In this village, for example, people have discarded the communal habits of helping each other; now it's everyone for himself. It's important to teach children responsibility to others. That's why I try to spend as much time as possible with mine. When I come home from work, I'm always with them. We all have different schedules in the morning, so we go in different directions, but in the evening we eat, study, and talk together, every day. My eldest son plays baseball, so on weekends and holidays we go to the games together. That's the best way to teach our children—just being with them."◆

SHIGEKO Masanao's wife Shigeko, thirty-eight, is an active, enthusiastic mother of three. She describes herself as someone who also tries to develop interests and relationships beyond the family. She attends lectures and concerts and belongs to a group that assists poor communities in Southeast Asia. She was curious to know my impressions of the countries I had visited. When she described her situation, she admitted to making a concerted effort to maintain her independence within the Nakasawa clan.

"I was raised in a nuclear family: my parents, two younger brothers and myself. We lived just a few miles from here. Until I married at twenty-six, I worked as a secretary for an electrical company in Susaka. Masanao and I met at a Young People's Society party. We courted for four years before getting married. We have a very equal relationship. In my mother's generation, if the husband said something, the wife had to obey; she had to put up with everything and was not allowed to complain. In my generation, anyone can say anything. My husband and I communicate equally. When we make big decisions, we discuss everything openly. It's a big difference.

"I had decided I wanted to marry a man with a multigenerational family. You see, when I was growing up I had a very close friend who lived with all her relatives in one house. I visited her all the time because when I came home from school there was no one at home. I envied her because she had a grandmother and grandfather. I really liked large families. Before I married Masanao, I worried a bit about his grandfather and the other adults in the family. Would they accept me, be nice to me? In former generations the grandparents had so much power that the daughter-in-law couldn't say a thing. But this family liked me, and I was in love with Masanao, so I told myself I would be able to manage. If I have retained a certain independence, it's mainly because I make an effort to do so. And the family understands what I'm doing. All that depends on the family, of course; some are very slow to change. I have friends who are in families in which they still cannot say anything. We discuss this a lot.

"I have other friends who married into a nuclear family situation and certainly, compared to this family, there is more freedom. But at the same time I feel I can learn from other family members. It's very clear who is responsible for what. My mother-in-law works in the fields; the great-grandmother

Nakasawa family members work together on the harvest

is in charge of keeping the bathtub clean and ready for use. I'm responsible for meals and laundry. And everyone is involved in raising the children. My children are not just my children but everyone's children. That's a definite advantage of a multigenerational family. Human beings need communication. They're always starving for conversation, especially the elderly, so living together is really good for us. We must have a gentle way of thinking and respecting each other.

"My friends all have three children, just as we do. The reason is usually the size of houses or apartments; they're too small for a large family. In the future, I'm sure it will cost too much even for three, no matter what the housing arrangements are. After the children grow up I will stay home, because my in-laws will be older and will not be able to work in the fields. I'll have more responsibility and will have to learn how to manage the farm.

"It is my responsibility, mine and my husband's, to teach the children all they need to know to have a good life. In today's world they need to know about the world, about other people, about their bodies and their sexuality. I will tell them about all these things.

"I want them to choose freely whatever job they want in life, but when I think about my first son, I begin to think that it would be good for him to stay with us, to run the farm. On the other hand, I feel sorry for him, that he has such a big responsibility and cannot have other choices. In the end I can't decide what I feel. I won't force him to stay, but I hope that one of the children will want to stay and live with us."◆

The Nakasawa family voiced many of the concerns that plague families in other parts of the world. Great-grandmother Setsu, born in 1911, told of poverty and work as a child, and of a time when women had little power.

Her stepson, Ichiro, the grandfather, spoke of discipline and obedience to his elders, and wondered about today's notions of democracy and individualism. Grandmother Toshiko told of how decision making within families has become more inclusive and shared, of women's improved status, and of "spoiled" children. Her son, Masanao, pondered the negative influence of money and his concern for teaching his children the notion of responsibility. His wife, Shigeko, told of a lonely childhood in a nuclear family and her choice to be part of a larger group, regardless of the tasks and responsibility it entails.

As we were saying good-bye to the Nakasawas, twelve-year-old Yoshiaki returned from school. He seemed already conscious of his responsibility as "first son," remaining calm as his younger siblings, excited by our visit, ran about, jumping up and down. They paid little attention to the adults who told them to behave, and no one seemed to think it mattered much. Like millions of families around the world, the Nakasawas gather around their table at night to share an evening meal. They discuss the day's events and the next day's chores. Grandfather Ichiro is pulled at by Hiroyuki, the five-year-old, and Setsu strains to hear what everyone is saying.

WAYLAND, MISSOURI, USA

It was three weeks before Christmas in 1994. As my plane descended toward St. Louis, I could see below me winding rivers, farms surrounded by green winter crops, and occasional ponds that sparkled in the afternoon sun. The Mississippi River appeared still swollen from its destructive rampage the previous summer, when it joined the Missouri and Des Moines rivers and flooded homes, towns, and farmland.

My destination was Wayland, a small farming community three hours north of Columbia, a university town halfway across Missouri from St. Louis. I traveled by rental car along an interstate express-way where towns, wistfully named St. Peters and Kingdom City, appeared among rolling hills. From Columbia, the drive to Wayland was on narrow country roads where endless stretches of harvested fields were interrupted only occasionally by clumps of miniature forests. Evidence of the demise of family farms rose up in these vast expanses of croplands: lifeless farmhouses and barns stood abandoned, some leaning sideways, ready to collapse.

Leslie Marshal Young, 88
Donald Young, 60
Geneal Young, 58,
Lisa Young, 22
David Young, 25

The family I was traveling to meet, the Youngs, have lived near Wayland for three generations. They grow corn and soybeans. Theirs is a story of a hard-working family faced with the changing economics of agriculture—the rise of large agribusinesses, with which few family farms can compete. The grandchildren, now young adults, have joined the quiet exodus from the land as these changes make it impossible for the family grain farm to support more than one generation at a time. Just months before, nature, too, had added to the Young's woes. Their farm was destroyed by the summer floods. Home, barns, and grain bins had all been lost.

LESLIE   Leslie Young retired long ago. Widowed three years before, he lives alone on his farm, which sits on a small hill across the Des Moines River in Iowa. It consists of a modest brick house, kennels, barns, a vegetable garden and orchard—all looking off over recently flooded cornfields. Leslie is tall, slight of build, and blessed with thick snow-white hair. His ice-blue eyes brightened mischievously at some of my questions. Admitting to a bad hip that "gives me trouble," Leslie nonetheless manages to tend his vegetable garden and orchard, and apparently enjoys living alone. His younger brother, he said, married his wife's sister. "Two brothers married two sisters. And both of us are widowers." When I asked about his childhood, the blue eyes looked straight at me, unwavering.

"My childhood? Oh, that's easy. It didn't last long. My dad hurt his spine working on a washed-out bridge when I was nine, so I had to make myself a man. I hitched myself up to the plow and started working. Nine years old with a fourth-grade education. You see, somebody had to work. There were nine of us kids. I was the second-oldest boy. My brother was six or seven years older, just out of the eighth grade, when the accident happened. He pulled me out of school and set me plowing. The other children went to school.

"Our main diet was cornbread mush with molasses, fried chicken—all things we raised. We raised our own sugar cane and made our own molasses. And we stuffed our featherbeds with straw. In one place we lived, we had three wooden shacks, like barns, covered inside with heavy paper. We boys had to sleep up in the loft; it wasn't sealed at all. And come the snow, we woke up with snow all over the quilt.

"I never went to town but two or three times until I was about fifteen years old. We were blessed; we worked hard. You see, I started out with a walking plow and a cultivator. Back then we didn't have all this machinery. I tell you, if I had left then and come back now, I couldn't believe it. Farming is gradually getting away from the individual operators. We're going into farming twelve thousand or fifteen thousand acres of land, and that's not good. It'll become just like General Motors, Ford, or Chrysler, where they end up controlling the prices. And they don't care as much for the soil. It's no good at all.

"I worked for my dad until I was twenty-four years old. I never drew a dime's worth of wages in my life. He'd give me a dollar or two the day after sales. When Elsie and I were married, I had to borrow money to buy her ring and my wedding suit."

The Young family: (*front*) Donald, Geneal, Leslie, (*back*) Dave, Lisa

As the octogenarian before me began to speak of his wife and of their courtship, he was transformed into a young man, alternately blushing joyfully and saddening at the thought of his loss. "She taught school in Wayland. I'd seen her several times in town. She was a plucky one, about five feet tall and ninety pounds. And two years older than I; we were twenty-six and twenty-four when we married. We started out broke but we made a little money. We didn't have it to throw away, but we really never wanted for anything. Elsie died three years ago; she had a heart condition and it just played out."

I asked Leslie who in his childhood had influenced him most. "My mother. She was a queen! I just copied her, I guess. She told me several times that I wasn't the only child she'd had, 'but I've given you more whippings than all the others put together.' She didn't talk much. She was busy; there was so many of us, she just didn't have time to devote to us kids.

"Our family would meet with other families pretty near every Sunday— there'd be anywhere from fifteen to twenty-five people—for a picnic. Neighbors visited each other in the evenings, five or six families together. That's totally gone. TV came in, and cars to come and go.

"It seems that churchgoing people are getting fewer and fewer. I've belonged to our church for over seventy years, and we've got the lowest membership we've ever had. Part of it is that there's no place for young people here. You send them to college to get an education and they don't come back. You see, it costs you $200,000 to set up farming—or you have to marry a rich farmer's daughter. That's why they're leaving; there's nothing for them here. They can't make a living unless one of them works off the land. And they don't have six or seven children like before. Rural communities are dying.

"Today's young people behave different than we did. Much different. There were nine of us kids, and we had little old kid spats, of course, but we never fell out. When my mother died, my sister took care of the estate. There wasn't much, but she settled it. There was no fuss or hassle. Seems to me like families don't get along that well anymore. And children demand so much more. We spoil them. We didn't have it, so we want them to have it. It's cost Donnie and me half of a fortune to get these grandkids through college. I put Donnie through for about ten cents on the dollar compared to what it cost for them. Now they have nine-hundred-dollar apartments and stereos. We're partly to blame.

"Elsie and I had only the one child because Donnie's birth was bad, very bad. Elsie had an awful time. He was born at home and the doctor was there. She was such a small woman, she had a bad time of it so she said, 'If you don't mind . . . ,' and she told me she didn't want to have more children. I would have liked a daughter but I never mentioned it; I never pushed her. She was a queen. I tried to be a good husband.

"From what I see, young men are getting irresponsible. Very definitely. When we were kids, sex and dating were very rare. Now they go out on a date and have sex. Many more men, and maybe some women, are stepping out on their mates. Our morals are deteriorating. TV is a terrible thing in this country. There's so much lovemaking and sex, sleeping together. Kids have only one way to learn—*observe*. They see you doing something and they're going to try it. A lot of these youngsters are brought up on television, from the very beginning. That's to blame for most of it. And we don't have a family life like we used to have. Both men and women are working, and they neglect the family. It all starts at home. Even my grandchildren—they make me feel like they don't need me. They're polite and all that but—as I say, I've spent as much on their college as their folks. They couldn't be where they are without me, but they act like it's all normal. The breakdown of families is causing it. But why are families breaking down? I don't know. Unless, as I say, it's because we're getting far from the church. And from each other. I read an article where a fellow had made a survey in some school: 25 percent of the first graders have been drunk before they go to school. There's no family life there. They just hatch 'em like I do pigs."

As we rose to leave, Leslie laughed at his last remark. Then, only seconds later, he shook his head with total conviction, saying, "I wouldn't want to be here two hundred years from now, believe me."◆

DONALD   An hour later, armed with a dozen doughnuts, I went to meet Leslie's son for a late morning coffee. Donald Young is a big man, sturdy in build and confidence. He is a young, energetic sixty, with a face weathered from years in the open air. He exudes vitality and appears somewhat impatient with his family's ways, in a gentle but insistent way. One would guess that he never wastes time—that he is a person who always has something *more* to do.

Don, as he asked to be called, graduated from the University of Missouri in 1955, went immediately into the army, and served two years in Germany. When he returned he began farming with his father. As soon as he was able, he started out on his own. He's been active in the community, serving on the University Extension Council at the county and state levels and as advisor to the 4H Club when his children were members. As we sat drinking our coffee, he mused on the difference among generations and how they relate to one another.

"It's strange, but the changes that bother my father are already the norm for us. It's what we've grown used to. It's our society, so we think nothing of it. But it bothers him greatly. And it's the same with our children: what bothers us about society is just their way of life. But people don't accept change readily.

"I was an only child, but I didn't think about it much. There was no pressure to live up to certain standards because I was an only child. I did farm chores; whatever is required of adults is what children start off doing. It definitely helped later in life. You have to accept responsibilities, learn how to be responsible for yourself. Tasks are given with the anticipation that they get done right. So you had to learn how to do 'em. Ours wasn't a talkative family; it was more a *doing* family. Both sides of my family have always been hard workers. They all had good work ethics. My grandparents were nearby, and we got to visit them often. It was always enjoyable, because I guess grandparents treated you a little nicer than parents did. In those days families were large, and they tended to stick together. My father gave me the opportunity to farm, and that was what I knew how to do, so—I just did it.

"Four or five years before Geneal and I married, Dad decided I needed to go it alone, so he split his operation and I took part of it. It was much easier then to start out on your own, because children grew up on farms and knew about farming; at some point they worked for other farmers or got their own land. Now, in rural communities, we educate our children to be competitive in the job market, for high-tech jobs. Consequently, they leave the land for those jobs.

"You see, most farmers chose farming because they are independent thinkers; they don't belong to unions or conform to a regimented type of work. They enjoy being their own boss. And to be successful you've got to be a very disciplined boss. In fact, the farm is really the boss. You'll probably be in debt all your life. A lot of farmers live very meagerly, but when they die, they pass on million-dollar estates.

"But farms are going to get larger and larger. With world population increases, food production will increase—but the problem is, will people have the money to buy it? We send corn and wheat to Africa, but they haven't got the jobs to provide wages for people to purchase it. And increased production will cause depletion of our soils and water. Where I've been farming there's been no loss of soil productivity, because it's the delta, flat ground. The ones who farmed in the hill country have lost a tremendous amount of soil. We're terracing the land, so when the water falls on the ground it only runs a short distance. I believe the conservation measures are justified. We're more aware of all this now. Maybe this country will start doing something to head off a crisis—instead of 'waiting to see.'

"We didn't encourage either of our children to follow our footsteps. I thought there were better occupations than farming. My boy helped on the farm. He was very talented and could do just about anything with little instruction. He could have been a tremendous farmer, but he chose not to. His interest was in computers and electronics, so consequently, we didn't encourage him to become a farmer. They just have to go out and do the best they can. Whatever is out there. They got their family values years ago.

"We didn't spend much time just sitting and having conversations on the philosophy of life with our children. There were things to do, to accomplish. We've only had two vacations in our lives. The others were just mini-vacations—two days, three days. When you leave a farming operation, you have to shut down everything, so you can't leave that often. We didn't get a babysitter and go off alone; the children were part of the travel.

"One of the things I feel that I accomplished in raising the children is their ability to make their own decisions. I felt that was very important. I started that when they were three and four. There are so many people who can't make a decision. That's one thing I wanted to instill in them. Even in the realm of punishment, I always gave them a choice: either they could accept the punishment or get a spanking. 'The decision is yours.' They had to learn early that there was a decision to make, that nobody was going to make it for them. I know it's paid off. Basically, the only thing I want for them is not to let anybody think for them.

"They've had more liberties than my generation was ever allowed. In my generation, if you argued, you'd be punished. I didn't go out in society much before high school, but our children's generation has been forced to become part of the society at age five or six. Lisa was doing adult jobs at church at age eleven or twelve. There's more emphasis on children becoming adults very early in life. It's more democratic. Definitely.

"The media have had tremendous influence, of course. Good and bad. Our children gained a tremendous amount of education through television. There have also been bad influences. Children don't learn to do for themselves as much. TV takes them away from the parents *and* takes the parents away from their responsibility to guide their children.

"Families have become so much more mobile, especially families that are not happy together. It's so much easier just to take off, get away from it. I don't know if people want to move, or have had to move in order to support their families. But this mobile society has broken down family structure. Years ago, families traded visits a lot and socialized. Now we socialize as much, even more, but it's not with families. It's through universities and other organizations. And we're gone from the home a lot. Cars have made that possible. We don't think anything about driving a hundred miles to go to a basketball game or to see friends. Back thirty, forty years ago, that was an all-day trip.

"Every family could probably live in harmony if they would return to the lifestyles of thirty, forty years ago. But we always want *more*. We have cars, the kids want to have a car. We have a TV, they want to watch cartoons, we want to watch the news. So we buy two televisions. It means that Mom has to go to work to 'keep up with the Joneses.' The driving forces are not *necessities*, but mostly *wants*."◆

GENEAL Don's wife is a woman of medium height, with curly auburn hair and a round face adorned with large plastic-rimmed eyeglasses. She wore a skirt and a sweater over a lace-trimmed blouse. Her presence exuded generosity and goodness. She seemed alternately shy and outspoken. After a while, I realized that her shyness emerged only when she was talking about herself; she spoke boldly and proudly when she told of her husband's or her children's accomplishments. Geneal had worked her way through school and college, become a secretary, and worked until her first child was born. She was proud to say that with what she had saved, she and Don were able to put a down payment on a small farm.

"I'm an only child, born and raised in Keokuk, Iowa. My mom was thirty-eight when she had me; Dad was forty-two. They'd been married for twelve years before I came along. My father was a delivery man for Mobil Oil, taking gasoline and kerosene to farmers. He was raised on a farm in a family of thirteen children. Although he never went back to the farm after serving in World War I, in Germany, he never lost sight of his roots.

"My mother was one of six children born in Minnesota. As a mother, she was a worry wart, very protective of me. She never wanted me to go anywhere; I could get hurt. I always resented it. It stifled me.

"I didn't give up my job until four years after we were married when I became pregnant. It was then I had to learn to be a farmer's wife. I was a city gal; I didn't know anything about farming. Since both Don and I were only children, I didn't want to raise just one child; I remember how lonely it was when I was growing up. When we had our own kids, we went to everything they were involved in. We went out of our way to take them here and there. We wanted to do it. I hope they'll appreciate it somewhere down the line. We were active in church and both of us were involved in extension work and still are.

"I belong to the Missouri Association for Family and Community Education, an organization devoted to voluntarism and to promoting the family and leadership development. We are affiliated with the Associated Country Women of the World. I'm just about to complete a two-year term as vice president for public policy for the statewide association. We're real concerned about the quality of television, the violence and lack of quality programming in prime time for children. We're also lobbying for more funds for the Children's Television Act and quality programming.

"I do volunteer work at the hospital, too, and we're hearing more and more about spousal abuse. We didn't realize we had this problem here. Back in my high school days we never heard of such things. We had the local town drunk, but never drugs or this violence.

"Our association is losing members because women are getting more involved in school boards and the city council. Women are getting more assertive —I know I am. I've become more assertive than I was a few years back because of my involvement with extension work and leadership in the women's association. They even wanted me to run for state president this year. Don said no. I'm glad he did, now, because we've had the floods and all the moving and sadness.

"I'm a lot more liberal with my children than Mother was. I wasn't allowed to go to the youth group at my church—the Lutheran Church. I never got to go on field trips. My kids went everywhere; we tried to get them into everything. They may not think they got to do much, but they got to do a lot more than I did.

"My mother never told me about married life or sexuality. Nothing at all. With my children, every time I wanted to bring up the subject, they didn't want to discuss it. Maybe I was hesitant or didn't feel I knew much myself, not having had any experience from my own parents. It was almost like a dirty word back then. I know Lisa is on the pill. She and Dave seem to know everything already, even about AIDS. I hope they're being careful.

"I hope they'll become successful, financially independent, and have nice homes. David didn't get his degree; he went to school for five and a half years and didn't graduate, much to my chagrin. But he says, 'Don't worry, Mother, I'll get my degree sometime.'

"As for Lisa, I don't really know about her goals. She got her degree in hotel and restaurant management from the University of Missouri this year. Her biggest fault is getting involved too deeply with the wrong guys. At one job she started dating her boss. The regulations said you couldn't fraternize with employees, so she had to quit; otherwise he would be fired. Then she moved in with him. My religious principles don't believe in that. We brought our children up in the church. I just hope we said enough good things ages ago that they'll come around someday.

"I guess I could have been a better mother. I read Dr. Spock and did the best I could. But no one teaches us to be a parent."◆

LISA   Blonde, athletic Lisa Young was dressed in an aqua jogging suit, ready for the drive to Kansas City and her new job as assistant manager of a motel. At twenty-three, she is an attractive, self-confident young woman, and appeared anxious to get on with her new life. Taking the time to reflect on her childhood and her views of family life was simply another task to be completed prior to setting off.

"I enjoyed growing up on the farm and in a small town because there's more personal identity there. The teachers know your name at school. In the city, you're just a number. The reason I'm not staying here is because there are no jobs. And I'm getting to the point where I want to do things you can only do in a city.

"My parents had a great influence on us. They were big motivators. They let me get involved in 4H, and in every activity I wanted at school. Dad always tried to reason everything out. I didn't like that, but now I know he was right. I get my stubbornness from Dad and my emotional side from Mum.

"We're a lot more advanced than my parents' generation. But they were closer to each other. They didn't have technology so they *had* to do things with each other. I want to be close with my family, to get along with them, talk to them. I also want my children to be more advanced than I am. I'd like to have my children young, that way I can keep up with them. I'd like two children, a son and daughter.

"Hopefully I'll start settling down. The person I settle down with will have to have a comparable job to be able to work things out. He'll have to understand that. Nowadays both members of a couple have to work to be able to survive. Two incomes are better than one, especially if you have children. Even if my husband makes a lot of money, I think I'd get bored if I didn't work.

"For a husband—the most important quality is communication, honesty, loyalty. I have a boyfriend now. It's a serious relationship. I hope it will work out. One day I was angry and I sat and wrote a list of everything I wanted in a man. I showed it to him and said, 'You have to be every one of these things or else.'

"Right now, I fear being alone. I don't know anyone in Kansas City. My title will be assistant manager/sales representative. I've had three months of training. Two days a week I'll go out and make sales calls, and eventually I'll move on to payroll and accounts payable. Hopefully I'll work my way up to a manager's position.

"It's definitely a disadvantage professionally to be a woman. I know for a fact that when I was interviewing for a job, one of the reasons I wasn't hired was because I was a woman. I wasn't 'authoritative' enough. I'm going to do the best I can, show them that I can do it.

"I know I'm going to call home a lot. I really don't want to go far away from my family. Lots of my friends have left Missouri, gone to California, but I don't want to do that—yet. I still want to try to be close to my family, especially Grandpa."◆

DAVE Lisa's brother, Dave, is three years older than she, but he appears to lack the outgoing self-confidence of his sister. He is tall and husky and has his mother's kind face. When we met outside his house, he was wearing sunglasses that he kept on indoors. His body language spoke of a person who is uncomfortable talking about himself, unsure of what life holds.

"The difference between my dad and me is that he's in the family business and I'm not. In most families, you used to do what your father and grandfather did, but I can't see myself as a farmer. Farming is too risky. I just don't want that much responsibility. It's fun to go home and drive the tractors for a while, but when you're a farmer you are responsible for your own income and livelihood. If you do something wrong, that could be the end of it. I don't want that much responsibility just yet. In a few years I might change my mind, but right now I don't want to farm.

"Most people in my generation feel the same. Everybody wants to do their own thing. I really wanted to be a computer programmer. After a while I realized that I'd sit in front of a desk or a computer screen twelve hours day. I'd end up a shriveled old man, all pale. It was a real revelation. I like my job working with a surveyor, but I haven't decided if I want to do it for the next fifty years. I'll stick with it for a while and see if I like it. For the moment I'm still in school, hoping to get a piece of paper. You need a diploma to get in the door anywhere. That's about all it's good for. Very few people have a degree related to what they're actually doing.

"I don't talk to my parents or my grandfather about what's going on in my life. I'm sure it annoys the hell out of them but—I just go ahead and do my own thing. I don't discuss my goals or problems with anyone, really. I don't feel the need for it.

"There doesn't seem to be as much respect for the older generation. It's not 'Yes sir, no sir' to your parents; it's just 'OK'—a lot less formal than it used to be. If you go back a ways, the elders were it. Whatever they said, you did. I don't think my generation rejects older people, but our parents' ideas might not apply to today's situations."

I interrupted to ask about his parents: Would he care for them when they got older?

"I never thought of that. Eventually it will happen. But I've never thought about it, actually. When it happens, I guess I'll deal with it.

"Right now, people are too greedy. Rather than making a little sacrifice so the rest of the world would be a better place, they're just trying to make as much money as they can. If you destroy something along the way, so what? It's not my age group that's like this; it's people in positions of power. The government is way out of control. I've never been in an activist group but I have my opinions. I vote. But I'm one little person in a sea of many. I'm just kind of existing and trying to stay out of everyone else's way.

"For example, marriage: I don't think there is a right age or anything. It's whenever you meet the right person and it feels right. Maybe I'll marry next week, maybe thirty years from now, maybe never. But I'd like a wife I can talk to, someone I'm comfortable with. Someone I can trust, who knows me, with whom I get along well. Someone semi-responsible. And I don't want a lot of kids. No more than one or two children, definitely. We've got too many people in the world already.

"I've never thought about parenting. I probably won't until I have kids. My parents seem to have done a decent job. I'm not sure how they did it. I know I'm not going to read a lot of books on the subject. Books were written by people who don't have my kids. I'll do what comes naturally."◆

The Youngs have tried to do all the right things for their children and community. Despite their involvement in church, agricultural associations, or school and parenting groups, they realize that the younger generation must leave, pushed by lack of opportunity close by and pulled by the excitement of a rapidly changing world far beyond the parents' experience.

Leslie Young's life was set out for him, and he made the most of it. His childhood was structured by responsibility to parents and siblings. Later, he saw to it that his child and grandchildren had more advantages than he had. His son, Don, has been a successful farmer who understands that the ways of the past are no model for his children's future. Times and technology have changed; so, too, have relationships and roles.

Employee, wife, mother, and volunteer leader are the defining roles of Geneal Young. Yet as one listens to her description of her volunteer work, one is struck by how she undervalues her contribution to her family and the larger community, caught perhaps in the mistaken belief that only salaried work is work. Lisa, her daughter, has reflected on how she wants to manage her life as woman, wife, mother, and professional. She seeks independence but admits her need for closeness to her family. Her brother, Dave, is far less sure of what he wants. Grandson and son of farmers, he realized early that farming was not a possibility for him. Afloat in choices with no model to follow, he seems at a loss to know what route to take.

BAMAKO, MALI

Bamako, the capital of the landlocked Sahelian nation of Mali, sits along the banks of the country's lifeline: the Niger River. Mali possesses few natural resources, but it is a land rich in a diversity of peoples and cultures: nomads, pastoralists, farmers, fishermen, and traders who once prospered from the trans-Saharan caravan trade.

In 1881, the colonizing French built a fort on a ridge above the river at Bamako, from which they could dominate the region's people. Since Mali's independence from France in 1960, Bamako has become a magnet for those who seek education, fortune, and power—and, increasingly, for those who flee rural poverty. It is a dusty, overcrowded city of nearly 700,000 people, where only the main streets are paved, open sewers line the alleys, and infrequent trash collection is a major health hazard. Yet bustling Bamako continues to attract hopeful migrants from Mali's remote villages.

I was taken by a Malian friend to meet the Sissoko family on the city's outskirts. A large group of relatives lives in a wide, enclosed courtyard and six adjoining rooms, each with a door leading to the courtyard. The Sissokos are among those who have sought a better life in Bamako. A generation removed from village life, they have prospered from the skills of the patriarch, Mahmadou, a retired mechanic. His earnings enabled him to send his sons to be trained in Germany. Five among them work there now, and when they can, they send money home. Luckily so: six years ago a stroke left Mahmadou Sissoko partially paralyzed and unable to work.

Kama Kante, 80
Mahmadou Sissoko, 63
Jala Touré, 49
Fathia Sissoko, 30
Aminata Samake, 24

Among those living in the family compound—or the "big family," as those interviewed called the house—are Mahmadou Sissoko's three wives, his mother, a sister, and the children of a second sister who, when she remarried, left her children in the big family. No one was quite sure just how many children live there—or how many adults, either. Estimates seemed to put the number at about forty. Over a period of a week, I talked with Mahmadou, his mother, his first wife, a son, and his bride of one year. Theirs is a story of a traditional multigenerational household that put great value on multiple wives and many children. Challenged by a more complex world and evolving needs, the family is in the process of reexamining its ways.

KAMA   Eighty-year-old Mme. Kama Kante was dressed in a long cotton robe with matching turban and sat ramrod straight in the family's courtyard. A spry elder with a pleasant, serene face, she took two ragged photographs from her pocket to show me how she had looked a half-century earlier. A tall, handsome woman indeed. She spoke of her life without the slightest hint of regret. Her only complaint was aimed at the behavior of today's children.

"I lived in a large family with my father and his brothers near Kayes [a remote town to the west, near the Senegalese border]. Each brother had one wife, and we were happy together. The men were blacksmiths, but they farmed as well. They worked in the fields in the rainy season and then at smithery in the dry season. My mother settled all our problems. I had two brothers and two sisters. There is no one left. They never came to Bamako; they died in the village. They had to stay there because that's where they worked.

"I got married at fourteen. In those days, if you weren't married by sixteen or seventeen it was said that it was because you weren't a beautiful girl. Now girls wait until thirty! Men should marry many women so that the girls don't have to wait like that."

Kama looked at me sideways, laughing. Then she flailed her arms at the children who had begun to gather around to listen to us, sending them off.

"When I married I didn't know the boy. He was from another village. The day of the wedding they prepared and washed me and wrapped me in a new *pagne* [traditional dress consisting of a long piece of cloth that is wrapped around the body]. That night they took me to my husband's village. You go first to a relative's house to be prepared, then they take you to the wedding room and you have to stay there for seven days. You can't eat anything but the porridge made from boiled roots of a certain plant, and they give you perfumed water to drink. You are all wrapped up; no one can see your face. An old woman stays with you during the time you spend in the wedding room. She is the one who prepares the porridge and gives you water to bathe with. If you are in your own village, friends can come and talk with you.

"I was married to three men. I had three children with the first and one with the second. [As is the custom, she counts only male children.] My first husband never beat me or made trouble. He was good. I was his only wife. And in those days, it wasn't the custom to have just one; most had two, three, even four. He was a mechanic on the railroads and had to travel back and forth. He left me home with the big family, his parents and relatives. We had three boys and a girl, but then he died of an illness. Someone put a hex on him. The family then gave me as a wife to my husband's younger brother, so I stayed in the same family. With him I had a son, and then I drank a traditional medicinal tea to have an abortion. He had abandoned me to go off on some adventure; that's how I got separated from him. I didn't stay in the family. I got married again and had another daughter. When he died I didn't marry again. I was then about seventy years old.

"People over seventy are living together now. They like that. But it's a problem, because if they are sick, how are people going to know? And people criticize their children, saying they have abandoned their parents. That can bring maledictions. Even if you have two nice houses and you put the elders in one, you are still criticized by people who say you abandoned your parents. Yet it's not the same if you abandon your wife. If a husband leaves to work in Mauritania, for example, they say he abandoned his wife and children because he doesn't have enough to support them. Men don't bother to divorce; they just go away. There are men who leave their wife and children and go to France for ten years at a time. Sometimes a husband doesn't even say where he is going. How are you supposed to find him if you don't know?" Kama laughed at her own words, then added, "Do you have men like that where you live?" I assured her that we did.

"Co-wives used to get along well, but not anymore. And their children even less so! Before the co-wives worked together in the fields, helped each other. There's no comparison with what goes on now. Women have changed; they no longer respect men. They're no longer submissive. Men don't behave or do what they are supposed to do. Each flees his responsibilities and duties. There is a change in men's character. When men don't do what they're supposed to do, women react. It's not good. Sometimes it's because women aren't good themselves.

"There have been so many changes in the way people behave! There was respect before. You couldn't say anything bad in front of an adult. You didn't address an older person by his name, for example. It was unheard of. But children couldn't care less these days; they insult each other, they don't respect older people, they do what they wish. When I try to tell stories to the children, they laugh at me. They say, 'Times have changed, it isn't the same as before.' They say, 'Leave

Mahmadou Sissoko and Jala Touré with their wedding photograph

us in peace.' One day they'll understand, but it will be too late for me. It's the fault of their education. Not at school, no. At *home*. They have independence, a certain freedom, and that's what weakens the family. Children only listen to those who beat them. And there are those who don't behave even then. They don't listen to their parents. They don't even think."◆

MAHMADOU   When it came time to talk with her son, sixty-year-old Mahmadou, Kama Kante instructed one of the teenagers in the courtyard to move the chairs to the far corner of the yard, far away from the shouts of the smaller children at play. Leaning on his cane, Mahmadou shuffled with us to the new seating arrangement. His leather sandals were hand-tooled in traditional Malian design, and a navy blue mechanic's overblouse covered his shirt and pants. He was obviously proud of his past profession. Mahmadou seemed to enjoy our meeting; as we talked, he wore a constant smile and easily ignored the commotion of the courtyard.

"I came to Bamako as a young man in search of work. There was a company that made cylinders for automobiles, and I had learned how to do that in my village, near Kayes. The owner thought I was a good worker. My wife is from my village, and they brought her here to give her to me. I have three wives and fourteen children, ten sons and four daughters. They're all here except the five who are in Germany. There's one who works in a bank, one who is studying forestry management. They have scholarships, of course. I have one daughter who goes to school, but the others were expelled because they didn't work hard enough. Girls aren't intelligent, and they're needed at home.

"I married my second wife in 1962, four years after the first. We have six children. Of those, only two go to school. The others went for a while and stopped. My third wife also has children.

"The changes I've seen since my youth are in the way people behave and their way of life. They are too clever, too individualistic; they don't want to behave well in society. They think only of themselves, not of the whole family. That's why I don't get along with all these children. I worked for them, and they don't pay any attention. Only those in Germany send money. Of my children who live here, four are employed. They're not yet married, so they should give their salaries to us. We would give them spending money, and the remainder would be spent on the family. But of the four who work, only one gives me money right now. Until I became sick I could work. I don't have a pension.

"The problem with children is their mothers. Everything comes from them. But it's not only my children who are like that. My friends complain about their children as well, that they don't do anything for their families. It's a general problem. In polygamous families, it's the husband who has to solve problems among the wives. When I think of being alone, I'm happy. I say to myself, 'Why did I marry three wives?' Actually, there's only one who makes trouble and gives us all a headache, so I don't regret having three wives—it's just that I chose poorly. Now the younger generation, the boys, want to be monogamous. Never two, they say!"◆

JALA Jala Touré, Mahmadou's first wife, was seated near a small metal stove that she had carried outside to prepare dinner. She was slight of build, and appeared even smaller due to the oversized, complicated turban that matched her long print dress. She smiled little, obviously judging our meeting an important but disruptive break in the family's routine. At forty-nine, she had the contented demeanor of a woman who enjoys the status and authority of "first wife."◆

"When I turned fourteen there was a wedding ceremony in Kayes, and then I was brought here. I was happy to come; I adapted to the city easily. I've been pregnant thirteen times. One time it was twins, but they died at birth. I am left with twelve children. Nine of them live here in this house; the youngest is five years old. I never used family planning. If I had had family planning when I was young, I would have spaced the children better. I can't speak for my daughters. I don't know what they will do—but it's not good to have so many children. I'm tired; I have no energy. Women worked much harder before—fieldwork, housework, the pregnancies. We are less burdened today. There are maids [young rural girls who come to the city to work in families for a year or two to earn money for their dowries] who help us and there are mills for grinding our meal.

"Men used to be very authoritarian and responsible. Now they do as they wish. They have become lazy. When they married two, three, four wives, they weren't supposed to give something to one wife and not the other. Now men aren't good with their wives. It's not moral, because our religion says if you can't maintain four women in equality then it's best to remain with one. Some don't have much money, and instead of raising the living standard of the family, they give what little they have to other women. It's totally irresponsible."◆

FATHIA AND AMINATA Another courtyard, about a half mile away from the big family's compound, led to the home of Mahmadou's thirty-year-old son, Fathia, and his twenty-four-year-old wife, Aminata. Their rented apartment consists of a small sitting room that also serves as kitchen and dining area, and, off a small corridor hidden behind a curtain, a bedroom and toilet. Stove, refrigerator, television, stereos and electric fan all testified to a fine dowry from the bride's family, which customarily provides house furnishings for newlyweds. When I arrived, Aminata had just returned from a friend's wedding and was dressed in a long, bright yellow dress, yellow shoes, and matching turban. She said the outfit was part of her wedding trousseau when she married, a year earlier. Just as we began to talk, her handsome young husband roared up to the door on a motorbike, anxious to join, if not take over, the conversation.

"I work in a car equipment store. I was an apprentice for four years after secondary school. My wife is a secretary in her father's business. She works on computers. We moved to this apartment two months ago because there's not enough room in the family compound. There are too many people. Even my brothers are obliged to sleep elsewhere; some sleep at their friends' houses or at relatives' houses. I support myself and want to stay here until I've enough money to get a house for us. Even if there was room at home, I'd still prefer to be here. This way I can avoid arguments and disputes with the

Jala Touré with daughter-in-law Aminata Samaka and grandson

relatives there. In Mali, when you get married it's sometimes hard to come to an agreement with parents when you live so closely. Little problems are always cropping up. My wife would prefer to be in the big family, but I'm the one who decides. I felt it was best to leave."

Aminata interrupted at this point to explain a custom relating to living in an extended family. "In Mali, it's expected that the daughter-in-law do the housework and cooking for the in-laws. I have friends who get out of work at four in the afternoon, go to the in-laws, and start cleaning and cooking. They eat with their husband and his family and then go home at eight or nine at night. These are customs left over from when we all lived together in a village. It's a big burden for working wives. It doesn't matter that there are many women in the family who could just as well do the cooking and housework; they believe they shouldn't work anymore as soon as the son marries."

Fathia joined in, saying, "Some women accept this and some don't. These local customs are petering out, little by little."

Aminata continued, "My mother-in-law doesn't think that women should work. She's against it. She told my husband that he shouldn't eat what our maid cooked for us. Fathia and I have arguments about this all the time. I met my husband over six years ago. I'd gone to secretarial school and was working with my father. When we met, he knew I was working, that I wasn't a housewife. He wanted to marry me. He liked me as a working woman, and that's what I am. I tell him, 'Maybe your mother didn't know I worked, but you did. So you shouldn't make a problem out of it now. If you don't eat what the maid prepares, too bad for you.'"

Fathia smiled, as if proud of the fact that his wife was outspoken in front of a visitor. He added, "That's why it's best to live here, because no matter what you do, there are always problems with the family. If you love your wife, the others say you are weak with her. If you buy her a nice dress, they get jealous. Living here, there are fewer problems with my father's wives, the sisters-in-law, all the others. From what I've seen and heard, this is the trend among young couples; they want to live away from their parents. You contribute to the upkeep of the larger family, but you don't have to live there. I want to live far from the family. It's for the best. I'll do what I can for my parents, but I don't want to live with them.

"I went to visit my brother in Germany once, and I've been to Morocco and to the Ivory Coast. In Germany I was an intern in a spare parts store. I saw how life is different there. It's everyone for themselves Here in Mali, it's not like that. The family, or your brothers, help you. Over there, you have to get on by yourself. You cook for yourself and make your own way. Here you take care of your parents, even if you don't have enough for yourself. But people are beginning to drop those customs.

"Polygamy, for example, it's not a good thing. At least not for me. There are always arguments and problems: the second wife doesn't like the children of the first wife or vice versa. Then there's competition among the women to have more children than one another. You end up with more than you can support. When you get home the wives are arguing, or you find your mother fighting with one of your wives. If you intervene they say you are impolite or insolent. Life can't be calm in such a home. I just don't understand why men want more than one wife.

"We don't want many children, three perhaps. We've discussed it many times, even before we married. My wife doesn't want many pregnancies for health reasons, and as for me, I know you have to have the means to provide well for your children. I would never have married a wife who wanted many children.

"The elders don't understand the new situation. Advice is always welcome if it's good advice—but not when it doesn't equate with reality. One of the things we don't agree on is children; the elders expect us to have many children. We know it's not good for us, or for Mali, because the population is growing so. But the elders think many children are good. My grandmother, for example, doesn't understand the reality of our time. She is completely out of date."

"My father had two wives," added Aminata, "and eight children. There were aunts, nieces and nephews, the grandmother, three maids. We were twenty-four or twenty-five in the house. I like having people around, even if I have to work more. I feel lonely here by myself. Since I come from a big family, I'd like to live that way—it's habit, my custom.

"That said, I don't want many children myself. I want to continue working, to prepare my children's future. And besides, you never know in life— it's best to have something for oneself."◆

The Sissoko family situation is not uncommon in Africa. The social and economic change that has taken place in the past three generations is immeasurable. Elders have witnessed that change, yet have managed to live much as their own parents did. Their children and grandchildren, however, have had to adapt to dramatic changes in modes of production and means of livelihood. The economic, political, and social realities that shape their world cannot help but affect family structures and values. Traditions are challenged and age-old ceremonies belittled. Often this means a weakening of family and community bonds as families are dispersed by the search for livelihood and are influenced by ideas from the larger world.

At eighty, Kama Kante is perplexed and chagrined by the changing attitudes of men and women toward each other, of children toward elders, and of all younger people toward the traditional family. If she regrets the demise of the institution of polygamy, it seems largely because this demise is accompanied by the disappearance of male responsibility toward the family. That she laments children's lack of respect of their elders is not surprising: in every country visited, elders voiced similar disappointments. Kama's son and daughter-in-law, members of what is likely the last generation to live within the traditional family structure, echo Kama's complaints that younger people are "too individualistic" and "totally irresponsible," as they themselves contend with a polygamous household that is fraught with tension and offspring who have emigrated across the hemisphere. The young Sissoko couple, meanwhile, speaks of the pressure the traditional family exerts on their lives, even their fertility. Like many of their generation, they have been lured into a nuclear family setting by the notion of independent living, away from the daily constraints of familial obligations. Far from family support groups, these young couples reinvent marital roles and develop new, more democratic relationships.

Families everywhere are adapting as best they can to changing times and mores. These three families offer examples of that adaptation from vastly different settings and cultures. Their common concerns emerge when they speak of changes they perceive in relationships and behavior, and the unknown futures faced by the young people. While these young people remain preoccupied with notions of independence and choice of partners and livelihoods, their elders look with nostalgia at the certainty and decorum that is lacking in today's family relationships. The elder Nakasawas, Youngs, and Sissokos are well aware that their lives provide no obvious models for the young who seek self-fulfillment in a complex world.

Two | Living Together, Growing Apart

We are separate but we are also together. And the grandchildren are
always at our side and happy to be with us.
                    —Hamida Sayeed El Shazli, 63, Seberbay, Egypt

On the cold steppes of the Ningxia Autonomous Region in north central China, we were introduced to families who live in caves carved into the cliffs and who herd their livestock throughout the region. Believing that their housing arrangements are not adequate for a modern people, the government is attempting to move them to rather bleak cement-block houses perched on the plains where everything—buildings, animals, people—is subject to icy winds or the blistering summer sun. They are being enticed by the promise of nearby schools and health care facilities—services that had until now been far away.

Yet many of the local people believe that the move will bring losses that are greater than any conceivable gains. The grandmother who proudly welcomed me to her spotless cave protested the government's plan, saying that their cave homes were warm, secure, and protected from the elements. She also fears that the move will break up close-knit families. "We want to remain here," she says, "to live together as we always have."

Among the forces that determine family living arrangements, choice appears to be the least consequential. Families may wish to remain in multigenerational groups but be unable to do so due a range of constraints: lack of housing, site of employment opportunities, available transportation, or, as in the case of the Chinese grandmother, government policy. Smaller, nuclear families are becoming more common everywhere. According to UN statistics, average household size in 1995 ranged from 7 persons in Algeria to 2.1 persons in Sweden.[1] UN statistics also note that the world's urban population more than tripled between 1950 and 1990. For millions of families, urbanization is synonymous with crowded, unsanitary slums or, for the more fortunate, apartment blocks that are towers of small rooms. Economic migrants from rural areas or from foreign lands attempt to find communities of peers in these strange, sometimes hostile environs. In a world that will soon be half urban, the re-creation of communities that share culture and identity is essential to easing the transition to urban life in enormous and anonymous cities.

The families quoted here, from Egypt, Thailand, and El Salvador, live in extended family groups, yet all foresee a time when that will not be the case. Here they discuss how their living arrangements are changing and how these changes may influence family structure and relationships.

SEBERBAY, EGYPT

To reach Seberbay, I traveled by train from Cairo to Tanta, a burgeoning city about thirty kilometers to the north in the Nile delta. Fifteen years earlier, when I passed through this area, it had been a vast stretch of open fields with villages scattered here and there. Now that pattern has been more or less reversed: one sprawling village after another extends along the railway line, broken from time to time by cultivated fields. The low-lying houses of the past have become three-story buildings; each house has columns emerging from its roof, promising that yet another story will be built as soon as funds are available. Between houses no land is left idle: fields are cultivated right up to their walls. The area has become a vast urban-like neighborhood in which the stretch of the horizon is no longer visible.

Abdel Fatah Mohamed Fath, 67
Hamida Sayeed Ahmed El Shazli, 63
Sayeed Abdel Fath, 46
Nadia Hassan Souliam, 45,
My Sayeed Fath, 17
Gamel Abdel Fath, 30

The streets of Tanta were crowded with pedestrians, each different from the other. A turbaned farmer's wife, balancing a huge covered basket on her head, walked behind her husband whose hands carried only a cigarette. Girls in head scarves and long straight skirts shuffled along, unable to take an easy stride. A woman wearing a cape-like veil, which fell to cover hands enclosed in black gloves, struggled to keep step with a man and two young sons. She walked cautiously, for only two eye slits in her face veil allowed a view of where she stepped. Nearby, a group of twenty-year-old women, dressed Western style, with earrings, flowing hair, and knee-length skirts, hurried along, close to one another. The diversity of women on the Tanta street would be echoed in the family I would meet in Seberbay, a sprawling village twenty kilometers away, across the plains.

Seberbay is an overgrown village where rural and urban life begin to meld. Children, dogs, donkey carts, and cars fill its streets. Sheltered from the tumult, the Fath home sits at the end of a narrow alley, surrounded by building of varying sizes. It is a four-story structure, containing an apartment for each of the village tailor's five sons. On the ground floor is the grandparents' apartment, where grandchildren are always welcome.

Hamida Sayeed and Abdel Fatah Mohamed Fath in front of their home in Seberbay

ABDEL FATAH   Abdel Fatah Mohamed Fath was seated in one of the two gilded chairs in a small sitting room. Slender and somewhat frail in appearance, he voiced his opinions in the assured tone of a traditional patriarch. He wore the customary gray *jellabah* and white cap, and gestured ceaselessly to his surroundings as he explained the family's situation. Abdel Fatah was a tailor, and, he explained, his good fortune was due to the small parcel of land he had inherited. When it came time for his sons to marry, he sold the land for the money needed to enlarge his home skyward. He added five apartments, a home for each of his five sons and their wives and children. Abdel Fatah is very proud to have been able to keep his family together.

"I was born here in Seberbay, the fourth of five sons of a farmer. At age fifteen my mother chose my wife. She was twelve at the time. We, too, had five sons. I've raised the family on the tailoring business. I began as an apprentice when I was twelve years old, so when I married I was already a tailor. I farmed a bit for our family food but tailoring was my main activity.

"As a boy I attended Koranic school and learned to recite the Koran. I was so good in Koranic studies that I didn't have to go to the army. I even taught my sons. Before only rich people could go to school. But now the standard of education is high; everybody must try to educate their children. My eldest finished a degree at the University of Commerce and now works at the Department of Health at the regional government here in Tanta. The second is an administrator at the health department; the third, an army officer. The fourth works at the Ministry of Youth; he had two years of teacher training. The fifth went to France and worked as a house painter to earn money for his wedding; now he's a telephone operator at Tanta Hospital.

"Many people have come to this village. It used to be open county all around. Village buildings had only one story and floors were made of beaten earth. Most farmers had at least two acres of land. Now it's all village, everywhere. Everyone builds up because there is so little land. We had kerosene lamps and slept on floor mats. Today we have television, radio, and video, and this beautiful furniture. We even have a good bathroom. I used to get from place to place on a donkey; now we have cars. Our country is progressing. Some change is positive, some not. Television and radio affect us and change our lives. Some films are about things we mustn't watch, like drugs and violence.

"Life has improved. When we were children we had one set of clothes, but today's children have many dresses, shoes; they have dolls, toys—they even have spending money. Now we eat fruits, vegetables, eggs, sweets, more meat, more chicken. In my youth there was nothing like that. And the government gives us health care as well.

"Families used to be religious and pray together; they were very close to each other. There were no problems. We all ate together, but that's not possible now. There are more children, more relatives. Life is better, but we don't share every meal with one another. Everyone has their own personality and wants to have their own place."

Abdel Fatah ended this comment with a gesture of futility, as if to say times were unfathomable, beyond his understanding. I asked about employment and migration, known to be crucial issues in villages such as Seberbay.

"People have to go to the Arab countries, Europe, even the United States to find work. They work for a time, then come back because their wives and children are here. Many don't return; they marry women from Europe or other countries and stay there. My sons won't do that."

Abdel Fatah appeared totally confident that he would be able to fend off any or all forces of family separation.

"There are many families who live in the same house, like we do. I like being with my sons, the children, the whole family. I can look out for them and they for me. Two of my sons asked my opinion on how to select their wives; the others chose for themselves, but they sought my agreement. When a son treats his wife badly or if there are any problems, I take it up with him and his wife. We talk together, examining where's the fault. I treat my son and his wife equally. I must solve their problems. I teach them the rules of the husband and the rules of the wife. They respect my opinion. If my sons' families need anything, they come and take anything I have. It's theirs.

"In the old days, women were like children for the man. Men decided everything; women didn't speak. With education women have changed: they talk with men, they even work outside the house. Because of economics and the expense of daily life, this sharing between man and woman is needed. When a man gets married and his wife is working, they share the expenses of daily life. In my opinion, it's better for the woman to be safe and stay at home. Only one of my daughters-in-law works, as a teacher. The others finished their education but they didn't look for jobs. They have children, two or three children maybe, and they are busy with their children. They don't think about working outside.

"I have fifteen grandchildren and more on the way. I want them to be happy, to live good lives and encounter no problems in life. Every generation depends on love and respect. I treat my sons' wives as my daughters, with love, as I do their children. Any problem they face, I must solve. They need the elders at every moment in their lives."

When I nodded in agreement, Abdel Fatah added, quietly, "I don't know about the future; in a moment everything can change. The future is the will of God."◆

HAMIDA   Tea and plates of assorted sweets arrived with a swish of flowing dresses as Abdel Fatah's wife and two daughters-in-law entered the small sitting room. Abdel Fatah told me it was time for me to hear his wife and, with a gesture, urged the daughters-in-law to leave with him. The small, serene grandmother, Hamida, is a young sixty-three. Her face, protected from the elements by a life of purdah, is unlined and nearly milk white. She wore a robe that resembled a Western nightdress, common women's attire in Egyptian homes. Her hair was covered with a white scarf tied tightly to cover forehead, ears, and neck. Seeming somewhat intimidated by my presence, she spoke softly, almost inaudibly.

"My father was a farmer here in Seberbay. We were five children: three boys and two girls. Two brothers have died and my parents are gone as well. My last brother is a farmer. His two children didn't go into farming. One works at the bank, the other at the Agricultural Association. Even though I attended primary school for six years, I only know how to write my name, but I can explain Koranic verses.

"I was twelve when I married. My husband didn't know me. His father saw me at the market where he sold his crops. He admired me and asked 'Who is this girl? Who is her father?' He brought his son to my father and we became engaged. I left my parents and came to live with his large, extended family. Every day I cried and pleaded to go back to my mother. I cried to my husband, his father, his mother, begging to go home to my family. My father and mother came and told me, 'You are now locked in this family. You must stay here. *This is your place.*' I was homesick but they just said, 'You must stay here.'

"My in-laws treated me like a daughter because their family didn't have any girls. I knew everything about housework when I came here but my mother-in-law said 'Forget everything you learned in your home. Every house has its traditions; you shall start over with me.' She didn't leave me on my own. We did everything together. I do the same with my daughters-in-law.

"My first child was born when I was fourteen. With every child I suffered for two days. I had problems with pregnancies: six times I had miscarriages at three months, maybe four months. All the children were delivered by a midwife.

"I didn't have any role in selecting my daughters-in-laws. I let my sons choose as they wished, all except my third son, the one in the army. I talked with him and selected his wife because most of the time he is with the army and leaves his wife with me.

"Although my husband is a tailor he educated all his sons and all of them have jobs. Two of them even went to Paris and worked as house painters. They stayed for two years but, happily, they didn't change from that experience. Not at all. Tradition is in a person's blood, and he takes it with him wherever he goes.

"This village used to be calm and quiet, but it has become noisy. Even our family has grown large and noisy. The small old houses have been replaced by big ones because people want their children to be with them. Houses are much better inside as well. We used to fetch water from wells, but now every house has running water. Life is much easier.

"Women used to wear clothes of very cheap cloth and have only two dresses, a dark one and one for special occasions. Now they have many outfits. Even the grandmothers! When they look at their daughters-in-law, how they dress, they want to look like them. When I was young, women stayed in their homes, but now when they finish their education, if they have a chance for a job, it's allowed.

"The negative change I see is that some wives push their husbands to live apart from the large family, away from the village. When my eldest son married the teacher, her mother didn't want them to live with us. She insisted they live outside this village, in a separate apartment. But when we built this house my son wanted to be with us. When my daughter-in-law saw that there was no hope of living separately, she finally agreed. From time to time her mother tries to find an apartment for them, but she has failed. They have three children. Either her mother or I took care of the babies while she worked. Now we have a good relationship, but sometimes it's difficult— when she gives the children to her mother, for example. But I accept; love is everything. My husband and I believe we must treat our daughters-in-law as our own girls. This will satisfy our sons and we will be a happy family.

"In this house each couple has their own apartment and manages their budget. Sometimes they come here for lunch or dinner but usually everyone eats in their own homes. They pay their own utility bills. We are sep-

Sayeed Abdel Fath and Nadia Hassan Souliam in their sitting room

arate but we are also together. And the grandchildren are with us. They come to see me every day after school. They don't want to leave their grandparents. The parents want them to go to bed upstairs, but they refuse. I've told them the history of our family, and my husband always brings sweets to keep here so that when the children come we have something for them. They're always at our side and happy to be with us."

Hamida was visibly pleased and proud to talk about her family. She was also anxious to learn about families I'd met in other countries. She said her son was returning to work in France and, then, with a wishful tone, she added, "If I had my own house, if I had money, I would go outside Egypt and learn about other places."◆

SAYEED It was late afternoon when I met the eldest son, Sayeed, who arrived directly from his office. Forty-six years old, he is a tall man, with the customary mustache and portly carriage of middle-aged Egyptians. He wore a Western-style suit and tie. As chief of the Planning Division at the Health Department of Tanta's regional government, Sayeed is a respected public servant, and he bears the serious demeanor common to eldest sons. Sitting in the gilded chair of his father's sitting room, he talked about his family: his wife is the only daughter-in-law to work outside the Fath home; their three children range in age from eight to seventeen.

"I went to school in Tanta. My grandfather would take me on his bicycle and return in the afternoon to fetch me. My parents always said, 'Pay attention only to your education.' I didn't have any chores at home—nothing at all. Only my studies. My father and grandfather used to tell us about the family, its history, and my mother spoke of her family as well. Ours was a close family, and religious; we read the Koran together.

"When I finished secondary school, I joined the army and while there I studied for a higher degree at the Institute of Commerce. When I returned I completed my university degree.

"I met my wife through a mutual friend and asked her father for her hand. Our children are seventeen, fifteen, and eight." At this point Sayeed looked up and laughed. "Yes, there is a big gap between them. We didn't plan for a third, but he came.

"The influences on our lives here? I think social relationships are changing. Life has become very complicated. People are more occupied with themselves and their work; they haven't the time to socialize as they did in the past.

"My grandmother use to organize the daughters-in-law to prepare meals for the entire family. Now our families live separately and each wife prepares food for her family. Among my friends, most couples live in separate houses, not with their parents. The generations get along but they live separately. Another change? In the past a man could marry more than one wife. It rarely happens anymore.

"Relationships are built on respect. We respect our elders and their opinions. My children must talk and behave just as I do with their mother or their grandparents. Like all fathers I hope my children will have excellent lives. Since my wife is a primary school teacher, she was responsible for our children's early education. For preparatory school, I was responsible. We belong to the Parents' Association at school; we know everything about our children's courses. But the future belongs to the children themselves, to their ability to be what they choose. We've given them everything we can. My daughter, for example—I give her anything she asks for. When she marries? Every father wants his son-in-law to be a good man. If he loves tradition and is religious, he wants his son-in-law to do the same."◆

NADIA   Sayeed's wife is tall, self-assured, and outwardly calm. She may dress in the customary long robe and white head scarf, but she has in fact stepped outside the Fath family traditions to continue her profession of schoolteacher even after the birth of her children. A stately forty-five-year-old woman, Nadia walked quietly into the room to take her husband's place in the gilded armchair. Her hands lay quietly in her lap as she spoke of how much she likes her work, of how committed she is to her children, to her parents, and their extended family. She admitted that the better part of her time is spent outside the Fath home, in which she does not feel as well-accepted as the less independent daughters-in-law. She spoke first of her childhood.

"We were nine in my family: seven children and my parents. My father was good to us; he let us study and work and didn't force us to marry at an early age. I was very lucky. I married at twenty-six. I'd been working in Tanta as a teacher for four years and was working on a university degree, which I completed after I married.

"The story of meeting my husband is a good one. I was teaching in Tanta and one of my students was a thirteen-year-old girl who admired my husband. The girl was young, but very mature in her mind. She went to my husband and said, 'If you want to marry, I have someone to suggest.' Then she came to me and said, 'Miss, I have a husband for you.' I laughed and said 'Go, go on—I don't want to marry.' She insisted, saying, 'I'm serious, really.'

"My husband came to see me at my parent's home and in one week the arrangements were completed. For the first two years we lived elsewhere, but when this house was completed we came here. I like it here now. Every Thursday we go to visit my family in Tanta. My mother is widowed and refuses to live with any of us; she wants to be free and independent. My sisters and brothers go by her house every day. Our lives are different from hers, of course; my sisters have all worked at some point, just as I do. Mother lived in the traditional way and that's very important to her.

"In the older generation, family ties were very strong; children were respectful because they were raised in a strict environment. Now parents are less strict with their children; they treat them almost as friends. Maybe this is good, I can't tell. I know I do it myself.

"I teach primary school, ages six to nine. I love my job. I prefer working with young children. I worry sometimes about the influence of television on them. It has had a great influence, especially on the younger ones. There is a TV now in every house. Cultural programs have helped young people to know more about everything, and through news programs, they learn about the world. But there are also programs that show bad things, with violence and sex. How can a family agree with that? The religious fanatics will use it against us. All families are experiencing these changes, always worrying about their children, about their future."◆

MY SAYEED   Sayeed and Nadia's daughter, seventeen-year-old My Sayeed, greeted me dressed in fashionable black pants, a green geometric-patterned blouse, dangling gold earrings, and the pride of a self-assured teenager. She was the sole woman of the Fath household who did not wear a head scarf. Her long, jet black hair was held back with a wide velvet ribbon, but neither her energy nor her enthusiasm was to be contained.

"Women used to be isolated from society. Men had all the authority. Women lived in a world of their own, inside, and didn't even *see* people. There was no role for the woman outside the house, no chance to voice an opinion in the family. My generation insists on our opinions. Women are half of our society. We are trying to expand our roles so that we can do everything like men. Of course we are cleverer than men in many ways. I take lessons in Kung Fu and play sports. My generation can go out, to committee meetings with boys and girls. They don't care if it's for boys or for girls; we are all Egyptians. That's what's important, and we must serve our country.

"We spend a long time on our education. They fill our minds with information we don't need. My generation loves reading: political issues and novels—and love stories. But due to the situation in our country, there's no time for love stories. Once I finish my university I'll be free. I want to be an airline pilot. There is a training program in Cairo I would like to attend. If my generation takes the opportunity, we will share complete responsibility for the society. We're interested in political issues; we read about them and want to participate. Egyptian women have natural inhibitions, but they should not be ashamed to participate.

"Television is both positive and negative: programs expose a problem but they don't show how to solve it. We need to know how to *solve* problems. I like programs which show social service in the community."

My's dark eyes looked at me intensely, wondering if I had another question. I answered the mute query by asking her views on marriage age and what she expected of a spouse.

"I'd like to marry after finishing university, between age twenty-two and twenty-five. I want to choose my husband, but my parents will have to agree. It's my choice, but also the choice of the parents. Boys and girls are now together in the university, in clubs, and all activities. This was not possible before. The man I marry must be understanding, one who shares my opinions as well as all responsibilities. I don't like traditional men who say that a woman must stay at home. And I don't want a large family. The population is increasing too much, and if we are to improve our lives, two children are enough. I prefer a man who has an open mind—a social, outgoing person who is willing to join me in service to society. Some girls say that when they finish their education they'll stay at home if their husbands have money. They say, 'Why not?' But money is not everything. I want to be self-sufficient.

"The conservative forces, the fundamentalists, insist that women be restricted to the home—but it doesn't mean that we accept it. We show them our country needs our efforts. We cannot stop; we must move on."

The young woman before me was so taken by her own words that she could barely contain her energy. Her opinions and ideas jumped out as if too long suppressed, surprising even her.

"There are extremist men here in Egypt but women have political rights in our society. If we need force, we shall use it. There's a women's organization that struggles for our rights. At the university there is also a small group of students who share these opinions. It's up to all of us to see that we don't fall back. Every woman moves walls—maybe slowly but we will achieve our goals. At school we get together to discuss the problems of our society. We learn about women in other countries; we ask about women working outside the home, what their opinions are. We don't accept things as they are.

"The majority of my generation insists that we struggle for our beliefs. When we finish our studies we will change the thinking of the government. We believe we will behave differently. And if the government doesn't agree with us, we will struggle. We must try, try, try."◆

GAMEL ABDEL   My's uncle and the youngest son of the elder Fath, Gamel Abdel had, at thirty, recently become a proud first-time father. Gamel is a pleasant-looking, outgoing man of medium height and build. He spoke eagerly of his time as a house painter in France and his return to marry a chosen bride.

"I worked in France for two years. It was difficult to be so far away from my parents, but my brother Mohammed was there, so I went to work with him. I had read that French people love the Egyptians. There was no problem. It was easy to find work and get along with the French. I lived with friends from this village.

"Before I left for France, my brother and I had worked as painters here. One day I was on the second floor of a house, painting the interior walls. Out the window I saw a girl on the third floor opposite us. I didn't speak to her—that is against our tradition. But I kept her in mind. When I was in France I phoned my mother, told her about the girl, and asked her to please go to the girl's family. I wanted to get engaged to her when I returned. But I still hadn't talked to her. She accepted and we married. We have a little baby. We want two children, but we'll wait a few years before we have the second. We will use family planning.

"The main problem for my generation is simply making a living. They want to get jobs, to live, but there is no opportunity. They want to marry, but they haven't any money. So they leave and work abroad. Without that money, they can't build a home. Some of them stay abroad. It's the main problem of this generation, even in this village. Many of my friends are discouraged: there's no job, no money, no apartment—and no marriage to complete their lives. I'm lucky my father was able to build this house; at least my wife and I have a home."◆

Before we left the Fath home, grandfather Abdel insisted on showing me through the house. He beamed with pride that he was able to provide a place where

Some among the Fath family during the author's visit: (*back row, left to right*) Nadia Hassan Souliam, her daughter My Sayeed, grandmother Hamida Sayeed, and two daughters-in-law with children, (*sitting*) youngest son Gamel Abdel with his wife and baby, grandfather Abdel Fatah, and five more grandchildren

his family could be together. And, he added, because in his old age he "wouldn't be lonely like all those people in the cities."

The Fath family is indeed sheltered under one roof, though their home is no longer a sanctuary from the vast outside world. Abdel Fath educated his sons well, and they, in turn, remain close and respectful of their parents. Yet the towering home is invaded by new ideas and images, which challenge traditional relationships. Well aware of the danger, the patriarch hopes to continues to guide his large family with equanimity. It is a family where relationships and roles are changing, yes—but in the context of a solid togetherness, both physical and spiritual.

BANGKOK, THAILAND

Bangkok residents represent 15 percent of the Thai population, yet the burgeoning city accounts for more than half the nation's GDP. It is estimated that Bangkok will swell dramatically in the next fifteen years, containing 41 percent of the population by 2015.[2] The nation's booming industrial activity is concen-

Thada Loca-apichia, 38

Weerawon Loca-apichai, 36

trated around Bangkok, and serves as a magnet for impoverished immigrants from rural areas. Thailand is becoming two nations: one urbanized, modern, and wealthy, the other rural, underserved, and poor.

Among the residents of Bangkok are hundreds of young couples who, increasingly, find the need for both husband and wife to work outside the home. One such couple is the Loca-apichias, the parents of two children, who must struggle to find time to be together and with their extended family.

THADA I met Thada Loca-apichai, husband, father, and businessman, in his office early on a Saturday morning. Saturdays, he says, are his to do with as he pleases. Apparently, this often results in spending extra hours at the office of his import-export business. It is housed in a small building built recently in the garden of an old mansion in central Bangkok. Thada was elegantly dressed in weekend sports clothes. A pleasant, outgoing man, he took obvious pleasure in discussing family issues common to working couples. He explained that he and his wife share a house with his parents and his two sisters. Of Chinese parentage, he is conscious that his father's strict ways may emanate from the fact that the father is trying to preserve Chinese ways in a foreign culture.

"My parents came from China in 1950. Each came independently to the south of Thailand, looked for relatives, and settled down. They married, then moved to Bangkok, where I was born. We are four children; I have a brother and two sisters, all younger than I.

"One good thing about Thailand is that immigrants are easily accepted. There's no trouble between races, religions, schools, languages. Among my Chinese friends, no one says 'I'm a Chinese'. It's not like the Irish who after three generations in Australia still say, 'I'm Irish,' which I heard often when I spent a year there. Your mother tongue may be Chinese, but when we go to school, we forget it. In public school everything is Thai; I have 100 percent of the rights of an ethnic Thai.

"My mother was a housewife but she gave private lessons in Chinese language because it was difficult for children to learn Chinese in the public schools. My parents were from the south of Canton state. They left because of economic hardship as well as political views. They were educated people. My mother was born into a wealthy family of landlords. She had to leave when the communists arrived. Everything was confiscated.

"My father was a farmer's son. He also had good reason to leave China because of hardships. He was twenty-two and held a degree comparable to a bachelor's degree. Here in Thailand he became a teacher. The government allows Chinese language to be taught in primary school during the daytime, but only after 5:00 P.M. in secondary school. So he taught day and night. But the popularity of the language faded as more people dropped the old ways. Then he started an association that serves the overseas Chinese in family matters: funerals, marriages, getting together, registration of relatives. The Chinese have heaps of relatives, so there is always work!

"We all live in the same house. It's a four-story apartment building. My wife and I live on the fourth floor, my parents on the second floor. We share the living room. Only my brother has moved out. My two sisters are not married and both work. The youngest is dating an older man, aged forty-five. He's a Thai from Canada. He married a Canadian, had a family, and is now divorced. My sister has dated him for over a year now. It's looking serious, but my parents are not happy about it.

"My father feels strongly about family and family history. He'd like to maintain the old ways. The generation gap is happening all over the world, but he won't accept it. My brother and sisters and I had a lot of difficulty with his views. All I could think about was going the opposite way, 180 degrees opposite.

"But I take it halfway. We live together with some difficulties. When I say halfway, I mean that I still want to be with them, to look after them. There's no government system to look after the elderly. Every family has to look after its own. My sister could be there but parents are happier with a son close by. I don't mind, but my wife has difficulties living with them. For the children it's fine; they get along very well with their grandparents. But we can't live with them forever.

"Being a working couple is difficult. There is more and more pressure in our society. Thailand is becoming an industrialized country like Korea, Hong Kong, and Taiwan. This change is disruptive, drastic. Labor is in demand, and young girls are flocking to the factories. This affects the life of couples because those who used to work as maids now go to the factories. Couples can no longer find child-minders, nannies. You can't have a baby if you work. In my case, one of my wife's relatives used to work as a dressmaker in her home. She agreed to stop that work and come to our house to look after the children. We compensate her at the same level she had in her tailoring business.

"We have two children but only one goes to school. We won't have any more. I would prefer to have just two and look after them well. Nobody can afford more. No matter how rich they are, nine out of ten of my friends stick to this, because there's no one to look after the children. It's the pattern of our generation. The wives are well-educated; they don't want to stay at home all day. They'd prefer to work, but at the same time they want to be mothers. This affects the care of the children."

Reaching behind his desk for the photographs of his children, Thada rose to show me two smiling children and an elderly man with his arm around the smallest. He sat again, saying, "I'm searching for a house or an apartment close to Chulalungkorn University because my son will go there in the first grade. By May we'll have moved out of my parents' home. Why am I doing this? Because of the traffic! You see, I want to live close to my wife's work and my son's school. It will be a different lifestyle. We'll be in a narrow space in an apartment on the fifteenth floor. We'll have to use an elevator; I'll become a full-fledged city man—all because of traffic.

"Right now we live about ten minutes from here. I drop my son off at the kindergarten around 8:00 A.M. and then drive my wife to the university. It takes forty-five minutes depending on how early I drop off my son. It takes another forty minutes to get back. So I start work usually around 9:30 or 10:00 A.M. We leave home at 7:30; two hours later I may be at my office. Traffic is the number one problem.

"I don't mind living in a very simple style—but getting rid of this long commute is the priority. My wife and son will spend the day on the same campus. But there's still the younger one; I'll have to find a nearby kindergarten. We can't get up at 5:00 A.M. and rush, rush, rush. It's too much. A lot of families feed the kids in the car because there is no time for breakfast.

"You see, at the outset, Bangkok had no urban planning. Then it was too late. Now the pollution is very bad. I know several people who are having trouble with it—the motorcycles, *tuk-tuks* [a local form of taxi, consisting of a motor scooter mounted with two passenger seats] cars, and the buses. You can't help but smell the fumes. There was a big campaign on unleaded gas and poisonous air, but we also have too much dust. Bangkok is probably the most dust-tainted city in the world because of construction. The municipal departments should be more strict. There are many health problems in the making.

"Since we both work, we split expenses. I pay for the house and utilities and my wife buys the consumer items, like baby diapers, milk, clothes. Because we live in a big family we have to contribute to the family budget. Each month we set aside a sum for our later days. We must. As for chores, we split them, too. My wife does the housework; I do the mopping.

"Thai society is becoming industrialized, and that will have a great influence on culture. First the economic change, then the cultural change. What will change? The Thai cultural scene is based on Asian customs and ways of thinking. We live in a big family like the Japanese, Chinese, and Malaysians. Parents and children are close; they respect each other. This will change because of industrialization and outside influences. Big families will cease; in each family there will be fewer people, more independence. The elders, as in Western societies, will take care of themselves. My parents expect me to be nearby. In the West you can request assistance from the government, but not here. One way or the other, you have to survive by yourself. Even if I move out, I have to be close in order to come often, buy their noodles, fix what's wrong with the furniture. They expect that. But I don't expect *my* son to do that. I imagine his way of life will be different. Maybe he'll live in a high-rise the rest of his life; nobody knows.

"I hope there will be more social discipline in this country in my children's generation. I hope they're not going to be cold-blooded or mean in business. What I can do now is try my best to support them. Education comes

first. No matter how hard it is, I have to put them through school and provide other experiences for them. I'll do my best to bring them up in a way
that prepares them to survive in the industrial world. I would like them to
have a nice place to live, a good job, and a good family. But if we don't prepare them, they'll have a lot of trouble when they get out of school. My parents didn't teach me about all this. We didn't discuss things like how to survive
in society, because we were immigrants. I'm more able than my parents in
this, in preparing my kids for the future. If they can continue to a master's
degree or a Ph.D., I'll not stop them. If my business succeeds, they can take
it over.

"The big cultural change is that I won't rely on them when I get old. Of
course I would like them to be nearby because I'm Asian; I'm still close to
that way of thinking."

As the conversation drew to a close, the young businessman smiled, adding
softly, "My parents and my children are very close, and there's nothing wrong
with that. But we do have problems with some things in the family. The best
thing is to be alone but close by."◆

WEERAWON　The following week I met Thada's wife, Weerawon Loca-apichai,
in her office on the grounds of the famous Chulalongkorn University. The
campus is a haven from the noise and scramble of Bangkok. The only discernible activity was the quiet parade of students from one building to another under the tall trees that shade the walkways. She took me to the patio
outside her office in the Accounting Department; there we could be alone,
undisturbed. Like her husband, Weerawon is of Chinese ancestry. She
wore a print dress, and her straight, shoulder-length black hair was held to
one side with a ribbon. Shy and soft-spoken, she seemed nervous about our
conversation, for we were sitting in full view of all who came and went to
her department. As time wore on, she seemed to forget our surroundings,
and her hands became agitated, a pair of dancing fans, especially when she
spoke about her children and their future.

"In our family, boys and girls were treated about the same. My parents
owned a grocery store and didn't have much time to be with us. When there
was time, we'd sit and talk, with my father especially. My life is much better than my mother's, because she had so many children. We were seven and
she still had to help my father in the store.

"My husband and I met in high school. We courted for a long time. We
share chores because we both work. The main worry I have as a working
wife is for the children, although I am truly lucky because I have someone
to care for them. But there's no park nearby, no trees. Just shops. The only
place where the children can play is a townhouse where they have playrooms
for children. It's a private home, an empty space where you can go and play.

In the neighborhood we know the people next door but not those farther away. There's not much of a community.

"Our main problem is the traffic. I'm sick of it. I leave here at 5:00 or 5:30. It takes about an hour to get home. The child-minder waits for me. We look forward to the weekend. Sunday is our family day. We do things together, just the four of us.

"I don't want more children. It's difficult to raise children in these times. I want them to get a university education and good jobs. I want them to be good people. I think the Western influence will affect them more than our Eastern traditions. It comes from the mass media. It influences my daughter's thinking and her lifestyle will change. They watch videos two or three hours a day. They like Japanese videos on aliens, monsters, robots. Can you imagine? Three to six year olds watch that!

"Eventually, once they are older, I'd like to start a business. My husband owns his business and it could become very successful but I still want my own." She laughed and relaxed with a mischievous smile.

Later, as we walked toward the campus gate, Weerawon added a last comment to our leave-taking: "There's too much materialism, development. I'm worried my children will be influenced by all this, that they won't grow up to be good people. Development is equated with money. I'm not negative about materialism; I'm just concerned about raising my children the way I want in this changing environment."◆

Thada and Weerawon, like so many young working couples, attempt to juggle responsibilities to their elders, their children, their work, and to each other in a constantly shifting world. Leisure—time to be together—is rare. City life seems to conspire to keep them busy just coping with daily life. It takes a conscious and continual effort to uphold and nurture relationships among the generations and with each other.

Urban life may be a strain on family relations, yet there is another, more disruptive force that is all to common in these times: millions of people have been uprooted from their homes, which taxes their ability to live together and to support their own.

SEGUNDO MONTES, EL SALVADOR

Segundo Montes is a "new" community, built in 1992, at the end of El Salvador's civil war. It lies in the Departamento de Morazan, a desolate region of poor soils and even poorer farmers. Former rebel soldiers, their families, and hundreds of returned refugees have settled there to rebuild their lives and livelihoods. After years of hiding, exile, or refugee camp interment, after years of depending on

Jose Calzans Martinez, 70

Santos Ramirez, 68

Paulina Martinez, 43

Elba Delia Martinez, 20

Santos and Jose Martinez, grandson Jose, daughter Paulina, and granddaughter Elba holding her daughter

each other for survival, hopes were high that this new community would serve
its members wisely, well, and equally.

One family that had such expectations of Segundo Montes is the Martinez
family. Their will to stay together and support each other, even in the most
difficult times, has been tested by war. Now, that will is being tested again,
by forces they little understand.

JOSE   Jose Calazans Martinez is a tall, dignified man with a thin face, deep-
set eyes, and a pointed nose. At age seventy, he works in the fields each morning but admits that he's getting weak, less able to work. He relies on his
twelve-year-old grandson to help him before the boy goes to school, and then
again when he returns in late afternoon.

As evening approached, we sat in a pair of dilapidated chairs in a
deserted market across the road from Jose's house. There we could be
alone and uninterrupted. We must have been an unlikely pair, sitting hud-
dled together in conversation in the last rays of mountain sun. We laughed
at the thought of what passersby might say. Jose began his story.

"I was born in Canton La Joya, here in Morazan. I didn't know my mother; she died in childbirth when I was three years old. My father raised me
until I was eighteen. When he died only a sister remained in the house. I was
the youngest of the boys. There were eight children in all—four boys and
four girls. Only three are left. Two brothers died during the war.

"My father was a farmer. At a very young age he taught me everything
relating to agriculture and how to work the henequen [sisal]. We made rope,
mats, and hammocks. I even learned how to plow with oxen. My father took

another woman and had three other children. We used to call them illegitimate because he wasn't married the second time. When my father died, she left with another man. The only story I can tell about my father is that he dedicated his life to work, and to teaching me everything he knew. Every night he would teach the Bible and the doctrine. He knew how to read. He had books by a priest called Jose Ricardo Garcia Mazo, and I studied those books all my life. They tell of the beginning of the world right through to its end. The only formal education I had was for a brief two years; I learned to sign my name, that's all. My father put me to work in the fields, so I couldn't continue school. It was because of the poverty in which we lived. All the other children abandoned him; I was the only one who remained. They were already men and left to work on other people's land. Maybe it was because he took another woman as his mate and they weren't happy with the stepmother.

"In spite of my lack of education, I still have the capacity to lead a straight life. I've never done anything criminal or been incarcerated for any reason. I've always lived according to what he taught me. He was a man who gave his services to others. As an adult, I, too, gave service to my community.

"When my father died, he left everything to me. After the nine-day mourning period, I asked my brothers to come for a reunion, to give each his share of my inheritance. My conscience wouldn't let me keep everything and I passed it on equally. Some of them sold their land to me.

"I married Dona Santos Ramirez in 1946. We lived in the same neighborhood, so we knew each other when we were little. We married after six years of courtship. I was twenty-two. Ours was a friendship, a very unusual one because we are still friends in a way.

"We had eleven children. Seven girls and four boys. Of the boys, only one is left. Two fell in the war; both were with the guerrillas. The other died very young. The remaining son works in a cooperative in Usulutan. All the girls are alive; two of them live here.

"I've followed in my father's footsteps as far as the education of the children. Just like he raised me and taught me how to work, to behave, it's the way I taught my children. I keep telling them about our family's good manners and behavior. That's the way we educated our children. The grandchildren, too. I don't have a single child who doesn't love me.

"When the fighting came this way we had to flee the army. We abandoned everything we had in the house, even things dear to us; we took only the clothes we had on. We reached Honduras after three days of walking. We stayed in the refugee camp for nine years. The army burned everything—beds, chairs, papers, everything. All our property documents and family papers were lost. We had to send to San Miguel for copies of documents to prove this land was ours. The same happened to our neighbors.

"One of my daughters was taken prisoner by the National Guard in 1984. She was put in the Mariona Prison in San Salvador for two years. She had been a teacher and was accused of being in the guerrilla movement.

"In my father's day, they didn't go through a war; the only war they used to tell us stories about was the Second World War. What was the reason for this war? Was it exploitation? Was it imperialism? Was it to erase the poverty of the people? In fact, I am worse off. The community leaders don't allow me to be part of anything. It may be because of my age. They formed a group in the community that was supposed to help the elderly, but it only lasted three months. Promises have not been fulfilled. Now we live off charity. The elders are suffering. They can't work; they have no help. They lack the barest of necessities. Some are alone; others have families, but their families don't want them anymore.

"The majority of elders would like to live in a retirement home. Not me. My needs are met by my children, who don't want to see me in disgrace. They are taking care of me. The community should look after their elders; they promised help, a home for them, but it never happened. We are wasting our last bit of energy working and earning a living."◆

SANTOS   Jose's wife welcomed us the next morning to their two-room house, a dark, damp, and untidy place. There was no running water nor electricity. Pigs and chickens roamed in and out among the litter on the earthen floor and courtyard. The kitchen was a long room with a single window and a disorderly collection of pots, plastic bottles, utensils, and trash. The second room was strung with a series of hammocks. In one a great-granddaughter still slept. At sixty-eight, the great-grandmother was bent by labor and age. She was a small and extremely shy woman who fondled her apron with hands that spoke of misfortune. Her fingers were twisted and gnarled, the fingernails broken, ragged. Throughout our talk she dried her eyes with her stained apron, expressing alarm about her husband's health and despair at the idea of never finding her dead sons' bodies.

"We were four girls and seven boys. All my sisters are dead but the brothers are alive, except for one who was killed in the war. He was a merchant who traded in tulle products and hammocks. The Armed Forces wanted his business so they accused him of being a guerrilla. They killed him and chopped him to pieces.

"My brothers went to school, but we girls didn't. My parents just didn't want to send us. My mother was a great influence on me; she taught me how to cook, how to behave, how to dress and have respect for others. She worked very hard; she died working. At times she had to feed up to twenty field hands during the harvest season. The year she died I got married. I was twenty.

"The war was a very sad time. While we were in the camps I received news of my sons. We haven't been able to recover the bodies. One died around Poloros—I think it's on the border with Honduras, far away. The other one fell in Morazan, near San Francisco Gotera. They killed him and then they burned the body. I'll never be able to find it."

Grief clouded the eyes of Santos Ramirez. She looked distant for a time before continuing.

"At the refugee camp, the soldiers would come and scare us. When we had to wash clothes, we had to go as a group to the river because if we were alone they would shoot at us. The international people tried to protect us, but it was not always possible.

"This is our home now. We fetch our water from a nearby well but I have to find young people to help me carry it. We talk of fixing the house because we cannot afford a better place, but I ask myself: Who is going to repair this house? There is no one. My husband is not at all strong. There is no one in the community to help us with things like this."◆

Paulina Martinez with granddaughter and daughter Elba

PAULINA   Paulina Martinez is the unmarried daughter of Jose and Santos Ramirez. She is a short, stocky woman with fine, smooth skin and the features that recall the indigenous peoples of Central America. She appears serene, although not quite enough to be called self-confident. Paulina has few expectations for herself. The daughter of devout parents, she is herself very religious. She has nevertheless borne three children by two errant men who failed to marry her or provide any support. Broken promises are at the core of her experience; she seems to be living for the sole purpose of serving those around her.

"We were eleven children; I was number three. We lived in a rural area and school was very far away. I first went to school when I was eight years old. I couldn't go earlier because I was making hammocks with my father. I reached the fourth grade, but had to stop to give the younger ones a chance to go.

"My father is a very good Catholic. He started teaching us the doctrine from the time we were very little. We even made our First Communion. He gave us advice and taught us good manners.

"There were aunts and uncles on either side who lived nearby then. I especially liked one of my mother's sisters. We loved her as if she had been our own mother. She had fourteen children and suffered a lot. She died young, at thirty-six. She had a stroke at the onset of the war. There are no relatives left now in this area.

"I met my [common law] husband because he lived nearby. We met, but we didn't marry. I stayed at my parents' house. When I became pregnant he found another woman, so I remained in my father's home. I was twenty-three when I had the first child.

"My father was very angry. I had to put up with an awful lot from him because in those days to have a baby out of wedlock was a big mistake. It was a grave sin to go with a man without getting married. He always promised to marry me, but soon he found a more attractive woman. Financially, he helped very little. Men promise things to women but never keep their promises. I fell for a pack of lies. He didn't marry the other woman either.

"I went to San Salvador to find work. I did housework—cleaning, washing, ironing, and cooking. My little girl was seven years old when I left her with my mother and sisters. I was there six years, but when the political climate became ugly, it was dangerous in the city, so I came back. My husband pursued me again, and I became pregnant with his second child. Later he wanted to take the children with him because he needed someone to serve him. When I said no he never helped me again. I managed to raise the children by myself. They are simply ignored and neglected by their father. But they love me as their mother.

"My third child is eight years old. I met his father when I traveled with the guerrillas as a teacher. I taught children to read and write in the towns we would come to. He, too, disappeared with another woman. I know where he lives but I don't contact him. Neither of the fathers comes to see their children.

"Being alone without a husband hasn't been a problem, because I'm with my parents. I don't expect to marry. When you see that things turn sour because men promise so many things, it's better to stay away from all that. Now my daughter has the same bad luck as me: her boyfriend left her with a baby girl. He, too, was a guerrilla; she worked in the office where he worked. They started making plans to live together. He made many promises—that he was going to build their home here—but it was all false.

"There's no responsibility on the part of young people. Both young men and young women refuse to accept advice from their parents. The young today have no education for responsibility. There's no order in their lives. In the past a couple would make decisions together; now a man likes to get one girl, then another and another, but refuses responsibility for any of them. And the girls are not strict with the boys. We must teach girls because they have their head in the clouds.

"In the camps, the idea was to form groups to prepare the food. It was difficult to get everyone to join in the effort; everything had to be on a communal basis. Camp life was difficult for the children, but anyone who knew how to teach would gather the children by grades and teach them what they could. There were international people who trained the teachers, who in turn taught the little ones. There were also classes for adults. This was beneficial because so many older people who hadn't had any previous schooling took this opportunity and learned to read and write.

"The camp years were good because they were like school to us. Women like me had an opportunity to work in many different jobs. My daughter, Elba, went to school and learned to type. One thing we learned was that women have the capacity to learn practical skills and don't have to limit themselves to kitchen work.

"My second child is a boy, now twelve; he was born in the refugee camp. He's in the fifth grade. In the morning he works in the cornfields and in the afternoon he goes to school from one to four. Then he works on the farm; he will probably be a farmer.

"For the time being I will live here. I've committed myself to taking care of my parents until they die. When we first came back here I was working in a store, but when I saw that there was no one to take care of our parents I decided I should be the one to take charge. They need me, so I will remain here.

"I believe that women now have more choices in their lives; everything is better for women. They have more freedom and can make their own decisions."◆

ELBA Paulina's daughter is twenty and the single mother of a nine-month-old girl. She works as a secretary in a nearby town. She is a beautiful young woman with a copper-tinted complexion. Very small in stature, she hasn't quite had time to shed her adolescent plumpness. She was ever so serious in answering questions, and asked many of her own.

"When we lived in a refugee camp I had an opportunity to go to school without having to pay. I finished the fourth grade and then took secretarial classes. Now I can be employed. If we hadn't gone to the camps I would have had to go away to the city to find work.

"I met my boyfriend when I was working in Perquin, during the war. When we started getting serious I told him he had to talk to my mother and my grandparents. He came, talked to them, and everyone was in agreement. But he left as soon as I was pregnant. He comes to see the baby from time to time, but as far as help, it's minimal. We women just don't have opportunities to have good responsible husbands. I think the best thing for a family is to have both parents raise the child. You can give the child anything of material value but he still needs love—the love of a mother *and* a father—as well as the father's presence in the home.

"We've had a lot of training in family planning, but many women don't want to use it. I see so many young girls with children already, in spite of the fact that they get this training. They have babies right and left. Until one has a solid home one shouldn't bring children into the world. It's the woman who must decide; she is the one who has to live with her decision.

"A woman should know the type of man she is involved with, what family he comes from and all. I wouldn't put too much emphasis on physical looks but on the inner qualities he has. I would focus more on his attitudes, on his behavior. I don't like men who drink or fight or are bad-tempered. The first thing is the marriage, the actual ceremony, because once this takes place there is more of a commitment. I want a polite person and then I'll wait a while to see what his attitudes are before taking the fall.

"When I compare my grandmother's or my mother's life to mine, I realize that women have more opportunities now. I hope that we will have even more and have a chance to develop and enjoy our rights. I'm thinking of studying more. There are scholarships that would make it possible for me to get my diploma and improve myself. The good thing is that at my office they don't hold you back; they counsel you and try to steer you in the right direction. It could be that staying here will be fine or that I will have to go to the city to find work.

"In that case I would have to leave the baby with my mother. I can see that only by leaving the baby here would I be able to provide for her."◆

Grandfather Martinez is a model family man and his family has a long history of generations and siblings helping each other for the common good. Their religious upbringing provided guidance on behavior and morality. Yet recent history has put all these factors to the test. Buffeted by war, flight, refugee status, and new ways learned far away, the tiny family struggles to make sense of their loved ones' deaths, abandonment, and the demands of the living.

The family-oriented, responsible grandfather and grandmother barely comprehend the behavior of their daughter and granddaughter or of the men who father the younger women's children. The women themselves are confused by their newfound value and the duplicity of the larger society. The extended family has been dispersed, and the formerly supportive community is now but an anonymous group of individuals attempting to survive. Social disruption has caught the Martinez family unaware, unprepared, and, for the most part, unsupported.

Each of the families quoted here—the Faths in a burgeoning Egyptian village, the Loca-apichais of Bangkok, and the Martinezes in Segundo Montes—is facing major transformations in family roles and living arrangements. Each sees the specter of the nuclear family looming in the next generation. Whether or not My Fath becomes an airline pilot, she will certainly not live in her grandfather's four-story home. She aspires to a partnership marriage in an independent setting. Bangkok traffic and outmoded ways have led the Loca-apichais to leave the extended family home for less inviting, less supportive quarters. At the same time they worry that their Asian traditions and lifestyle will be overpowered by global pop culture in their children's time. The elder Martinez feels forsaken by the community in which he placed his peacetime hopes, and his granddaughter speaks of going away to seek a better life.

Like so many families elsewhere, these families wonder if, and how, they will remain together in the years to come, when powerful social and economic forces seem to push or pull them apart.

Part Two

Generations and Genders

Three | Cherishing Our Wisdom

The young say we're not good for anything, that we have outlived our usefulness. Don't they know that if they have a decent life now, it's because we've lived through hardships and suffered a lot for the youth of today?

—Ruben Chicas, Morazan, El Salvador

One hundred and one elderly couples sat facing each other across long, narrow tables, women on one side, men the other. Many were quite frail. A few women wore formal kimonos; the husbands appeared ill at ease in cumbersome suits. It was Elders' Day in Japan, an annual occasion when families and communities pay homage to their oldest members. The ceremony in the town hall was organized to honor local couples who would celebrate fifty years of marriage during the coming year. Traditional dances and songs, a fine meal, speeches by local officials, and a good dose of politics marked the occasion. The mayor spoke eloquently:

> Greetings to you the couples celebrating fifty years of marriage. Congratulations that both members of the couple can be here. You married in the middle of World War II without ceremony or fancy clothes. You overcame hard times and contributed to our city and country. After Japan's defeat, you worked to rebuild the nation; what we have today is because of your willingness to work hard. We thank you for the lives you have led. Now, you must enjoy life and be healthy.

Some elders fell asleep; others smoked, chatted, or watched the parade of officials come and go. Each speaker voiced similar words of appreciation until it was time for a response. Slowly, a sturdy, white-haired octogenarian rose from his chair, saying:

> We are moved by the speeches and greetings given us. We married midway through the war. Our weddings were simple, and when we went to war, our wives were left behind to work. We've lived a long time. Now we have the opportunity for a happy life, to take care of ourselves and try to be good citizens.

Years of work etched on faces disappeared into smiles. Heads nodded and wives poked dozing husbands. As an onlooker, I was moved by this public display of respect, yet found myself saddened by the thought of how seldom we express such appreciation of, and gratitude to, our elders.

The preceding chapters examined how we lived together a generation or two ago, and how our families are adapting to new times. Many of the older family members spoke of the profound and varied effects recent changes have had on their lives. The elders Setsu Nakasawa and Kama Kante still live in extended, multigenerational families. Leslie Young lives alone, by choice. Grandfather El Fath counsels the younger generations in a house built for that purpose, while Thada Locha-pichai does not expect his children to live with him in his later years. Grandfather Martinez cannot rest or retire.

This chapter will focus more closely on elders. They, and their families, will describe the realities of contemporary "elderhood" and the demands it places on families, communities, and public policy.

The twentieth century witnessed an increase in average life spans of nearly thirty years. Even in the less developed nations, the rise in life expectancy has been dramatic. In China, for example, the State Family Planning Commission notes that life expectancy rose from 35 years in 1949 to 70.8 in 1996. (It should be noted here that some nations, due to the HIV pandemic, are currently witnessing a net decline in life expectancy.)[1]

From approximately 1 percent of the world population in 1900, people over sixty represented 10 percent by 1999 and will comprise 22.1 percent by 2050.[2] Indeed, the fastest growing segment of the world's population is the group aged eighty or over.[3] This ageing of global population is a demographic phenomenon that has profound consequences for families and nations because it coincides with changes in family structure and roles due to economic transformations, advances in education and technology, and the democratization of relationships. Younger generations will wait longer to inherit family property; communities will have to provide amenities in public transportation, leisure, and health care for their older citizens. These concerns are of such importance to the world community that the United Nations declared 1999 the International Year of Older Persons, urging governments to focus their attention on the 1991 UN Principles for Older Persons—independence, participation, care, self-fulfillment, and dignity.

In this chapter, individual elders attest that standards of living have improved "unimaginably" since their youths in the early twentieth century, yet complain that the fast-paced, mobile, electronic world of today often surpasses the older person's ability to adapt to emerging technologies and lifestyles. Once the guardians of family history and traditions and arbitrators of family disputes, elders were revered and respected. In many cultures, they were the only source of information from the past and from the world beyond the family. As one retiree said, "Our grandfathers were the radio." Today, telephones, television, radio, films, and the Web bring faraway places and far-out ideas into the sanctuary of the home. Elders here note that traditions and values once passed on from generation to generation seem of little relevance in contemporary society, and are often judged as passé—or, worse, irrelevant—by the young.

In addition, images of befuddled or incompetent older people are common in the media, undermining the perception of elders as vital participants in the community. The results of all these forces are feelings of alienation and uselessness—and, at times, anger at what they perceive as a lack of respect. When today's elders speak of the seniors they knew as children, of the manner in which their own elders were revered, obeyed, and feared, the changes are all too clear.

Some elders quoted here live in secure multigenerational families, others choose to live alone; some care for grandchildren almost daily, while still others feel abandoned by children who live far away. When a spouse dies, loneliness and insecurity often increase. In this context, the situation of women is of special concern, as they tend to live longer than men and have fewer resources and skills. Among elders over seventy-five years of age, almost two-thirds are women; many, of course, are widows.[4]

The end of one's working life can bring years of isolation and inactivity or of leisure and friendship. As more couples work outside the home, we are witnessing a revalidation of grandparents' usefulness in an active caregiving role. Some grandfathers discover the joys of parenting for the first time, realizing that their work life had deprived them of that experience with their own children. Lenin Passos, a retired Brazilian engineer, remarked, "The difference between being a father and a grandfather is that when your own children behave badly, you beat them. When your grandchildren do the same—you kiss them!"

Here we listen to what the elders themselves are saying about the economic and social changes they have witnessed and about their relationships with the younger generations. Not surprisingly, questions of independence, of more democratic relationships within the family, and of responsibility arise across the range of social and cultural situations. In the process of conducting these interviews, I met eighty year olds who had immigrated to the Amazonas in their late sixties as farming pioneers; I met a seventy-five-year-old Rio slum dweller who raises children no one else wants. I met elders who were independent and feisty, and others who are disappointed by the lack of community support for their older citizens. Each of them, in different ways, share the challenge of continual adaptation to rapidly changing—and confusing—times.

AMMAN, JORDAN

On the outskirts of Jordan's capital, Amman, is a new neighborhood called Hay Nissan. It is set on a treeless hillside, served by unpaved streets.

Modest homes are under construction everywhere. Haja Mohamed Hussein Jaffe, matriarch of the Masshour family, lives in one of those recently built homes with her son, an office employee (whose interview appears in chapter 5). Seven people—Haja, her son, his wife, their three children, and Haja's unmarried daughter—live together there.

Haja Mohammed never attended school and married, she said, "when I was twelve, maybe thirteen. My husband died many years ago.

Haja Mohamed Hussein Jaffe, 76

"We lived in a tent, as Bedouins, and now people live in stone houses that have electricity and water. It was better before, not complicated. The same is true for the relationship between relatives. When we lived together, we always did things together; neighbors and the family had contact in their daily lives. Now? No. Nobody knows the other.

"Years ago, women always worked on the farm and followed the sheep. Now the woman is mostly in the house and can talk with the children, with everyone together. Before they didn't speak to the husband. Once when I spoke to my husband, he said, 'Go away and never come back to this house.' So I went to his father and he took me back to my house and lectured my husband. 'You must talk to her and let her stay in this house.' My father-in-law was an elder, so my husband had to obey. There was great respect for the elders. But now, customs have changed.

"We ate fresh meat and yogurt and chicken and eggs—everything was fresh. Sheep and goat and cows, camels, we had everything. Now, because I don't see the food myself, because I don't raise it, I don't like it. I don't eat that frozen chicken or meat. And bread from the shop I won't eat at all. Who made it? Were his hands clean? I make my *own* with my *own* hands!"

Haja Mohammed has lived the transition from tents to frozen food, from total submission to family tradition to the democratization of relationships. Her reluctance to eat what some unknown person has touched is, for many of us, an anachronism: we rarely know where or how our food is grown, much less who has touched it. It is indeed difficult for the young to comprehend the breadth and depth of change these elders have experienced in the last century.

At the same time, living longer and in better health has allowed our elders to be and do more than the grandparents they knew. Another widowed grandmother, in a remote province of China, spoke of the change she has taken in stride, as well as the role she has played as a family helper in the transition and as a link with the crucial element of family history.

NINGXIA HUI AUTONOMOUS REGION, CHINA

In the steppes of central China, camels grow thick shaggy coats to protect themselves from the elements. Life is harsh, cold, and windblown. The predominantly rural population struggles to wrest a livelihood from a high desert environment with little water and poor soils. It is a region inhabited by the Hui, descendants of Muslim merchants of Persian origin who, in the thirteenth century, followed Genghis Khan's Mongol armies into China. The Hui have retained their language and distinctive culture—in which Islam and Confucianism sometimes combine—because the region remained isolated and relatively undeveloped until the late 1950s.

Yinchuan, the regional capital, stretches across naked plains; it is a large city dominated by boxlike, utilitarian architecture. Homes are heated by coal and industrial smokestacks belch black coal fumes at all hours of the day and night. During my predawn walk, I covered both nose and mouth to protect myself from the acrid smoke. The cold streets of December were yet to be filled with the hundreds of cyclists who would appear an hour later on their way to work.

In one of Yinchuan's cement high-rise apartment buildings, we climbed four flights of stairs in near darkness to find the Baos' apartment. They are a Muslim family that lives in a twenty-five-square-meter apartment consisting of a small kitchen, living room, and two bedrooms. One bedroom was filled with a double bed, shared, I was told, by the granny and granddaughter. The second bedroom housed the parents and their thirteen-year-old son. The sofa in the sitting room where we sat

Bao Guoren, 50
Guo Xiuying, 46
Ma Yuzhen, 84
Bao Weiwei, 16

was covered with pink towels—for protection, I suspect, more than decoration. The cement floors were bare, but the furnishings were comfortable and attractive. A collection of vases and an antique tea set were displayed in a glass-doored bookcase. The family, adults and children, were swaddled in layers of hand-knitted sweaters, as the coal stove didn't quite succeed in chasing the winter chill. I, too, kept my coat wrapped tight.

GUOREN Bao Guoren, fifty, has been employed by the Telecommunications Bureau for many years, first as a postman and now as a telegram encoder. His father was an illiterate door-to-door coal peddler who did all he could to send his children to school. Guoren dropped out of secondary school to help support his parents and four siblings. Only recently, he passed a test that allowed him to become a senior technician. A rather small, slender man, he described himself as "quiet," saying he spends his weekends at home or, occasionally, with colleagues. He rises at six each morning to jog forty minutes in a neighboring park. His one passion, he admitted, is watching television news programs, "Everyday, no matter what else I may be doing.

"I grew up here in Yinchuan. All the villages around us have now become part of the city. Both my parents came from one of those villages. My father's influence on me was profound, in particular, his sense of duty to raise his family well. He taught us to be honest and didn't allow us to misbehave. He passed away in 1981.

"We have both a son and a daughter, and I treat them equally, although I admit that I do sometimes favor my daughter. I insist that they rely on their own efforts. Since I'm just an ordinary office worker, they cannot depend on me or my influence to get them ahead. That's why I teach them self-reliance. They have to build a career through their own efforts. Our hope is that both will graduate from university, although as parents, we shouldn't interfere too much.

"Together, my wife and I earn about 500 yuan per month [U.S. $60]. We give our salaries to my mother and she manages our budget. Since prices are constantly increasing we struggle to make ends meet. If we want to buy something, we discuss it and then I ask my mother for the money. As long as our budget can permit the expenditure, my mother agrees.

"My wife is very good with my mother. She respects her very much; so does my daughter. And for this I'm grateful. Since my daughter is the only granddaughter my mother has, the two of them have become inseparable."◆

XIUYING   Guo Xiuying and Bao Guoren were introduced by relatives and married in their early twenties. She is a teacher on the staff of the Women's Federation of Ningxia Hui Autonomous Region. The federation oversees child care and family education services for the entire region. Although born to a poor, rural family, Xiuying studied so hard and did so well that she was able to obtain scholarships throughout her schooling, including university.

The Bao family during the author's visit: (*left to right*) Bao Guoren, Bao Weiwei, Guo Xiuying, the author, Ma Yuzhen, Bao Shuwen, and cousin Bao Jie

"I never knew my grandparents, but my parents told me that they were very poor. My grandfather was a sharecropper for a landlord near the city of Kunjung. They couldn't make a living there, so they left and became wandering beggars. They eventually died of starvation in Mongolia.

"After Liberation [by the Communists in 1949] our family worked on a commune. We were five children. Mother passed away when I was thirteen; my younger sister was only two years old. My father raised us alone. He was a very typical Chinese peasant; he worked hard and was a very honest man. He told us to be upright human beings and to follow what the Koran says. He is dead now.

"My oldest brother is illiterate because he had to work the land, to support the rest of us. All the others are university graduates. When I graduated I worked to support my younger brother, then he supported the next younger.

"When I married, my father told me, 'You must treat your mother-in-law well; that is what a Muslim should do. The Koran teaches that people must keep a harmonious relationship in the family. It is our duty to support and care for the elders. My mother-in-law is the head of our family. She may be in her eighties, but her mind is very clear. She can do everything.

"I'm very lucky to have her; she takes care of the household so I am able to work without worrying. When I come home I help her with the chores. Granny takes responsibility for the meals; I wash the dishes and my husband cleans the floors. He also buys the grain and coal because someone has to carry it up the stairs. We use coal for cooking because Granny is afraid to use natural gas; she thinks she might forget and cause an accident. And she doesn't like television; she says it confuses her.

"Generally speaking, the grandparents' generation is more influenced by tradition, the Koran, and the concepts of Confucius. Our children live in the modern world, so they are pulled in two directions. It is confusing to cope with both. I believe parents play a greater role than the elders in children's upbringing because the parents know the psychology of the children and how to bridge this gap.

"That said, my mother-in-law teaches our children well; the methods she uses are very appropriate. She doesn't scold or upset them, and the children are willing to accept this kind of upbringing unconsciously; it is simply part of their lives.

"If my husband and I disagree with Granny, the children are always on Granny's side, saying, 'You shouldn't say that. You should respect the elders.'"◆

YUZHEN   All the while we talked, Ma Yuzhen did little to hide her joy with our visit. Her plump, wrinkled face smiled constantly and her gnarled arthritic hands punctuated her words with gusto. She wore the traditional white cap of Hui women, a navy blue jacket, and gray pants. Beneath the pants, heavy long underwear protected her from the winter chill. When she began to tell of her youth, Yuzhen's heavy-lidded eyes filled with tears. She was born and raised in an earthen cottage, and she described her early life as desperately poor.

"My parents, grandparents, and five of us children lived in two rooms. We all slept together on an earthen kong [a sort of bench that is heated from below]. We raised sheep and sold mutton in the market.

"At fifteen I was married to a herder. We had a few sheep of our own, but mostly he herded the sheep of others. We used to sell garlic illegally to earn some cash. Sometimes my husband bought coal at the mine and sold it door to door. It was a very poor life. So you see, to have a home like this was unimaginable.

"My first child came when I was seventeen; it was a son who was stillborn. In all, I had thirteen children, but only five survived. Some died soon after birth, others lasted a few days. There was no one to help with births, only an aunt who cut the cord and washed the baby. It may have been tetanus that killed them. I don't know. Peasant life was too difficult—too many hardships."

Yuzhen pressed food on us at every pause, saying, "This food—fruit and cookies—were unimaginable in my childhood. My parents had a miserable life; no words can describe the misery. The only thing we had to eat was gruel. Even millet was a delicacy. Now, look: you and I can share these cakes together!"

Repeatedly Yuzhen expressed gratitude to Chairman Mao for bringing easier lives to the peasants of China. Repeatedly she patted my hand, which she held tightly in her lap. "I'm a widow without a state pension but I have eleven great-grandchildren, all living in the vicinity of Yinchuan. They live happily and all have work.

"My children and my grandchildren are all doing very well, earning salaries. They know that everything comes from hard work. I only hope that my grandchildren will have successful careers. You see, you should never be satisfied with the present; it's important to always try to do better. But for me, as long as I live I'll be content with my present life. I am very healthy. I go to the market to buy our food and cook for the whole family. As soon as they return from work, their meal is ready."◆

WEIWEI Yuzhen, above all, feels useful. Despite her difficult early life, and the children she has lost, she is fulfilled by the role her family has given her. She is respected by her son and his wife. She manages the household income and is adored by her grandchildren—even more than she knows. Shuwen, her thirteen-year-old grandson, and his cousin Jie, fourteen, nodded affirmatively as her sixteen-year-old granddaughter, Weiwei, a high school student, spoke of their grandmother. Dressed in the teen attire of a white sweater, brown ski pants, and sneakers, Weiwei first spoke of her personal hopes, saying, "If I pass the university entrance exams, I'll become a journalist. It's a good job: I would meet a lot of people and travel. That's my ambition.

"It's my grandmother who has the most influence on me. I'm closer to Granny than to my parents. Five days after my birth I was brought home and Granny has looked after me ever since. Even now we share the same bed. She taught me so many things it would be impossible to say all I've learned from her— to treat others with kindness, to be honest, kindhearted, always willing to help others.

"Granny has an influence on all of us. She tells us stories about our family's history and about what kind of life she had. Because religion is very important to her, we are strict observers of all the taboos, like not eating pork. My father doesn't smoke or drink because of her. Families who don't have an elder with them are free to disregard the taboos."

The girl hesitated a moment, then smiled as she recalled an incident that demonstrated her reliance on her grandmother. "I once traveled to Beijing with my parents. I was very excited to visit so many different places there, but after two or three days I was homesick. I asked my mother if we could go home four days early."

Laughing aloud at herself, Weiwei admitted, "I missed my granny."◆

Yuzhen is surrounded by a loving family. Her daughter-in-law is grateful for her help; her grandchildren welcome her counsel. The strain inherent in living with one foot in an impoverished past and another in the grandchildren's world of school and television are minimized by the knowledge that she is useful to others. In her loving home, she is unaware that living arrangements for the elderly are about to be challenged by demographic trends.

In the 1970s, demographers in the Peoples' Republic of China began to sound the alarm about the nation's escalating birthrate, predicting environmental and social collapse if family size was not reduced. In the 1980s, the "One Couple, One Child" policy was encouraged, even enforced in some cases, in an effort to avoid overburdening the nation's natural systems, productive capacity, and institutions.[5] But for every well-intentioned policy there is usually an unforeseen, problematic consequence. In this case, what emerges, foremost, is the issue of elderly care. If there is but one child for two sets of grandparents, what are the consequences for the elderly in later years? Would a couple like Guoren and Xiuying have to support two sets of grandparents? Will the government step in instead, taking responsibility for the ramification of its social policy?

China is facing a dilemma already apparent in Europe and Japan where birthrates have been falling since the mid-twentieth century. Yet everywhere, the ratio of active workers to inactive "senior citizens" is diminishing rapidly, raising questions of dependency, long-term security and pensions, and "late life" care. Added to the economic and social consequences of what is known as population aging is a worry that the dark side of family life, elder abuse, seems to be increasing. Studies in England, Canada, the United States, and Scandinavia reveal that from 4 to 12 percent of older citizens face physical, psychological, and financial exploitation. In the United States, according to the National Center for Victims of Crime, neglect is the most comon form of maltreatement, accounting for 58.5 percent of all reports in 1998.[6] Many other elders, though they do not face abuse, speak of how they feel rejected by the younger generation.

The care of a growing elderly population presents governments with demands for adequate pensions, health care, and institutional support. Faced with the financial burden of these needs, governments are inclined to shift responsibilities back to families, which in turn brings up the gender dimension of the aging population. When elders are no longer able to care for themselves, the tasks falls to the family—most often to its women. The consequences for women's lives are momentous. Policymakers and employers, who recognize the considerable burden that falls on those who care for aging parents, predict this burden will have an increasing impact on women's lives as population aging continues.[7]

In the mountains of Minas Gerais, Brazil, I encountered a family where three women were bound to the care of an elderly patriarch. They spoke of how that responsibility circumscribes their life choices, and thus those of their children.

LIMERIA, BRAZIL

Twenty-four hours after my arrival in Rio, I traveled to the region of Minas Gerais by one of the thousands of buses that crisscross the immensity of Brazil. As the bus made its way out of Rio toward the city of Muriae, nature demonstrated its superiority in the running battle with manmade objects: the grass has broken through concrete sidewalks, and houses were covered with vines and mildew. Further north, in Minas Gerais, humankind's impact on nature was more obvious. Once covered by Atlantic rain forest, the region is now denuded, its beauty marred by deep eroded gullies cut into the red-orange earth. Fields, hills, mountains—everything is cracked open by the force of rain on unprotected soil.

The next morning, Easter Sunday, we set out on horseback to visit Joao Araujo de Silva, an elderly farmer and widower whose farm lies hidden in a narrow valley of the range known as the Mountains of the Spiders. Its steep hillsides have been cleared for cattle raising and, according to my companion, the area is among the most neglected in Brazil, renowned as bandit country. The nearest paved road is forty-five kilometers away; horses or ox-drawn carts are the usual means of transportation.

The three Araujo family homes are well separated one from another, each on a hillside, each whitewashed with a tile roof. The grandfather's home boasts indoor plumbing, even though the bathtub sits in the middle of the yard and kitchen wastewater was thrown out the window. It is a simple house, with an earthen stove, a table and three chairs, and a cupboard of amateur workmanship. On the day we visited, its interior was spotless, everything in its place. In the grandfather's

Joao Araujo de Silva, 84
Erlicia Aruajo, 45
Wilma Falco Araujo, 40

bedroom there were three beds, one of which was his. The others served as sofas to sit on as we listened to the elder tell of his life.

JOAO Joao Araujo is a very tall, slim man, somewhat bowed by age, and his angular features immediately called to mind a fighter of windmills. His bright blue eyes are those of a young man but age has taken its toll: his hands trembled as they rested on his lap. His grandfather, he explained, had come from Portugal, traded in gold, bought land, and "even owned slaves." His father became a schoolteacher who was moved from town to town. They were eight children, six brothers and two sisters. Only one brother is still alive, and lives in Rio state.

"When I arrived here, at age twenty-four, there was only one other man, a surveyor. There was no road. You had to wade through rivers. I actually built the first bridges here. A huge forest covered the area. There was lots of wildlife, even leopards—and big dogs that chased the leopards. I used to go into the forest early in the morning and hunt, especially a two-kilo bird called chororó. They're like big chickens.

"Life was difficult. People were very poor. They chopped down the forest to plant corn, but that didn't work. Now it's just pasture. I had four horses and a mule then. One horse was as sleek as a jaguar, but thieves stole all my animals.

"I married when I was twenty-four. My wife was not even sixteen, and very beautiful. She had lovely hair, a beautiful brunette. She had a lovely body, too. I had seen her in Limeria. She and her sisters had their bedroom on the street side of their house; I could go under her window on horseback and chat through the window.

"People were scared of her father. He was tough. One day when I went to Limeria, he called me over and said, 'I've got a daughter to be married. If you're going to marry her, you can hang around; if not you'd better get lost.'

"I replied, 'If you think I'm good enough to come into the family, you can set the date.' After we married I stayed seven years with the father-in-law, working with him as a sharecropper. We had eight children in all, three boys and five girls. [One son, Walter, is interviewed in chapter 6.] One died at age twelve from an illness; the others are all dispersed—Limeria, Rio, or here.

"My wife's grandmother used to live with us, and my wife looked after her parents and uncles. Now it's the daughters who care for me. They all live here, and there is no ill will between us. I get on well with my children and my daughter-in-law. We're not rich, but we have remained together here.

"We never used to keep our children too close to us, perhaps, but they respected us. The father had to give the children permission to go out. I think it's more difficult for young people today because parents don't look after them properly. Now they don't need their parents' permission for anything. There's no order. My grandchildren go where they like. My son Cesar is fifty-four years old, yet if I ask him to go to Limeria to buy me a pack of cigarettes, he certainly won't say no.

"I pray to God every night that my grandchildren are successful. I hope they will live honestly and treat people well, that they'll be friendly with everybody. Every night I pray to the Almighty that He give us health and peace and happiness."◆

WILMA As Joao prays for his family, the younger generation wonders about what will come to pass upon his death. His land will be divided in six parts (two of his daughters have relinquished their inheritance), and the ten acres will hardly suffice for six large families. Meanwhile, three women—two daughters and a daughter-in-law—share responsibility for the aging Joao, who needs constant attention. One daughter, forty-five-year-old Maria, had become blind from diabetes two years earlier. She, too, now requires assistance to manage the simplest of tasks.

It is her forty-three-year-old sister-in-law, Wilma Falco Araujo, who is closest at hand to do the caretaking. She and her husband share Joao's house, and thus the responsibility for his care. Wilma is a small, dark-haired, attractive woman who has four children—boys ages seventeen, sixteen, fifteen, and a seven-year-old girl.

"My family is from Ancourados, twelve kilometers from here. My parents are still alive. I have five sisters and four brothers. I met my husband in the square, walking around. Our parents knew each other, but we hadn't met.

"We would like to move into town, to Limeria, so that the children could continue school there. The school here only goes to the fourth grade, and my sons have completed the four years. We could manage it, but my husband doesn't want to leave his father. He wants to be here when his father is sick. That's why we've stayed on. The girl is starting school now and is very happy. I would like one of them to leave this peasant life. It's backward here in the countryside. There is nothing, even for the children. We want so much to leave. It seems like a dream."◆

ERCILIA   Joao's second-eldest daughter, Ercilia, is, at forty-five, a discouraged woman who appears much older than she is. Her home is but a few hundred yards from Joao's house. She is a strong-looking woman, but her gray hair was matted and her teeth suffered the decay so common in a region where people chew on sugar cane stalks to keep hunger at bay. She asked us to sit outside, away from the house, saying she wanted to ensure a private conversation. As soon as we sat down, she burst out emotionally, saying she wanted a better life for her two sons. She wants to educate them "so they could get jobs someday, not have a life like mine."

"I never went to school; I wanted to, but my mother wouldn't let me. I don't read and write well. What little I learned, I learned from my brother when I was still unmarried.

"I lived here in this house as a child. We worked in the fields, planting, weeding, or harvesting coffee. We girls did housework, as well. I used to dream of a different life. I wanted to go and live with my sister in Rio, but my mother wouldn't let me. I went to São Paulo once, before I was married, but since then I haven't been anywhere.

"I've been married fifteen years and have two sons. I couldn't have more because they were Caesarian births. My husband's life is a bitter one; he's been a farm laborer for thirty years. His father was very backward, and when his coffee plants didn't take, he hired himself out as a day worker. My husband doesn't have anything. He would like to buy some land, but we have no means to do so. Let's hope things are better for our children, that they have a more tranquil life. I would like to move so that the children could continue their education. I just want them to be able to get good jobs.

"Families have changed, to be sure. Children are changing, too. My sister married a widower with eight children and looked after all the children, and now they don't give her the time of day. There is much violence against women here, mostly related to drinking. It's real madness! It's happening in many families. And children are going off, leaving the elderly parents."

Ercilia looked up toward the house. She sighed deeply. Turning toward us, she added, "At least all my sisters and brothers get along well." Her hand rose to rub tears from her eyes and she turned away, adding, "Everything is fine here."◆

Two brave women care for an old man in a remote valley where their children are deprived of education and, their mothers fear, a better life. Wilma and Ercilia are in what is known as the sandwich generation of caregivers.

Still raising their own children, they also care for the older generation. This scenario is bound to become more prevalent as the number of older citizens increases in the next decades.

Another trend we now see, for a variety of reasons, is grandparents cast in the role of caregivers to their grandchildren. When both spouses work, they may depend on their parents to provide partial child care. In the United States, for example, in 1994, 16 percent of preschool children with working mothers were cared for by a grandparent.[8] In developing counties, emigrant parents may leave their children with grandparents until they can earn enough to send for them. In other cases, like that of the Kiyimba family in Uganda, grandparents care for the grandchildren who have been orphaned.

KAMPALA, UGANDA

Uganda's capital city is a jumble of modern buildings, gardens, markets, and neat one-family homes, makeshift shelters in growing slums, and garbage dumps where street children play. It is also a city of wide tree-lined streets that climb up and down its hills, where the famous Makerere University and dozens of churches are spread. Kampala's friendly people are eager to give directions when the lost visitor enquires. The couple I was to interview lived on the outskirts of town, in a residential neighborhood that we, their daughter Anne Kaddumakasa, and I, reached by taxi.

Benedict Kiyimba, 69
Anne Kiyimba, 62

The Kiyimba house was at the end of a quiet unpaved street and the flower garden surrounding the home was a testament to Anne Kiyimba's fascination with plants. When I mentioned the beauty of the garden, the family laughed aloud, for they enjoy teasing their grandmother about the "jungle" she has created.

The Kiyimbas lived an ordinary life that combined work, churchgoing, and childrearing. Grandfather Benedict began his working life as a teacher and then turned to community work. He retired at the level of district commissioner. Anne is a retired schoolteacher. Both were proud of their children's accomplishments and had looked forward to enjoying their later years surrounded by children and grandchildren. When HIV struck Uganda, their children's generation was most affected. The Kiyimbas now care for the three children of their deceased daughter and worry about another daughter—my companion, Anne, who has been widowed by the disease, leaving her the sole supporter of seven children. (Anne, who works for an AIDS patient support group, is interviewed in chapter 10.)

BENEDICT Benedict Kiyimba is a soft-spoken man who peppers his stories with smiles and humor. He began the couple's story by saying, "My wife and I have been married for forty-five years and haven't been apart for a single day! We met at a bus station and I didn't want to leave her even then. I decided to take her bus rather than my own.

"My father was a humble peasant and I was the first to be educated, so we started life in a very humble way. I was twenty-seven; she was just twenty-one. We were both teachers and we've been blessed with three daughters. We're very proud of our daughters. Unfortunately, one—the middle one—passed away a year ago. She was such a beautiful girl. The other two are doing well and help us. Especially Annie. She always comes to see how we are doing.

"Originally I thought I could relax in my old age because I had discharged my duty as a parent. But when the deaths began I felt I had to step in and do whatever I could. Beti died at thirty-eight and left us three children, all of school age. One is retarded due to a malaria-caused cerebral hemorrhage at age two. She is seventeen and can't walk or talk. She has the mental age of a small child, and goes to a boarding school for the disabled. Her brother was by another father, who lives in the United States. He used to send some money for his son's education, but lately he has neglected his obligations. I've written to him but I've received nothing. It is their school fees that are forcing me to continue working. And we are afraid for Annie, who is now alone with seven children.

"I have a pension from the government. It's negligible but it's a pension. I had thought, 'I can live happily with a meager income,' provided I was doing something in which I believed, something I thought was good for my children and my country. The archbishop of Kampala had started a community center, a place where people could go either

Benedict and Anne Kiyimba on their wedding day in 1947

for relaxation or to study. They wanted somebody with experience, so I offered my services. I volunteered in the community center for six years; then I was administrator of a home for the disabled for ten years.

"My daughter, Anne, is following in my footsteps. She is close to my way of thinking—not working only for money, but for the good of others. Money is not everything. Because of our efforts, she can help the victims of AIDS.

"As I mentioned before, family life has become more complex. When I was around twenty, people wouldn't care if they had many children at home. They grew their food; they didn't have to buy it. Life was simple. People lived with the income they had.

"With the change in attitude toward the extended family, people tend to care only for their immediate families. They are not keen to invite the extended family to live with them. They can't afford it. It's a pity, because I obtained my education not because my father was rich but because of the extended family. So that aspect of family life is being lost. People no longer wish to have many children. When they have four, they say, 'That's enough. I don't want a fifth one.' That's another change: it's no longer possible to maintain a big family. Life is too expensive. And now? We have to worry about these orphans. How are the retired elders going to educate them?"◆

ANNE Benedict's wife, Anne, sixty-two, is a warm, outgoing, and trusting woman. Her years of teaching are evident in her manner. She is just five feet

The Kiyimbas with daughter Anne Kaddumukasa (*left*) and grandchildren

tall, but she is endowed with endless energy. Her pleasure in receiving us was evident, even if it was to bring forth painful memories—stories of loss upon loss. Unlike her husband, she frowns on her daughter's desire to work with AIDS patients.

"My parents had only three children; one was a priest, the other a nun. I was the last-born. My father was a catechist in the Catholic Church. He died when I was four years old, so my sister, the nun, took me to live with the sisters. I grew up mostly with them. I would go home to my mother only for the holidays.

"I finished my training at the Teacher Training College at age nineteen and started teaching primary school. I met my husband at the bus park. It wasn't love at first sight, but later on. But once he visited my home, the family liked him very much; he was very humble and polite to them. They thought he could make a good in-law. From the time I met him until we married was just five months.

"We raised our children well, but now look what has happened. So much grief. Anne—she insists of working with the dying. I worry about her. And we must raise these orphans. We must. We will."◆

The Kiyimbas are part of a global phenomenon: the increasing number of grandparents who find themselves caring for AIDS orphans, who numbered more than 13 million in 2000, according to UNAIDS.[9] In some of the most affected countries, we are witnessing the disappearance of the middle generation, the young adults, leaving the very young and the old to care for each other.

Responsibility for the family's young, late in life, is not an unusual occurrence. As more couples are obliged to work, elders are increasingly called upon to provide care for the grandchildren. In the United States, the Census Bureau estimated that in 1994 four million children lived in a household headed by a grandparent, a 40 percent increase over the previous decade.[10] In some cases this may provide a sense of pride and usefulness to otherwise lonely elders. In the case of Benedict Kiyimba, however, it entailed returning to work after retirement. He was fortunate to have found paid work. Ageism is endemic in the workplace; many elders are turned away by employers who want young workers. That, too, may change as the marketplace is forced to seek competence from a healthy aging population.[11]

Another trend we see is that of elders caring for elders. Choosing not to live with the young, preferring to remain independent or to live among other older people as long as possible, elders themselves become caregivers.

PETERSBURG, WEST VIRGINIA, USA

A four-hour drive from Washington, D.C., Petersburg is a county seat of just over ten thousand inhabitants. Today forestry is the pillar of Petersburg's economy. The scattered family farms have turned to raising cattle and, increasingly, laying hens. The area attracts sports hunters, who roam its forested hills in search of deer and, more rarely, bear. Many of the town's young are attracted to the military or to life in nearby cities.

Oscar Halderman, 99
Velma Lahman, 72
Sandy Mowry, 52
Bart Mowry, 17

In a valley just north of Petersburg, the Halderman farmhouse sits in a picture-book setting of rolling hills and cattle pastures. As we drove into the farmyard we were greeted by an ancient collie dog, lame and nearly blind. Physical ailments also plagued the dog's owners, Oscar Halderman and his daughter, Velma Lahman. Both had suffered fractured bones in the recent past and were not as agile as they would have liked. They welcomed us at the back door of the two-story farmhouse and led us through a hallway that had been rearranged as a sitting room to the kitchen that also serves as Velma's bedroom while she recovers from a broken hip.

OSCAR Oscar Halderman is a slender, distinguished-looking man, who stands tall in his ninety-ninth year and, I soon learned, was of lively and youthful mind. Indeed, he answered questions before I had a chance to formulate them. Known locally as "Cussin' Oscar," he boasts of drinking a beer a day and chewing tobacco. Since his daughter has difficulty standing, Oscar does most of the cooking. When Velma had hip and knee surgery, Oscar took care of all her needs. The spring sunshine filled the room as I sat facing the feisty elder. His clothes were neat and well-ironed because, he announced, he does the ironing himself. Through thick eyeglasses that were held together with tape, his eyes searched mine for reaction to his comments.

"I was born in 1896, the ninth of eleven children. My great-grandfather came from Germany with his brother and settled up here in Holland County. My mother was born in 1861 and lived to be eighty-six. Of her children, only one died as a baby; the rest lived long lives. They're all dead now. And to tell you the truth, even my brother's kids are dead.

"When I was sixteen, I started working at a paper mill. Got paid fourteen cents an hour. Five years later I was drafted. It was 1918. They sent us down to Mississippi for training and nearly starved us. Gave us things my dog wouldn't eat. And they worked us like horses. I never got to go across to Europe.

"I moved back to the farm and got married in 1920. I met Alma in church. We courted for about a year and then eloped. We didn't want to go to any expense. Her father was dead. We just called her mother once we got back to tell her. We had two children, Velma and a boy. My son passed away nine years ago.

"I've lived a long time because I was honest. I never cheated a man out of a dollar! I always worked hard. I don't know why I stay healthy. I don't do much. I like to watch TV; I watch all the shows. I've got nothing else to do. But I don't like ball games. When they play that football, I shut it off. I like to listen to the news on the radio. But I don't worry about the state of the world. Why bother, to tell you the truth?

"I take care of the dog, feed my cats. I don't go out much. I don't even go to church anymore. Once in a while I go to Petersburg for the ride. I feel good—in fact, the last time I saw a doctor was six years ago. Sometimes I feel dizzy or lose my balance, like I'm drunk. Back a couple of years Velma used to drive me because I gave my car away. You see, I drove until I was ninety years old; then I thought it was time to quit.

"I have four grandchildren, and one lives nearby. He comes up every week or so. I don't go around to visit them very much and they don't visit me like

they used to. Back in my young days, on Sunday, we always visited family. But now they don't. Nowadays when a man reaches sixty-five years old,
he's called a dummy. He's not smart anymore.

"When I die, I hope I go to sleep, I don't want to cause any trouble. When
I go, I want to go all at once. To tell the truth, the majority of the people I
know—they're all dead. The young people, I don't even know them. They
don't pay attention to me or tell me anything."◆

VELMA   Oscar's daughter is seventy-two years old and somewhat disabled
by arthritis. She is small in stature and was wearing a T-shirt and pants—
the same attire as her grandchildren, whom I met later. Like her father, she
wears eyeglasses. She has a lovely face framed by short-cropped hair. In recent
years, Velma rarely leaves the house. She fills her day with telephone conversations with the neighbors. A few months before she had purchased a radio
scanner that allows her to listen to the police and fire department frequencies.
She and her friends call each other to discuss what's happening on the police
radio. It keeps her from getting lonely, she explained.

"My husband died when I was forty-two. Imagine, thirty years ago! Someone
was cutting a tree up in the fields and it hit him on the side of the head. He
was in the hospital for a while, then suddenly he had a heart attack.

"My dad worked at the paper mill and my mom, of course, just kept house.
In this area the only job you could get was housework, so I worked in other
people's homes until I married in 1940. My husband was a truck driver. Four
years later my husband was drafted and sent to Germany. We had both a
son and a daughter. I did a bit of everything—farm work, gardening, caring for the henhouse.

"Everybody lives so far away now, they never get to see each other. Especially
the older people. My great-grandmother lived with my grandmother. Elders
stayed in the home—just like Dad lives with me. I'm lucky that my family is close. I have a neighbor whose children are both far away. What
would happen if she got sick? Old people don't have anyone to depend on.

"If the neighbors hear somebody died, they'll bring food or something like
that. When I was sick some people came by, but it is not as it used to be.
Not like when I was growing up. I think they are too busy to pay any attention. I have a couple of women friends who really help me out. They are about
my age. Another neighbor comes by now because her husband is dead. I call
her every day and I talk to Lucy, a friend who is paralyzed. I call my granddaughter often. And there's another woman up here who is eighty-seven years
old. We all have radio scanners so we can pick up police radio calls. If anything happens—a fire, an accident—we hear the police. We hear the ambu-
lance. It's not very long before we call each other and talk about what is going
on. The telephone is our community network."◆

SANDY   That evening I visited with Velma's daughter, Sandy Mowry, fifty-two, who was working late at the office of the family trucking business. Sandy is a woman of medium height, with reddish blonde hair and fancy eyeglasses. Her desk was cluttered with an accountant's papers, and I suspect she leaves the desk only to go to her house, right next door. She wakes at 5:30, she explained, to do the housework and then comes to work. Leisure, she added, is not part of her routine. Soft-spoken and somewhat self-deprecating, she made light of the fact that the family rarely has "much fun."

"Our family was very close-knit. Dad was a farmer, my mother took care of the family and made all my clothes. She's a very independent person. She wants to live up there on the farm. Elders seem happier in their own sur-roundings. My grandfather is happier there as well. We take him wherever he wants to go. He wouldn't want to be in a nursing home. As long as he is independent and can manage for himself, there's no reason to put him in a nursing home. Mother is very independent; once she tackles something she doesn't let go. But if something would happen, either my brother or I would take care of her."◆

BART   Sandy's seventeen-year-old son, a senior in high school, is Oscar's great-grandson. A handsome young fellow, he stands at medium height and is a successful amateur wrestler. He said he's had a girlfriend since he was twelve and knows what he wants in life: to marry at twenty-three and have three children. In talking about his two sets of grandparents, the young man appeared admiring.

"Both my grandmothers had interesting lives. Grandma Lahman worked until she got real bad arthritis. At Christmas we got together at her house. She always told me great stories about the old days. And great-granddad tells his stories over and over again. The one about walking seven miles with his girlfriend—with a gun. He has lots of great stories."◆

Later, when I met Bart's paternal grandmother, she told me that he comes by her house or calls her every night—always. He is part of her routine; she waits up for his call.

Most members of the Halderman-Lahman-Mowry family live within fifteen kilometers of each other. Distance is not a barrier to their relation-ships, but, due to each family's work, they don't have occasion to see each other often. The television, telephone, and the radio scanner are the elders' antidotes to lack of visits. The older generation seems proud of their inde-pendence knowing that if they are in need, their children are close by.

Since none of the children or grandchildren wish to be farmers, questions of inheritance of land are not crucial to the next generation's well-being. For some elders the question of inheritance is a great preoccupation, especially those who have worked all their lives hoping to leave property, a business, or productive land to those who follow. An elderly Tokyo craftsman and his family worry about the escalating costs of inheritance.

TOKYO, JAPAN

In the heart of Tokyo, one still finds neighborhoods filled with small, family-owned factories: printing workshops, carpentry stores, cardboard container producers, and small iron works. The Iinuma family lives in such a neighborhood, where people stroll the narrow streets and call greetings to their neighbors through open factory doors.

The Iinumas own an iron works that employs seven people; five are family members. They manufacture made-to-order metal stairs and gates. Their story is similar to other "family productive units" in Japan's large cities, to which rural families migrated in the early decades of the twentieth century.

The family group consists of the rural-born grand-parents, their second son, who runs the business, his wife, their two sons, aged sixteen and eleven, and an

Masaichi Iinuma, 69

Aguri Iinuma, 69

Akiko Iinuma, 43

Kiyoshi Iinuma, 41

Masauni Iinuma, 11

unmarried sister, who is inseparable from her two dogs. The three generations live in apartments above and next door to the small factory. The Iinumas believe they are fortunate to have been sheltered from the corporate, commuting life by their home-based business. Yet they worry about the survival of their lifestyle. Real estate prices have so escalated that when elders die, younger couples are not always able to pay the mandatory inheritance taxes. Elders who spent a lifetime building a business for the next generation see their life's work—and their children's future—at risk.

We met on the second floor, above the workshop, in the younger couple's kitchen. Every inch of space was used, every object and utensil neatly arranged. We sat on benches around an octagonal table covered by a paisley cloth, sipping tea and discussing the object of my visit.

MASAICHI I learned that nine years before, the sixty-nine-year-old Masaichi Iinuma had been partially paralyzed by a stroke and had retired from daily business affairs. His speech remains somewhat impaired, but he paid that no mind; his will to tell us as much as possible about his family was far stronger than his disability. Dressed in a smart tweed jacket and shirt, he reveled in the attention given to his family story.

"We were poor farmers from the Yamanachi region. It's a mountainous area where farming is difficult. In 1922 there was a great flood and our land was covered by huge mud slides. The family sold everything to come to Tokyo, thinking they would find jobs here. Two years later the great Kanto earthquake destroyed Tokyo—everything. Once again, they had to start over.

"We were six: my grandparents, parents, my brother, and me. At first my father worked for a company that made heavy metal safes. It was hard labor but he liked it. My mother worked at a military base, sewing uniforms for soldiers. Their salaries were very low, so my father thought he should try to be independent. He quit his job and started this business with my grandfather.

"When I was a small child, houses were very large and there were lots of children in each family. During the war the large houses were destroyed, and when people rebuilt, they didn't have much money, so the homes are much more compact now.

"During the war we produced pipes and bolts. I was called into the military, of course, and was sent first to Manchuria, then to Taiwan. My brother didn't survive the war. He was sent to the West Carolinas Islands, and when the troops landed there, the ships carrying supplies and food were sunk; only the soldiers managed to land. They had nothing. There was no food or fresh water on the island; it was impossible to farm. Every soldier perished.

"When Tokyo was bombed, our business was destroyed and many customers were lost, even killed. We began again from scratch, and started producing base structures for stairs.

"When I was twenty-five, my cousin was sent here to marry me. Her family are still farmers—although I'm not sure they'll continue farming because none of the young are willing to do farm work. Many want to move to Tokyo. We have four children: three boys and a girl. Kyoshi is my second son. The eldest has worked for the Seiko Corporation since he graduated from college twenty years ago.

"This is a good family; we work hard. Our family history demonstrates enormous courage—always starting over after so many difficulties. I tell the youngsters these stories to teach them that if you try hard, you will always succeed. I think it's very important to hear stories about your ancestors.

"One change I've noticed is that people used to think work was the priority, not education. Children played and enjoyed themselves after school. We had classes on the significant people in the history of Japan, on morals and behavior. Neighbors were like relatives; we helped and cared for each other. After the war, education drastically changed. People have lost a sense of responsibility and good morals because of the way they are educated. Relationships between neighbors have decreased because of nuclear families. The elderly are confused by these changes.

"Since I became disabled, I've realized that people should be more caring for those who are weaker than they. I often walk in the nearby park where we elders get together to talk. The grandmothers, for example, say they can't agree with their daughters-in-law. I think you shouldn't be so stubborn as

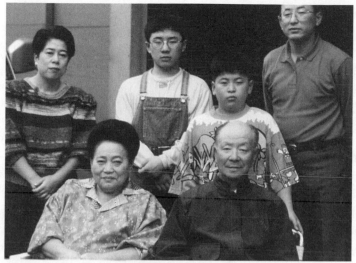

The Iinuma family in front of their factory/home: (*seated*) Aguri and Masaichi, (*standing, left to right*) Akiko, Toshikazu, Masauni, and Kiyoshi

you get older, because the daughters-in-law are going to take care of us. We should be much more flexible.

"The only thing I worry about now is how my sons will manage this business once I am gone."◆

AGURI Masaichi's wife is a short, stockily built woman who wears her jet-black hair swept up into a neat bun. She seemed at peace with her life and surroundings, yet she repeatedly stated that she is "just a country woman." She offered few opinions and asked no questions. She told about her eleven sisters and brothers, and how, at age twenty-three, she was sent to Tokyo to marry Masaichi, a cousin she had never seen.

"It was difficult to adjust to city life. People ridiculed me for my rural ways and dialect. And since my family were farmers, I had only worked in the fields; there wasn't much I could do in the iron industry.

"My mother-in-law had died during the war. So there was only the father-in-law. He was a difficult man, very demanding. It was an unhappy time. For my mother it was worse; she had both her parents-in-law and was treated very harshly. Her mother-in-law used to complain about the meals my mother prepared. When mother visited me, she thought I was fortunate to have only a father-in-law to criticize me.

"My husband makes all the family decisions about spending money—on food, on education. I never make any decisions myself, but I do discuss them and give my opinion.

"When I was young there wasn't much difference in how boys and girls were raised. As long as they were healthy, we thought that was fine. Love matches never happened; it was always the parents who decided who we were to marry. These days, you are free to decide whether you want a love match or an arranged marriage. It's a good thing. Our marriage was just a joining of cousins—for family convenience."◆

AKIKO Akiko is a very attractive forty-three-year-old woman, who was dressed youthfully in a blue pleated skirt and a short-sleeved cardigan sweater. Her hair was stylishly short. She exuded enthusiasm and spoke almost hurriedly, as if I might leave before she could tell me all her thoughts. Her father, she said, was a high school teacher; the family had lived on the school premises due to his position.

"We were a nuclear family mainly because of my father's housing situation. I attended school here in Tokyo, and that is how I met my husband. When we first married, we had our own house in another area of Tokyo. When I had my children, I stopped working to devote myself to raising them. Then, when my father-in-law suffered a stroke, I came to help out. We moved to this house two years ago.

"Before deciding to move here, my husband called our family together— our two sons and me—to talk about how important the family is. He explained that since we would be living with the grandparents, they would necessarily be involved in educating the children. The children and I should accept this as a good thing. He told me that we four would be the center of the family, and if we remained close, we wouldn't have any problems. This reassured me, so we made the decision to live here. My in-laws live down the hall; they have their own kitchen, so we eat separately.

"This family's business is truly that—a family business. My father-in-law is the chairman of the board, my husband is the president, and we are the hired officials. We all have our salaries. We're not the kind of family where the husband leaves in the morning and comes back in the evening. In fact, we are together too much: We work in the same building. I see my husband morning, afternoon, and evening. We discuss everything and ask the children about their ideas. Decisions are never made alone.

"Although I've known my in-laws for a long time, I still have problems because we are from such different backgrounds. If I do something for my in-laws that I think will be nice, they might interpret my gesture totally differently. But for the children, it's good to learn about their elders. They sometimes deliver dinner to them, and in that way the children learn responsibility by doing.

"In Japan, as you know, the wife of the son takes care of the in-laws. Daughters can't care for their own parents if they are married elsewhere. My younger brother cares for my parents because I'm here. His wife is a good woman; she always says that if my parents become ill, if they have any problems, she will take care of them. But my mother might refuse; she might say she wants one of her daughters to take care of them. We just don't know what will happen."◆

KYOSHI   It was a week later when I returned to the Iinuma home to talk with Akiko's husband, Kyoshi, the manager of the family business. Akiko was waiting for us with homemade soup and cakes, which she served in the formal dining room, seating us on cushions around a lovely lacquered table. Kyoshi, a slim and athletic man, wore light blue jeans and matching shirt. Rather than sit on the cushions, he balanced his weight by crouching on his heels, conveying a feeling of nervous energy. At first he seemed hesitant to give anything but brief answers to my questions. Only after an hour did our exchange become more of a conversation. He began by talking about the difference between his lifestyle and that of a "salaryman"—the Japanese term for a white-collar worker.

"There are certain advantages to working in a family business, close to home, especially compared to so many men who must commute far from home. Also, since this is my business, I can decide when I'll work. If I am tired I can stop. It's up to me.

"The other advantage is that when my children return from school, I can spend time with them. And my children have their grandparents with them; that's very important to me. In nuclear families, with no grandparents, the relationships between grandparents and children barely exist. My children and their grandparents meet every day; they discuss what happened that day and share ideas. My children have learned to respect their elders; they observe how I work and develop an appreciation of their parents' efforts."

Kiyoshi and Akiko Iinuma

A brief smile crossed Kyoshi's face at this point; he added, almost sheepishly, that working at home deprives him of private time. "Since I don't have to commute to an office, I'm never alone. Other men have time to relax coming from or going to work. I relax by going out with people in my neighborhood. We go out drinking and singing karaoke.

"I feel sorry for my wife, because she is always with my parents and the children. She can't go out as much as I do. Among our friends there are couples who live with their parents and there are some who are divorced. Often couples get divorced due to problems with in-laws. For the elders, their son is their blood relation. His wife is not. The daughter-in-law and the grandparents have disagreements about raising the children or preparing meals.

"The relationship between my wife and me is very good. She is very patient with my parents, and we share responsibilities for the family. She is responsible for financial matters and I manage the factory. We view each other as the best person to talk to. We discuss everything—the community, the children, the elders. We haven't had much conflict with my parents since we came to live here. It's because my wife is so understanding. Another woman might have had more difficulty."

Kyoshi paused. Softly he began to voice his concerns for the future. "I worry about the children and this business. I'm not sure they will be able to keep it. Real estate prices have increased so drastically that if grandfather dies I'll have to pay a huge amount. I fear that I might not be able to raise the money. Some people have had to sell their businesses in order to pay the tax. And if I die, my children wouldn't be able to pay the taxes. Will they want to work in this sector? You get dirty; you have to carry heavy things. It's dangerous. Among our colleagues and friends I never hear that their children are taking over the business. Young people prefer office work; it's considered with more respect."◆

MASAKUNI   Kyoshi's fears for the future remain inconclusive. For the time being, the generations live and work together in harmony. The problems of cohabitation are minimized by an understanding daughter-in-law and the will to give the children a multigenerational upbringing. Questions of inheritance, taxes, and family-owned businesses are, for the moment, but far-off worries. That said, eleven-year-old Masakuni, the youngest grandson, dreams of becoming a sailor on the open sea, scanning a horizon that he never sees in the center of Tokyo.

When asked about his family, Masakuni replied, "Sometimes my grandparents tell me stories. They talk about life in the past, about the war. The fact that all that is so different from the life we have makes me want to listen.

"I haven't decided yet what I want to study. I help out my father when he asks me to; it's fun—but I'm not sure that's what I'll want to do later."♦ Whether they live in an apartment in Tokyo or the suburbs of Kampala, elders' preoccupation with the next generation is universal. They are concerned about continuity, inheritance, and tradition. The elders who speak here have a variety of living arrangements and relationships with their families. Some still live in multigenerational settings while others choose to be independent or to live with other elders. Some continue to work while others care for their grandchildren, as a family necessity or for pure pleasure. Meanwhile, the care of the elderly family members themselves falls disproportionately to the women of the family.

Those who are in their later years have witnessed dramatic changes in attitudes, the physical world, and technology during their lifetime. Yet perhaps the most important change is immeasurable: the evolution of the concept of individual rights, of the value of each individual, which in turn has lead to the democratization of relationships within the family and in society. It is clear that some of the elders quoted here are confused by this trend. And what we hear from them begs a question: With these changes in perception of individual worth and rights, has the notion of the individual's responsibility to community and family kept pace?

Responsibility to our older citizens is a case in point. The quality of life of our elders requires attention from policy makers and families alike. If our elders are living two or three decades longer, planning for useful and fulfilling roles in their later years becomes a necessity. When the primary school children of 2000 reach middle age, nearly one quarter of the world's population will be over sixty-five years old.[12] Questions of pension policies, elder-friendly housing and transportation, part-time employment, legalities of elder care, medical and nursing care, continuing education and leisure for senior citizens are but a few of the challenges before us.

The goal is independence, participation, care, self-fulfillment, and dignity for all elders.[13] If we utilize the talents of older persons to meet these challenges, families and society will greatly benefit. But if we are to do so, it is crucial that we rethink our attitudes toward age; what was considered old when life expectancy was fifty years is not at all old when it is more than seventy years. On the contrary, the healthy elder years can be a period of personal growth and creativity. Older volunteers are readily found in schools, religious institutions, nongovernmental organizations, and public service. Older family members provide a perspective on our families and the world that our children are unable to obtain elsewhere. By listening to our elders we can learn much about how to design policies and communities in which families can support all their members in a caring and productive manner.

Four | Womanhood Transformed

With the fright, the shyness, the shame, we cannot aspire. How different my life would have been if I'd known about this self-esteem when I was young.

—Albertina Sosa de Marroquin, El Salvador

In the summer of 1976 I traveled to several developing nations interviewing rural women. One day, in central Tunisia, I found myself sitting across the road from a rural health clinic where a crowd of women and children sought medical services. One by one, I talked with women who waited their turn to tell me their stories. At one point, a nomadic woman who had been working in the adjacent field approached me and said, defiantly, "Why do you talk to all those women and not to me?"

Surprised but pleased by the woman's fearless approach, I urged her to sit with us and tell her story. Barefoot, wearing a torn cotton robe held together with safety pins rather than the traditional silver brooch common to nomadic women, she was clearly living on the harsh edge of poverty. She told of her family's years of wandering with the seasons—south to north, then north to south—as keepers of sheep herds belonging to others more wealthy than they. There was no permanent home for herself, her husband, and their four children, she said, because the family moved with their few possessions every week or two throughout the year. I asked if the children were able to go to school with the family moving so often. The woman smiled proudly and answered, "Yes, the children attend school."

I added, "Both girls and boys?"

The woman looked at me aghast. Her eyes proclaimed disbelief at my ignorance. She hesitated and then, as if talking to a simpleton, she answered, "Of course both girls and boys. The whole world had a year for women, so women are important now. Girls *must* attend school."

That this nomadic woman, without a television, radio, or even a fixed residence, had heard about the United Nations–sponsored International Women's Year proclaimed in 1975, one year prior to this encounter, was a revelation. That she affirmed its message of gender equality was a tribute to her own strength and a measure of the power of an idea—the radical idea that women could aspire to rights and opportunities hitherto available only to men.

The twenty-five years since that first International Women's Year have taught us much about the status and needs of women, and have seen the lives of women transformed. Access to education, broadened legal rights, and a worldwide democratic feminist movement have increased women's self-confidence and independence in many societies. In addition, in just about every nation, economic imperatives and women's search for fulfillment have thrust women into the workplace. By 1990, women made up 43 to 47 percent of the workforce in the industrialized countries and the numbers have only grown in the last decade. Those women with access to modern contraceptives have been freed of the fear of unplanned pregnancies and permitted to manage their own fertility.

At the same time, the century began with some alarming statistics on the status and well-being of women. In 2000, UN statistics note that two-thirds of the world's 920 million illiterates are women. Women own barely 2 percent of all land and occupy only 14 percent of parlimentary seats worldwide. Worse yet, one in every three women has been subjected to violence in an intimate relationship, 75 million pregnancies per year are unwanted, and every minute of every day a woman dies of pregnancy-related causes. For girls, we are far from reaching parity with boys in primary school attendance, and even farther behind in higher education.[1]

Recent decades have witnessed an additional, and disturbing, trend affecting the lives of women—and of families everywhere: due to the emigration of men in search of work, to divorce, to widowhood or simply to abandonment, the number of women-headed households is on the increase in most societies. In some nations, female-headed households comprise 30 to 40 percent of all households, with numbers even higher in rural areas. This trend requires that women attain a measure of economic independence without which their financial and physical well-being, and that of their families, remains elusive.

The widened roles and increased autonomy of women challenge family hierarchy and traditional male authority. At the individual level, for women, the multiplicity of roles required by tradition and contemporary reality, by motherhood and work outside the home, carries significant psychological and physical burdens, but also exciting challenges and opportunites. While women's new status is condemned by those who oppose all but a passive, homebound role for women, it receives encouragement from those who recognize the benefit for men, family, and society when women are full and equal participants in both the private and public spheres.

RIO DE JANEIRO, BRAZIL

Rio de Janeiro is undoubtedly one of the world's most beautifully situated cities, surrounded by mountains and bordered by the Atlantic Ocean. It vibrates with a unique culture, forged from the ways of its indigenous peoples and of those who arrived, as immigrants or slaves, from around the world. Five and a half million people live there, some in great wealth and opulence, others in unimaginable poverty. The beachfront buildings house the elite; the mountains are dotted with shanties. In the weeks following my arrival, I would meet families from both neighborhoods, including that of a retired Ambassador, who had emigrated from his middle class provincial home in the Amazon basin, to seek a career in the foreign service.

Maria Carmelita Guilhon, 76
Manoel Emilio Guilhon, 78
Madalena Guilhon, 50
Teresa Barros, 28
Ricardo Sarmento Costa, 34

Ambassador Manoel Guilhon and Maria Guilhon greeted us warmly. Their apartment is on the fifth floor of an elegant apartment building in the Leblon district, a few blocks from Rio's famous Ipanema Beach. Their sitting room windows look out over the distant bay. The room is tastefully decorated with antique furniture and silver-framed photographs of children and grandchildren. On one strategically placed table is a photograph of the career diplomat and his wife with Pope John Paul II, taken at a papal audience in Rome.

In the ensuing hours, soft drinks and homemade vanilla cakes were served, along with large doses of gracious Brazilian hospitality. The elder Guilhons described their generation as one that worked hard to achieve what they did. They have no fortune to leave their children, they say, but are proud to leave them a good name. Each spoke of the significant social and economic change she or he had witnessed and admitted to the strains of adjusting to changes within the family. Indeed, the three generations of Guilhon women reflect three totally different lifestyles, three different visions of womanhood.

MARIA Seventy-six-year-old Maria Carmelita Guilhon is a small, delicate woman who appears easily ten years younger than her age. She was dressed in loose, flowered cotton pants and shirt. She appeared to be a generous and serene woman, free of any pretensions whatsoever. One of four daughters of a family from northern Brazil, she had planned to become a primary school teacher. She married her sweetheart instead. After fifty-three years of marriage, she is proud to tell of her eight children, fourteen grandchildren, and two great-grandchildren.

"I'm from Belem do Pará. I was raised in a traditional family. I left only to marry. My husband was my only boyfriend and my only love.

"I adored my mother. She was a gentle person and spent a lot of time with us children. Her influence made me feel dedicated to my children. My father was a well-known businessman. He had one of the most famous import shops, things from Paris. But he lost everything when a ship sank at sea. Soon he fell ill and died. I was just seven at the time.

"We went to live with my grandfather. He was very traditional and, as head of the Income Tax Authority, was very respected. I was very close to him. He lost his wife before I was born and used to go to church every day.

"When I was young there were few universities in Pará, so I attended a course for schoolteachers. After I graduated, at seventeen, I fell in love with my husband, so I never did teach. My husband is also Paraense. We were both from honorable but not rich families. We courted for nearly six years. Then he went to Rio to take the foreign service examination. A year later he sent for me. My mother wouldn't let me go unless I was married, so I had to marry by proxy. My father-in-law was my proxy husband. I came to Rio already married to meet my husband! It's a lovely story. I still love my husband as I did before. It's very rare. I would never have thought it would last so long. And here we are!

"The moment we married, I started my family eight children, five girls and three boys. The girls came first, then the boys. When my oldest was five we went to Mexico. Only one was born outside Brazil, the fifth, a daughter who was born in New York. As a young wife and mother raising children abroad, it was difficult. But since there was a lot of love between my husband and me, I was strong enough to deal with it.

"Families have changed a great deal, even my own. Three of my children are separated or divorced. I can't understand it. Families are splitting up. It's gotten worse in recent years. I don't think people *try* to keep families together. My husband and I do our utmost to get as many family members as possible together at one time. I have a few friends who have permanent marriages, but among their children there are fewer and fewer.

"My case is very rare. I think love is the main thing. Before my children married, I said, 'There's no point in getting married if you're not in love.' Because sex is one thing, love is another. One of our granddaughters came with her boyfriend to ask us advice before she married. She wanted to know what they should do to make their marriage work. I told them first of all, love, then respect, each other. You both have to give up something. If you can do this, the marriage will work. Young people aren't prepared for marriage; they separate over little things.

"My daughter Madalena got separated because her husband liked another woman. Margarita also wanted to separate. By the time they came to us to talk about it, it was all over. It's very sad. My eldest son separated from a first wife, with whom he has no children, and from a second wife, with whom he has a son. Now he lives here with Mama and Papa! His son comes from time to time. He's very affectionate. He was a little beast when the parents first separated, but with our love, he changed.

"Luckily, my children have all managed to create new families, even after divorce. I don't understand how that can be, but I think it's lovely.

"When my mother sent me off to Rio, she said if my husband was good to me, I should back him up in everything. That was her advice. She didn't tell me about sexuality in marriage. In those days, we didn't talk about it. We learned from our girlfriends or from books. With my own children, I made sure they read things. We talked about drugs and relationships. I thank God every day that none of my children used drugs, and none of my grandchildren, either. I know many people whose children are on drugs or dying of AIDS.

"I hope this new generation will stay on the right track. I tell my grandchildren how they should behave because their grandfather is leaving them a fine name. He doesn't have a fortune, there's little money, but the name is clean. I want them to observe their grandfather and understand what they are inheriting."◆

MANOEL   At seventy-eight, the ambassador is a tall, distinguished, white-haired gentleman, descendent of a French naval officer who settled in Brazil in the eighteenth century. During his thirty years in the diplomatic service of Brazil he was posted in Europe, North America, and Latin America, and his observations about his homeland were affected by that experience. His manner was that of someone who is at home in all surroundings, eager to encounter all newcomers.

"My grandfather had no higher education. He was seventeen, eighteen years old when he started working in commerce. His children went to university, and one of them became governor of the state. My father was an agricultural engineer but also a politician. He traveled to the interior of [the state of] Amazonas, to the different cities, and to a town where he became the mayor. My mother traveled with him. We were four children, but only two of us remain now.

"I applied for the diplomatic service because I wanted to get married and needed a job. We had no inclination to be diplomats! My wife and I have been married fifty-three years— and when I was named consul general in Lisbon, we took eight children with us. The oldest was twenty, the youngest three months. All that year, I listened to the cries of children, especially in the first hours of the morning. But in my opinion this is good, because you become more human in spirit and you build a stronger family. Today I could never have eight children. Never. This belongs to the past. There are too many people in the world; it will be a big problem in the future. Now that I'm retired I like being with my grandchildren. A grandfather has more time than a father. I'm able to be the nanny or nursemaid. All my time is for my grandchildren.

"My concerns about the future of Brazil and our family? It is a haunting question. It has a political basis. Brazil is facing a serious crisis, various crises: morality, ethics, the economy, the lack of great politicians, leadership. We don't have any idea what is going to happen in the next month. For my grandchildren and great grandchildren—I wish for them peace and conscience. And love, especially for the people in Brazil who have no bread and milk. And a new world, better than the last one."◆

MADALENA Manoel and Maria's fifty-year-old daughter, Madalena, dresses with style and possesses a spirited self-confidence. She is one of the directors of CEMINA (the Women's Project Center), a nonprofit feminist organization that works with poor women on social justice, health, and environmental issues. She guided me around the office and introduced me to colleagues and friends, but as we began our conversation, we realized that the noise and activity around us was distracting. Madalena suggested we continue the discussion in the garden of the nearby National Museum. For the next three hours we sat on the edge of a fountain, dangling our feet over the still water, as Madalena told her story. She is the mother of two grown children and is divorced; she reclaimed her family name, she said, when she left her Portuguese husband and returned to Brazil. She spoke of her involvement in social justice work and how it had changed her life goals.

"I'm a journalist. When my parents were posted in Portugal, I was about to take the university entrance exams to come to Brazil and study journalism. But I met my husband and fell in love. It was passion right away. So I stayed in Portugal, got married, and went off to Africa with my husband. When we returned to Lisbon, again I wanted to come to Brazil to study. My husband refused. He didn't want me to study or work. That was a big problem in my marriage. To preserve the marriage, I didn't do either. But I was very unhappy about it. I'm not a housewife. I'm not the motherly type. I like my children, but I'm not a passionate mother." Madalena laughed aloud at her own admission, then added, "But I am a passionate grandmother.

"I wanted to study. I always wanted to be a journalist. I said I wouldn't marry until I was thirty. As it turned out, I got married at twenty-one and had two kids! Life sometimes takes you where you don't expect to go.

"My marriage didn't satisfy me as a person. We had a lot of things in common, things we both enjoyed—to go out, travel together, listen to music. We were friends. To a certain extent, I think we held each other back. He started to travel for his work and, without us knowing how or why, our marriage began to fall apart. Then he fell in love with another woman on a trip. What had kept us together was more friendship than a husband-wife relationship. We weren't in love with each other. Sexually it was weak. I felt very dissatisfied with my little life; it was too restricted. I needed something more.

"When I decided to separate from him, I began to think about returning to Brazil. There was no reason to stay in Portugal. Once here, I got a job at a jewelers and attended university at the same time. You see, I was a journalist but I couldn't live on a journalist's salary. My daughter was then nine, and my son five. Certainly their life has been more difficult financially than if I had stayed with their father. He remarried and has eleven-year-old identical twins by his second wife. He and I are on good terms. When he comes here we go out with the children. His wife doesn't like that and doesn't want any relationship with me, either. I don't know her. We invited her to lunch

Four generations of Guilhon women: Madalena, her granddaughter
Juliana, Maria Carmelita, and Teresa Barros

once but she didn't come." Madalena leaned forward over the fountain's waters, laughing, "Since I talk all the time, perhaps she's a little scared of me. I don't know.

"If my husband hadn't fallen in love with another woman, maybe we would have separated later, when the children were bigger. Maybe not. Perhaps I would have had lovers. Who knows? My life would have been very different. But I'm sure that I'm more satisfied with life now. Thank the Lord! Because you have to have courage to break out of a marriage that is not bad, but not good either. When we separated, I began to live as I really wanted. Politics, activism, boyfriends. For a time it was a little exaggerated! Then you get tired of it.

"When I returned to Brazil I wanted to change my life radically. The war in Angola [for independence from Portugal in the early 1960s to 1975] had politicized me. And one of my brothers drew me into clandestine political activity in Brazil. Then an amnesty was declared [after the military regime relinquished power in 1985] and political parties were allowed. So I became one of the founders of the Worker's Party. When I had joined the clandestine organization, one of the groups was working on feminist issues. So we formed a group to discuss our ideas. We worked in the *favelas* [slums], holding meetings with women about sexuality and violence. I became politicized as a feminist at the same time.

"In 1985, I went to work for a feminist politician, a deputy from Rio state. Through her I met the women who joined to create this women's organization. We wrote up a proposal and managed to get support. We now have a radio program for women and a documentation center. We work on domestic violence and all sorts of legal issues."

Madalena leaned forward, reaching out with both palms facing upward, saying, "Feminism brought a revolution to my life—more so than my divorce, more than politics. It made me give myself a value and see everything from a different angle. The relationship with my children, with other people, with the whole world, is better—changed. Feminism gives you a different philosophy of life: to look for the truth, to live more truly and securely. Feminism is basically against authoritarianism. It doesn't say do this or do that. It gives you autonomy. That's the basis of it. It affects your work. It affects everything."

Leaning back again, with a smile, as if recalling a humorous incident, she continued: "My children were a little resentful of my work—my commitment to feminism. When they were young, I was away a lot. But now they understand it was important for me. I was alone and I would have been unhappy if I had nothing to do except look after them. And they benefited from it as well. My women friends see my children as two incredible people. They say, 'What did you do?' I think it's what I *didn't* do. I didn't keep after them, telling them what to do, but showed them by my example, by my life, what you *can* do. I don't remember having told them anything or given moral lessons. It was my way of living that influenced them.

"Being a feminist in Brazilian society is easier nowadays. I began my involvement in 1975, when it first started here. I'm a feminist, yes, but feminism has matured, just as I have. I'm less of a firebrand. Not just me—the whole movement. We used to be very aggressive because we had to be. But we don't have to now. Feminism is now part of society. Feminists are invited to give their opinions; their ideas are important to society. The new generation sees everything in a new way, even the question of marriage. We've had a strong influence on them, to be sure.

"Until I was married, I followed my parents' example, very conservative and traditional. Get married and have children. Be a good housewife. I wasn't very religious, but I used to go to church. But after I separated, I completely rebelled. It was difficult for my parents. I was, after all, a woman who had been married, who had children, and here I was, making my own living. Slowly they began to accept it. They have no influence in my life—how I spend my money, what I do, how I dress, where I go. They admire me now because they see me on television or mentioned in the newspapers. I succeeded professionally; I raised my children well. I did it all by myself. They admire that. If anything, *I* have had an influence on *them.*

"The traditional family—with mother, father, children, grandparents— that's changing a lot. There are so many different types of families in today's world—a tremendous diversity. So you can't think of the old model of family. The family is evolving, and I think it will continue to do so.

"The new generation is far better than ours. My son, my son-in-law, they're different from the men of our generation. The husbands of my friends and nieces are more mature. They treat women as equals. They don't think a wife has to stay home and make dinner; sometimes they do it themselves. It's not a problem as it was with us. It doesn't matter if the house is a mess. The young are more involved with the problems of the country, with external things. I think they're more outward looking, more involved with the outside world.

"As for my son, I don't know if he's going to be a feminist man. I educated him to be one, but sometimes children rebel against their parents and want to be exactly the opposite. When he was thirteen or fourteen he used to rebel. Not against my ideas, but because I wasn't there. Today he agrees with me. He thinks it's wonderful that I'm a feminist, that it's good for me. I don't know if he will choose a feminist wife, but I know he is very sensitive with women. He is concerned about them. He even encourages *me.*

"Feminism has had a huge influence on society, even though plenty of men resist and disagree. Women are getting ahead in politics and economically. They are changing the model of civilization. Take ecology, for example. It was always part of our philosophy. It wasn't a separate issue; it was part of the feminist agenda: more equal relations among people and with nature. Feminism was the first movement that actually began to talk about gender roles. Why does a man have to be like this, or a woman like that? Why can't a man cry or wear a ring in his ear? We began to question our roles. But this is still a *machista* society. Woman took huge steps, and men were left behind.

"We try to sensitize people to women's reality. The public image of women is terrible. It's still naked women selling tires or cars. We're pushing for feminist images, which depict woman neither as the housewife nor as the woman who conquers and eats up men. Just a woman.

"On a personal level, it's difficult to find a man who is at ease with equality. Men are very stuffy; they have lots of prejudices. At my age, they are either married or narrow-minded. Or they want men! Difficult? No. I'm not unhappy because I don't have a man. But I miss having one. I'm not unhappy, because I've made the most of my life. I'm going to do a lot more, too! Travel, be committed to good causes, have women and men friends."

Madalena stopped speaking. Then, raising her arms over her head and a wide smile crossing her face, she added, "Life is beautiful."◆

TERESA As night fell on Rio and its lights lit up the bay and surrounding mountains, we set out to visit Madalena's daughter, Teresa Barros. The night was clear, and high above us, Rio's landmark, the statue known as El Cristo, hovered in the sky. Closer by, within earshot, one of Rio's overcrowded favelas dispatched its din. Teresa and her six-month-old daughter, Juliana, greeted us as we emerged from the elevator in their high-rise apartment building. Teresa is a very slender, almost fragile, woman and has a matching gentle manner. She is a graphic artist who recently started her own graphics business. Teresa considers Juliana's father, Ricardo, her husband, although they are not legally married. Soon after we arrived Ricardo returned from work, and the young couple proudly showed us around their apartment and the terrace with its view of the mountain and statue looming above us. Teresa and Ricardo are a handsome couple, comfortable in each other's company, each listening attentively as the other spoke. Ricardo offered to change the baby's diapers and keep her occupied while Teresa told us her story.

"I was born in Africa. My parents were living in Portugal, and about the time mother got pregnant, my father was called to the war in Angola. I was the first child. I have one brother and two half-brothers from my father's second marriage. I lived in Portugal for my first nine years. We lived in the same apartment block as my paternal grandparents. I was very close to them.

"When my parents were having problems it was difficult for us children, especially not knowing what was going on. My father used to disguise the situation. There was a good deal of prejudice about divorce then. When we came to Brazil it was even more difficult. My mother had to start from zero. That's something I can understand more now, but at that time I didn't.

"Some months after coming here, we became curious and asked questions like 'Are we going back to Portugal?' and that kind of thing. So mother explained their separation. Yes, I guess that affected my relationships later on. I used to be very shy with boys when I was ten or eleven years old. I saw my father once a year when he came to Brazil. There is a definite connection between us; we haven't lost that. But I'm not close at all to his second wife. I would even say distant.

"I studied graphic design at the university here and worked part-time in educational television. Ricardo and I met through common friends and started living together. My grandfather was very disappointed in me. When Ricardo wanted to go to England for a degree, we gave a party to celebrate our departure. My grandfather was very disappointed that there wasn't a priest. He expected someone to come bless us.

"The major influence on families is the women's movement—how women of my mother's generation changed things for us. Things have changed so much: the role of women in the house and work, having their jobs and lives. Men don't have to be the machos anymore. There's more open dialogue; we are able to talk about a lot of things. That's a big change, the dialogue.

"Ricardo and I discussed how life was going to be after the baby, how we would take care of her. We do everything together. After Juliana was born, we realized that every moment together is wonderful. We are trying to find our own way. Among our friends everyone is trying to avoid being like their parents.

"I've started my own business in graphic design. I use the computer to design printing jobs. There's still discrimination against women, for sure. When I worked for a company I could see that. But I never felt it stopped me from going ahead. When I got pregnant I decided to start my own business and be more available to the child. We still aren't married—there are no papers between us."◆

RICARDO   As Teresa rose to prepare a pot of tea, Ricardo emerged from the baby's room to join us. He is gentle-mannered, much like his wife. An engineer, he works for the Brazilian National Institute for Technology, where, he said, he is in charge of production management. He spoke softly, and suggested that we go to the far side of the room, to sit at the dining table, conference-style.

"I have one brother and one sister and am close to both of them. We didn't really have a traditional Brazilian upbringing, although it was a serene childhood. My father and some friends had a place outside Rio, and we lived all together, about twenty children in all. My parents are still living and I get along very well with them.

"When I met Teresa she was living with her mother, so we had to meet at my place. When she decided to move in with me, her mother supported the idea. So we gave a family lunch. Her grandparents were not very happy; they didn't know how to react. But later they decided to support us. They liked me. One of the reasons I decided to study in England was because of Teresa's father. He had remarried and was living in London. He was a missing link in Teresa's life. She had had a very nice relationship with her father, but it was completely cut off by the divorce. So I finished my master's degree and applied for a doctoral program in England, first in London and then at Warwick. We spent eighteen months there.

"When I met Teresa I was coming out of another relationship which was much more conventional. To get married officially didn't seem very important to either of us. There was no point in creating a lot of expectations unless it was important for Teresa and me. But it doesn't mean we can't change our minds. I was struck by the fact that in our generation, few relationships last. In my address book I have a hundred or so names, and I can't find any couple that has been together ten years, married or not. I don't think marriage is the point. We've been together almost ten years; we've known each other for thirteen. My parents would rather have me married; they hold out the hope that we'll marry one day. My brother, for example, has more or less the same story—although he decided to marry after eight years. That's how I know there's hope, because I see the happiness of my brother's decision.

"We wanted a child and, when we came back from England, I was about thirty-four. I didn't want to wait; I want to be able to play soccer with my children. For Teresa, I think it was earlier than she would have liked, but she's very happy now. When Juliana was born, I took time off so I could be with her the first month. When I returned to work, we moved Teresa's office into this building, on another floor. She was breast-feeding so she had to be close by. After six months we decided to get help, a woman who comes to look after the house.

"I try to help around the house, but I used to do more. Since money is tight these days, I'm teaching evening courses. When I get home late I'm not anxious to do household chores. I feel a bit guilty sometimes. We're not unusual. Many couples help each other now; it's becoming part of married life. We have friends who live much as we do. There has been a good deal of social change and, as I mentioned before, couples are rather unstable. What has also changed is the attitude of the young about sexuality due to the HIV/AIDS epidemic. We know many young people who have died or who are HIV-positive. It has contributed to more monogamous relationships in our generation, for sure.

"I want to be a good father to Juliana, to be involved in her life from this age onward. More than anything I'd like for her to become what she wants to become." ◆

Three generations of Guilhon women have evolved rapidly in lifestyle and self-confidence. From the patriarchal family traditions of the grandmother to the feminism of the mother to the daughter's egalitarian domestic partnership, the Guilhon family has been transformed by the trends of the past half-century. Due in part to the resources available only to those of their social class, they have managed these transformations without any major disruption of family bonds or financial well-being. Such adaptations are not always so smooth, especially in families that are surviving just a step ahead of poverty.

DHAKA, BANGLADESH

Bangladesh is the most densely populated country on earth, and one of the poorest. According to UN statistics, per capita income in 1999 averaged $299 per year. Poverty, coupled with demographic expansion, has led to landlessness, emigration, and the breakdown of extended family support systems. It has also led to a dramatic rise in women-headed households through divorce, abandonment, and migration. According to government studies, 45 percent of women-headed households suffer chronic food shortages, double that of the population at large.

Employment creation is a national priority, since nearly half of the population of 137.4 million is age fifteen or under. In recent years, the gar-

Shahida Begum, 33

ment assembly industry has expanded, and is now the fourth-largest employer in the country. Hats and clothes of all types are assembled for export to Europe and the United States. Of the nearly 400,000 garment workers, 64 percent are women, half are under age twenty, and 30 percent are illiterate.[2]

According to Mashuda Khatun Shefali, director of Nari Udduf Kendra (Center for Women's Initiatives), an organization that assists female factory workers, "It is the only organized sector where women have employment opportunities. But there are big problems. The women are overworked, underpaid, and suffer from dangerous working conditions. Many young girls come here to earn their dowry and are caught in a double bind: they are proud to be earning money and supporting their families, but they are self-deprecating because of the controversy surrounding their break with local custom. They are considered 'lost women,' or 'dirty girls, prostitutes,' simply because they work outside the home." Mashuda Shefali arranged for me to meet a number of garment workers at their homes after work. Among them was Shahida Begum, a worker in her early thirties who is raising her children alone.

Of medium, but frail, stature and a prim charm, Shahida Begum is a bundle of energy. She was dressed in a faded yellow sari and wore gold stud earrings in her pierced ears. Her round face smiled contentedly as she told of her pride in being an independent wage-earner. Her home consisted of one rented room in which Shahida and her four unmarried children, ages twelve to sixteen, live. The building was very old; both latrine and kitchen were outside in the unlit, damp corridor, and both were shared among several families. The one-room home was spotless, but badly in need of paint. The only furnishings were a large bed, a chest of drawers and shelves placed high up the wall. She and the daughters sleep in the bed; the boys spread a mattress on the floor. "It's safe here," Shahida explained, as if that in itself made everything else worthwhile.

"I was born in Hazaribagh, here in Dhaka. My father owned a small hotel, but he died before I was born. When I was fourteen, my brother arranged my marriage; he did the negotiations and counseled me.

"My husband was a laborer in a shoe factory. He was very lazy, idle. He beat me often. We had five children. With all the children, we began to suffer, especially trying to provide food for them. When my fifth child was one and a half years old, I decided to have a tubal ligation. I didn't want more children because my husband wasn't taking responsibility for us. I went to the family planning hospital and told them that my husband was abroad, that my mother would give the permission to have it done.

"When I told my husband about the ligation he was furious. It was a terrible argument. I said more children were not possible since we weren't earning enough. He didn't agree and said 'Go back to your family. I'm not keeping you anymore.' My family was poor, and with five children I couldn't burden them. I decided to go to the garment factory. I began work as a helper at 125 taka [approximately U.S. $3] per month. My mother took care of the children. And my husband continued to threaten me.

"Two months later I was promoted to machine operator. My salary increased to 470 taka. My husband then tried to get me back. He was only interested in taking my money and spending it on himself. When my salary increased to 700 taka, he threatened me: 'You are my wife, you have to come to me where I am.' I used to go to a hotel with him, for an hour or half an hour, just to do the duty of a wife. After that he completely forgot me and didn't want to take any responsibility.

Young garment workers who live in the Nari Udduf Kendra–sponsored hostel in Dhaka

"By then my older daughter was about thirteen. According to custom, this is the right age for marriage. I saved enough for a dowry for a good man and somehow managed to find a fellow who seemed suitable. But the dowry request included a refrigerator. I went to my husband's older brother, who was better off, and asked if he could donate money for the dowry. He agreed and gave me the money. But I had to solve the problem of the father: without a father, nobody will take a girl. I had to find my husband and have him negotiate the marriage. He said he would take care of everything, so I turned the dowry money over to him. Suddenly we learned that he had disappeared with the money. The marriage could not take place. My husband had taken the dowry to get himself a second wife. He sacrificed his own daughter. His own daughter! I'm still upset when I think of it. It was the most terrible thing in my life. I couldn't manage to marry my daughter. And she was so upset.

"One and a half years later I found another nice man for her; they married and are living happily with his family. She's better off than we are. Her husband is strong, active, and nice. She visits me every Friday. That's why I'm happy.

"I also have two sons, thirteen and twelve. The oldest works in a tannery; he earns 1,000 taka a month and gives his money to me. The second son is an apprentice in a lathe workshop. The two younger daughters are in fourth grade. I want them to be working women. Since my husband remarried, he hasn't given us any money. His relatives come all the time saying they want to bring him to me. I say 'What for? He'll take my money and make more trouble. I want to live in peace with my children.' He used to beat me with the end of an umbrella."

When Shahida spoke these last words, the youngest daughter, Roona, barely twelve years old, jumped up from the corner and shouted excitedly, "He used to beat her with a big stick and when we tried to stop him we, too, were beaten."

Shahida nodded and continued: "Most of the women I work with have similar problems. Many are married but are heads of households like me—either abandoned, divorced, separated, or something like that. The younger girls come from poor families where parents can't afford a dowry or from families who don't have a son to earn for them. That's why they send their daughters to the factories.

"I'm a machine operator. I usually work on collars or pockets, parts of shirts and jackets. The working conditions are good; there are electricity and windows and bathrooms. I earn 2,000 taka a month, and that's if I get overtime. With four children to support, my earnings aren't enough for clothing, school costs, medicines, and our food. I pay 800 taka just for this room. This is the cheapest area of the city. We could earn more money if management paid us overtime, but they usually don't. We start at 7:30 and work to 4:00. From 4:00 to 8:00 is overtime, but it is an unpaid obligation.

"They always pay us late, and if we complain they criticize us. We wanted to create a trade union so we organized the workers and collected signatures. They sacked forty-one workers, including the leader. I was the women's leader and second to him. We are frightened because of the arrests. Since we are weak and poor, we had to follow management's decision.

"My mother was very proud that I was earning money. She died last year. She was poor but she tried her best. She always said, 'If there is trouble you should come back to me. I'll help you raise the children.' She helped me 100 percent, taking care of the children, encouraging me. This was possible because her husband was dead—otherwise things would have been different. My father would have beaten me or my mother.

"I have a brother and a sister. The brother works as a construction worker. The sister is trying to go to Indonesia to get a job there. She owns a small parcel of land and has rented it to get the money to go. Last year she tried to go to the Middle East, but they tricked her. She didn't get her money back. If she succeeds this time, I hope she'll help my son get a job there. This is one of my last hopes.

"That's why I want a better salary, to support this family. I want to give them a good chance in life. But I don't have a proper education. I have to stay here; if I go to another area I'll have trouble finding a job, and it's not safe to leave two teenage girls alone at home in an unknown place. This place is safe. I'm familiar with it and the children are comfortable here; they have friends and relatives nearby.

"My husband is remarried to a young, beautiful wife. But I've not divorced. I want to stay married, because if anybody knows that I'm single or divorced, men will start bothering me. I don't want to remarry, so why get divorced? Like all the other women I know, we have nominal guardianship of our children but we don't divorce because of the importance of social identity. It's better being married even if we're not with the man." ◆

When women like Shahida tell of their mistreatment and efforts to provide for their families, the words of Lic Zoila de Innocenti, a sociologist at Jose Simeon Canas University in San Salvador, come back to me. When I asked about the trends influencing family life in El Salvador, she replied almost bluntly, "The socialization of patriarchal culture runs throughout society and has consequences for everything: the economy, health, education, and, of course, violence. In the past, merit went to women who put up with the most; what has changed is women's unwillingness to accept double standards or its violence. My grandmothers on both sides remained silent about my grandfathers' mistresses. It was considered a private affair, as was violence. My mother kicked my father out for too much womanizing. We children were glad she did. Women are less willing to accept poor treatment now."

But that change is far from universal. Women's understanding of their rights and self-worth has yet to reach millions of women, particularly those who have little access to education. Even Shahida, as strong and self-sufficient as she is, understands that society doesn't accept women's independence easily: to be secure socially and physically, she must retain her married status, no matter how irresponsible the spouse. A similar situation was encountered in a neighborhood of Egypt's great capital.

CAIRO, EGYPT

Menshiet Nasser is a vast, crowded squatter settlement on the edge of Cairo. Ninety thousand people have built homes in a random pattern on a hillside high above the railroad tracks. The overgrown village is a monument to human ingenuity and initiative, a vibrant community of homes, markets, and cottage industries. Street hawkers and music add volume to the seemingly chaotic scene in the streets of Menshiet Nasser, where crowds make their way to tiny shops, and overburdened donkeys carry wares into narrow alleys where sales are negotiated through open windows. As an illegal squatter community, Menshiet Nasser does not benefit from municipal services. This was all too evident when my companion and I stepped from her car at the outskirts of the settlement and were assailed by the stench of two dead goats rotting in the gutter.

Karima Aboukhadre, 68
Farida, 43
Hoda, 28
Heba, 15
Amira, 12

Marlene Tadros, my companion and interpreter for the next days, is a leader of the Center for Development Services, an organization that works with low-income women, providing skills training and low-cost loans. The family she was taking me to meet was described as having "a very active grandmother."

Like most houses in Menshiet Nasser, the home I visited was built little by little, without architectural expertise or much apparent forethought. The stairway seemed to lean sideways, and the concrete pillars were rough and unfinished. A series of rooms followed no set pattern; sometimes one stepped up into a room, while others required a step or two down. The furnishings were sparse and worn. I learned that nearly twenty people dwelled in this makeshift home.

KARIMA Karima, the matriarch, was dressed in a dark gray housedress, sleeves rolled up and collar open. Her gray hair was pulled back in a bun covered by a gray scarf. Her nose was straight and pointed, almost sharp. Several of her lower teeth were missing, which gave her a pensive expression. She never turned her eyes from those to whom she spoke and showed no hesitation to tell her story. On the contrary, she wanted to tell the story of every family member.

"I was born here in Cairo. My father came from Dairout el Sharif in Upper Egypt. He came here as a soldier and sent for his wife. My mother's people said that Cairo was a bad city, so they took their daughter back to the village. I was only forty days old. That left my father alone with me. 'I can't do anything with an infant!' he said. He asked his brother to care for me and left forever. I don't know if either of my parents remarried. I don't know anything about them. I think my father's family were farmers.

"My uncle was a donkey cart driver. He had a four-wheeled cart and carried things from one place to another. He had a daughter and three sons and raised me with his children. Then he married me to a seventy-year-old man!

"I was ten years old. He was seventy! My first child came when I was twelve years old. By the time I was nineteen, I had four children. Then he died. He left me nothing at all. And I was glad he died. He gave me everything bad. He was old, disgusting, dirty. He even smelled bad."

Karima's gestures of disgust were convincing indeed. She shook her head and, taking my hand, added, "Let's not talk about him. He was old. Is there anything more upsetting than being married to an old man? I'm still upset at my father for abandoning me. I was so beautiful, just as beautiful as an actress.

"I drank all the bitterness of life—all the bitterness of the entire country—but I raised my children." Karima wiped her eyes. Then, making a plucking gesture to each eye, she said, "I put my children in my eyes, two here and two here—and went on.

"At that time the Jews were here. They were my neighbors. Then Gamel Abdul Nasser said, 'No Jews will stay in Egypt!' One of my neighbors, a Jew named Salem, came to me and said, 'Karima, do you want to work?' and I said, 'Yes, where?' He said, 'In the school here.' The building belonged to the Jews; it is still a school, even today. 'You could work and live in the school,' he said. The school secretary was a Christian who told me, 'God will let you work with us.' So my job came from a Jew and a Christian. Hamdullah! In gratitude I named my grandson Salem, after the Jew who gave me the job.

"I was like a maid; I did the cleaning. My pay of three pounds was enough to feed the children because bread was very cheap. I was able to raise my children well. I worked there forty-one years, until I was sixty years old. Because of the patience I had over those years, God gives me back a little: a pension of 150 pounds a month [approximately U.S. $50].

"I didn't remarry because I was afraid for the children. I thought, 'Shall I repeat what happened to me—all the pain and suffering?' I was afraid to get someone who would mistreat the children. Men used to make passes at me; a widow is always vulnerable.

"When my daughter married, I went to live near her. Wherever they lived, I lived close by. If there is any money to pay, I try to pay. My daughter's first

Karima at home in Menshiet Nasser

husband had no money, so I built this house for him. At first it was just a very large room; now it has electricity, water—everything.

"My first child is the one who died. His wife poured gasoline over herself, and when he tried to save her, she said, 'Okay, you too!' She threw the gasoline on him and burned them both, even his face. He left three children, and I took care of them until they got old enough to leave home.

"The other son is very spoiled. He has stolen from me. He doesn't work. You can raise children, one will be fine, the other is not, and you can't do anything about it.

"Family life has changed a lot. The way I brought up my children isn't suitable anymore. I used to say, 'Stop doing this,' and the boy would stop immediately. Now if you tell a little boy to stop, he would say, 'What do you want?' I don't know what happened. It's ghosts, the genies!

"Also, in our time we didn't have television. If a man talked to a girl, she would immediately be afraid, but now on television they see women dancing naked and kissing men. My granddaughter Amira saw a man kissing a woman on the TV. She sat staring, and I slapped her. She cried and ran to her mother, who got upset. We never had this kind of thing. Television spoils everything. I wish it would stop. But they won't stop it because it employs people. Even the TV has changed. In the 1960s everything was very decent. There was no lust shown—people hugging each other and kissing and naked." At this point Karima began to laugh. She looked around to see if anyone could hear her, then added, "Before, even when they were hugging and kissing, they at least had their clothes on.

"Look at me, I'm really tired. I am used to being the man *and* the woman so I am very strict. But tell me now, after forty-one years of work, where is all the money? Where did it go? I spent it all on my children. I've no mother, no father, so it was all for them. I should have buildings and apartments and cars. My children say since there is no man your age for a husband, we'll get you two twenty-five year olds! Karima's laughter came deep and hearty; her head swayed with mockery. "I say, 'No man! Just a car and a villa on the Nile.'"◆

FARIDA Karima's forty-three-year-old daughter looked like a younger version of her mother—a bit stout and with the same color hair and the same direct manner. She nursed her four-year-old son while we talked. Occasionally he would get up and play in the next room, then come back to sit in his mother's arms. Nursing, she explained, was her method of birth control.

"Everything has changed in the last generation. It's not the same way of life, of marriage, or of raising children. They're all aggressive in this generation. They have the characters of crooks. When this generation takes over, they will destroy Egypt.

"I had a similar situation to my mother, except my first husband did not die, he left me—so it's the same. My three children were small when he left. I came in one day and found him with another woman in *my* bed. He got up and beat me. I said, 'I won't sleep with you anymore. I won't stay with you.' He threw me and the children out of the house. He gave nothing for the children. Nothing. I got my divorce papers and went to work sewing, making T-shirts. Because I was a good worker, the owner allowed me to bring the children. Even now, if I need money, I work for a while."

"My second husband was twenty-seven years old when he saw me. I didn't know he wanted to marry me. After three years he said, 'I want only you. I have no brothers, no sisters, and you are my whole family; I want you.' We married, and ever since he has cared for me. He never asked me for anything. I own this building and rent out five or six shops downstairs. I write the contracts and rent them. He never asks for anything. What else does a woman want except this kind of freedom? This kind of peace?

"He likes my children. He likes the way I raised them. But life is becoming very expensive and he can't really provide. He's a construction worker. He makes around 15 to 20 pounds a day [approximately U.S. $4 to $6] but it's not enough, especially since there is no work for five or six months at a time.

"This house is a big place, but some people live in houses so small the men have to go out and stay in the streets during the day. What bothers me is that sometimes the men come back very late because they work; they have no time to spend with their family. They just wash and sleep. There is no time to see them. Women are starting to work more. They have to, to feed their families. Some husbands don't want the wives to work; it's one of the things that is upsetting women.

"The husband wants to prove he is the man. Just like he smokes or drinks to prove he is a man. The last penny in his pocket he spends on cigarettes to show off. Women work because we have many children and have to help the men. Even with many children, men refuse to let their wives work. It's jealousy; the men are usually jealous. Many women work behind their husband's back.

Farida and two of her children

"A woman who has married several men consecutively has to have children from each man. I had only three children and was happy with them, but then I remarried. I had two more girls, but then I had to have a son. But God gave me three! I breast-fed for three years and I never got my period. But as soon as I stopped I got pregnant. This is why this boy is still nursing. He's quite old, but I don't want to stop breast-feeding him because I don't want to be pregnant. I never took the pill. It makes you fat.

"I have five children by my second husband, so he has raised all eight of my children. Everybody envies us, our family. They keep asking, 'What did you do to this guy?' and I say, 'I didn't do anything; it is God.' My husband was a man and still is, but if he gets tired in any way, I will carry him on my shoulders. If he is a bag of bones, I will carry him!"◆

HODA   Farida's daughter Hoda is a tall, plump, pretty woman of twenty-eight. Her pale yellow dress accentuated her youthful olive skin. On the day that I met her, she was a very frightened young woman. She did not regularly reside at the Menshiet Nasser house, but she had taken refuge there temporarily following a marital dispute. Her husband hadn't been too violent this time, she said, but he had threatened more than the punches to her face. Their third child was barely a month old.

"We are told not to upset any man. I try not to cause problems with my husband because he always beats me. If I was strong I wouldn't have taken those punches in my eyes. I have nothing except my husband and my house, so I wait until he cools down and then go back. He's a driver. People upset him a lot and he gets very tense. Then he beats me. He is still good because on ordinary days, he's a gentle person."

"We fight because he wants more children and I don't. We've been married thirteen years, since I was fifteen. We have three children—a girl and two boys. He wants another girl. Some women want to have many children to keep the man so he doesn't go and get married again. But I don't want that. Three children, that's enough. I have an IUD. He told me to take the IUD out because for him having many children is a source of pride.

"He'll probably come back tomorrow to take me home. We'll fight because when I am here I'm not afraid that he will beat me. After I go back, I get back into line. He's a thin man, but I can't hit him back because it's a shame to beat a man.

"He's the one who's providing for us. How can I dare beat him? In other countries a women can hit a man, but here she can't do it. Being beaten hurts inside a woman. So imagine a man being beaten; it leaves an even worse feeling. It's his dignity." Hoda paused for a moment as if searching for other reasons to defend her husband. Then she added, "And he provides for me.

"When I watch my mother feeding him and being nice to him, I get upset. Then he comes home and punches me. Nobody talks to him about it—not my sister, not my brothers, nobody. You're supposed to solve your own problems between yourself and your husband, because that's our custom.

"I didn't like him at first. He saw me and came to talk to my father. My mother told me that my father had accepted him, so I said, 'Okay, if my father accepts, I'll accept.' But now, thank God, I like him, not like before. Love came after marriage." Hoda broke into a huge smile and, with a twist of her head, added almost teasingly, "With every punch—comes love."◆

HEBA AND AMIRA Several days later Marlene Tadros and I returned to Karima's home, having made arrangements to talk with Farida's daughters Heba and Amira, ages fifteen and twelve. They are already promised in marriage. As the conversation wore on, Marlene became distressed about their impending marriages, and expressed her concern.

Heba is the first child of Farida's second marriage; she no longer attends school. "I do housework or if my mother wants groceries, I go. I also went once to sew T-shirts. I worked for three months. But my fiancé doesn't want me to work. He says we don't need the money. I said, 'It's not a matter of money, it's also a matter of learning some skills for my future.' He disagreed. He won't let me work.

"He's twenty-two years old and a cart vendor. He sells women's accessories. He goes around the neighborhoods with his cart. He's my brother's friend. Usually, that's what happens: brothers like to marry their sisters to their best friends. I like him."

I asked her if she believed she was too young for marriage. "I don't know, maybe. But my father says that I should 'write the book [marry officially, on paper, only].' It will be a marriage without consummation. I'll stay in my parents' house. The marriage will not be consummated until my husband can afford a home. But you see, I have to be tied to someone. It's because of my age. People gossip. 'Why is she not married?' Every time I stop to talk to someone, people gossip more. So it's safer if I'm tied to someone; then nobody can talk."

Amira, the younger sister, has just turned twelve. Shy and withdrawn, she is still a plump little girl yet she announced proudly, "My fiancé is also chosen. In a few months' time he'll be ready, not like Heba's would-be husband. Mine is ready; he wants to make the full marriage. But we've decided that we'll just write the book. Consummation will take place in a year's time."

At this point Farida interrupted her daughters, attempting to explain what was planned, "The girls' brothers are the ones who pressured their father to get them married. They don't want the girls to know other people, to go out. They want to protect our honor very early."

Amira, the shy twelve-year-old, added, "I've met him. I like him very much."

Marlene Tadros looked at Farida and said, "She is a twelve year old, for God's sake, she likes everybody! The legal age is twenty!"

Farida interrupted defensively, saying, "My mother says she got married at ten. Why shouldn't I marry these girls? When they are old like this they should get married. Just look at her body!"◆

Anatomy is destiny, it is said, and for the adolescent Amira, having a woman's body has prompted her brothers and parents to propel her into an early marriage. The women of her family are strong and resourceful; both Karima and Farida have shown that they could survive without the support of men. It sometimes seems, nonetheless, that they have yet to take their self-worth to heart. They cannot resist the powerful demands that their men—and society—place on their person and bodies, including having more children than they want or can afford, and accepting domestic violence as a matter of course.

In a small town in Uganda, a quite different story emerged when a young woman told of the formidable consequences of stepping outside of the roles prescribed for women.

FORT PORTAL, UGANDA

The ride from Uganda's capital, Kampala, to the western town of Fort Portal took us through stunning countryside. The rural homes were neatly cared for and many had flowering gardens out front. Everywhere, children abounded. As we neared Fort Portal at nightfall, we could make out the Mountains of the Moon against the night sky; on the other side lay the troubled nation of Congo (then Zaire).

At breakfast the next morning, sitting on a sidewalk patio outside the hotel, I watched the town's activity. No personal cars were visible—just trucks, minibuses, and bicycles, transporting people, bananas, furniture, charcoal bags, and huge cans of milk for door-to-door distribution.

Jocelyne Bajanja, 25

I was to meet with Gertrude Bajanja, a longtime volunteer for the Fort Portal YWCA. Gertrude is in her mid-fifties, quite small in stature, but with a manner that would command respect anywhere. She owns and manages a sawmill and furniture shop on the edge of town. She said she was training an errant daughter to run the business. When I explained the reason for my visit, Gertrude suggested that I speak with the daughter, saying, "She was a soldier in the army and has had children by three different men." Jocelyne Bajanja had fought in the National Resistance Army led by Yoweri Museveni, now president of Uganda. "She is somewhat typical of the young women who were caught in Uganda's civil war and who now search for stability, security," her mother said.

At twenty-five, Jocelyne Bajanja is a slim, almost wiry girl, with a quick smile. She was wearing a pink skirt, yellow T-shirt, and white jacket. Her home was a mud-and-stick house, tucked too closely among others in an area where chickens and naked children ran about chasing each other. To find more privacy for our conversation, she took us to her mother's furniture factory, where she worked. There, seated in the office, she talked easily of her years as a soldier, admitting right away that she had made mistakes, had learned, and was getting on with her life. Young Jocelyne does not dwell upon or regret her youth's hardships and foolishness; her story was laced with laughter.

"I was born here, the fourth of eight children. I went to school until I was sixteen, when an army battalion came to town. I saw women wearing uniforms and handling guns, and said to myself, 'Why don't I join these people? I have handled a gun; I know how to use it.' Soldiers had come here before, but they were men and were harsh. These people had discipline. I asked a woman soldier about women in the army, saying, 'Are they suffering?' She replied, 'No, we get food and clothes and do what the men do. If you follow orders, nothing is going to happen.'

"The next day I saw the soldiers on parade—men and women—marching and singing. I went home and told my mother I wanted to join the army.

'You?' she replied. 'You hear a bullet go by and you run under the bed.' She thought I was joking and didn't pay attention to me. I took some clothes, a few books, and snuck away.

"You see, when I was a little girl I looked up to my cousin, who had studied and become a policeman. I wanted to be like him. There were women in the police, too, and I liked their uniforms." With a wide smile, the young woman before me rocked back and forth on her chair, laughing at the thought of her childish ways.

"In the army they trained us just like the men. When there was guard duty, we had to guard. When there was fighting on the front, we went to fight. Whatever men did, we did. Wake up early, go running, sing military songs, political education, march—left foot, right foot—all that. I also trained in radio broadcasting. They taught us how to handle guns, to clean them and to shoot, to take cover by digging holes. When the enemy attacked us, we killed them and they retreated. It was frightening. Luckily I never saw anybody I shot at.

"When the war was over, I stayed in the army and learned to work the switchboard. That was when I got a man and had my first child. I was eighteen. The father worked as a doctor in the army. But when he started befriending many girls, I said, 'No, I might get diseases. I think we must stop here.' So I left and went to another town. Mummy came and said, 'It's not right to have this baby here, let me take the child home.' My son now lives with my brother, a forester, who makes him study well. He's seven years old. His father doesn't send any money or school fees.

"I had a second child by another man. He, too, was an army man. He was from Mbara. I didn't want to stay with him because when a woman soldier marries a man soldier he starts mistreating her. Always criticizing, wanting to be served.

"When I had the second child I was ill, and Mummy came and said, 'You are sick. Why don't you come home and rest.' She persuaded the officer to give me a pass to go home and rest. Eventually I asked to leave the army. I'm planning to stay here and help my parents. I work, go home, and have a family around. I have just had twins with a nice man. I'm happy with him. I love him. We met here in Fort Portal, and we plan to get married. But first we have to save enough money so I can take him to my father.

"He is nice to me. He helps and shares duties with me. Since the twins were born, he has helped, fetching water for me, washing the babies. He behaves well. He is respectful of old people on the street. He doesn't drink beer. He studied until the seventh primary grade, but had to stop for lack of school fees. He is a mechanic. His father is dead, but his mother lives here in town. I visit her now and then. She is happy about the twins.

"We talked to each other about how many children we'd have. I told him I don't want many children. But he wants three. He wanted to take my other children, but Mummy and I decided it was not good. It's not good to carry children to another man's home. He can love them at first, but later he might change. I'll probably have another child with him, since he wants three.

"We don't have much leisure. We stay home, we play cards and listen to music. Sometimes we go to see a film. I like to see films where people are fighting—in other countries, not here like we used to, but in America or Germany. I also like adventure films.

"I don't see many friends. Young people are drinking too much. And there are many couples who don't stay together. If they feel something is wrong, they leave. The husband goes to the bar and starts drinking; he comes home and beats his wife. I've seen that, and I don't want a man who drinks. I told my fiancé the very first day, 'I don't want a person who drinks or who slaps me.' He said he wasn't involved in that kind of thing. But I studied him for five months to see what he did. I know what I want and I can say it. Men and women must talk to each other.

"My life is very different from my mother's, of course. I want to be like her; whatever she does I want to do. I didn't realize this when I was young. Now I'm old enough to see what is good and what is bad. I see a person who loves me and those who don't. When he has money he brings it, and when I get my money he says, 'Take good care of it.' We discuss whose needs are most urgent. We make the decisions together.

"My plans? I'd like to get experience like my mother, to learn how she works. I want to get involved in women's groups so that I can teach like she does. I was never taught anything about how one gets pregnant. I knew only about labor, about childbirth. That's all. I knew nothing about relations with a man. I just learned when I was with them. I don't want any more children. These are enough. I want them to study and get jobs. I'm going to get pills at the family planning office."◆

Regardless of her sense of humor and matter-of-fact delivery, Jocelyne Bajanja's early life had not been an easy one. It might not have ended so well had she not had the support of a wise mother who was not quick to judge, always ready to counsel and assist. Like so many women elsewhere, Jocelyne had taken a very difficult journey before finding a life of safety and security for her family, and a man who recognized her right to dignity and respect. Another woman, a midwife I met in El Salvador, told of an even more difficult learning process.

AGUILARES, EL SALVADOR

The road to Aguilares, a few hours north of San Salvador, passes through a series of villages of little distinction. Most consist of groups of iron-roofed shacks made of palm leaves, stalks, and plastic covering. Their streets are littered with piles of rain-soaked, rotting garbage and car carcasses. Aguilares is a bustling market town. Its health center, the Unidad de Salud, is an over-crowded, stretched-to-the-limit health post, not unlike countless others in El Salvador. Serving a population of 60,000 people, it has only six doctors. It also serves as a training center, offering programs for midwives and nutri-tion workers. I had arranged to meet a midwife who had completed the train-ing program a few months earlier.

Rising out of the center of a small cornfield three miles east of town, the Marroquin family home and clinic is a small thatched structure divided into

Albertina Sosa de Marroquin, 57
Porfirio Marroquin, 50
Rosa Vila Sosa, 38

two rooms—one a large room where hammocks are strung and belongings stored, the other the birthing room and midwifery office. The house was as neat as a pin the day we vis-ited, the hardened earth floor swept dustless. Barrels for catching rainwa-ter from the roof leaned against the outside walls; additional water is fetched from a well down the road. There is no electricity; kerosene lamps are used for nighttime deliveries. On the wall near the front door, a large poster had been nailed to the wall: a man and a woman face each other; between them is an equal sign.

ALBERTINA   Albertina Sosa de Marroquin is a diminutive woman who bare-ly reached to my shoulder. Her bright blue eyes were rendered even brighter by her blue shirtdress and white bandanna. A smile seemingly wider than her face greeted us, and she insisted on showing us her home and workplace. Then, shaded by a porchlike overhang, we settled down to talk in front of the house. I was to learn later, from Albertina's husband and her daughter, that her life of misery had led her to drink and to some destructive behav-ior, a fact she withheld in her interview.

"I was born in Apopa and lived there all my life. We didn't move, even during the war [El Salvador's twelve-year civil war, in the 1980s and early 1990s]. We came here three years ago, looking for land to work. My husband is a farmer. A rich private owner donated this land because he saw I was helping so many people. We have the land, but we can't afford to build anything more than this hut.

"When I was small something happened to my mother's feet; they turned inward. It might have been poliomyelitis, I don't know, but she could only crawl on the ground like a baby. I was about seven years old and I watched her suffer. Then my father abandoned us. We were five children, two girls and three boys.

"That was a very difficult time. I went to school for only one year, and when I reached eleven I went to work cutting sugar cane with a machete. I earned thirty-five cents a day. My father never supported us. We had to live on what my grandmother and we children earned. I remember how much my mother suffered all those years, not only physical mistreatment, but also harsh words. My father would tell us to look for him at the market and he'd give us something. When we met him, he'd say, 'You idiots don't deserve anything,' and he'd throw five cents at us. We had to pick it up among the rocks. He had another woman. Men are all like that. They abandon women with many babies, and the children suffer.

"When I was thirteen, my life of grief and suffering began. A man kidnapped me. He was eighteen years old. He was not my boyfriend; I knew him, but I didn't want to go with him. He took me to his mother's house and locked me in a room for a month. He forced himself upon me. I never consented. I didn't want to do it. There was no love. I was a child. Then the police came and arrested us.

"The boy threatened to kill me if I said I didn't love him. The judge sent me to jail for five days. He had paid the judge. It was impossible for me to return home. I was disgraced; I feared my mother and grandmother would punish me. Even though I'd been locked up so I couldn't run away, my folks wouldn't believe me.

"People say that I was a pretty girl and that they felt sorry I fell into the hands of this man. We lived together fourteen years. There was no marriage, but he's the father of my seven children. Life with him was pure hell; I have scars he gave me when he came home drunk. In the beginning he didn't drink; he just threatened abuse. Later on he became a drunk. He brought women to the house and ordered me to feed them. I milked forty-five cows every day. I would get up at 12:30 A.M. to deliver the milk at 3 A.M. We were *corraleros*, hired hands, paid by the day. On payday he would take my money and leave us totally helpless. He never provided anything for the children.

"One day I was ironing, and he arrived and started hitting me. He grabbed me by the hair and dragged me on the ground. It was at that moment I found the courage to stand up to him. I started to hit him with a broom handle. I hit him in his private parts with my knee and grabbed him by the neck. He lost face. In his eyes he'd been disgraced. I fled with my children and went to my brother's place.

"Of my seven children, two are dead, and the rest have their own families. One is in the United States, but I don't know anything about him. He was a sergeant in the national police. I heard he was in California, but he has never written. My daughter lives in San Salvador. Today's generation

Near their home in Aguilares, Porfirio Marroquin and Albertina Sosa
Marroquin with their visiting grandson, Alberto

is changing. Thank God, there are many of us strong women who have started to do away with the abuse we suffered from the men in our lives. The
Secretariat of the Family is doing something about this problem. [The Secretaria
Nacional de la Familia was created and directed by Dona Margarita de Cristiani,
then First Lady of El Salvador.]

"Who taught me the most? Poverty was the best teacher! When I was a
girl I wanted to be a midwife like my grandmother. I don't know how she
learned, but she was a local midwife. Now, thank God, with the new
emphasis on literacy, I've learned to write a bit. In 1991, I took courses in
literacy, self-esteem, and family problems. I worked side-by-side with doctors to learn midwifery and how to keep a record of all the deliveries.

"The self-esteem course, Capacitacion, teaches us our value. It says, 'We
women have suffered so much, so much ill treatment, so much misery.' I cared
for my children when they were little but I didn't take care of myself. I said
to myself, 'The child is important, I'm not.' Or I would say, 'My husband should
eat, not me.' Why? Psychologically speaking, I'm damaging myself because
I don't love myself, I only love others. I don't feel worthy to think of myself,
of the value of being a woman; I think that I'm worth nothing.

"The self-esteem class opened my eyes. I know who I am. I used to be scared
to death. I always felt like a worm, the smallest and most undesirable of all
creatures. Now I can even talk to doctors!

"Imagine: to deliver a baby it costs 100 colones, but if it's a baby boy it's
150! We have to ask ourselves, 'Why is it that women are worth less? Where
is the self-esteem?'

"The man I lived with would arrive home drunk and hit me. Now I see the hospital full of battered women. They lie to the doctors, who don't know how to treat them if the women don't say how the injury happened. They say they fell off the bed. Yes, bruised and purple! We see newborns also hurt, because husbands actually kick the mothers in the stomach. We have to teach women about self-esteem, what it means to love ourselves.

"Many girls get their first sexual experiences at home; they are raped by their uncles, their brothers, or other males in the family. Or perhaps it happens in the streets; that's very commonplace. Once it happens they feel so low, they think very little of themselves. And parents don't talk to their daughters; sexuality is not discussed. When the father of my children kidnapped me, I didn't have any idea what was going to happen. In those days these things were taboo. Today, when girls get to be about twelve years old, we explain the facts of life to them.

"Before, no one dared say anything. We were afraid and ashamed of society's opinion of us. Everything was hush-hush, but the truth is that there is so much injustice. All men want to do is to shack up with other women. We want this to stop. So we are becoming stronger. Society has burdened us with so many taboos. Women become desperate with so many children crying and yelling. I tell my neighbors we must organize to educate the next generation about this.

"My life would have been different if I had been to this self-esteem class when I was a young woman. With the fright, the shyness, the shame, we can't aspire to anything. It took a lot of courage to go to that class; I didn't know what I was getting into, but made up my mind that I would go and I did, with God's help.

"I first met my current husband when I was twenty-eight years old. But it wasn't until much later that we got together. He had been my friend. When I was sick, he started visiting. Then he proposed to me. At first I did not want any more relationships; I was sick of having men mistreat me. I told him that all men are cut from the same cloth. But he is a good man compared to others. My life has become much easier. Because of him I have my training and people look up to me. My husband respects me, and I'm happy. I'm also training him, passing on what I learn so he can tend to the patients when I'm not home.

"We are seeing changes in family and community life, and I feel happy. I have this ability to help others. This has made me better. When I was young I didn't know about self-esteem. One has to be mature to put the puzzle together. In the self-esteem classes we learn that boys and girls are neither superior nor inferior, that God created everyone equal. We are all here to accomplish something."◆

PORFIRIO   Albertina's husband is fifty years old, a tall, attractive man with unusually bright green eyes. His gentle demeanor inspired confidence immediately. He said he'd had many girlfriends but had never married. Then he met Albertina. A member of the Evangelical Church, he believes his faith helped Albertina abandon her previous "unruly ways." His devotion to, and pride in, his wife was total. They had married in a church, and they had a home of their own and a profession. Life was good.

"My father was a farmer, but my mother died from a breast tumor when I was eight months old. There were three of us children. I started helping my father when I was eight. Then, two years later, my father remarried and had two more children. My stepmother was mean, so we went to live with our grandmother, about three kilometers away. We felt unappreciated, humiliated, isolated by my father's absence. He gave all his time and care to the other wife and children. When he died the family fell apart. My sisters went to live with my aunt. I was twelve and almost a man, so I left home to find work. I started roaming the countryside and became unruly, not having to answer to anybody.

"I met Albertina in the town of Apopa. Two years later, we started going together, sort of dating. We were married ten years ago. With this parcel of land we can grow enough to feed ourselves and have some left over to sell. My wife wishes she could have her maternity clinic, with water and electricity, right here. Maybe someday we can fulfill our dream."◆

ROSA   Rosa Vila Sosa, thirty-eight, is Albertina's oldest daughter and lives and works far away in San Salvador, where we met in her home. She is an attractive woman but appears overly shy, unable to think of herself as anything other than the hardworking mother of two sons. Each boy has a different father; neither spends much time or money on his son. The fact that Rosa has managed to purchase her house is a source of great pride. She works seven days a week selling fish, striving to assure that her sons will be educated and her house remain hers. The sad story of her life reveals how her mother fled the brutality of their home to find refuge in drink and other men.

"I remember my father with sadness and fear. I was the only one responsible for the household. My mother would leave, and we couldn't go with her because she always had a man to go to. My father gave her a real rotten life and he demanded that I do the work of a grown-up woman. Our life was hell. If we were left with my father he would beat us. If we lived with either one, it was bad. Neither was a good parent.

"When mother left we suspected she had another man, so we felt miserable. We didn't know what to do. She would leave for weeks, sometimes months. I couldn't live with my father because the stepmothers would be mean to us. My father was a criminal; he even burned my feet. I still have the scars. I wanted to go to my mother, but she had problems, too, and the area was totally devoid of food—nothing to eat but roots and leaves. I worked on the same farm as my father. Imagine: at eleven years old I was working like a grown man. I lived full of fear, constantly expecting the worst.

"He never touched me as a woman, sexually; he was only after other women. He abused me physically in every other sense, though. The women he liked were loose women, but as a rule, they hardly lasted more than a day. I was glad these women would come, because in a sense they would share in the work, and he would be interested in them and leave us alone. I felt like a slave. I went to school thanks to my own effort; neither of my parents can say they helped me. I managed to get a health diploma after eight years of schooling. When I finished I worked in a clinic doing bookkeeping, lowering the mercury in thermometers, serving as a receptionist. The last year I worked was in Environmental Health on mosquito control.

"Now no one will hire me because I am thirty-eight years old, and besides, I have no money to go looking for such a job. If I look for work it means I won't be earning anything. The day I don't work is the day we don't eat. My hands are tied.

"What I can't forgive is the lack of love of my parents toward me. The love they didn't give me is the love that I give my children. I never want them to lack what every child should have, the parents' love. This way, they can never accuse me of not caring for them.

"The older boy is very calm in nature. He knows I'm the only one who will help him when he needs it. At times it takes great sacrifice, but he understands this. He must learn to be responsible and learn a trade so when he has his own children, he will take care of them with love and no vices. There's so much delinquency among young men. I wish he could continue studying but he doesn't want to. That's why he is attending mechanic's training.

"I came to La Zapanila to sell fish. I met a woman here who became my good friend. I told her of my problems, the lack of money, the constant struggle. She thought about it and came up with a possible solution. She knew that this land was going to be subdivided into small lots and the payments were low enough for me to afford. We started paying about 50 colones a month [at the time, approximately US $1], and I was able to buy.

"My brothers had no idea what to do; they didn't have a trade. It's the result of the way my parents raised us—if you can call it that. They never knew how to guide us. Each of us left and did whatever we thought was best for us, but our parents never gave us any direction at all—no schooling, no guidance. It was as if we were wild puppies. The brother who lives in San Francisco didn't want to leave; he wanted to study. He became a military man because he had no help from anybody. He is a sad man.

Rosa Vila Sosa and her youngest son in front of their San Salvador home

"Now my mother wishes she could see him, but it's too late. She says she is sorry for everything she did. She wants to give us what she didn't give us before, but it's too late. We don't need her anymore. Things would have been different if she had met her present husband years ago. She has found happiness, finally, and has changed tremendously. When my father kidnapped her she was very young and ignorant. My father grew up in a desolate, ugly place where there was nothing to eat, no future of any kind. Places like that somehow create people who grow up like savages. He's still alive, but we don't want anything to do with him.

"I don't think of getting married again. There are many men out there who would like to have us take them in. We know better. We don't pay attention to them. They are very tricky and soon would make our lives miserable. We would end up selling the house and they would run off with the money. You have to be smart. For now, I want to push these children ahead to a better life and to continue working. That is my goal. I want to save money so we can fix the house and educate this last child. He's in the second grade and very smart; I think he'll want to study."◆

Rosa, relentless worker and devoted mother, is among the hundreds of thousands of Salvadoran women who are heads of households due to the civil war, migration, or abandonment. She is also a contributor to the statistic of out-of-wedlock births, which account for 75 percent of all births in El Salvador. She has never shirked her responsibilities; she does what is expected of her without question. Deprived of even one day a week for leisure or rest, Rosa struggles to keep poverty at bay.

Worldwide, the increase in women-headed households continues unabated due to divorce, abandonment, widowhood, and, in some rare cases, personal choice. The tragedy behind the statistics is that households headed by women are the poorest of all households in all societies. As one researcher explained, "Female-headed households are being formed not through women's emancipation or through any desire or economic capability on their part. They are being forced to manage the households through a combination of economic, demographic, and social factors which hold no advantage for them in any form. They are the end products of a pauperization process and represent the poverty situation in its most acute form."[3]

Examining the reasons for the lack of responsibility on the part of other family members, particularly husbands and fathers, is one step toward a solution. Salvadoran sociologist Zoila de Innocenti brought her insights to the predicament, explaining, "To feminists, people say: 'You are taking women out of the family.' And we reply, 'No, we are trying to get men *into* the family.'" But as long as female-headed households are a reality, they need to be supported by their societies, rather than ignored or scorned.

The stories told here demonstrate the obstacles women encounter in making their way within the family and in the larger world. A common thread that links these stories is the importance of women's ability to earn a livelihood; another is the power of a sense of self-worth. The first often results in the second, but where either is missing, a woman's life is diminished.

Maria Guilhon's life has been structured by a patriarchal home—service to her husband and the rearing of eight children. It is an experience many affluent women of her generation share. Her daughter and granddaughter work full-time in professions of their choice, the daughter divorced, the granddaughter as yet unmarried.

The Bengali garment worker, Shahida, made a decision about the quality of life she wanted for her four children and chose to take control of her fertility. She was consequently discarded. She, like Rosa in El Salvador, is single-handedly holding her family together and is justifiably proud of it. But in Egypt, although Karima has supported her family since she was widowed at age nineteen, she has yet to question the tradition of early marriage or of total male authority. She takes pride in the fact that her twelve-year-old granddaughter has a fiancé.

In rural Uganda, Jocelyne, the ex-soldier, made some youthful choices she regrets and lived through some grim experiences. With the support of a strong and loving mother, she has learned how to manage her life and found greater stability and fulfillment. Albertina, the Salvadoran midwife whose early life was marred by violence and psychological abuse, has likewise had the opportunity to see beyond women's subservient condition. Her training in auto-estima has given her a sense of purpose and pride.

These interviews reveal how education, economic independence, legal equality, freedom from violence, and control of their own bodies and fertility are trends that are reshaping women's experience and the quality of family life for women, men, and children everywhere. Unfortunately, women and their families are far from achieving the attention and investment that their situation warrants. Experience has demonstrated that such attention and investment increase substantially only when women are in the chambers of power, in parliaments and ministries. At present, women are very poorly represented in policy-making institutions of government: in 1999, women represented only 11 percent of parliament members worldwide.[4] Women's increased presence in key institutions of both government and civil society is one of the major challenges of the twenty-first century.

Five | Manhood Revisited

Society has started to appreciate the importance of being a member of a family, rather than a member of a company. Men are now able to say publicly that they have to go to a meeting for their child's orientation. Before it was not possible. Men are changing, becoming more flexible. It's a good change.

—Emmy Saito, Tokyo, Japan

It was a bitterly cold December in Ningxia Province. The two buildings in the modest compound I was visiting were hidden from passing villagers by a six-foot-high wall. The one-level main house sat in the center of a courtyard in which a single hen strutted and clucked. The interior was simple, its furniture consisting only of the long, benchlike beds that ran along the wall, heated from beneath and piled high with quilts.

It was here that Jin Xuefu, a fifty-four-year-old Tongxin County employee, reflected proudly on his responsibility as son, father, and grandfather. His concern for the changing times was not unlike that of many men of his generation in the countries I visited. His personal story, however, was particularly harsh. Born of illiterate peasants, he was eleven years old before he could attend primary school. His father and grandfather both opposed schooling, wanting to keep him as a farmworker. "I was concerned," he explained, "by the fact that my legs were not very strong, and that if I were to become a real man and earn a living for my family, I must learn something that would enable me to do so. I was determined to get an education.

"Luckily I did, because I was just twenty when my father died. I then had to shoulder the responsibility for the whole family. I supported my two sisters until they married. My younger brother lived with us until five years ago, but since his family expanded, there was not enough space. We are now four generations living together. It is sometimes very difficult to organize family life in such a big family. I'm the one who has the heaviest responsibility; I have to look after everything in daily life, to coordinate the relations among all the family members, to see they are united.

"There are not many problems in my family because I support my mother, and when I retire I'll have a pension and so will my wife. Economically we won't have to depend on the children very much. It's my sons' generation that I worry about. Within ten years there will be big change.

Jin Xuefu (*seated at left*) with his family

I've already prepared for it. Within this courtyard, I've put up a wall to separate the houses. I will build new houses for everyone. You see, this depends on me as the head of the family. If I treat the family well, they find that each of them has a place, they are united, and live harmoniously, they will not feel the need to separate and go away.

"I've even planted more fruit trees for the family's future. They will benefit from the fruit probably after I'm gone."

Being born male has long been a guarantee of privilege and authority in both family and community. In return, manhood was associated with the capacity and responsibility to provide for one's family. There was a structure to male roles; rights and responsibilities were well-defined. Jin Xuefu was well aware of those responsibilities; this awareness fueled his determination to get the education that would compensate for his weak physical condition.

The families interviewed in earlier chapters reveal that the foundations on which male privilege once reposed have been weakened in the past century by a series of economic, technological, and demographic transformations. It is no longer possible for men to provide easily for large extended families as they did in the past; as a result, their authority is diminished and, some say, so is their self-confidence. At the same time, increased access to education, expanding concepts of democracy and gender equity, and women's more active participation in all sectors of society have combined to transform roles and relationships among generations and between the sexes. Contraceptive technologies have had enormous impact on people's lives: planned parenthood allows men to provide for a desired number of children and women to look beyond the role of mother. The resulting shifts in authority and family decision making are present to one degree or another everywhere. Some men express confusion about changing gender roles and how to adjust to the new times. There are others who, when their traditional authority is no longer assured, shirk the customary responsibilities of son, husband, father and provider. Still others, enjoy the release from strict gender roles and happily participate in more democratic, equal partnerships.

OMUTA CITY, JAPAN

My plane landed at Fukuoka on the island of Kyushu, the southernmost of the four main Japanese islands. Kyushu is known for its rice and coal production. But coal mining is on the wane; cheap foreign coal and petroleum have undercut the energy source which once stoked the engines of Japan's industrial miracle. My destination was Omuta City, a coal mining town where the local labor union had agreed to introduce me to a family of miners who were facing the loss of their traditional livelihood. The Miike Labor Union

Umematsu Tanaka, 77
Shidzue Tanaka, 80
Kunihiro Tanaka, 51
Seiko Tanaka, 50

offices were housed in a large, wooden prewar building. The office walls were decorated with old photographic portraits of dead miners, victims of local mine disasters. Mr. Yoshikawa, a slight, self-effacing union official welcomed us and proposed to drive us to the home of the Tanaka family, in a rural area twenty-eight kilometers from Omuta City.

The Tanaka home was located along a winding country road. The modest one-story house was surrounded by a vegetable garden which, I later learned, is tended with the utmost care by eighty year old Shidzue Tanaka. During our visit, we sat on cushions placed around a formidable tree-trunk table hewn of a tropical hardwood from the Philippines. It could easily seat ten people. Kunihiro proudly announced that it was a gift from his parents to himself and his wife— adding, with a wink at the table's indestructible bulk, "and our descendants."

UMEMATSU   Umematsu Tanaka is a small man with rounded shoulders and a happily crinkled face. His eyes squint ceaselessly, as if still straining to see as they did for so many years in the darkness of the coal mines. Umematsu and his son, Kunihiro, are lifelong miners, but the younger Tanakas, as is the case in so many families, have chosen a different course.

Umematsu was hesitant at first about telling his life story. Shidzue, a distinguished looking woman with dark brown hair, appeared more at ease than he with our conversation. Born in a mining family, she had worked as a volunteer in the union office for twenty some years. That experience had given her an ease with people. Her husband, on the other hand, had few contacts beyond his miner colleagues. In a barely audible voice, Umematsu began his narrative.

"I was one of five children in a family of farmers. My mother died giving birth to a sister when I was five years old." He hesitated a moment, adding sadly, "I have no memory of her face. None at all. Years later, when my father died, there was no use staying in the countryside to try to farm alone, so I came to Omuta to join my brother, who worked in the mines. I was then twenty-one years old.

"I was put to work running machines that pumped water out of the mine. A year later, at the beginning of the Sino-Japanese War, I was drafted into the army and sent to China. During the war my brothers and sisters moved away, so I lost touch with them. There was little to bind us together. My elder brother was killed in the war. His widow, Shidzue, was living in Omuta City with her young son when I returned from the war." The elder raised his head to catch my eye, adding matter-of-factly, "So I married her. We had four more children together.

"Work in the mines today is much different from when I started. But I can't say anything against the colliery; I didn't have an accident all those years. I worked safely until the end, thank God. I retired at fifty-five and went to work for a civil engineer building roads. By the time I was seventy-three the Ministry of Labor banned people over seventy from road crews. Only one of my sons became a miner. The others have gone off, to Tokyo or to Omuta City. I have three grandchildren in Tokyo, two here in the family, three in Omuta. Since I was separated from my family because of the war, I feel happy that my children and grandchildren are healthy and doing well. They are living a much better life than we did. They have few worries and can live in peace."◆

The Tanaka family in front of their home: (*left to right*) Seiko, Kunihiro, Shidzue, and Umematsu

KUNIHIRO Umematsu's miner son, Kunihiro, is slim and athletic, a man with a huge smile and easy wit. He seems to struggle with a store of unspent energy, difficult to curb. Dressed in a light blue knit shirt and beige trousers, he appeared ready for a game of golf rather than a commute to his night shift in the mines. His smile rarely wavered; he was proud to say he had known his wife since childhood and added with another grin, "We get along well together."

He began by speaking about his work. "After graduating from junior high school, I attended a three-year training school for coal miners. I've been a coal miner ever since. I'm in charge of supporting the miners who prepare tunnels. The shifts are eight and a half hours each: six in the morning, three in the afternoon, or nine at night. We change every week. There used to be three mines here. Only one remains open. There are two thousand miners left from a count of fifteen thousand union members years ago." For the first time, Kunihiro seemed to lose his upbeat tempo, stating flatly, "I'm the last miner in this family.

"My father worked nights and mother volunteered at the union, so beginning in elementary school, I helped around the house. I rinsed and cooked the rice and took care of my younger brothers and sisters when they were small. That was the way of life then." With a shrug of regret, Kunihiro mused, "Unlike parents today, mine didn't push us to study.

"Seiko and I have two sons. One is married and lives nearby; the other is at the university. They realize that coal mining is over and there aren't many opportunities in this area. Many young people have to move to the cities. They don't want to; they would rather find work here. When my older son joined a locally based company he told them he didn't want to move away. He'd worked there just a short time when the company asked him to move to another city. He refused and quit the job. It would have taken him away from us, his family. Now he works for a small company that makes video equipment. In March I'll be a grandfather. I think I'll worry a lot more about my grandchildren than I did about my own children. I didn't interfere with my sons much. I let them do whatever they wanted. It's nice to have the sons around. There are two generations living in this house, my father and myself, and we hope that when my elder son has the baby, they will all come live with us.

"My generation differs from my father's in the way we interact with society. For him, the range of friendships is rather limited. When he worked he knew only people from work. I play tennis and badminton and sometimes serve as a judge for athletic meetings. I have friends from all different areas. And we talk a lot in our family. Compared to other families and my own childhood, I think we are much more frank. I used to tell my children, there are school rules and it's your responsibility to follow them. You can't claim only your rights—you have to take responsibilities. It's the same for the elders. I tell my children, if you do nice things for the elders, you'll be treated nicely when you get older. If I did not take good care of my parents, maybe my children would not take good care of us. We talk and discuss things a lot. Of course we have family disagreements, but we can talk freely with one another. When I disagree with my wife, we talk it out and come to a decision. We don't get emotional. In Japan the rate of divorce is increasing and one of the reasons is that one person insists on his or her opinion. My wife and I do a lot together, we play tennis and badminton together; sometimes we travel together. I could say to her, 'You go there alone,' but instead I say, 'Let's go together or with your friends.' We have to help each other in today's life. Japanese men are rather old-fashioned. I don't think I can fully agree with women's independence because I want the woman to take care of the family. My generation feels the way I do. But I don't know where I should draw the line."◆

SEIKO   While her husband talked with us, Seiko Tanaka had prepared a light evening meal because Kunihiro was soon to leave for his night shift. Her bobbed black hair and print dress gave her a girlish look; she was constantly coming and going, with food, drink, and smiles, concerned that her in-laws, husband, and guests were well attended. She works in her sister's hardware store and happily noted that "women's work has weakened strict obedience to in-laws and made our relations more comfortable.

"My in-laws are kind and my husband is understanding so I'm happy in this family. Women lead an easy life today, much easier than before. We can even make our own money; before, it wasn't allowed. I do the washing and morning cooking before I leave for work. My mother-in-law prepares the evening meal. We don't have any specific rules on who should do what; it comes naturally." Seiko then hesitated before adding, with a wide smile and a gesture of mock surprise, "My father-in-law even helps me clean the house. Imagine that!"◆

The Tanaka family's adaptation to the economic and social changes of the last half of the twentieth century has by all accounts been harmonious and successful. Umematsu, who couldn't be a farmer, followed his brother into mining; when another brother was killed, he married his widow, as was the custom. Kunihiro followed his father into mining, albeit with more education and more interests beyond work. Members of the third generation could not become participants in a failing industry, but they attempt to remain close to their family. The roles of women were transformed, by voluntarism and then by paid work, which in turn altered male behavior within the home. But as Kunihiro states, although the men in his generation support women's new independence, they still worry about where to "draw the line."

The changes in roles, authority, and family decision making to which the Tanaka's allude are present to one degree or another in all societies. Some families adjust to the new relationships with ease; others find it difficult. What is certain is that men and boys can no longer assume that they will follow easily in the footsteps of the preceding generations or that the birthright privileges that once came with being born a male are immutable. As political and economic systems change, so, too, do roles, relationships, and responsibilities to one another.

In the Tanaka's community young people have the choice to go outside, beyond the community, to find employment. In some regions of the world, pushed by need rather than opportunity or choice, family members must suffer far greater separations in order to secure a livelihood. In 2000, the International Labor Organization estimated that 130 million men and women were participants in the international migrant labor pool. Many nations' economies rely heavily on the remittances of citizens employed abroad. For example, the estimated $700 million that Salvadorans living abroad send back to El Salvador each year is more than the country earns from coffee, sugar, and all its other exports combined.[1]

In Bangladesh, half of the people living in the countryside own less than half an acre each. The result, in a predominantly rural nation of 137.4 million, is an almost limitless supply of laborers—far more than Bangladesh can hope to employ within its borders. Here, as in many other developing nations, citizens desperate for work fall prey to gangs of traders in human exports, who demand large sums to arrange work in and travel to foreign lands. Such trafficking achieved worldwide attention when, in June 2000, the bodies of fifty-seven Chinese men and one woman—would-be illegal immigrants—were discovered inside a refrigerated truck as it arrived in Dover, England. Becoming an economic exile or a temporary "guest worker" is the lot of millions in Bangladesh and around the world. Some are fortunate and have good experiences; others don't. In all cases the families left at home rely on their lonely provider.

BAIRAPURA, BANGLADESH

We left the capital of Dhaka early one morning for the journey to Bogra, a large town several hundred miles to the northwest. My travel companion was Rokya Buli, a middle-aged community development worker who had offered to introduce me to several families in her district. We traveled by four-wheel-drive vehicle and numerous river ferries before reaching Bogra at nightfall. The following day we set out for Bairapara, a village similar to the thousands of villages that dot the flat countryside of Bangladesh. Its inhabitants are mostly farmers who struggle with fears of overflowing

Mohammed Abdur Rouf with his two wives, Shahinur (*left*) and Belli, and children

rivers and destructive monsoons. Others hope to rise out of the constraints of rural poverty by seeking work abroad—among them is an electrician named Mohammed Abdur Rouf.

Mohammed welcomed us warmly to his home, which, like most in the village, consisted of an enclosed courtyard in which women are free from prying eyes and a one-room house woven of thick fibers. The earthen floor of the courtyard had been swept spotless; in one corner the family

Mohammed Abdur Rouf, 40
Belli Abdur Rouf, 38

latrine stood half hidden by flowering bushes. Inside the house, a bed, a large wooden storage trunk, two chairs, a gas lamp, and assorted utensils were the only visible possessions.

MOHAMMED   Mohammed is easily six feet tall and visibly underweight. His broad smile and freshly ironed white shirt seemed to accentuate his gaunt features and pasty complexion. He invited us to sit on the trunk as he told his migrant's story.

"My father was a farmer and had sufficient land for our family. Our nightmare began when the Jamuna River covered our land. From then on our poverty increased. The damage was caused by erosion: the fertile earth was swept away, gone. I'm the only son, and there were four daughters. We managed to eat because my father and I both worked on other people's land. When my father died I came to Shariakandi with my four sisters. I bought this plot; it's not farmland, it's only good for a house. I trained to become an electrician but here I couldn't earn enough to support the family. We were suffering. I thought I should do something. I was twenty-six when I was fortunate enough to get a job in Singapore. One feels terrible leaving one's country behind. I was very homesick.

"The biggest problem of the journey was fear. The traders take your money and send you off with other laborers; they don't bother to take you to your job. By plane to Bangkok—I had never been in a plane—and then a bus for many hours until we reached Singapore. I liked Singapore and Malaysia. What fertile, green country! It was a magnificent experience. I worked on a construction site at the university. I didn't know how to work with aluminum or glass, but I learned. I was told that I had good behavior. We were well treated and the boss paid for our housing. I went there on a two-year contract. At first, I got $12 every five days, but when the Ministry of Labor gave me a work permit, my salary increased. After one year I received a cable from my wife saying that one of my sisters had died. My boss paid for my return home. I worked in Singapore three years in all, and built this house with what I earned. But we are suffering now. I want to go back. But it's not possible. You see, it requires money."◆

BELLI Mohammed insisted we look at the photographs of his time abroad. A happy, well-fed young man smiled from the album's pages. Belli, his diminutive first wife, sat with us, straining to see the photos. She appeared older than her thirty-eight years: an orange sari fell from her body at angles, leaving no discernible roundness. Even her delicate hands were thin and bony. When we sat alone later in the day, she said that she remembers the years of her husband's emigration with deep sadness. Married at fifteen, she was a twenty-four-year-old mother when her husband left her in charge of their baby daughter and four sisters-in-law. Since he returned she has given birth to two more daughters.

"I cared for my husband's sisters while he was away, as if I were their mother. I had to make do with the 500 takas (approximately U.S. $13) which he sent each month. He borrowed money to go to Singapore and I had to see that it was repaid. Just think, we had to eat and repay debts with 500 takas. Every month I took a loan, because after paying his travel debt, I had little money left for food or school fees. When he returned he brought money and some goods, which he sold—saris, cassettes, pants, sandals. With that money he cleared his debts and finished buying this house. After three years in Singapore, all he was able to do was buy the house; that is the result of the separation. There's nothing else. Except another wife. With the money from Singapore part went to pay off the loan, part to build this house, and part was used to marry another wife. Now there is another woman who lives in poverty, and he beats her just like he does me. That's what men do. He has a second wife and has two daughters with her. And no income. Sometimes he finds work, sometimes he doesn't. All day yesterday he looked for work but didn't get any. We didn't have anything to eat last night."◆

Labor migration is a livelihood strategy that is expanding rapidly in all regions of the world. Mohammed Abdur Rouf's guest worker experience was a positive one compared to most, despite his inability to make it work as a long-term family survival strategy. Others are not always as fortunate. Remittances may increase family security temporarily, but the overall impact of migration for work on family unity, parenting, and spousal relationships is profound and poorly documented. Women left behind suffer particular hardships. Being without an adult male often undermines their status as well as their physical and economic security. The long-term impact on the migrant worker and his or her readaptation upon return home is also little understood.

A study by the Bangladesh Institute for Development Studies notes a phenomenon that, alas, applies to other poor regions as well: "In the final analysis we see that to cope with the deteriorating economic situation in rural areas, relatively new households were adopting the strategy of male out-migration, leaving the households to be managed by women in the absence of a surrogate male head. For households with little or no assets the strategy adopted by the male was in the form of divorce or abandonment of wife and children."[2] A story from the West African nation of Mali confirms the harmful consequences of this "strategy."

BAMAKO, MALI

Mali has less than one-tenth the population of Bangladesh, yet the two countries share a poverty level of over 50 percent, a custom of teenage marriages, and an average family size of five to six persons. Each also has an ever-expanding need for employment for its young. One unemployed father was very candid about his plans to leave his family and "escape" despite the fact that he had suffered from the abandonment of his own father.

Nansa Diabite, 70
Assetou Bagayoko, 52
Sekou Coulibaly, 33
Maimouna Coulibaly, 30

The Bagayoko-Coulibaly home, in the center of Bamako, consists of two rented rooms that look out on a central courtyard shared by five other families. The furnishings are sparse; mattresses placed directly on woven floor mats serve as couches during the day. High on the light blue walls hangs a series of photographs of family members of different generations. Several among them are of two or three women together; I learned later that these were portraits of Assetou Bagayoko's cowives.

Assetou, a receptionist at a nearby health facility, shares her home with her seventy-year-old mother as well as with a son, his wife, and their two children. Her mother, Nansa Diabite, is an impressive figure who had dressed for our visit in flowing *boubou* and matching turban, twisted and

Assetou Bagayoko (*second from right*) and her dependents: (*left to right*) son Sekou Coulibaly holding baby Fanta, daughter-in-law Maimouna, and mother, Nansa Diabite

tied with flair. Gold hoop earrings, bracelets, and watch added to her modish allure. Nansa had been married twice, each time to men who had other wives. She left the first husband when her daughter was two years old because he went to live far from her parents. The second husband was a veterinarian and "was kind enough to send my daughter to school." Since she had no children by him, she inherited nothing when he died. It was then that she came to live with her daughter.

ASSETOU   Until Assetou's eyesight deteriorated to the point where office work was out of the question, she had worked as an executive secretary, earning better pay than in her current job. As it is, her salary provides for ten people: she helps out her mother, Sekou, his wife and two children, and four more of her nine children, who "come by from time to time."

Assetou married twice like her mother. Both husbands had other wives. From her first marriage she had four children and "a host of problems" with her three cowives. She attributes the problems to the fact that she was the only educated one among them.

"They were jealous of me and the fact that I worked. They made it very difficult for me, and my husband wouldn't intervene. We divorced. Then I met a man who worked with my uncle. We married and had five children. He was very difficult. He beat me just like the first husband. I couldn't take it anymore. We are divorced. In all I had nine children. Neither of the husbands wanted to keep their children. They don't help with them—no money, nothing. If a woman can work, the husband doesn't care about her.

If she can't work, she must stay with the husband—no matter what. Sekou's father doesn't even help him find a job. I paid for him to get a driver's license, but he can't find employment."◆

SEKOU While the women prepared tea in the courtyard, tall, lanky Sekou, dressed in traditional Malian robes and embroidered slippers, told of his predicament and plans.

"I've been living with my mother for ten years. I'd been at my father's house before, but he wouldn't give me any money, so I came here. If I have money, I go to see him; if not, I can't go. Everything would be fine if I had work. As it is, I have to live here with my mother. I want to get out of here, go off on an adventure, abroad. I want to go to Paris. I have friends there. Lots of my friends want to leave. But I'm stuck with this marriage. I didn't want to get married, but they arranged it because we had been going out together and the families intervened. I had to. It's eleven years now. If I had the opportunity, I would abandon her. I don't know how to get rid of her. If I could, I would pack my bag and go. But I have nothing. Mother has nothing. It's not possible.

"Between the parents," he reasoned, "it's always the mother who is on the children's side. A man only cares about the children of the woman he loves. After a divorce, her children don't matter."◆

Sekou's daughters are ages one and eleven. He has witnessed the difficulties his mother had in raising children without support from their fathers; he observes her daily struggle to provide for him still—yet he dreams of escaping familial responsibilities, just as his own father escaped his.

Sekou's wife, Maimouna, is a pretty young woman with a heart-shaped face; she was eager and proud to describe their meeting and courtship. "We chose each other; that is the way it is now. Young people can make love matches." Maimouna knows that her husband wants to leave Mali in search of work; she is unaware that he is among a growing number of men worldwide—as documented in the Bangladeshi study—who see no alternative to their poverty but abandonment of family responsibility.

The fact that one quarter of the world's households are headed by women raises the question of how well men are adjusting to change—how willing or able they are to assume the responsibilities of son, husband, father, and provider in times of social and economic transformation. Malian sociologist Tieman Diarra believes the crisis of authority and responsibility in families is of economic origin. "In families which traditionally relied on a patriarch, it was his duty to provide for the family . . . often a large group of people. Because of the current economic—or in the case of Mali, ecological—situation, the family head is no longer able to fulfill that function, to provide for so many. As a result, his real and moral authority is eroded. With the advent of market economies, excessive materialism, and the push to consume, obedience to an outdated patriarch is replaced by individual aspirations. Responsibility for the family group diminishes." In sum, the patriarch of patriarchy appears to be defaulting on his responsibilities, leaving women to struggle on in a world still controlled by men.

But Dr. Speciosa Wandira Kazibwe, then Ugandan Minister of Women, Youth, and Culture and currently vice president of Uganda, questioned the image of the traditional patriarch as reliable family provider. "Male responsibility? Was it ever a reality?" she asked, as we spoke in her office. It was housed in a war-maimed building with broken windows and doors, cracked tiles, and leaking ceilings. The war had also claimed the ministry's office furniture, looted during the violence. The scarcity of precious light bulbs forces workers to rely on occasional window light. Kazibwe. Dr. Speciosa, as the minister is known affectionately, is not one to be deterred by work conditions. She continued: "Women and children did most of the work in nonmonetized economy. Men had authority but no responsibility. It was women who provided food and herbal medicines, so men didn't have responsibilities; they only had to discipline the children of different wives. Now the economy has uprooted people from villages and the burden is being carried more and more by women—for it is women who know how little people are eating.

"Women are doing everything because the children are in school and the men are off. Women's roles haven't changed—just broadened. We are trying to make men responsible—responsible for the first time."

Dr. Kazibwe's analysis underlines the urgent need to better understand how the ongoing inequities of patriarchy, further complicated by the disruptive trends influencing the lives of men and boys in the era of globalization, have contributed to the hardships families face worldwide.

Far to the west of the Ugandan capital, on the road from Kasese to Bushenyi, I met one family that belies the minister's pessimism.

BUSHENYI, UGANDA

We'd traveled through mountains of lush banana plantations and then dropped to the nascent Rift Valley, where the land turned to dry scrub flatlands. After Kasese, the road climbed through a volcanic **Peter Asiimwe, 74** mountain range where bananas trees—and men peddling **Ben Asiimwe, 20** bicycles piled high with bananas—were everywhere.

Just before Bushenyi we turned off the road to stop at a modest house hidden among banana trees and towering corn stalks. It was the home of Peter Asiimwe, his wife, and their two teenage children. The two-room house was built with mud-plastered walls over a wooden frame. The furnishings consisted of three chairs, a table, and a three-year-old calendar hanging near the entrance. The impression was one of extreme tidiness; nothing was out of place.

PETER Sitting just inside the doorway, sheltered from the sun, Peter Asiimwe looked terribly thin, and delicate of frame and features. His luminous light brown eyes almost matched the color of his worn woolen sweater, and he sported a Chaplinesque mustache. Painful peptic ulcers, he said, prevent him from working as much as he once did.

"Every morning I wake up and start tending the coffee plants, the banana plantation, or the vegetables. That's how I live. I don't have any activity apart from my farm. You see, I want to educate my children and the farm is the only source of income. But I worry because I'm growing lame and getting thinner and thinner.

"My income doesn't meet our expenses, but my wife works and brings money to the family. She is at the market now, selling her vegetables. She makes handicrafts and digs for others [works as a laborer on others' farms]. I'm a lucky husband to have my wife's contribution. I couldn't support us alone. My parents were also farmers. They were married in church; I'm their firstborn. I've never moved from this place. We grew our food—millet, banana, sorghum, groundnuts, and beans. It was not for sale, only for our family. I went to school up to primary three, no higher because education was not important then. Land was plentiful. Everyone was free to build where they wanted. The climate was good for growing; there were enough trees for firewood and for building. Today, the population is increasing. You have to buy your land. There is often drought; the trees have been cut. In addition to our food, we have to grow cash crops to pay for our families' needs: school fees and clothes. Even beer has become a cash crop. We used to make it only for the family; today we sell it.

"We are struggling to give our children an education. We had eight children but the firstborn died in her teens. She had polio and was crippled from the waist down. Just two remain at home now. We are trying to shape their future. We want them to be independent of us. For parents, the main worry used to be that a boy grew up and got married; a girl was brought up to be a housewife. Today it's different. If you don't give a daughter an education there's no hope for a good marriage. If you don't give a boy an education there's no hope for his future.

"When I stopped school, I first worked on others' farms. Then I met a family friend who was a shoemaker. I admired his work and asked if I could work with him. I stayed with him for two years, until I was able to make shoes satisfactorily. Then, in 1953, I met an Indian man who set up a small shoe factory and I went to work for him. That job gave me a lot of money and experience. The Asian man promoted me. I was able to get ahead; I taught others and had a lot of friends. I even looked different from people in the village because I had something appropriate to wear.

"Following independence in 1960 my Asian friend went away. He was very kind to me; he left all the equipment—tools, materials, and his contacts. He left me everything. It was a gift. But the business depended on ordering materials from abroad. When I worked with him, he was the one who ordered everything—materials like leather, machines. I didn't know about importing. My education didn't permit me to know how to order things. I had to eat the capital he left with me. Then, during Idi Amin's regime, the Asians' shops were given to others. Mine was still officially in the Asian man's name, so it was given to another, not to me. The army came, escorting the people who were given the properties. The building was taken and I was chased away. Many people lost their business or houses like that. We had to vacate our homes and sleep in the swamps. It was lucky we had the swamps, otherwise we wouldn't have survived. All our things were confiscated and looted. They stole my goats and cut down the banana plantation. They filled their lorries with bananas or anything they found. That is how my failure started. My children are grown now. Those still at home contribute to the family's income. During the holidays they work to pay half their school fees. The boy works for other farmers when he can."◆

BEN   Peter's son, Ben, is a twenty-year-old student at Mushanga Secondary School. He is the physical opposite of his father: tall, broad-shouldered, and strappingly healthy. But his father's ways have marked him: he speaks in the same thoughtful way, the same low voice. Ben likes religious music and sings in the church choir. He studies a lot, he said, and is obliged to study by candlelight in the absence of electricity.

"We don't have a radio either, so we get our information from newspapers at school. I'm about to take my secondary school exams and if I could, I would like to go to university. I want to study social work and social administration; then I could help the people around me. I come from a poor family but I'm fighting for the opportunity to go to university.

"When I come from school I either work in the garden or brew bananas into alcohol, into beer, in order to raise school fees. I'm against drinking alcohol, but if there was no alcohol consumption, I wouldn't have a source of income for my school needs. That's why I do it. It's a problem for me: I discourage alcohol drinking in my family, but at the same time I promote it for others. Most of the young people my age aren't helping to build our country. They don't work; they just drink alcohol all the time. Alcohol is a big problem."◆

Ben's concern for the destructive consequences of alcohol abuse was echoed among families in most of the countries I visited. Like domestic violence, alcoholism is often a silent tragedy, hidden in shame. In El Salvador, a wealthy and well-known Salvadoran businessman, Jaime Hill (interviewed in chapter 9), is a recovering alcoholic who created the Fundacion Antidrogas de El Salvador (FundaSalva), a foundation for the prevention of substance abuse. His personal experience led him to create an institution dedicated to education about, and prevention of, alcohol and drug abuse. When we met at the foundation, he passionately denounced the destructive power of alcohol.

"It actually breaks down the whole family system. It's the drug that causes violence. I'm not talking about hating people, killing people; I'm talking about violence in the manner I address you, in the way I talk to myself. Alcohol causes violence in the home, and when that happens, the family is destroyed. If the family is shattered, the whole society is destroyed. For me, alcohol is the most harmful drug we have in Central America."

BANGKOK, THAILAND

Klong Toey is a famous low-income quarter of Bangkok. Many who take refuge there are but a few years removed from Thailand's rural areas. It lies not far from the port of Bangkok, and many residents of Klong Toey work in and around the port. Children, dogs, trash, and stench fill its narrow alleys as does the laughter of its residents, and open sewers stretch along either side of the passageways. The social worker who accompanied me there explained, "People have shelter, food, and, yes, TV. There is no 'basic needs' problem here. It's privacy and public services that are in short supply. And security. The residents of Klong Toey are squatters; their cement homes could be summarily destroyed if Bangkok's Port Authority decides it wants the land."

Kwan Singtoh, 56
Moy Singtoh, 51
Suvhit Monpowana, 31

The Singtoh home is one among the hundreds that crowd Klong Toey's alleys. A concrete-block structure, it has four small rooms: a kitchen, sitting room with a television set, and two bedrooms.

KWAN The family's fifty-six-year-old grandfather was about to leave for work at a child care center where he is a security guard. He had a calm, self-confident manner as we talked together in an open area, a sort of makeshift playground near the house. Dozens of children gathered around, and occasionally he shooed them away. Despite the distractions, he told of his rural origins and why he had come to Bangkok as a young man.

"When my parents died we had to parcel up the land, to share it among all the children. There wasn't enough for each of us to raise a family. We are separated, all over the country. Only one brother stayed on the land. I thought

I could find a job and earn more money here in the city. Now I provide for my family better than on the farm because there you get money only once a year; here you get a salary every month. If we don't get expelled, we are fine. We are happy here."◆

MOY The happiness of which Kwan spoke seemed less than complete when, later, I talked with other family members in the quiet of his home. The central object in the sitting room was the refrigerator, the only furniture, a couch upon which we sat. Quan's wife, Moy, is fifty-one years old and, like most of her neighbors, of rural origin. Although she complained of living in one of the world's most polluted cities, she believes that her mother's life on the farm was far more difficult than her own. For one thing, she told us proudly, her tubes had been tied after her seventh child. To supplement her husband's income, Moy sells homemade noodles on the street.

"On good days I earn 100 baht [approximately U.S. $4 at time of interview] per day. I invest 60 of it for the next day and we have 40 left for eating. My husband earns about 3,000 baht [U.S. $120] a month; he gives it to me. It is our custom that the wife controls the money. But what he earns is not enough. Sometimes I have no money because he spends it. He likes to drink alcohol. He spends 60 baht per day on drink; that's a lot. He says if he doesn't drink he can't sleep. When he's drunk he scares people and insults everybody. We quarrel. I think I'm going to separate from him. I've had enough. Every day he's drunk. Some days he hits me and pushes me around. It was the same for my mother; she also married a man who liked to drink. The big problem for wives in this community is being afraid of the husbands who are drunk. Drinking. Alcohol, drugs, and the sniffing. In this area, I hear violence everyday. Everybody goes out to work and comes home tired. The husbands use drugs. There's not enough money. There is always violence in the home. Anytime, night or day.

"When my husband wasn't drunk he used to help me sell the food and help in the house. Then he changed. Most men don't like to work in the house, don't like to help the wife. Some men are ashamed to help. Now it's changing; men are getting better. They understand women more than in the past. My son-in-law, for example—he's a good man."◆

SUVHIT The "good man" Moy admires is thirty-one-year-old Suvhit Monpowana, who works in the shipping department of the Bangkok Port Authority. He is one of seven children, and his father died when he was a small boy. A graduate of commercial high school, Suvhit was proud to say that his younger brother was about to finish university, a goal to which he had made monthly contributions.

"My mother taught me how to take care of the family, of children and a wife, because before I got married, I wasn't good. I spent time going places just like other men. But when I got married my mother said, 'Do this, do like that.' She told me not to go anywhere to see girls. She said I should help my wife in the house. Some of my colleagues like to drink. Every day they invite me to drink with them, but I refuse. I don't have the time. I just want to work and save money for my family, for my children's education. If they go to university they can get good jobs. When I have the time, I spend it with my wife and children at home."◆

Suvhit relishes "family time," and he is not alone. As is illustrated in chapter 3, elderly men often say, with a tinge of regret, that they have more time to be grandfathers than they had to be fathers. The competitive work ethic, say many, is a cause of men's alienation from close family ties and hence of family disunity.

BISHOP, CALIFORNIA, UNITED STATES

The Owens Valley of California lies between the Sierra Nevada and the White and Inyo Mountain ranges. Stretching north-south for 120 miles, it was once rich with wildlife and the Navajo-Paiute people camped and hunted its vast

Alvin Bowman, 70

Bob Mora, 42

plains. Today their ancestors live on reservations, but their influence on local culture is present everywhere, even in the name of the county: Inyo County, meaning, literally, "the dwelling of the great spirit." The reservation I visited is in the town of Bishop and includes approximately 1,000 people who live in small homes well-distanced from one another and who find employment either in the local tourist industry or, more often, far away from the valley.

Alvin Chief Bowman (*rear*) with daughter Barbara Mora, three grand-daughters, and son-in-law Bob Mora

For generations, the men of the Bowman-Mora family have had to leave home to find work, often in military service or the mining industry. Its patriarch, Alvin Bowman, is a Navajo born to a herding family in Arizona. He, too, served in the army; he too, had worked in the mines. Just a few weeks before we met, his beloved wife had died. He lives alone now, visits her grave each morning, and remains distraught at her passing. As I approached his home on a narrow unpaved driveway, a blacksheep dog greeted me unsuspiciously. The hand-built house is a warm, welcoming dwelling, cluttered with photographs and mementos on the walls. Scattered magazines, blanket-covered couches and chairs, and a well-used kitchen all seem to be waiting for Alvin's daughters to come and clean up. Two carpets, which he said were made by his mother, hang on the walls; beside one is Alvin's faded photograph of his mother in the traditional Navajo skirt and blouse.

ALVIN Alvin Bowman is a tall, slim, distinguished man with delicate hands and a lovely smile. His turquoise Navajo jewelry set off the bronze tint of his skin as he spoke softly of his family. He began, however, with a question, "Why does anybody want to talk with us about our family? It's such a sad story."

He began by saying that he had only two years of schooling because his father needed him to help with the herding. "My mother wove blankets. She took them to the trading post and got enough money to buy sugar, coffee, and potatoes. Just enough to keep us going."

He proudly recalled that he had left home as a teenager to ride in rodeos, the only Indian allowed in rodeos at the time. But I learned later from his daughter that he had lost his only chance to become a professional rodeo rider when he chose to remain with his wife at the birth of their first child. The couple eventually had eight children; two died at birth and the six others were forced by the family's poverty to attend "Indian schools." There, as boarders far from home, they were systematically "de-Indianized": separated from one another, forbidden to braid their hair or speak their language. They were taught to be ashamed of their Navajo-Paiute origins. The entire family was scarred by the experience.

"My first child was a daughter. She went to college for two years and then married a Cree Indian in Oklahoma. He was an alcoholic and one day he beat her to death. Their children came to live with us. One of my sons joined the army and fought in Vietnam; he returned addicted to drugs and alcohol and became a recluse, right here in Bishop. My last son was an alcoholic; he died at twenty-six, the alcohol got to his lungs. Another daughter ran away from the Indian school into an abusive marriage in which she endured years of beatings and abuse. [This daughter is interviewed in chapter 10.] Why would anyone want to read a book about me? It's such a sad and lonely story."◆

BOB The following day I went to meet Alvin's son-in-law, Bob Mora, who is married to Barbara, the daughter who ran away from the Indian school.

The Mora home is a mobile unit parked at the end of an unpaved driveway. Wood is stacked outside, ready for winter heating. A goat and a tiny black mongrel dog guard the yard. Inside a fire was going in the stove. The dominant color of the interior is brown and beige, which matched the colors of the Navajo carpets that covered the sofa.

At forty-two, Bob Mora, a heavyset and quiet man, is an employee at a local supermarket. A baseball cap covers his long hair, which is tied back in a ponytail. A large turquoise ring, given to him by the tribe's elders, signifies his position in the Paiute community. Sitting in the warm cluttered living room of his home after a day's work, he reflected on his experience as boy and man.

"I saw my dad only on weekends when he came home from the mines. I don't feel I know him as much as I would like. We didn't have much contact. My mom was the one who taught us how to behave.

"As soon as I turned eighteen, I joined the navy, right out of high school. Some friends had done the same and I thought I knew what I was getting into. It was glamorous and all. How wrong I was. There is such a conflict between our traditional life and the need to earn a living in the modern world; it warps our values. You have to be very aggressive with everyone. For me it was hard; it went against my nature. The whole way of thinking is different. There are a lot of harmful things, psychologically. After work they expected you to go out drinking, partying—all very macho. So much behavior and motivation is built on this aggressiveness and competition, and putting down someone else, whether in business or relationships. It's very offensive to elders, to women and children.

"American white culture has failed to a certain degree and now they are reaching for meaning in our Native American traditions. One of the things I believe is that boys are pushed into very ugly behavior, thinking that it's being 'manly.' It's the opposite of being a man—which for me is being responsible and caring and nurturing your family. It's all turned around.

"As a man trying to function in that environment, it was stressful. You have to be aggressive all the time. You have to put on an act. Around aggressive people you have to be aggressive, or you will be pushed to the back. If you don't fit in, you will lose your job or assignment. You get passed over. It's the opposite of cooperation. They say, 'We are together, etcetera,' but it's not the reality. It's 'me, me, me.' Where I work now, it's that way. If you aren't aggressive, you aren't worth having around."♦

Bob Mora struggles each day with the conflicting demands of traditional and "modern" manhood. His experience is similar to those of men in cultures that have been catapulted into the industrialized world in a generation or two. In his case, the struggle included bouts with alcoholism, drugs, and a dissolute lifestyle. Then, relying on the traditions of Native American culture, Bob found an equilibrium. He now serves as a tribal elder and teacher of young men.

Bob Mora's comments on the travails of competitiveness in the workplace echo those of an elderly gentleman in Japan.

TOKYO, JAPAN

Eighty-year-old Takeo Takano resides in an affluent neighborhood of Tokyo where houses are veritable small mansions and quiet gardens abound. Takeo is a retired lifelong employee of the giant Japanese corporation Mitsui. He lives with his daughter, also a Mitsui employee, her artist/sculptor husband, and two **Takeo Tanako, 80**

Emmy Saito, 40

grandchildren in their garden-encircled home. There are two houses in the garden, the large one for the young couple and their children and a bungalow for Takeo.

TAKEO Essentially blind, yet adept at finding his way around with a guiding cane, Takeo Takano came to greet us in the garden and then led us to his sun-filled study. He sat facing us, clutching his white cane, fingering it with delicate hands almost as if playing a flute. Once we learned about his family, he told about his years as an executive of his corporation, which sent him to work abroad. He pondered aloud about the corporate work ethic that had governed his life—and that he hopes is now changing.

"When I was representing Mitsui in Argentina, the company driver once asked me, 'Why do the Japanese work even on Sundays?' He said that Sunday wasn't just to go to church but to have a rest, that it was important for people to rest and enjoy themselves. I began to think about it and ask, 'Why do we have to work so much?'

"Competition is the reason we work so hard, of course. Yet because you work so much, there is also competition between your professional and family lives. I started to wonder why I had taken my family with me to Argentina. They were with me, but I never spent time with them. All I did was work. For a lot of people at Mitsui, once they take off their Mitsui identity tags there is nothing left of them. They have no personal identity. After retirement people don't know what to do. Many retired men get depressed. It's important for men to face this problem. Young women employees, for example, don't stay after work. They don't want more money by working overtime; they'd rather go home to their families. We have to learn to do this."◆

EMMY Takeo Takano's daughter, Emmy Saito, is an interpreter and translator at Mitsui's headquarters. She is a very elegant young woman, energetic and self-assured. She is married to a well-known Japanese artist/sculptor and architect, Sumio Saito, and believes that her closeness to the artistic world has helped her avoid the rigidities and competitive work ethic of corporate life. For this she was grateful.

"Japanese society is a male-dominated society. Women have to squeeze themselves inside somehow. It's difficult for us, to be sure. Men should try to understand their families more. I think the change in demographics is going to have an influence on how men behave toward work, families, and toward working women. Just in the past five years, between the birth of my first and second child, I've seen a change. My boss had expected me to quit my job after my first pregnancy; he had that kind of attitude. But when I was pregnant the second time, he told me he was looking forward to my return to work in about a year. Society changed in those five years. When that same man was going to have a first grandchild, his daughter was scheduled for a C-section. He worried about it, and was very happy to announce publicly that he was going to visit his daughter. Society has started to appreciate the importance of being a member of a family, rather than a member of a company. Men are now able to say publicly that they have to go to a meeting for their child's orientation. Before it was not possible. Men are changing, becoming more flexible. It's a good change."◆

It is true that "men are changing." In all the countries we visited, both men and women agreed that education, travel, and improved communications have opened new vistas and roles to them. Both adjust as best they can. One can argue that the changes are more beneficial for one sex or the other, or that change has resulted in more stress on one sex than the other. But it is clear that the pressure for men to provide for families in times of limited economic opportunity is often overpowering. Women's entry into the paid workforce could, thus, be interpreted as a means to ease that pressure. Some men recognize this; many do not.

AMMAN, JORDAN

In chapter 3, we met an elderly Palestinian woman, Haja Mohamed Hussein Jaffe, who lives with her son in a newly constructed neighborhood of Amman. Hers was a story of resistance to modern ways of life. Her son's story

Naser Hussein Masshour, 46
Adla Mohammed Masshour, 38

is yet another story of adaptation. The steps leading to the Masshour family's new home were exceedingly steep, a mark of homemade miscalculation. We entered a large, simply decorated room: unpainted cement floor and walls, mats and thin mattresses against walls, cushions here and there. The Masshour family is of Palestinian origin; most its members have lived in exile in Jordan since 1967. The home shelters ten people: Naser Masshour, his wife, their six children, his unmarried sister Adla, and their mother.

NASER   Naser is a frail, soft-spoken man with dark, darting eyes. He deferred to his mother at all times, even when she interrupted the voicing of his opinions before we were able to talk alone.

"As a father, I have to carry a heavy load. Children need many things in life. I don't allow them to go in the street, for example, I must give them all the things they need, advise them how to live, and give them as good a life as I can. I want them to be educated. This is my aim. What I want is what they want. Doctor? Fine. Lawyer? Fine. Farmer? Fine. I want them to be good people. When my son asked me what he should study at university, I said, 'You choose. It's your life.'

"Luckily, I've never had to go abroad to find work. So many others have to do so. I am an office employee; this way I was able to keep the family together. My mother and father, for example, have always lived with us. My father was a very good and brave man. He was only a farmer, and he suffered in order to send us to school. He spent time with us, advised us. He loved us too much. He talked about the family history, about my grandfather, their hard life. For my children it will be very difficult to live the way I do. There is so much change. In the past, for example, women worked as farmers and did everything around the family home, but they didn't go very far. Now women go in planes to other countries. Sometimes a woman wants to work. I agree, but she should not forget her children. She must be careful to give them time, to teach them, to make them grow with her. My sister works as a kindergarten teacher, but, you see, she never married. She has no obligations as wife and mother."◆

Naser Hussein Masshour (*second from right*) with his sister Adla (*far right*), and his dependents

ADLA Adla Masshour, Naser's sister, does not think she is without obligations, regardless of the fact that she is unmarried. On the contrary: in talking about her work, she explained that she returned to school at age twenty-
four in order to acquire the skills needed to help her family financially.

"I had completed only the third grade. When we came here after the
1967 war [with Israel], my father was elderly. I was obliged to help my family. I had always wanted to go back to school, and when my father passed away,
I decided to do so. I had to complete primary and secondary school before going
to college. Many women are doing this. Life is too costly, with housing, education, and health expenses. Women want more for their children, a good education. They work so as to provide these thing for their children. People used
to gossip about me going out to work, but I didn't care because I had a goal."◆

This mix of stories and opinions illustrates some of the effects of modernization and social change on men and family relationships. The oft-found need
to leave one's family to find work; the pressure to pay more attention to work
than to one's family; the stress of competition, sometimes leading to dysfunctional
behavior; and a resistance to women's changing roles are but a few of the concerns mentioned repeatedly by those interviewed. Some of the more positive
examples of how families cope with the complexities of change are found in
the younger age groups or in societies where leaders, institutions, or public
policies have focussed on the emerging needs of contemporary families. Such
is the case in a small town north of Shanghai, China.

TAICHANG, JIANGSU PROVINCE, CHINA

The houses in this semirural area are very impressive. They appear to be
small apartment buildings but are, in fact, simply multigenerational homes
for large rural families that are taking part in an experiment to bring
industry to rural areas. Families continue to farm but are employed by small
industries at the same time.

The Zhang family's large house is typical of the multigenerational homes
in this area. A vegetable garden monopolized what would otherwise be the

Zhang Yeuqin, 56
Zhuang Jinsheng, 42
Gu Yongyi, 33
Zhang Yanfeng, 30

front yard; only a half-dozen cabbages remained unhar-
vested, wizened by the December cold. The welcome
we received was a demonstration of the warmest possible hospitality. Grandparents, two young couples
and two grandchildren live together in the large
two-story building; all took part in our visit.

YEUQUIN The elegant and outgoing grandmother, Zhang Yeuqin, is a factory seamstress. She was orphaned as a child and was too poor to go to school,
as was the case for millions of children prior to China's revolution in 1949.

Zhang Yeuquin (*second from right*) with her family: (*left to right*) son-in-law Zhuang Jincheng, daughter Yanfeng, granddaughter Xinyi, and daughter Yanpin

Two of her three daughters and their families share the house with Yeuquin and her husband. One daughter manages a small shoe factory; the other is an accountant at the local health clinic. The women all wore hand-knit sweaters, warm trousers, and tennis shoes to ward off the chill of the unheated home. The sons-in-law are both of rural origin; each had struggled for an education which would open the way to a better life than that of peasant farmers. One is a driver for a local factory, the other an employee of the village council. A seventy-six-year-old great-grandmother came to greet us when we arrived but was unable to participate in our conversation; her mind had lost its clarity. She sat for a time, observing and sipping the green tea we were ceaselessly served. Her daughter-in-law, Zhang Yeuqin, continued by telling the story of her childhood.

"I was three years old when my father died, six when my mother passed away. Both died of illness, but I don't know the cause. A younger sister died as soon as she was born, so I was an only child. My grandmother looked after me. There was no grandfather—just my grandmother, who lived by weaving straw slippers. We were very poor. Once in a while we had rice to eat, but most of the time it was porridge. My husband is from this village. We played together as children. He was a farmer but didn't own any land. We were both eighteen and he came to live with me and my grandmother, in our hut. Two years later, he had to go to the People's Liberation Army. He stayed for eighteen years, stationed in Shanghai. All that time we saw each other only once a year due to army regulations. It was difficult for us. My three daughters were very young, so I couldn't leave them. I grew rice and cotton to support us and my husband sent money from the army. Once demobilized, he became a truck driver for the County Transportation Company and he's home every weekend.

"We built this house in 1986. We had a hut for a house before, now we have this large bungalow. That's the important change. Our home shelters three couples and the children, all one family. Our life is much better now.

"We decided that our sons-in-law would come live with us because we think that daughters are closer to their parents. Our sons-in-law's families agreed to let them come here. Neither of the husbands was a first son. One is a second son, the other, a third. If either had been his parents' only son, it would not have been possible. We've also decided that my eight-year-old granddaughter will bring her husband to live in this house, and my grandson will bring his wife.

"At first we used to eat together, but when the families grew bigger, it wasn't convenient. Both young couples have their own kitchens, so we, the old couple, eat one year with one, the next year with the other. Each couple keeps its earnings.

"I'm happy to have my daughters and their families around me. At home women have much more say in things now. Especially in my case, since my husband is not at home, I make the decisions. My opinions have much more weight than in previous generations. My children respect me. In China, when a child is born, it usually takes the father's name. In our family, one daughter took my husband's name and the other kept mine. We want to keep the family together."◆

JINSHENG Zhuang Jinsheng is Yeuquin's eldest son-in-law and is deputy director of the Township Association, a type of town council. Heavyset with a large round face, he is a bashful man with a benevolent, kindly manner. He was obviously proud when telling of his struggle to get an education.

"My father led a difficult life as a fisherman; they went out in very small boats. We didn't have enough to eat or wear; we were always cold. After the liberation, he contracted typhoid and they didn't have the proper treatment for it. I was eight years old when he died. My two elder sisters married before he died, so only my mother, brother, and I were left at home. We had a very difficult time. My elder brother still lives with my mother; he is a harbor boat pilot.

"My mother didn't want me go to school; she wanted me to work the farm, but I was eager to study. When I was in the third grade, she threw my book bag in the fire. When I finished primary school once again, she said I had to work on the farm to help feed the family. I still insisted on going to school and, luckily, received a scholarship to finish senior middle school. Because of my education, I was able to become deputy director at the Township. It wasn't easy for a peasant's son. It's the result of my efforts and heart.

"I married at twenty-seven and came to live here. My sister's husband acted as go-between. I was poor and didn't want to get married, but my mother-in-law came to our house to talk about it. My wife and I had several meetings and decided to marry. Our society provided me with the opportunity; otherwise this would have been unimaginable. Just as there is no comparison between my parents' life and mine, my children have more opportunity than I did. My son will work in more scientific ways."◆

YONGYI The importance of education for Zhuang Jinsheng and his generation cannot be underestimated. To move beyond the life of daily physical toil and illiteracy is something that his parents could never have dreamed. The same is true for Gu Yongyi, the second son-in-law. He is thirty-three years old and a driver for the county-owned electronic parts factory.

"I was born of a peasant family in the next village. I was the fifth born of four boys and two girls. After high school, I did three years of military service and then became a driver for the head office of a township enterprise. It's local driving, so I'm home every night. My elder brother also lives in his wife's house. It is very unusual that the eldest son live with his wife's family, but people accept it. It's a major change. My wife carries her family name, and now my daughter bears my wife's name as well. If a son-in-law lives in his wife's home, the first child should take the wife's name; the second child should take his name. But now there is only one child allowed!

"My daughter and I are very close. I have a more flexible schedule than my wife, who has to work very long days. When there is no work for me in the afternoon, I come back home. So I have more time with my daughter. I hope she will study well and have a good job in the future. But no matter what she becomes, she's my daughter. You see, in this area, before Liberation, there existed the idea, and the practice, of male superiority over women. But now, so many years after Liberation and all the change, the belief that men are superior to women is gone; it no longer exists."◆

YANFENG Yongyi may be too optimistic about the depth of the change that has taken place in China. But as the two son-in-laws demonstrate, the younger generation, raised in a period of more egalitarian relationships between women and men, are redefining gender roles even in a strict tradition-bound society. Yongji takes delight in his fathering duties and, recognizing that he has more leisure than his wife, has crossed the boundaries of strict gender roles. His wife, Yanfeng, deputy manager of a shoe factory is duly appreciative.

"In my mother's time, women were looked down upon in one way or another. Even though all women worked, they were still not treated with equality. Now as long as women have the ability, they may do anything. There is more respect. My daughter can even keep my name, and I can keep my mother's. Because my work requires so much time at the factory, my husband and I share household chores. He does most of the housework and cares for our child. He's a good man."◆

One hears these stories of changing roles in nearly every country, but of course, they are often seen as the exception that confirms the macho rule. In Brazil, a father and son had strong personal views on the changes taking place.

MURIAÉ, MINAS GERAIS, BRAZIL

An old, wide, leather-seated bus, a common sight in rural Brazil, had carried us from tiny Limeira to Muriaé, a large market town bustling with early

Lenin Passos, 69

Leir Passos, 41

Ircema Passos, 63

morning trade. We were met there by Lenin Passos, lawyer, politician, pilot and hotel owner. "Doctor" Passos is semi-retired and lives in his hotel situated thirty kilometers from Muriaé, in the denuded hills of the Forest Zone.

LENIN The Hotel Y Juca Pirama—which means "the man who is going to die" in the Tupi Indian language—is a big blocklike establishment that accommodates up to ninety guests. It is nestled against a hill surrounded by a bamboo grove mingled with pines. The tiny forest is just big enough to go for shaded walks or to imagine what this region was like when Lenin Passos was a child. Lenin is a big man, with heavy features and soft blue eyes. He was dressed in a light blue shirt and beige trousers, dapper dress for a man who spends his afternoons watering his flower garden and playing with his grandsons.

"I was a lawyer, trying to earn a decent living; I didn't have time to be a father. But with my grandchildren, I have time. My children studied in Rio, so we spent holidays together and I let them do what they wanted. I told them, 'The world is for those who study. Whoever is more intelligent will get ahead.' I'm really raising my children through my grandchildren. They live with me, they study with me. They do theater with me. They like to spend time with me. It's the patience of older people they like. You have more time, more patience, when you're older. You can tell them family stories they should know. My grandfather, for example, came here in 1883. He was an engineer who spent his life running hither and yon, surveying land for others. He had eight children and named them all after great people. My father's name was Vivaldi, his brother was Edison, another, Ibsen. My father continued the custom, so I got to be Lenin.

"Of my grandchildren—four grandsons and two granddaughters—the girls are the top students. Women are entering nontraditional fields, but with great difficulty. It's tremendously difficult. In Minas, there are female judges, and one chief of police is a woman. You can see things changing, but it takes so

Lenin Passos and son Leir in the garden of their hotel

long. Men are afraid of women taking their places. I have a niece who graduated the top student in electrical engineering in Fundão University in Rio.
She speaks English fluently, as well as French, German, and Portuguese. She
still can't get a job because she's a woman! What else can I say? The
director of EMBRATEL, the telephone company, is her mother's cousin. When
she graduated, we spoke to him about her. We did everything we could to
get her in. They just kept saying, 'But she's a woman.' Such is our country!
Let the woman go wash clothes and cook!"◆

LEIR   Lenin's son, Leir, just turned forty. Two years ago he gave up the profession of electrical engineer to settle nearby and manage his aging parents'
hotel. With dark eyes, greying temples, and a sensitive manner, he is a handsome man, at ease, unhurried and pensive. He and his second wife, Jaciara,
an agricultural technician, live in a small house reached by a cobbled
path which leads downhill from the hotel. The house was filled with sun,
flowering plants, and musical instruments. It was there that Leir spoke of
his marriages, his divorce, and his obligations to his children.

   "I was twenty-six when I married the first time. My ex-wife is from Muriaé.
We went to São Paulo for my job, but she had problems being away from
her parents. In my family, when I left home we would embrace and say good-
bye and off I'd go. But in her family, they would all cry. We divorced, and
she now lives in Muriaé. It's convenient to be so near the children. Our relationship has been civil but when I remarried, it got better. She remarried,
too. I was alone for two years before I met Jaciara. I didn't know what I wanted.
Jaciara is a more independent woman, an agronomist by training. Her parents were divorced so she understood my predicament; her father was an alco-

holic, a fine musician, but an alcoholic. Jaciara had to give up her job to come here, but she thought more of me than of her career.

"The divorce didn't affect the children much. They were four and five years old when we separated; they're twelve and thirteen now. I see them every weekend. By law, my financial responsibility to the children is total. I have to pay their keep until they are eighteen. The law in Brazil is very serious. It's the same whether you are rich or poor.

"Family relationships have changed considerably. In my father's family, between brothers, it was more united because they lived close by each other. Since then Brazil has developed in such a way that families are dispersed. I think it's better not to have your family too close. They don't allow you to make your own mistakes. You don't have to live close by to have their support. And you might pick up their vices too. Between men and women, relationships are changing due to women working. It's better now. If a woman stays at home as she used to, problems are greater. She doesn't like staying at home and invents problems. The advantage of working outside, apart from earning money, is that problems at home come into proportion. There's more dialogue. But in Brazil most men don't want to see their wives go out to work. I believe it is beneficial—but most men don't think so. Machismo has diminished, but there's still a lot. A man on his own can't provide for a family, so he has to put his wife out to work, but he still remains "machista." The problem comes when she starts to earn more than he does. There is a lot of ignorance in this country.

"Most of my friends have their heads screwed on the right way. Their wives are educated and weren't raised just to get married. That's how it used to be: girls stayed at home and got married. Now they study. My father always said that women should study hard and if they wanted to get married then they could better choose who they wanted. He told my sister that if she didn't want to marry and was educated, she would have had other alternatives. I learned a lot from my father. We don't learn how to parent at school, we learn from our parents. Your father brings you up one way and your mother another way. I tended more toward my father, because his ideas were more liberal."◆

IRCEMA   Leir's mother, Ircema, is a small, elegant woman who for many years has devoted her spare time to working with the poor of Muriaé. She is certainly far from being as conservative as her son's words imply. When asked what she thought about Leir's divorce and remarriage, she replied, "These multiple marriages today are a good thing. It will go on happening. I don't think you should stick with one man all your life just to satisfy society. I'm not against changing husbands."

Then, looking at me with a mischievous smile, she added, "Although changing husbands is just changing defects! This is happening because women

are more independent now. Today women are presidents; they're not tied to the kitchen, waiting for the husband to have lunch. There are no more slave women, as there were in the past. I think men are losing their status."◆

Is Ircema's conclusion a just one? Is it necessary that men lose status if women are to gain some? Feminists have long claimed that partnership—women and men, together, braving an increasingly complex world—is the only viable way to cope with the realities of contemporary family life. Successful families are partnerships built on mutual respect and caring, in which men and women, old and young, have a voice.

Yet, as might be expected, any perceived challenge to traditional authority and power has both personal and social repercussions. According to those interviewed, there are men just about everywhere who view women's entry into the paid labor force as a disturbing trend, especially in times of shrinking economic opportunity. Feelings of vulnerability at the individual level can be, and are, easily exploited for political gain. More democratic relationships between men and women are viewed as a danger by those who wish to retain power. It may be that the rise of religious fundamentalisms—Christian, Muslim, or Judaic—is in part a manifestation of the frustration and fear felt by some men. It certainly stands to reason, since fundamentalists of all stripes share the common belief that women should return to submissive, homebound roles under the authority of family males.

What is also evident from these interviews is that competition in the workplace often requires that employees pay more attention to their work than to their families. Amy Saito, her father Takeo Tanako, and Bob Mora have had different experiences with the same phenomenon.

That said, feelings of alienation and vulnerability among men originate in trends other than those of the workplace. The traditional or customary foundations of male dominance have been slowly eroded by more equitable laws covering everything from education and employment opportunities to divorce and child support. Sexual harassment, long a constraint for women entering the workplace, is, like domestic violence, condemned by human rights law although, as is the case regarding so many laws, enforcement lags far behind.

Still another challenge to traditional male dominance came from advances in reproductive health sciences. With effective contraceptives for women, male dominance in matters of sexuality and reproduction has ended; women are becoming full partners in planning families and in negotiating sexual relations. This is true, however, only insofar as contraceptives are available or their use is permitted by a husband. For the sons-in-law in Taichang, China, planning families and even naming children for their wives' family is a remarkable benefit of their partnership marriages.

It is important to recognize that women are not the sole beneficiaries of efforts to create more equality between the sexes. Progressive legislation provides opportunities—and encouragement—for men to become more involved in family life. Parental leave, job assignments that consider the needs of spouse and family, and dual custody of children in case of divorce are examples of how the workplace and the legal system can be more family friendly and considerate of husbands and fathers. As Lic Zoile de Innocenti, a sociologist at University in San Salvador, points out, "To feminists, people always say, 'You are taking women out of the family' and we reply, 'No, we are trying to get men into the family.'"

In many places, it is working. Attitudes are changing. Leir Passos wants his wife to work, wants a partnership marriage even in a culture that his father condemns as macho. Fathers-in-law like Umematsu Tanaka are joining daughters-in-law in household tasks, freed of the constraints of customs which prohibited friendship or affection between them. Young fathers are becoming more involved with their children's education. Increasingly, it is expected of them. Grandfathers like Lenin Passos are "fathering" their grandchildren with enjoyment and pride, free to be educators at last.

That said, the malaise hovering around the evolution of gender roles permeates world society. Patterns of authority, responsibility, and power are in flux; more democratic relations in family and society are being formed everywhere. And so are the sad cases of abandonment of families by men who seek only to improve their own lives. The men and women who speak here on the shifting responsibilities and expectations of manhood—of being provider and husband, father, brother and son—give evidence of the tremendous transformations now unfolding.

Six | Changing Childhood, Challenged Parents

Mom and Dad were like a pool of water. When you went out and got thirsty, you could come back and get a drink and were refreshed. Then you could walk away and continue on your journey. If ever you needed to come back, you knew where the spring was.
— Barbara Mora, Bishop, California

The eighty year old Chinese grandmother, a retired schoolteacher, sat quite still, reminiscing. Wrapped in a worn silk jacket, she warmed her hands by rubbing them constantly, attempting to ward off the December chill of her Beijing apartment. "In my family, boys and girls were treated the same. Maybe my mother loved the boys more than the girls, but my father liked girls very much. All four sisters had senior middle school schooling. We all had the same opportunities. It was my father who influenced me most. He had a very modern outlook. For example, in the Ch'ing dynasty people wore pigtails. If they cut their pigtail, it was to signify that they had accepted modern civilization. Some disapproved, of course, but my father let us cut our pigtails. We four sisters were the first in our school to do so. We were allowed to go swimming, skating, and we even rode bicycles; all these things were allowed, even encouraged, by my father. We wore white blouses and white shoes for these activities, and when we came home we would wrap the shoes up in newspapers and place them under my father's bed because my mother didn't like us to wear them. My mother still wanted us to bind our feet. My father wouldn't permit it."

Parents have far more impact on their children's lives than they may realize. The emotional and psychological development of the child commences with the first interaction with parents. Throughout the series of interviews conducted for this book, participants were asked, "Who was it that influenced you most as a child?" Answers, regardless of country or social class, fell within the same narrow parameters: "Both my parents." "My grandparents." "My father taught me how to work." "My parents taught by example." "My mother taught me how to behave." "I learned from everyone because we all lived together."

Women often cited their mother as the critical influence, since she taught them how to do "women's work." Many men said that their fathers taught them about work life and religion. Very rarely were teachers or religious figures mentioned as significant influences.

In the last two chapters, women and men told of their struggles with the new roles and behavior required in a rapidly changing world. That struggle continues into their years of parenting—for which, again, there are few models, given the swiftly evolving environment in which they must function. Large families where siblings help care for one another are fewer and fewer; so are the extended families whose members live nearby and contribute to a child's ethical and emotional formation. Fewer, too, are families that adhere to the strict gender roles that hitherto defined both parents' and children's lives.

When both mother and father seek salaried work outside the home, parenting and child care practices are necessarily changed. In the industrialized world, many nuclear families must rely on outside help with child care. The less developed nations have begun to face the child care dilemma as well, and pressures are bound to increase as traditional ways of life recede. With both parents away at work, schoolteachers, religious institutions, and public child care facilities are becoming more influential elements in guiding a child to adulthood. Families herein tell of how they raised, or are raising, their children—the strategies employed and the problems encountered.

QUEENS, NEW YORK, USA

The taxi from La Guardia Airport streaked along a highway and barely slowed down when we entered the quiet working-class neighborhoods of South Ozone Park in Queens, an outer borough of New York City. Tree-lined streets of garden apartments and narrow single-family homes, traversed by early morning bicycle riders, finally led us to the home of African American septuagenarians Dorothy and Harvey Mangum.

Harvey Mangum, 78
Dorothy Mangum, 76
Richard Mangum, 48
Derren Ameer Mangum, 22
Ann-Marie Shepperson, 31

The Mangum home is a small, neat house, surrounded by a well-kept lawn and flower garden. The interior features thick carpeting, comfortable armchairs, a glass-caged doll collection, and dozens of photographs of family gatherings and smiling children of all ages. I was asked to sit on the large pearl-colored couch in a sitting room crowded with plants. Fritzy, a dog in her late teens, barely noticed my arrival.

DOROTHY   Dorothy Mangum, seventy-six, is a distinguished and graceful woman with white hair and a lithe, athletic build. She was dressed in a bright pink blouse, blue jeans, and a leather belt.

Dorothy Mangum, grandson Derren Ameer Mangum, Harvey Mangum, and son Richard Mangum (*seated*)

Once we had settled down with our coffee and homemade cookies, Dorothy Mangum seemed perfectly at ease telling about her family and childhood. "I was born in Harlem, the youngest of six children. We lived on 138th Street." Dorothy smiled as her thoughts took her back in time. "We lived in what people would call tenements. It was a real neighborhood. The church was just across the street, and our school was only a few blocks away.

"My mother was a housewife, my father a musician. They were both from Barbados but they met here. We lived with my mother's sister and her husband. They didn't have any children, so we were like their children. My mother's sister died in the spring of 1923, and my father died that October. My uncle was kind of attached to my mother and didn't want to be away from the family, so he and my mother married. I was five years old. I didn't know much about my father, so I loved my uncle and he loved me. He died when I was fifteen.

"I was one of six children, and my oldest sister was married and had four children. The whole gang lived in that apartment together. We all had our chores to do. My mother sometimes did laundry for people. She was the strongest person I've ever known; she knew how to handle everything, how to solve any problem. She taught me to be fair to everyone.

"My stepfather worked in a factory as a stock clerk, and my brothers got jobs at hotels as waiters. That's how we got along. In those days, there wasn't too much advancement for young black men. The difference between opportunities for white children and black children wasn't really discussed, not like it is today. Everybody was interested in earning a living, getting married, having children, and supporting the family.

"I was the first high school graduate in the family, but I couldn't afford to go to college, even to the city colleges. They were free, but you needed books and things. A friend of mine worked for Clairol, the beauty company, and helped me get a job there. I started at $8 a week; I gave my mother $5 and kept $3. When I married I continued working for Clairol; by then I was making $14 a week. I was twenty-one; he was twenty-two. We moved in with his mother and brother. It was a six-room apartment, and we had our own bedroom. A lot of young men had gone off to war. Both my brothers were in the service. One was sent to Japan, the other to Germany.

"During the war we both went to work at Sperry Rand, where they made gyroscopes for airplanes. When I was expecting my second child I stopped working; I stayed home and then had a third child. We began to think about moving out of the city [Manhattan] because we had a two-bedroom apartment with a family of five. I knew we could save the down payment if I went back to work. So that's what we did.

"Between my husband and my mother we managed to see that the children were taken care of. Ricky, the youngest son, was a little over two; Claude was four and Carol must have been nine or ten. By then my husband worked for the subway system from three in the afternoon to eleven at night. I had a daytime job with the Immigration and Naturalization Service. Luckily my mother lived just a block away. I prepared the children for school; my husband fed them lunch; my mother would pick them up in the afternoon and take them to her house until I came home at five-thirty.

"The children were always supervised. Everybody had their homework to do and they had to do chores, like washing dishes. It took them forever, but they managed. Once in a while, when things didn't go well, I would say we needed to have a meeting about family spirit. Everybody had to pitch in.

"As a mother, working was hectic, to be sure. I would only get to see Harvey late at night when all the chores were done. I could get by on about five hours rest. Many of my colleagues would go out together on Saturday or Sunday, but having been away from the children all week, I felt I couldn't go; my duty was to do family-oriented things in my free time.

"I really feel my children got more attention than children whose parents were home all day. For example, when I would be ironing, Ricky would read the newspaper to improve his reading. If I decided to watch the news, we watched together so they learned. We tried to find things to amuse them at home, without going into debt. We always had friends who were in the same situation, where both husband and wife worked. We went to their homes and they came to ours.

"There were those who didn't approve of mothers working outside. Once I asked a woman, 'Where do you work?' and she answered 'I don't go out to business,' as if that was bad or something.

"When my daughter got married, they lived with us for two years. When they had their first child they moved out. What I'm proud of about her is that after she had four children, she went to college and graduated with a bachelor's degree. Her husband and Harvey looked after the children.

Her husband was a policeman, so he worked odd hours. Since she went to night school, Harvey would go straight to their place after work and stay with the children until her husband came. Eventually she obtained her master's degree, all by night school."

Dorothy Mangum hesitated a moment, as if perplexed by an idea. Then she added, "You know, I wanted my children to love me, but if they didn't, it wouldn't bother me, as long as they are good people—and I told them that, too. I just feel that way. I think parents have to sacrifice their time. Childhood doesn't last long, so parents should make the most of it, devote more time to their children, take them to places like zoos, to broaden their outlook. Not just send them to the movies, but go with them and see what they are seeing. Try to guide them. We tried to do that. In fact, we were married twenty-five years before we went on a vacation by ourselves.

"I didn't have time to belong to the PTA, but I always looked at the children's schoolwork, and even learned something by reading their books. I think many young parents aren't prepared for parenthood. They think a child is like a possession. I see young people with a baby, all dressed up, as if the baby is possession, not a real person.

"You know, I don't know whether you are born a certain way or whether it's your environment. A little of both I guess. But sometimes I hear people abusing their children verbally—telling them they are never going to amount to anything. I never thought a parent would talk that way to a child, saying, 'You're no good' just because the child didn't do its homework. Why not say, 'Listen, you did badly this time, but try to improve, to do a little better the next time.' That's the way we build children's confidence. And we have to."

Once again, Dorothy Mangum was overtaken by memories; a faraway look captured her face. "I was fortunate that I found a husband who was very understanding. He came here from the South, from the Carolinas, when he was about ten. His father worked as a janitor in the tenements. People used to say that if a man is good to your mother, he's a good man. Harvey was very good." ◆

HARVEY Grandfather Harvey Mangum, seventy-eight, has stark white hair like his wife and a lucky space between his front teeth. Sadly, he is not as fit as his wife; for the past fifty years he has suffered from a degenerative spinal condition which causes a slow, halting gait. He is a soft-spoken gentleman who was no less anxious than his wife to tell the family's story. He told how everyone he knew was on welfare during the Great Depression, including his own mother. He had found employment with the Work Projects Administration (WPA), a federally funded jobs program, clearing Staten Island of its swampland. A longtime employee of the Transit Authority, he retired over twenty years ago. His words were punctuated from time to time with a broad, joyous smile.

"It's been a great life. I baby-sat in this very room and learned about Sesame Street! Derren, my grandson, would be there on that couch; we'd be talking and he'd fall asleep, and I would put him to bed. My daughter had four children and wanted to go back to school to get her degree, so we babysat for them. I would go from my job to her house and stay until she came home. Dorothy and I enjoyed it because we knew we were helping them.

"Being a grandparent, there are all advantages—no disadvantages. Because I love them. There's no secret for guiding a family—no secret; it's just love. They need to make the most of themselves to get ahead. We always taught them, 'Treat people like you want them to treat you.'

"It's been a good life and it still is a good life. I guess I'm very fortunate, because all of our children turned out to be pretty good citizens. I'm proud of what they've done and accomplished. I just wish it on everyone—that they are, or could be, as fortunate."◆

DERREN   The grandson who, as a child, slept on Harvey's couch, is now twenty-two, a recent college graduate and an aspiring musician who has organized his own musical group. A handsome and outgoing young man, Derren Mangum remembers the time spent with his grandparents while his parents attended law school. He recalls the caring atmosphere with affection.

"We spent so much time at my grandparents. I was very little, but I remember playing with the old dog, Fritz, and Grandpa would read me stories and books about nature. I would always fall asleep in the chair. I was lucky to live so close, only a mile away.

"As far as important influences on me, it was definitely my parents and grandparents. I've come to appreciate their influence more in the last couple of years. When you're always with your family, you don't really understand their influence. My parents kept me moving in the right direction and put things in perspective.

"That's one thing that's important for me: what each generation does for the next. We have to be responsible, because there were so many things my parents and grandparents didn't have, and yet they gave them to us. My family has done so much for me; now I have the responsibility to do whatever it takes for them."◆

RICHARD   Derren's father, Richard Mangum, is a lawyer and a prosecutor for the State of New York; he reaffirmed his son's statement on responsibility when we talked the next day.

"My parents' example—that's the only standard I know, the one I use. We taught the children by example because that's what my parents did. With my sons, I talk about what I expect from them. They don't question it.

"Parents work and share the home duties. You provide the right example, set your goals, and do what you are supposed to. I'll do anything necessary to protect and shield my children. You know, you never stop being concerned about them."◆

ANN-MARIE Another Mangum grandchild, Ann-Marie Shepperson, thirty-one, is a teacher. She, too, is sensitive to the strong family bonds espoused by her parents and grandparents, saying, "When we were growing up, my mother worked as a paraprofessional and, at the same time, went to school to get a bachelor's degree. Sometimes I would wake up in the morning and find her at the table, typing a paper, knowing she didn't sleep at all. I began to realize the difficulty my mother was going through in raising a family and going to school at the same time.

"In terms of my grandparents on both sides, the comfort of knowing that they lived in the same block and were there for you gave a sense of stability and security. Seeing what they went through in life influenced me.

"As a teacher I see so much change in the way families educate their children. And there is animosity coming from parents toward the school and its teachers. They send their kids to school and expect us to be baby-sitters. But when we try to talk to the children or discipline them, most parents don't like it at all.

"When I was growing up there were consequences for things we did. If I didn't do the right thing, something would follow, something that I didn't want to happen—be it a talk, a spanking, being put back in a class. We didn't argue like children do now; we didn't try to blame someone else. If a teacher said we did something wrong, that was it. Today, with parents' busy schedules, they are not as heavily involved as before. Kids blame their problems on the teacher, and, of course, the parents side with the kids."◆

For days after meeting the Mangum family, I marveled at their family story. It is one of inspiring familial solidarity and of parenting built on intergenerational partnership. Both husband and wife worked full time while raising three children. That they value children and family above all else is the reason for their success. Vacations, time together, outings with colleagues—all were sacrificed for the good of the family. Once the children married and had children of their own, they chose to live nearby and the grandparents rearranged their lives so that the young working couples could study for advanced degrees without the worry of child care. Now the grandchildren attend the best universities in the United States. The family is solidly united, thanks to the grandparents' devotion and a willingness by all to take turns helping one another. Dorothy and Harvey built a strong partnership based on respect and responsibility. It is a partnership that inspired their children, and now their grandchildren.

From China comes the story of another grandparent's contribution to parenting. On the outskirts of Shanghai, in a high-rise apartment building among a dozen others, I met a retired factory worker and grandmother who, like the Mangums in New York, doubles as a child minder.

SHANGHAI, CHINA

Shanghai is more of an experience than a city. Its thirteen million inhabitants all seem to be on the streets at the same time, in cars, trucks, on cycles—going, coming, shadow boxing, or, like one group outside my hotel window at eight in the morning, dancing the fox trot to 1940s band music. The vitality of the city is legendary, of course, but it is also indescribable. To walk its streets or stroll in its gardens is to encounter pure wonderment at the creative energy of the Chinese people.

We climbed two flights of stairs to reach the apartment that is home to grandmother Hu Xiuying, her husband, a son and daughter-in-law, and one small granddaughter. They share two rooms, plus a kitchen and bathroom, all crowded with the belongings of four adults and a child. Each room had a small walking space, which could be converted to other uses at a given time of night or day. I learned that yet another son leaves his infant son with the grandmother as well, and that he and his wife often sleep in the apartment. In this crowded space it might be considered a blessing that Hu Xiuying's husband is a long-distance truck driver and not often at home.

Hu Xiuying, 59
Huang Chang, 31
Chi Wenmei, 30

XIUYING   Grandmother Hu is a small woman with a large smile. Dressed in a hand-knit gray woolen cardigan and black slacks, she talked of the way her life had unfolded.

"I come from a peasant family, but my parents worked on other people's farms, so I wasn't needed for fieldwork. We were four children. My two elder brothers finished primary school, but my sister and I didn't go at all. At the time it was the custom that girls stay home to help in the house.

"My husband and I come from the same village. Our marriage was arranged by our families. There was no courtship. The matchmaker just came to my parents and told them about my husband. My parents then said to me, 'He is a good boy and is working in Shanghai. You will have a better life there than in the countryside.' Since my parents believed it was a good marriage, of course, I accepted. I was nineteen years old. I didn't see my husband until the wedding day. Because we were poor, the marriage ceremony was very simple. We just made a new quilt and then lived together.

"I was very happy to come to Shanghai; it was a place I was longing for. I found work making bricks on a tunnel construction site. My husband and

I get along well; I've had a happy life with him. We discuss everything together; we are equal and decide things together. As for our money, we put it together and use it as needed.

"I have three sons. One works at the glassworks, another in a plastics factory, and the third is a hotel employee. I have one grandson and two granddaughters, one child for each couple.

"The baby of the son who works in the plastics factory lives here because the parents' lodgings aren't big enough and there's no running water. They keep their things there, but in fact, it's more convenient here. We all live in this room. I look after the baby, because a child has to be two or three years old before it can be sent to kindergarten. When the parents have free time, they come to see their baby and help me with housework. When they sleep here, they share the room with me. When my husband returns we put up a screen.

"I have a television in my room but I have no time to watch it. I have no leisure time, because my granddaughter is constantly naughty and the baby needs a lot of attention. Besides, there are many things I don't understand because I don't have much schooling.

"I think my grandchildren will have a much better life than we have. Life will get better generation by generation."◆

WENMEI Chi Wenmei is the daughter-in-law who resides in the apartment with her husband and four-year-old daughter. She is a small, delicate woman with hair that fell halfway down the back of her white sports sweater. She held her head to one side, as if always wondering what question would be asked next. Wenmei is also of rural origin, although both her parents became factory workers. Her mother died of liver problems just after retirement from a chemical factory; her father has since remarried. Wenmei

Chi Wenmei, her husband Huang Chang holding their daughter Chi, and grandmother Hu Xinying

operates a loom at a textile factory where, she says, the shifts change continuously and noise is a constant problem. She is hoping to find less demanding work and, someday, to have a home of her own.

"I married when I was twenty-five and came here to my father-in-law's apartment. My husband and I met through an uncle who lives nearby. Our courtship was considered rather long, five years.

"The money arrangements in our family are good: my mother-in-law has her own small pension, my father-in-law is also a pensioner. My husband and I, together, earn about 750 yuan, and I give 120 yuan to my in-laws each month because we keep the baby here. [1 yuan was equivalent to approximately U.S. 10¢] We share tasks like marketing and household chores. We all put money in a drawer, and whoever is going to buy food takes the money. When I come home, I clean up the house.

"After I give money to my mother-in-law and pay for my daughter's kindergarten, we still have some left to buy things. But it's difficult to save for big purchases.

"I think the one-child policy is very good. We get subsidies for child care from the government and a single child subsidy from both our factories. They also provide milk for my daughter. Even without the policy, my husband and I would have had only one child. We don't want more children. With contraception there is no danger we'll have another child. I've had an IUD for four years now; it's very good, no side effects at all.

"My mother's generation followed the tradition handed down for thousands of years: they all obeyed their husbands. It was just a matter of course. But society has changed. Women have status in society. We both work and have incomes. Why should I listen to a husband?"

Wenmei was obviously enjoying herself being so outspoken. She laughed aloud, adding, "My husband does what I say. Of course, if I say the wrong thing, he will not follow me."

Suddenly looking serious, the young woman continued, "I think my daughter's generation will have a difficult time because they are all single children. They are very self-centered. When they get married, they won't be like us. Will they tolerate each other? For this generation of 'Little Emperors,' it will be very difficult. They all want to be first, to have their own way."◆

CHANG Wenmei's husband, Huang Chang, resembles his mother; his wide smile and trusting manner are nearly identical to hers. He took me to meet his supervisor at the Yaohua Glass Works, where I learned that the factory's production of automobile windshields and highly technical glassware is primarily for the export market, some for limousines in the United States. It was obvious from the interactions at the factory that Chang is a respected employee. As we sat in his apartment hours later, he told how, as a high school graduate, he chose to go into the military for a while. After two years he returned and found employment at the glass works.

"Military service is not compulsory, but I joined the army because I wanted a job. If you do military service, you get training. Then you are assured of a job when you are demobilized. Besides, I was young and liked the idea of going off to the outside world. When I came here I was first apprenticed to an old worker, a master craftsman. I worked with him for three years before becoming independent.

"My father is a very hardworking man who works seriously at everything he does. This is what influenced me. As for my mother, she is a great woman and is very careful about family relationships. She keeps the family together. This, too, has been a good influence on me.

"I know that my parents had a very difficult life bringing up all their children, and I will do my best to see that they have a happy evening of life. Whatever we can do, we will do. That's why we would like to live together. The only problem is the housing conditions; maybe we can move to a bigger place. But I want to live with them so that I can look after them.

"I have to be a good son and be loyal to my father, but for my daughter I want to be a good father. When I have leisure time, I spend it with her. We take her to the park. I explain everything to her. I want her to understand the world. At home, I take every opportunity to teach her. This way we'll become closer. She is only four years old; she can't understand some things yet, but this is what I do.

"My father never took me out. He went to work, then came home to rest, and there was little contact. He had to support a family of six, which is a very heavy burden. He had no extra energy or leisure time to give us. But I have only one child. I can devote all my love and leisure to this one child. And there are more equal relations between husband and wife these days. We share the household tasks so we can take the child out together. We never go out without her.

"We want our daughter to see everything. I just hope she can go to the university and then get a desirable job. I worry about her, though. I worry that these single children think only of themselves. There won't be any family harmony because husband and wife will each be an only child. They are all very selfish. Not caring about others is a terrible thing. And when they marry, they will have two pairs of parents to look after.

"I discuss this with my colleagues; we all have the same fear. It's difficult to educate our children because the older generation is spoiling them. When I want to punish my daughter, for example, the grandparents stand between us and say, 'No, you shouldn't do that.' I don't want my parents to get angry, so I stop. The child knows very well what's going on; she knows she will be rescued. It's the same for all my friends.

"We are lucky because we live with my parents, and my daughter sees how to respect family members. She knows that you should be good to your parents and grandparents. If we were in a nuclear family, maybe she would be more spoiled. When I buy food, I put it on the table and I tell her, 'Take this to Grandpa or Grandma or Uncle.' We teach her that when you have something you have to share it with the family. An only child doesn't have to be spoiled. You just have to teach them how to behave."◆

In the hours spent with Chang and his family I caught a glimpse of the "Little Emperor" problem. Four-year-old Chi demands constant attention. Fortunately, her parents are well aware of their predicament. They are among those parents who are learning to guide their children in vastly different circumstances than those of their own childhoods. They share tasks, resources, and decision making, and do their best to meet the needs of their parents and their daughter.

Of course, this is not always the case. Working mothers, if unaided by their spouse, are in a particularly stressful situation facing a lack of leisure and an overload of chores and responsibilities. In addition, in many societies, working mothers are frowned upon and single mothers are scorned. In Brazil, I met a single working mother who was determined to build better lives for her daughters, in spite of—or perhaps, in part, because of—the hardships she herself had faced.

NUEVO FRIBURGO, BRAZIL

The bus ride into the mountains above Rio was breathtaking. For two and a half hours we climbed into lush mountain terrain to where, in 1822, Swiss immigrants founded a settlement on land ceded them by the short-lived Brazilian emperor Pedro I. Perched at an altitude of 865 meters, Nuevo Friburgo is now a summer resort, and also boasts factories that have earned it the title of Brazil's "capital of intimate apparel." I was to meet a family of factory workers.

The Pereira home, perched on a hillside, had been built crazy-quilt style at different periods. One of its courtyards was used as a dining room, **Helosa Pereira Shuenck, 57** and it was there that the family assembled to greet us: grandparents, mother, daughters, aunts, and cousins. It was the eldest daughter, Helosa, who guided our visit.

At fifty-seven, Helosa is a beautiful woman—tall, slender, and dressed with flair. Helosa is one of seven children. She has but three: one daughter works as a hairdresser in Florida, another is a secretary in Rio de Janeiro, and the third is a schoolteacher in Nuevo Friburgo.

Helosa was widowed at twenty-nine when her husband was killed in a car accident. She was pregnant with their third child. She moved in with her parents and raised her three daughters by working in a undergarment factory for twenty-five years. She noted, matter-of-factly, "I was allowed to retire early because I worked in a polluted environment. Normally retirement is only after thirty years." She had not remarried and, as she explained, single parenthood had not been easy on her.

"I was married only five years when I was widowed. My husband was a mechanic and had his own repair shop. One of my brothers worked with him as an apprentice. My brother swore in front of my husband's casket that he would help me. But he did nothing. I had to sell the shop to him for very little. Today he has three houses, two telephones, two cars—all from that business.

"Three years after my husband's death I met a man I liked. My father refused him because there was a mentally ill woman in his family. Imagine! My father is a dictator, and things have to go the way he wants. He actually beat me up on account of that man. If I had rebelled against him, my mother would have suffered. He still bosses me around even today.

"As a child I couldn't go far in school. We lived in a rural area and the school only went up to fourth grade. We came here when I was sixteen; I wanted-ed to go to night school, but my father wouldn't permit it.

"I had girlfriends at the factory who attended school after work. I was desperate to go. But father wouldn't let us even put our noses out the win-dow at night. If I had studied, my life would be different today. I would have been able to earn more and defend myself when my husband died.

"When my daughters wanted to go to night school, my father said, 'No, they will only play around with men.' I was strong and said, 'You didn't let me study, but you won't forbid my children.' So they went and finished their schooling. They have good heads, thank goodness. Like anyone else, they have their defects, but I don't lose any sleep worrying about them. They live like other young people, go out in the evening, go to nightclubs. Thank good-ness I managed to fend off their grandfather.

"When the children were little I met men who liked me and said, 'If you didn't have your children, we could go around the world together.' If I'd been crazy, I would have left them and gone. But from the moment you have a child, you have a big responsibility. You have to give up a lot of things. That's how I think and that's how I act.

"For a woman alone it's difficult. She loses her husband, she works out-side the home, raises her children alone, is both mother and father. No one helps her. If a man loses his wife, two or three months later he has anoth-er one. I think women are much more responsible than men. We are all the same, all sisters all over the world, and much more responsible than men.

"That's why I say I wish I could be young these days! It's much better now that women have a certain autonomy. I wanted to study, but I couldn't. Now,

Helosa Pereira Schuenck (*right*) with mother Etelvina Constancia, and daughter Helenice

if a woman wants to study or live elsewhere, like my daughter Ana Silvie, it's possible. When she left for Florida I was sad, but I was also happy that she did what she wanted to do. If you know that your children will go off the rails or do stupid things like take drugs, you have to worry. But if you know they won't get into trouble, that they will look after their own lives, then you have to trust them.

"I didn't raise them for myself. I said, 'If you want to go, go. The house is here. You can always come back.'"◆

Having worked her entire life to raise her three daughters, Helosa has encouraged them to study, to go abroad, to do whatever their hearts and minds seek. Her vision of parenting resides in her children's development as fully individual human beings. Unlike her father, she treats her daughters as responsible adults who should be hindered neither by gender nor by education. On the other side of the globe, I met another strong single mother determined to live by similar precepts.

YINCHUAN, NINGXIA AUTONOMOUS REGION, CHINA

Yinchuan is the capital of the Hui Autonomous Region, a region in Central China settled by peoples of Persian origin who came over the silk route following the armies of Ghengis Kahn. The Hui people are Muslims and the region had remained fairly isolated until it received government investments in the late

Shan Yichang, 67

1950s. "The Hui are traders and like commerce," explained Shan Yichang, an associate professor at the local education college. "Our ancestors came here as traders and have continued as such. They're not very good or patient as farmers."

We found the entrance to the professor's ground-floor apartment by passing through an alley where small, closetlike structures sheltered an array of bicycles. Huge chunks of coal, waiting to be broken up into usable cooking pieces, were piled near the door.

Yichang is the mother of three; one daughter and two grandchildren live with her. She ushered us past the small, cluttered sitting room to her sunfilled bedroom, which serves as a second sitting room. It contained a double bed, a desk, a single bed, and a glass-fronted bookcase, filled to the brim with books and stuffed animals. No carpets covered the cold cement floor, but traditional Hui spiced tea was served to warm her guests.

Yichang teaches an advanced linguistic psychology course designed for certified teachers. She comes, she explained, from a long line of teachers. Her grandmother created a school for Hui girls in Beijing; her mother was a teacher, and four of her seven brothers are professors. "The teaching profession is greatly respected," she said. "It is a noble job. But we live very simply because the income is not high.

"When I was teaching in the Hui Middle School in Beijing, the principal was transferred here to the Ningxia Autonomous Region as the new governor in 1958. He wanted to take several teachers of Hui nationality with him. I said I was willing to go. My eldest daughter was six, the next one three, and the last was only ten months old.

"I was married at the time. My husband was a journalist at the *Beijing Daily* and could not come with me. He passed away in 1964.

"To come here without a husband and also work was going against Hui traditions. This is a rather backward region, and the religious influence here is very strong, especially in the less-advantaged areas.

"It was difficult for me as a single parent. Luckily I had an aunt who took care of the children. The most difficult problem was the limited financial resources. Also, I found it difficult to educate the children as I wanted. Whenever I had time, I tried to teach them, but there was so little time. With my grandson, now, I pay great attention to the development of his intelligence. Each time we go out, I teach him something different. I never take him out without a purpose.

"Among my friends who are single mothers, we talk about how difficult those times were. I never thought of remarrying because I had three children. I didn't want to have another family and create problems with the first.

"I had to distinguish myself through my work, make people respect me for my accomplishments. Being a woman, I had to be very careful, because of what one would say about me. I don't want any gossip about me; that is the saddest thing for anybody.

"For women, the important thing is to be independent economically, to work and have your own money. This is what brings change to women's lives and status, both in the family and in society. If women are deprived of education, no one will employ them. No employment means no independence. And what does that mean? You cannot raise your voice, in the family or outside."◆

For single mothers Helosa Schuenck and Shan Yichang, the importance of educating their children is indisputable. From their own personal experience as working mothers, they recognize the advantages of education in being able to provide for one's family and having the personal liberty to develop to one's full potential. They are especially determined to see their daughters educated, aware of the difference a good job and financial resources can make to a woman's life.

UN studies have documented the fact that more than one quarter of the world's households are headed by women, and that this trend is on the rise.[1] Whether they are highly educated professionals like Professor Shan or unskilled workers like Helosa, they face the difficulties of both structural and social discrimination. Single working mothers are often judged harshly and suffer from the lack of support available in large families. Their lives are frequently plagued by the absence of coherent, child-focused employment policies and social service systems.

The multiplicity of roles required of women by tradition and daily reality carry significant psychological and physical burdens for them and, by extension, for their families. Single mothers are particularly vulnerable.

Unlike the single mother who is criticized for leaving her children to go to work, the single father is seen as an almost heroic figure. Although they may confront some of the same practical challenges, such as affordable child care, the stigma of single parenthood does not seem to touch men.

(*Seated, left to right*) grandson Xue Qiao, Shan Yichang, the author, Yichang's daughter Gao Hong and son-in-law Xue Jianwei, (*standing*) grandson Xue Yan

The age-old difference in society's expectation of female parents and male parents is even evident in the English language in the connotations of the verbs *to mother* and *to father*. *To mother* connotates the act of nurturing and responsibility for the welfare of the child. *To father*, on the other hand, is associated with procreation alone. Until fairly recently, when the feminist movement began to call attention to the absurdity of strict gender roles, the two concepts stood separate and at odds. Fortunately, that, too, is changing.

The Susaka City, Japan, municipal employee, Masanao Nakasawa, whom we met in chapter 1, is an actively involved father of three. He shakes his head at what he sees as a lack of parenting around him. "People are so self-centered now; in this village, for example, people have discarded the communal habits of helping one another. Yet it's so important to teach children responsibility to others. That's why I try to spend as much time as possible with mine. When I come home from work, I'm always with them. We all have different schedules in the morning, so we all go in different directions. But in the evening we eat, study, and talk together. Every day. My eldest son plays baseball, so on weekends and holidays we go to the games together. That's the best way to teach children, just being with them."

For Masanao Nakasawa, finding time to be with his children is not too difficult. He lives in a small town, has a fine income, and lives barely five minutes from his office. For millions of other fathers, there are multiple constraints on parenting time, ranging from work environments to social attitudes to simple lack of resources or opportunity.

MINAS GERAIS, BRAZIL

In chapter 3 we met the family of Jao Araujo, an elderly Brazilian farmer on an isolated farm in Minas Gerais. His youngest son, Walter, is, at thirty-seven, a man who appears to have lived a hard life. He is small and narrow-shouldered, with dark eyes and **Walter Araujo, 37** a beard. His front teeth, above and below, are missing. With a smile and a gesture of futility, he announced he was father to seven children. "Seven children! If we had known about family planning, I wouldn't have had all these children."

Walter laughed aloud, but he truly meant what he said. "The last child was a difficult birth so the doctor offered to tie my wife's tubes. We said yes, of course. If you are living in rural areas and have land you need hands for labor—but we don't have enough land to warrant all the hands."

When we arrived at his home one Sunday morning, Walter was watching a soccer game on a black-and-white television which sat in a corner of his bedroom. It was an unkempt room with soiled walls and discarded clothes everywhere. His wife had gone to visit her mother, a two-hour walk to the east. Children of all ages, his own and their many cousins, gathered around to listen.

"All my children attend school except the two eldest, who have completed the four years available here. The oldest is thirteen, Maria Cristina. The youngest is five. I want the best for them, but we can't give them what they deserve. The girls work in the fields. I'd like them to learn to sew because I think it's very hard for women to do fieldwork. In Brazil, if you don't have education, you need land. If you don't have land or an education, you have to go to the cities. Only 5 percent of those who go there make good.

"The world has changed, but parents aren't keeping up with the changes. There is a lack of guidance. Parents aren't passing on what they learned from their parents, so children are learning from whomever or wherever. Parents should know what is good and what is bad so their children don't have to learn for themselves. Drugs, for example, are destroying families. Limeria is our nearest town and it has drugs. Some children have been taken by them. If the parents are no longer in control of the child, well, that's all it takes.

"I think it's a lack of communication among family members. Most fathers don't talk to their children, so there are misunderstandings. They're not giving them a moral base. If fathers talked to their children, they could direct them. Fathers don't treat their children with much respect, yet they expect children to respect them. Parents use swear words and tell their children not to. Parents are to blame; they get the children they raise."◆

Walter Araujo's emphasis on the role of the father and the importance of good parental communications was a common refrain in conversations with families everywhere. Yet in our fast-paced work life, men often have difficulty finding the time to spend with their children. Indeed, the culture of the workplace has tremendous influence on family life. Fathers who spend ten or twelve hours at work, away from home, are obviously less available to their children as teachers, guides, or advisors. They may want to spend more time with their children, but cannot. In the case where the mother also works, substitute child care becomes a major preoccupation and expense.

Toshihisa Tanaka, fifty, is an executive with a nonprofit organization in Tokyo. I met him at his home in Chiba one afternoon. Both he and his brother are married to professional women; each couple has two children.

"The workplace has a very important impact on families. Men work all the time; it is very difficult for marriages. We should help our wives more. In my organization, I know a man my age who takes holidays occasionally so he can care for his children. Since his wife works also, he sometimes has to take care of the children. I don't think it would be possible if he were working in a commercial company as do the majority of men in Japan.

"The basic idea of the husband and wife relationship is that we have to cooperate in bringing up our children. It's obvious that orking conditions have an influence, a great impact on this role."

Shared parenting is in fact a rather new idea, one that has emerged from need as well as more democratic relationships even within the more traditional family structures. Sayeed, the eldest son of the Fath family, whose interview appears in chapter 2, is a prime example of this trend. Sayeed is chief of the planning division at the Department of Health of the Tanta Governorate. His wife, Nadia, a grade-school teacher, is the only working daughter-in-law in the traditional multigenerational family that Sayeed's father governs. Sayeed's three children, he says, benefit from his wife's pedagogic skills, while his own style of fathering recalls his father's.

"Since my wife is a primary school teacher, she was responsible for our children's early education. For preparatory school, I was responsible. We belong to the parents' association at school; we know everything about our children's courses. But the future belongs to the children themselves, to their ability to be what they choose."

Sayeed and his wife are the transitional generation in the Fath family: she is the first wife to work outside the home. Their commitment to shared parenting and to a child's right to "choose" a future is rooted in traditions and behavior that give them a sense of security and purpose. For others, the transition has occurred without a sense of continuity, with less positive results.

FORT PORTAL, UGANDA

Yovanni MMK Muirumuba, a retired schoolteacher, sat in the front room of his cement-brick cottage, looking off at the mountains that form the border with the Congo (formerly Zaire). His eyeglasses were held together by tape and his treasured pipe had also seen better days. Yovanni Muirumuba's concern centered on a diminishing regard for the obligations of fatherhood. He reminisced about how his illiterate father had so wanted him to be educated that he walked and carried him, through the bush and over mountains filled with wild animals, for more than a week in order to deliver him to a village where he could attend school.

Yovanni MMK Muirumuba, 68

"My father was a herder who wore only animal skins, but he knew that education was going to be important. He wanted his children to have the advantage of education.

"Among fathers today, there is an 'I don't care' attitude about their children. In past generations there was more concern for children. The attachment and sense of responsibility is just not there. I am caring for two grandchildren because my son, their father, sent them to me for schooling. He lives thirty miles from here. I assumed he would help us out, but he hasn't. He doesn't even come to see the children. I am substituting for him, but that is not what they need.

"The fatherhood thing is missing. Part of this lack of paternal responsibility is purely economic. They say, 'I'm struggling to keep my nose
above water and then comes another child.' They shun the child because they
are already struggling."

Stories of those who default on their parenting responsibilies are not uncommon in any of the countries I visited. What is more common, however, are
the stories of parenthood sought and enjoyed. Due to their own childhood
experience, the road to confident parenthood, for some, has been troubled
by lack of positive experience, but in the case of a young Brazilian, it has
been nonetheless wise.

CACOAL, BRAZIL

Cacoal is a large town deep in the Amazon state of Rondônia. A number of
indigenous groups live deep within its rainforests, and it is now also home
to settlers who arrived to cut the forest and farm the land about twenty years
ago. The town has few paved roads; most houses are built of local wood, and
one soon gets the impression of being in a pioneering culture.

Three generations of the De Witt family are among those pioneers. The elder
couple, who are interviewed in chapter 8, came from the south of Brazil in 1970
with several members of their extended family. One among them was an
infant granddaughter, Monica, who is now married and a proud mother.

Monica lives a few blocks away from her grandparents with her policeman husband, Natalicio, and their two-year-old daughter. The couple are

Monica Witt Braga, 22

near opposites: Monica is a plump, round-faced,
sandy-haired woman of medium height; her husband is very tall and slender, with jet black hair.
They share a gracious and serene demeanor. They met, Monica explained,
when she went to apply for a job in a clothing store that Natalicio managed.
She blushed when she added, "It was soap opera romance."

Their small house, set back from the dirt road, is painted dark green. Inside,
leather chairs, a couch, and a bookcase are the only furnishings. Natalicio's
framed pencil sketches hang on the wall alongside a huge photograph of the
faraway ocean. Toys were scattered everywhere. It is a modest home, yet equipped
with refrigerator, television set, and gas stove. Monica proudly announced
that she roasts and grinds their coffee, of which she served innumerable cups
during our visit.Monica wanted most to speak about how she is raising her
daughter—who is adopted, and valued all the more for it—and the contrast
to her own upbringing.

"Our family is spread all over Brazil, some in Minas Gerais, some in Espirito
Santo. I was born there and moved here when I was two years old. We moved
first to Colourado, thirteen kilometers from here, when the government gave
out plots of land in 1977. But my father got malaria and became too weak

to work on the farm. We moved to Vilhena where he started delivering fish by truck.

"We are two boys and two girls. I was ten when I first went to school because we kept moving and it was difficult to go to school. And there were so few teachers in those days. I didn't even manage to finish the first year. At one point my father decided to send my brother and me to my grandmother here in Cacoal so that we could attend school. As a result, I'm very close to my grandparents.

"I still haven't finished school; I'm working on the eighth-year diploma. I was the oldest child, and my mother was very rigid with me. I wasn't allowed to have friends around. We were so isolated, outside of town, but I couldn't go out as young girls do. I had to stay and help my mother. She is very nervous and used to hit me with a stick, without reason. Whatever I did for her, it wasn't good enough. When I was nine, I would get up at six to make coffee, wash up, and fetch water from the river. I carried the water bucket on my head, and my neck would hurt. I washed our clothes and cleaned the house, but my mother always complained that it wasn't done well. When I was sixteen, my mother started making candies to sell, so I was out in the street, selling the sweets. Everybody felt sorry for me. 'Monica works so hard. You don't let her out. Let us buy her something nice to wear.' With my father it was even more difficult. My mother never gave me any opportunity to talk with her or my father. Even today, it wouldn't enter my mother's head to talk to me. I have no memories of conversations with her. It was very difficult for her to be close. I don't remember ever receiving a kiss from her.

"I learned a lot from my childhood. I treat my daughter completely differently. I think a mother should be a friend, and listen to what you say, and teach you how to live. At a certain age you should know what is right, what

Monica Witt Braga with daughter Jessica

you should and shouldn't do. It's important that I give my daughter lots of love and attention. It's something I never had.

"My daughter is adopted. I underwent two years of hormonal treatments to become pregnant, but it didn't work because it wasn't my problem. We found out my husband has a low sperm count. He was the one who should have been treated. When I married I was very slim, but with the hormones, I got fatter and fatter. I still have an excess of hormones." The young woman was saddened by her admission; looking down at her hands she smoothed the folds of her dress. Then with a smile, she joked, "If I do get pregnant, I'll probably have twins! We want to wait a while, and if I don't become pregnant, we might adopt another child. I would like to have three in all.

"We don't intend to hide from our daughter the fact that she is adopted. Lots of people know. If she had been my real child, I couldn't love her more than I do. I used to sit here crying because I loved her so much! You would never know her mother let her go. It affects children very much, the way their mothers deal with them. All the love she didn't get when she was inside her mother, she is getting now.

"We were lucky because a doctor helped us with the adoption. He found an unmarried girl who didn't want to keep her baby. What's so sad here is the number of abortions. Lots of people have abortions even though it's against the law. There are contraceptives, but people can't afford them. They get pregnant and are afraid to tell their mothers. One of my acquaintances got pregnant; she was almost seven months along and no one knew. She had the child and abandoned it. You see, there's no sex education in the schools. Young girls are ignorant or ashamed to buy contraceptives. I think mothers should talk to their daughters, help them so they don't have problems that lead to abortions. Fathers are important, to be sure, but the most important is the mother. For anything that happens, you run to Mama.

"I'd like to give my daughter all the things I didn't get as a child. I hope God will help me. I'd like her to study. There's not much to do in Rondônia, so she must get an education. If she wants to go to college, that's fine. I would like to give her everything."

Monica had begun to cry, as if listening to her own words had stirred something she had never known or expressed. She stood and hurriedly offered us another cup of coffee. She passed around a plate of biscuits and then took her place once again beside us. After a long silence she looked up, wiping her eyes, saying, "I've never had an opportunity to talk like this. It has done me a lot of good."◆

Monica's joy in adopting a child is one shared by parents everywhere who have taken on the responsibility of raising a child born to someone else. In the borough of Brooklyn in New York City, I met parents who had adopted a baby girl from an orphanage in a distant Asian nation. The parents told me that their desire to be parents, to offer a loving home to an orphaned child, met with resistance from some adoption agencies. In the eyes of some, they explained, their parenthood should not be allowed because theirs is a same-sex union.

BROOKLYN, NEW YORK, USA

Park Slope is a Brooklyn neighborhood of tree-lined streets with handsome three- and four-story brownstone and brick buildings. In a typical brownstone, two flights up, I found the sun-filled apartment of Camilla Brooks and Margaret Egan, two professional women who live with their daughter, four-year-old Miranda. Twelve years ago, Camilla and Margaret decided to join their lives and form a family together. A little less than three years ago, they completed their family, adopting Miranda.

Camilla Brooks, 47

Margaret Egan, 43

The apartment was littered with toys and small furniture suitable for a preschooler. It was a holiday and Heidi, the cat, and Miranda were watching a children's program on television when I arrived.

CAMILLA I was greeted by Camilla, a gentle and gracious woman with long, curly brown hair. She grew up in Boston, Massachusetts, attended college there, and went on to obtain a master's degree in arts administration at Columbia University. After working in the theater and art school communities, Camilla turned to social work and trained to become a psychotherapist.

"I had a rather traditional childhood. I grew up in a nuclear family with my grandparents close by and saw them regularly. There were relatives in the towns around Boston and they were very much in our lives. When we met at family events there were probably twenty to twenty-five people there. My grandmother was from Scotland and was the kindest, most accepting, nonjudgmental person I've ever known.

"My father died in 1976. My parents loved each other, supported each other all their lives; they were a model of a loving couple. My mother is almost eighty now. She remarried ten years ago. Her husband is ninety. They are amazing.

"When I was about thirty I began to explore and question my sexual orientation. I had had a loving and long-term relationship with a man but had often wondered about my attraction to women. I met Margaret at a health care center for artists where we both worked. It took a while, but after a couple of years of ups and downs we decided to build a life together.

"When my mother learned about my decision to live with Margaret, she said, 'I wouldn't have chosen this for you,' but she has included Margaret in our family.

"Early in our relationship we began talking about having children, but it took seven years from talking to having Miranda. When gays and lesbians adopt it is such a thought-out process, because it has to be—a very conscious deliberate process. I was anxious to create a family because of my age. I was the one pushing for it.

"We considered having a donor; Margaret was going to bear the child since I have some physical problems that could preclude pregnancy. But Margaret was starting a business and she, too, had some health concerns. We then began to think about adoption. But how? We weren't very good candidates for domestic adoption: two women. Some states prohibit gay adoption. Many religious organizations facilitate adoptions, and that can be a barrier as well. Also, a person putting a child up for adoption might be more likely to choose a heterosexual couple living in the nice suburbs rather than two women living in Brooklyn. That's the reality. Although within the gay community there is a baby boom at this point, some gays and lesbians consider it a radical idea to adopt a child. So the criticism comes from both the straight and gay communities

"We eventually settled on an international adoption, and decided that I would be the adoptive mother. Luckily the laws in New York state allow second-parent adoption; Margaret can be a legal parent as well. That is not the case in every state. Should anything happen to one of us, the other is protected and so is our daughter.

"Miranda had spent her first fifteen months in an orphanage and in some kind of foster care. She is a bright, happy child, outgoing and well-adjusted. I think this is due to the good nurturing she received from her caregivers.

"My mother was a bit apprehensive about us adopting, but not anymore. Just the other day she said, 'Miranda is a wonderful addition to our family.'

"We're both Miranda's moms. Sometimes someone on the street will say, 'Oh, she's lovely, who is her father?' We reply, "Miranda has two moms.' Her

Margaret Egan and Camilla Brooks with their daughter, Miranda

school is wonderfully supportive of our family configuration. It is important that we live in a community where there are other families like ours,
families that are biracial, multiracial, gay or lesbian parents. To me that's
very important in terms of Miranda not feeling isolated or different. There
are five adopted children in her preschool class: two from Russia, two
from China, and one from Guatemala. We know lots of adoptive parents.
When we become parents we identify more with other parents than anything,
be they gay or straight. When you have a kid you form a community of people who share issues and you get support from them.

"For Miranda I have the hopes that any parent has: that she be happy
and productive in her life, that she finds something she loves to do, that she
finds somebody she loves to share her life with if that is meant to be. If not,
that she finds satisfaction and happiness.

"I hope that she'll not be too burdened by being an only child. I worry
about that. I think if we had more space and more money we would adopt
another child—and if we were younger.

"I sometimes wish we lived closer to my family. I have a niece and a nephew—
older, twenty-six and nineteen—but to see Miranda bond with the twenty-
six year old makes me so happy. They are her closest relatives, and that is
important to me. When we are all gone, they will be her relatives, her family.

"Family is about how you care for one another, how you nurture a child
to grow and develop, and love them and give them support."◆

MARGARET   Margaret Egan, an information systems architect, is a New Yorker
of Irish ancestry with lovely red hair and a contagious sense of humor. She,
too, took several turns in her career before finding her calling. And she also
comes from a large, close-knit family.

"I grew up in Larchmont, New York. I was my mother's twelfth pregnancy
out of thirteen. There are seven of us—six brothers and sisters. I have sixty-
three cousins on my mother's side. It was a very close family. We would have
dinners for twenty-five people every week, cookouts, lots of drinking. My
father was a very devout Catholic, a daily communicant, and the church was
a great part of our lives.

"I went to parochial school and then to the Scared Heart Convent for high
school. The Catholic church did a real number on me. I still feel an affin-
ity to that faith, but I struggle too much with its politics.

"I met Camilla in 1986 and we've been together since 1988. She is my
soul mate, my emancipator. I love her joy of living, her intellect, and her
love of music. It took us time to understand what it meant to be a couple,
to learn to be together. When I told Mom, I said, 'I have wonderful news to
share—although it might not be great news to you.' Her response was, 'I just
want you to be happy,' which is what you pray for any parent to say. But

she also struggled with our situation morally; it was stashed away in a [mental] drawer somewhere.

"My second oldest sister, the one who raised me, 'dis-invited' me to her home when I came out. It hurt me very deeply. I am the same person, the sister whom she love and raised. I can't tell you how that affected me, what it is like to have your history rewritten.

"When we started down the road to adoption, I had to be convinced. I was not at all sure I wanted to do it, to give up all sorts of things and take on such a responsibility. We sought out a counselor who helped us understand how we could become parents together.

"Now with Miranda—my love for her is grander and richer and fuller than anything I could have imagined. I never knew my heart could grow so big in my chest. I was so happy that my mom met Miranda and gave us her blessing before passing on.

"I hope Miranda will live in an accepting world. I want her to know self-love, self-acceptance, and to value education, to be whoever she thinks she is, not who I think she has to be—and I know I'll have to work on that every day. I want her to be healthy, in her body and spirit. She will be subjected to lots of different prejudices by the nature of her skin, her eye shape, having two mothers and being adopted, but I think there is enough love all around us to help heal those hurts.

"To me, the idea of family is all about acceptance—an open heart."◆

We are living a period of profound change in all areas of public and private life. It has been in many ways a liberating time. Notwithstanding ongoing backlash, the definitions of *family* have at least begun to expand to make room for loving, nontraditional families like the one formed by Camila, Margaret, and Miranda.

It has also, for many, been a confusing time, when shifts in traditional attitudes to marriage, education, and child-rearing seem all too daunting to those involved. In the case of a well-to-do family in Amman, Jordan, those changes are articulated by three generations of women whose own upbringing differs considerably from the way they now guide their young.

AMMAN, JORDAN

On a quiet residential street of large stone villas, I was invited to the home of an elderly Palestinian widow where she, two of her daughters, and a granddaughter welcomed us. Ornate gilded chairs and a room-sized Persian carpet were the centerpieces of the elegant sitting room where we talked and were served homemade pastries and tea.

Kaoukab Yasin Tota, 71
Sara El Sherif, 45
Dalia El Sherif, 21

KAOUKAB Grandmother Kaoukab Yasin Tota was wearing the head-covering *hijab*, a long dress, and thick eyeglasses. She told us that she was born in Jerusalem, the eldest of four children. When she was fourteen years old she was married to a man fifteen years her senior. Her first child was born just as she turned fifteen. In all, she bore eleven children.

"I had a beautiful childhood. My father was a religious person but not a fanatic. He was a friend to Muslims, Christians, Jews, the British. Because Jerusalem is a town of all religions, everybody was very close. We left Jerusalem in 1948, following the Israeli assault on Deir Yassim; we were terrified.

"We have strong family ties, but the way of life has changed. People don't have time for one another; everybody is so busy. And we Palestinians are dispersed around the world.

"Women used to stay at home but now it's not possible. They must work. If a man wants to ask for the hand of a woman, he makes sure that she works, otherwise he will not marry her. They need each other to work.

"I didn't have much schooling, but my daughters went to Egypt to university. My husband agreed; he was an open-minded person. I brought them up properly; they were responsible, and I trust them. My daughter Nawal goes out at night. I never did that. I rely on her as if she were a man. I am confident they know how to behave."◆

DALIA Kaoukab's granddaughter is twenty-one and a student in sociology at Amman University. She spoke of her mother's family in Hebron, saying she couldn't adjust to their traditional attitudes toward women and girls.

"I can't manage there. They're too strict. You have to dress and behave in a certain way. Sometimes I feel like I'm not a human being. You want to be treated as the males in the family are treated, but you aren't. Why? Because you are female.

"A boy is taught to talk in front of anyone, to be brave, not to cry, to do this and that. While the daughters are taught, 'Help your mother; do this; you've got to do that.' The son is taught to talk, to be tough. Girls are taught to be shy. A woman always has to listen to the views of her husband, father, or brothers. A woman has the same right to work outside the home, but she can't do what she chooses. And once she is married, her main job is to have children. I don't say that's not good; it's just that life is more than that."◆

SARA Dalia's mother, Sara El Sherif, forty-five, is a graduate of the University of Cairo and has lived in North Africa and traveled widely with her husband. A modern woman, she has nonetheless revealed some hidden fears for her daughter's future.

"Things have changed so much. I have to live in my mother's generation, my daughter's generation, and my own. I have to do things my daughter accepts, to be able to protect her from doing wrong things, to guide her. Her generation is completely lost. They try to do things that other people are doing. And since their parents do not allow it, they do it behind their parents' backs. It is a lost generation. I don't want that to happen to my daughters.

"When my daughters were ten and eight, I sent them to summer school in London for three months. They lived in an English family. There were young people from many different countries. My daughters learned a lot, but some of it was negative."

Sara hesitated a moment, as if wondering if she should go on, then added, "They picked up concepts like excessive liberty, arguments, attempting to emulate the other girls."◆

For parents throughout the world, parenting in an increasingly complex world presents a worrisome dilemma. Parents want to protect their children, do the best for them, provide them with the tools for life in a global economy and culture—yet traditional attitudes and fear for their well-being often make them hesitate. Pressured by the society around them, parents feel vulnerable and inadequate. These three generations of Palestinian women are an example. The grandmother and granddaughter met change head on, the middle generation, the mother, who goes out into the world daily, has observed the pitfalls and chaos of overly rapid change.

Giving children the tools and the self-esteem to meet a changing social, technological, and economic environment is the common goal. How to do so remains, often, a trial-and-error effort.

Smaller families, working parents, a more mobile, competitive society, and less leisure time are factors that are reshaping families and the relationships within them. Widespread democratization and expanding rights have led to increased individual independence, which in turn calls for strong commitments to individual responsibility. This, too, presents a challenge to today's parents: respect of community, elders and responsibility toward others are qualities that must be instilled at an early age.

How do we best provide for children's needs if not by assisting parents to better provide for them? Truly child-centered policies would ensure free public education, child care, after-school programs, community centers, and recreational facilities. They would be based upon government and business sensitivity to the needs of parents and the importance of parental time. As we learned from those interviewed, the influence of parents is profound in shaping an individual's life. From privileged children of the affluent to the dispossessed children of the poor, our children are in need of more parenting, not less.

Seven | Youth's Search for Life Maps

I hope I can do as well as my parents have in raising a family. One of the most important things is to be able to provide security and a stable environment and make sure all necessities are met.
—Derren Mangum, Queens, New York, USA

Its doors open and its passengers strapped in, the plane waited in the afternoon heat for late boarders on the Dhaka to Singapore flight. To my right, a window seat was empty; I surmised I would gain a seat companion by the delay. Suddenly a group of Bengali boys in their late teens crowded silently into the plane's cabin. Scrubbed spotless and dressed in secondhand Western shirts and pants, their composure was as frayed as their shirt collars. Cowed by inexperience and fright, they remained silent as fashionable flight attendants directed them to their seats.

One among them was told to sit next to me. Lanky and awkward, he took his place, eyes lowered. He appeared to be struggling with a bad case of panic. The instructions for passengers, loudspeakered in English, served only to exacerbate his anxiety. One way of dealing with fright is, of course, paper shuffling. He threw himself into it. Over and over he counted his papers: passport, permits, documents of all sorts, each with its official seal. There were health certificates claiming the boy was free of tuberculosis and hepatitis, a nineteen-year-old birth certificate, and a permit to enter Singapore as a day laborer.

I had encountered many such migrant boys and men going hither and yon in search of work: Tunisians in France, Senegalese in Cameroon, Salvadorians in my Washington neighborhood, all sharing the pain of exile made necessary by poverty or, at times, fear. I wanted to comfort this seatmate, but alas, we shared no common language—only an awkward silence. I was left to wonder how many relatives counted on this frightened boy's earnings, what young girl dreams of his return, and why the hands of fate conspired to send him away, to build yet another shopping mall in Singapore.

The United Nations defines *youth* as those in the fifteen to twenty-four age group. It is the period during which biological, psychological, and social maturity is transforming the individual, the bridge from childhood to the world of the adult. Today's youth number one billion, comprising one-sixth of the world's people.[1] They are taking their place in the most rapidly changing society ever known, and all too often, they are doing so without without life maps.

These young people's childhoods were vastly different from those of their parents, and their parents are at a loss to provide guidance in a world they no longer understand. Livelihoods that sustained their families for generations are no longer viable. Education and technology appear to be the panaceas of their generation, yet both remain out of reach for millions of youth. In many countries of the developing world, rapid urbanization and economic imperatives have torn families away from the large extended family group, leaving youngsters without the guidance of multiple adults in multiple generations. The reality of costly education, lack of employment opportunities, domestic violence, HIV/AIDS, gangs and drugs, juxtaposed with a view of a television-inspired dream world, contribute to youth's confusion. Forces such as a growing demand for gender equity and evolving sexual mores often confound parents and youth alike. Concepts of individual worth, social equality, and democratic ways have been positive factors in the transformation of family relationships and society. And, knowledge of a wider world, unknown in their parents' time, pushes youth to be more demanding of themselves and of their futures.

One billion young people stand at the threshold of adulthood. Their future opportunities, or lack thereof, will shape the political and economic future of their nations and of world society. Here young people express their aspirations, speak of their present families, and muse on the families they will one day create.

BAYAD EL ARAB, EGYPT

A three-hour drive south along the Nile from Cairo brought us to the outskirts of Beni Suef, where we turned off to Bayad el Arab. We drove to the edge of the great river, to a point where an island stood a few hundred yards offshore. By honking the car's horn, we signaled to a boatman on the island to come fetch us.

Nasra Kamel Mohammed, 22
Mahmoud Abdulaziz Al Wahab, 16

He rowed over to take us in his dinghy across to the small island's landing, beyond which stretched the gardens of half a dozen families; one was that of the Al Wahab family.

The irrigation ditches crisscrossing the island traversed the land belonging to Abdulaziz Mohammed Al Wahab, a sixty-four-year-old farmer whose family has farmed on the banks of the Nile as far back as anyone can remember. He owns about 1.5 acres of land, a cow, a buffalo, ducks, chickens, and

Mahmoud, his father Abdulaziz, Nasra, Fatma, Kazma, and Nasra's
two children

three donkeys. Living with him are his wife, his two youngest children, and
a daughter-in-law whose husband is a construction laborer in Saudi Arabia.
Their home is constructed of cement bricks and includes several small buildings close together—one a barn for the animals, another a kitchen, and still
another the sleeping quarters. Drinking water is drawn from a well, but the
family takes its washing water from the Nile. There is neither town nor school
on the island. Attending school entails a boat trip across to the mainland
and a six kilometer walk.[2]

Grandfather Al Wahab has had two wives and has fathered ten children.
He divorced his first wife long ago, but still visits her and their six adult children. When we arrived, he was working in the family market garden,
wearing a turban, white shorts, a shirt and white waistcoat. His face told
of a gentle man, but he exuded energy and was loud and forceful in his speech.
At one point, while talking, he realized he didn't have on his djellaba, a traditional robe. He left abruptly to find it, in order, his wife explained, to be
properly dressed for visitors. He told how he married at seventeen and was
not allowed to go to school because as an only son he was needed in the fields.

His wife, Kazma Ahmed Seed, fifty, said she had been forced to marry
a cousin at age fourteen. He beat her so often that after three weeks she gave
him all she had, her dowry, in order to get away. Kazma was fragile looking and very thin; when I put my arms around her to say good-bye, I could
feel her protruding shoulder blades. She said she couldn't put on weight because
of so much work in the fields.

The family didn't know quite what to expect of our visit but was extremely hospitable. As the interviews progressed, we began to joke and laugh together. They served us huge round maize bread, scrambled eggs in ghee, and cheese

made from their buffalo's milk, spiced with red peppers from the garden. Abdelaziz and Kazma were noticeably affectionate together, deferring to each other and exchanging approving glances.

NASRA   The young daughter-in-law, Nasra Kamel Mohammed, now twenty-two, told us she had married at age seventeen and came to live with her in-laws. She has two children and is expecting a third. She said she would like to rest a bit before having another. Her round, cherublike face was dotted with blemishes which, she explained, were caused by "the pesticides in the water." Her teeth showed signs of neglect and she appeared much older than her years. During the hours of our visit, even as we talked, she never once stopped scrubbing the family's clothes, which were piled up for the weekly wash.

"This is the first time my husband has gone abroad. There isn't enough work for two men on this land. He sends letters but no money. I have two daughters and am now carrying another child. After this one, I'll rest, and maybe have another one later. For now I take care of the children and help my mother-in-law with housework, fieldwork, and laundry, and I take care of the small animals.

"My daughters will go to school, and I want them to finish. Here they let only the boys go to school—not the girls. But I'd like my daughters to find employment and live in different conditions. I'd like them to marry an employee; that's better than marrying a farmer."◆

MAHMOUD   Abdulaziz's youngest son, Mahmoud Abdulaziz, is sixteen but already as tall as his father. When he returns from school, he works with his father in the garden. He admitted to having difficulty studying: there is no electricity on the island, and his only time for study is in the evening. Mahmoud was a shy boy, but as soon as we were walking alone, away from the family, he became more animated and talkative.

"I'm in the second year of high school. I don't want to be a farmer. I'd like to study and become an engineer. I don't want to stay here. If I could, I'd live away. I'll go to any city, but not a village. There are many opportunities in the cities if you can learn new things. I'd like to go abroad, maybe to Saudi Arabia like my brother. And when I marry I want to live far away from my father.

"I'd like my wife to be educated, but I wouldn't want her to work, just stay in the house. Perhaps I'll have four children, but not more because salaries don't cover the cost of more."

Mahmoud paused for a while; then, almost wistfully, he added, "I want to go far away. There is nothing to do here. Nothing at all."◆

Nasra Kamel Mohammed mixing bread dough with her son

As we were rowed back to the mainland and waved to the young man who stood watching us leave, it occurred to me that Nasra and Mahmoud's island life is symbolic of the dilemma facing so many of their generation: isolated youths, cut off from the currents of progress, yet aspiring to independence, opportunity, and more democratic relationships. Such is the story of two teenagers I met in Uganda.

BUSHENYI, UGANDA

In chapter 5 we encountered a frail, elderly cobbler, Peter Asiimwe, who owns a small farm in western Uganda. He spoke of the poverty brought on by political upheaval and war, and of how he, as a parent, isn't able to provide as he would like for his children. The day we met he was waiting for his wife to return from selling their vegetables at market. We sat in

Ben Asiimwe, 20
Efrance Asiimwe, 15

the morning sun outside the modest home, built of branches, mud, and palm fronds. His son Ben told of brewing beer to pay for his chool fees; he was disturbed that he had no alternative for earning money, given the negative influence alcohol has on his peers.

BEN A tall, handsome twenty year old, Ben sat on the second of two chairs owned by the family as we talked. Like millions of young people the world over, Ben knows there is little his parents can do, or know how to do, to improve their lives in a rapidly changing world.

"I attend a boarding school fifteen kilometers from here. Once a week, my brother takes me on his bicycle. When I come home on weekends, I either work in the garden or brew banana beer because my parents can't afford to pay the school fees. I help in the coffee fields, but our production has declined because I'm away at school and my father is often ill. My mother sells vegetables and gives me some of her earnings, but it's not enough. I brew beer and do errands for people to pay for my books.

"In my studies I have learned about other countries: Germany, Russia, Great Britain, France. I would like to visit France because I've studied the French Revolution, its people and philosophers. I hope to be able to learn more.

"My sister attends school, too. But, you know, in my mother's time it was difficult for girls to survive, because they were despised and weren't allowed education. Now girls have become important and people are interested in them. Women participate in all spheres of national life, in the administration, in politics. I think all girls will be educated in the future.

"When I marry I want a wife who has a good education, who is concerned about social issues, and who upholds our African traditions. She should be cooperative with everyone in the family. It would be good if she had the same profession as I. I'll have only three children, I think, because I don't know if I will have the money necessary to do well by them. The economy is such that it might be difficult to educate more than that."

Ben became silent for a time. He then spoke quietly about his fear of AIDS. "AIDS is all over Uganda. Right here, in this village, many have died. I'm hoping God will protect our family. I know that it is transmitted through sexual interaction and transfusions. My generation is well aware of that. But, then there is alcohol, and when they drink, they do silly things.

"If I could finish university, I could get a job and help educate my brothers and sisters. I could also help the people around me. I'll be the first in my family to graduate from secondary school. During my father's youth, people were not concerned about educating their children. That is why illiteracy is so high. But my generation is struggling to get ahead. We want a better future. That is one of the major changes in our society, this young generation reaching for education."◆

EFRANCE   Ben's fifteen-year-old sister, Efrance, is not as optimistic as he is. She joined us in front of the house and spoke of seeing the future close in on her.

"I wasn't allowed to take my exams because I haven't been able to pay the fees. I help in our sorghum fields and sell vegetables at market, but it's not enough. If I were able to finish school I would like to go to university. I want to be a nurse, because when the doctor finishes with the patient, there is much more to do to care for them. But I don't think I'll be able to continue because I don't have any money. The fees are 20,000 shillings [U.S. $20] for one term. I still owe some from the last term. I have to pay it before

I can return. And we are asked to buy textbooks for math and English. It adds up to far too much."◆

Ben and Efrance live in a remote region of East Africa, yet their situation and aspirations resemble those of countless young people. They struggle to learn, to better themselves, hoping to lead useful lives. They want to help their siblings and their families. They speak of service to their country, of what they would do if educated, of responsible parenthood. They speak of more egalitarian relationships between women and men than their parents enjoyed. And they know the dangers their generation faces. When one hears their aspirations—and learns about the realities of their situations— it is difficult to overcome a sense of loss: the lack of opportunity for this gen- eration deprives our world of immeasurable talent and service to others.

Elsewhere, in more affluent families, youths who have the advantage of material security and education express fears of a different sort: they worry about the consequences of rapid change and the dangers of affluence.

QUEENS, NEW YORK, USA

In the Queens neighborhood of South Ozone Park, Dorothy and Harvey Man- gum, the retired couple we met in chapter 6, worked hard to ensure that their children and grandchildren would have opportunities not available to them. Their children received college educations. Their son, Richard, is a professional, as is his wife. They in turn were able, and will-   **Derren Ameer Mangum, 22** ing, to pay for the education of their son, Derren, and he earned a degree from an excellent institution, the University of Virginia. Instead of confronting a lack of opportunity, Derren faces problems that come with limitless choice and changing values.

Derren is tall, with light brown skin and movie-star good looks. His smile lights up those around him. He was obviously enjoying his newfound responsibility for running a small music business.

"I have my own music group, and we started a company, a production and publishing group. At college we started getting into music and organ- ized a group. When we graduated we decided to keep it going. We're doing rap and hip hop music. I do mostly production work. I write lyrics, do the graphics, the business side, the promotion, the management of people.

"Business acumen is almost as important as the music. A lot of people will work for eight hours, five days a week on somebody else's agenda, doing what the company wants them to do. You've got to put the same kind of effort into your own agenda. The rewards aren't the same, and maybe you won't be as secure financially, but I get more rewards out of this, even though I get ter- ribly tired. But when it's music, and coordinating things—hey, I'm happy.

"When I think of my values, my ethics and morals, I have to give credit to my family. I may not be very religious, but I think of myself as a moral person. I do better than a lot of people I know. Where does it come from? It comes from my family.

"Societies, especially American society, are becoming more individualistic. The individual's concerns are overly important. Such thinking affects the family structure. Right now I can't think of just me as important; my family is important. If more people thought this way, it would save a lot of trouble. You can't be selfish, with concern only for your goals and your ideals, because they affect everybody—and you are affected by everybody. I think it's important to maintain the family circle.

"Of the friends I knew before going to college, many didn't finish school. Some never knew their father or had parents who had split up. What was normal to me wasn't necessarily normal for others. At one point, a friend told me I was the only person he knew whose parents were still together. That's a pretty sad statement. That's one thing about my group of college friends, each one of us had the image of a strong father figure. A lot of people don't have that, especially in the black community.

"I have a special relationship with my brother. Being the oldest, I have a big responsibility, especially when our parents try so hard to raise us well. There's just so much they can do. You can rely on your parents, but there is just so much you can tell them, and just so much you will listen to. I've tried to advise my brother, and hopefully he will have an easier time because he had an older brother who looked out for him. Ours is a very important relationship to me.

"It seems like relations between men and women are getting better, especially compared to the old days, when women were shoved off to the side. In my generation, everybody is more or less equal, but there are still a lot of things that haven't changed. Any way you look at it, women are still underappreciated generally by a male-dominated society. There are more women in higher positions, but not nearly as many as there should be. It's good to see women in those situations; it's so important in our community. On the other hand, there's so much single parenting going on where the mother is the primary parent, unmarried. You don't see much of the father. It's unfortunate.

"In many ways I'm closer to my mother than to my father, just by the mother-son relationship. The serious discussions are always with my mother as far as my relationships with women go. I believe that everyone is equal, but I also believe there are differences in this equality—vast differences between men and women. The big question is always the debate about sexuality. It's all right for a man to run around, but if the woman does, she's wrong, or she's this or that—the double standard. This starts all kinds of arguments. Reality is that we do have a double standard. As a woman, your sexuality has more of a risk just by the ability to get pregnant. Nature seems to dish out more diseases to women and pregnancy is a much bigger risk. A man can go out there and he knows he's not going to get pregnant. But he has responsibilities. Being a responsible male, you should know you have less risk—but more responsibility.

"Awareness about AIDS, for example, is getting better, but in reality it's still a mystical kind of thing. Everybody knows about it—AIDS, AIDS—but they also think it's something that affects mostly homosexuals. People don't really understand the danger. When they hear that one in every 250 people is HIV-positive, they don't believe it. They rationalize, saying, 'I haven't slept with that many people; I'm responsible; it's a problem of gay people and poor people and drug addicts and people in other countries.' I think people need to wake up. You can't do everything you want; you can't live your life for pleasure all the time. This disease is outrageous; it hits humanity at its worst possible moment, during the reproductive years. My mother's cousin died from AIDS. So for me, it's very real. I've got proof right here in this family.

"As for me, thinking about having a family seems kind of far off. I worry about the future because my career path is not solid yet. I haven't yet begun to think too much about marriage or a family of my own. I look forward to it, though. It's something everybody looks forward to. It's going to be exciting. I hope I can do as well as my parents have in raising a family. One of the most important things is to be able to provide for your family—security, a stable environment, and make sure all the necessities are met.

"For a wife I'm looking for someone like myself: someone with strong personal goals, ambitions, and someone who will push me to do as much as I can. I'd like a woman who is a career person, who has a strong sense of family and responsibility, somebody who is into solid commitment. I see marriages being tossed around, like friendships. That's not what I want. We have a history of long marriages in our family, and that's important to me.

"I'd like somebody who wants to have children, who has strong family ideas, that's the most important thing. I don't know how many kids I want to have yet, but I worry about the way things are today and how it will affect my children: the education system, safety, just being able to provide all the basics, plus a cultural education. I worry about the environment in which my kids will grow up. The city is tough. I had to become really street-smart in high school. I was lucky, but I don't want to put my kids at risk of violence and drugs. I was a teenager when crack started to hit Queens. People I knew in the neighborhood started selling it. Others started using it. Their lives were ruined, either by the drugs or by the violence that comes with it. It's crazy. And kids have to know how to deal with it."◆

Derren has been lucky, he says, guided as he is by a strong supportive family. Like Ben and Efrance, he places great value on family and a responsible family life. Like them, he is frightened by the specter of HIV/AIDS and the dangers of drugs, gangs, and violence that lurk in contemporary society.[3]

Indeed, the youth of this new century are confronted with a host of confusing and dangerous forces, and parents are unaware, unprepared, or, sometimes, unavailable, to provide the guidance needed by their youngsters. Winone, a teenager from northern Thailand is a case in point. Her journey in search of better life has left her in ill health, humiliated, and with few dreams.

MESAI, THAILAND

We were to leave Bangkok in the evening for an overnight bus journey north to Ching Rai and Mesai. My travelling companions were Oranan Chanlerdfa, a former sex worker who helps rehabilitate young girls in the "trade," and Dao Phosree, a trained social worker who works with her. They had given me instructions on how to find them in the incredibly crowded bus depot: I was to go to the Emergency Women's Shelter counter, a service set up by Khunying Kanitha, founder of the Association for the Promotion of the Status of Women, the organization for which both

Kam Namsai, 59
Nilo Lung, 54
Wimone Lung, 18

Oranan and Dao work. The association was created to provide guidance and protection for young girls who arrive in Bangkok, unprepared for the dangers of the big city. I found my companions as planned. Twelve hours later, in time for a soup and rice breakfast, our bus arrived in Mesai, a town that straddles the Thai-Burmese border. Not far from the bus stop, we could see border flags flying, and when we visited the border crossing later in the day, huge signs proclaimed, "Welcome to the Golden Triangle."

We hired a scooter taxi to help us find the home of Wimone, a former sex worker who had once been sheltered by Khunying Kanitha's organization.

Asking directions in a series of crowded neighborhoods, we eventually found the Lung family home. The modest five rooms were enclosed by walls of woven bamboo. They were sparsely furnished but decorated with the ever-present photo of Thailand's monarchs and assorted Buddhist images. There was a cupboard filled with blankets, a sofa, two chairs, and a table. We sat on a straw mat on the tile floor, watched over by a small, silent television set. It was a house that the father, a construction worker skilled in plastering and tiling, had built himself. The mother is a street food vendor, selling soups and noodles in a stall not far from the house.

The family, I learned, had come from Burma in 1977, fleeing poverty and constant civil war. There were thirteen children—seven boys and six girls. Two have since died; eight reside in Mesai. Wimone is next to the last.

WIMONE Known as Gao in her former profession of sex worker, Wimone is, at eighteen, a tall, plump, quiet young woman with short hair, a round and serious face, and bright dark eyes. She is very fashion conscious; she admitted her dream is to own a dress shop. She told us she had attended school from age seven to eleven.

"After I finished school, I lived with my older sister, Bang, for more than a year. I love her very much because she helped me and taught me many things, the right way to do things. She lives in Ching Rai and is married with one child.

"After a year with her, I came back to help my mother with her business. I wanted to get some training, but my mother didn't have enough money for that. I stayed for more than a year. It was then that some neighborhood girls asked if I wanted to go to Bangkok to work. I wanted to earn money and get ahead, so I said 'Okay, I'll go with you.'

"Three of us went together. I had just turned fifteen, but I looked older. The plan was to work as housemaids, but once we got there, we couldn't find a job. We heard of someone who had hired two girls. I went there with my friend to ask about a job. The agent sent us to a place that turned out to be a brothel. I didn't know it at the time; I thought I was going to work as a housemaid. My friend said it wasn't a bad place. Then I saw what it was, and that they were going to beat us if we didn't do as they said.

"Normally I wouldn't want to do that, but I saw all these other girls do it. And they had money. So I agreed. Nobody beat me. I worked there for more than a year.

"For each client, I got 300 baht [U.S. $12] but I had to give it to the mama-san. In principle I was to get 50 percent, but if I had to go outside, to a hotel, I might spend the 50 percent because they deducted the cab fare. I stayed one whole year and never had any money because they kept it and deducted too many things. For example, if one night I had ten clients, they paid 3000 baht. That means 1500 [U.S. $60] for me. Mama-san would write it in her account book. But I never saw the money. They never gave me money to spend; they just wrote it down. When I was sick they paid for the doctor and the antibiotics, and deducted them. They charged me for my meals—two meals a day. We didn't even have nice clothes; we had to share clothes with one another. After one year I had no money, no clothes, nothing.

"The clients were mostly Thai, sometimes Chinese. There were no Europeans because it was a low-class place, not like a members' club. The clients drink a bit and then they want the girls. Most of them wear condoms, and I always used the pill.

"Some girls didn't want to work and were beaten. The mama-san treated me well because I did what she wanted, but she still kept my money. After a year I found a way to escape. I fled to the slums with a woman friend; there we couldn't be found.

"I left with nothing, just one dress. I have a brother who lives in Bangkok, but I didn't go to him because I was ashamed that after one year, I didn't have even one baht in my pocket. Also, I wanted to earn money before trying to go home.

"I went around Bangkok, to the movies, to the clubs, looking for a paying friend. After a few weeks some people asked me to work in a go-go bar in Patpong, the red-light district where I had worked before. I stayed there for two years. Everything was expensive. I had to buy my own food, pay rent, buy clothes. I didn't have much chance to work with foreigners, with Europeans, because of the language. When I worked in the brothel, somebody helped translate, but in Patpong you have to speak yourself. If not, there's no work. That's why after two years, I had nothing.

"Finally I found a boyfriend. We met at the go-go bar and we liked each other. We lived together for about two months. When I got pregnant he didn't want me anymore. I went to his parents to ask their help, but they didn't want me because of my work. Then someone told me about the Emergency Home in downtown Bangkok. There I could have the baby at the hospital and it would be free. In the meantime I worked at a bar; I couldn't dance, but I could serve drinks and earn a little.

"The month before the baby was due I went to the Emergency Home and stayed until I had my baby boy. I didn't want to give him up for adoption, so the social worker wrote to my parents and my sister. She told them everything, and they came to take me and the baby home. They forgave me and treated us nicely. I am lucky to have such parents. But they gave the baby canned milk, sweet milk. They didn't know it was wrong and neither did I. He began to have diarrhea every day. I took him to the doctor several times. He would have diarrhea for two or three days, then take some medicine and it would cease. Then they'd give the milk again and the diarrhea got really bad. When he was four months old he died."

Winone turned away, facing the empty wall near her. Oranan reached for her hand and spoke softly in Thai. Oranan then asked her if she was still a sex worker.

"No, I don't want to do that anymore. I have only had the one boyfriend, by whom I got pregnant. Nobody around here wants me for a girlfriend because I'm not interested in doing that. I just want to help my parents.

"The girl who went with me is still working in the brothel. For her it's a job. She doesn't want to escape; she is afraid to try. For her, it's comfortable and easy. She gets food, clothing, and because she's honest and stays, sometimes they give her money.

"It's sad. Every couple of days two or three girls leave here. They know they're going to be prostitutes but they don't care. They are twelve, thirteen, or fourteen years old. Most of them know exactly what they will do. And many are virgins. That's the biggest problem: child prostitution. The clients think that girls eighteen or twenty are already tired or that they will get HIV. So they want the eleven-, twelve-, thirteen-year-old virgins.

"I try to warn them, to stop them, but the girls don't believe me. They say Bangkok is a good place and there is lots of money there. The young girls need money. If they don't go, they stay here and have nothing. Many come back with gold or money and buy a motorcycle for their family. In the neighborhood they say I'm stupid, because I went for four years and came back with nothing.

"Now I'd like to find a man who is a little bit older, twenty-five, twenty-six, or maybe more. He would have to be someone who could forgive my past and start anew. He'd have to help support me and my family. I don't want someone who talks about my past. I will tell him about it: I must. Everybody knows, and one day he'd find out and get hurt. That would ruin everything. It's not easy.

"My dream is to have a shop, a small clothing shop. I'd like to have good dresses and do sewing. I don't know sewing, but if there is a chance to learn I would like that. I don't want to go back to school to get trained. I think I can do it by myself.

"The trouble is my health is not always good. I have a lot of stomach pain. When I was pregnant I went to a doctor who checked my blood, but he didn't tell me anything. I didn't go back to check after the birth. My mother worries about me, I know."◆

KAM   Wimone's mother is a look-alike of her daughter: a chubby woman with bright, dark eyes. Deeply shy, she spoke almost inaudibly and smiled only once, when she told of her grandchildren's visits during school holidays. Nearing sixty, she spends her days selling the soups and noodles she prepares before dawn. She has little capital, and has to invest 60 baht a day for ingredients of the soups she sells for 100 to 110 baht per day, leaving her total daily profit at no more than 40 to 50 baht [U.S. $2].

"I barely make enough money to buy the ingredients for the next day," she confided. "And then I have to take care of the family. It leaves no time to think.

"I was born in Burma. My parents were farmers. They didn't own land; they worked for others. Both were killed in the civil wars. I don't even remember their names. I was completely cut off. Cousins of my husband's father took care of me like a daughter, but I never went to school. I don't know how to read or write. My husband and I grew up together and married when I became nineteen. Like my parents, we were farm laborers. We had thirteen children, but two died.

"I'm happy with my life here, but I am worried about Wimone because she has nothing. I looked for her for four years. I asked for news everywhere.

I hoped for a letter every day, and when the social worker's message arrived, I felt happy that I'd have my daughter back. I went all the way to Bangkok to bring her home. Now I worry about her health and her future. She doesn't want to go back to school to be dressmaker or hairdresser.

"My shop is the only dependable family support. What is going to happen if I die—especially to this daughter, who causes so many problems? How is she going to support herself? I try to teach her everything. I'm always talking, talking; she has to think about her future. My life is perfect if my children don't make trouble. Only Wimone worries me."◆

NILO   As we sat in the shuttered sitting room of their home, Nilo Lung, husband and father, expressed the same preoccupation for his daughter's future. I could barely make out his eyes in the shadows, but his hands rested calmly on his knees while he spoke. Only when we discussed Wimone did he become agitated. At fifty-four, he was a shy man whose pride resided in his trade and in his success at bringing his family to safety.

"My father died when I was very young, so I had to learn everything by myself. As a boy I saw a lot of people die by shooting, in the fighting. There was always so much fighting in the civil wars. Every day soldiers beat the farmers. It was difficult to find food. I promised myself I would find a place where life would be better.

"I'm a construction worker and know my job well. Life has improved for us but there is not always enough work. I cannot compare myself with rich families, of course, but I am happy with what I have. I have my work and my wife has hers. If I were to think about the future and wish for this or that, it would make me unhappy. It's better that chance comes by itself.

"Now education is more important than it was in my youth. If children don't have education, they'll have a hard time earning a livelihood. In the past girls didn't have to learn, because they would marry and stay at home. Now they watch TV and get ideas about how other people live. They need to learn more to prepare them for life.

"Wimone, for example: I want her to be a good girl and to begin anew, to forget everything about the past. If I die or my wife dies, I want to be sure she can take care of herself. The most important thing is for her to be a good girl and to have an honest job."◆

The Lung family is one among the innumerable families who have become victims of forces they do not fully comprehend. Their daughter, in her youthful desire to improve her situation, found herself duped into becoming involved in a dangerous and damaging life. Nothing in her family's experience had prepared them to avoid such dangers. Solidly united as a family, the

Lungs wanted only their daughter's safe return and an opportunity for her to begin anew.

BAMAKO, MALI

In Bamako, we heard similar stories of young rural girls seeking fortune—or in the Malian context, a trousseau—by going off to the city to become maids. There, too, there are organizations that attempt to protect the young and naive. Young people raised in villages where everyone knows them are sadly unprepared for the anonymity and predatory forces found in the city.

Mme. Jacqueline Urbain is somewhat of a heroine in Mali. She created the Association for the Advancement of Family Maids (Association pour la Promotion des Aides Familiales) for the purpose of assisting rural girls who turn up in Bamako, often to be exploited by the families that "employ" them. In addition to economic exploitation, some girls fall victim to rape or coerced sex by the men of the family. The day I met her, she introduced me to a village girl who had just given birth to a baby boy. The young mother had been "dishonored" by her employer and feared returning to her village. Jacqueline Urbain was going to accompany her to her home village and explain to the community that the girl was an innocent victim of exploitation. Doing so, she explained, might give the girl a second chance at life.

Oum Coulibaly, 20
Doumbia Natene, 17

Jacqueline also introduced me to two girls who had come to her office seeking work: Oum Coulibaly, age twenty, who had recently arrived in Bamako, and her friend, Doumbia Natene, a seventeen year old who had been working for a family for the past year. Doumbia explained their reason for coming to Bamako.

"I live in a village 200 kilometers from here. My father used to be a marabou [religious counselor], but he is old now and can't earn much. We are seven children from his two wives. In our village there are girls my age who have nice things, are well dressed, much better than I am. My family is too poor to buy those things, so my brother gave me the money to travel to Bamako to find work. When I have enough money I'll be able to buy things for myself.

"Three of us came together. We walked around the neighborhoods looking for work. At one point some girls asked if we were looking for work and said their mother was in need of maids. That's how I got my job. I wanted to stay until next year, but my brother is going to get married so I will have to go home to help with the wedding."

Her friend, Oum, seemed anxious to add to our conversation. I asked her if her parents had allowed her to come to Bamako on her own.

"I have a brother here, so I stayed with him. He is the one who sends money to my parents. I want to earn money for my own wedding. Last year my parents chose a fiancé for me, but I didn't like him. Everybody in the village knew I didn't want to marry him. I don't like him at all. His first wife died after fifteen days, and people believe that if a man marries one wife and she dies, the second wife will die also. I'm afraid to marry him. So I came here.

"I want a man who can earn money, who will be able to provide for the family and for his children, all their expenses. I'd like him to love me and my parents, especially my mother. I don't want a man who argues and fights. I don't want a man who brings trouble."

Wimone, Oum, and Doumbia have each reached out for a better life, little knowing the risks they might encounter. Their rural-based parents are also ignorant of the dangers that lurk in the cities of a rapidly modernizing world. In China, the daughter of a more affluent and educated family has received more guidance, yet, as is the case for many young people, the protective environment in which she has been raised is not always to her liking.

BEIJING, CHINA

The ubiquitous high-rise apartment buildings of China's capital are seemingly indistinguishable, but their interiors do vary in the size of rooms or the quality of building material. It was a dreary winter morning when we climbed the stairs to the relatively spacious apartment in central Beijing allocated to Professor Liu Gengshang and his family. In fact, he and his mother, wife, and daughter share two adjoining apartments.

Professor Liu is the director of teaching and research in the Archival Department at China's Peoples' University. His family's apartments are sparsely furnished, the concrete floors bare of carpets. They share a common kitchen

Geng Yuhui, 80
Yu Xiaoxuan, 44
Liu Gengshang, 50
Liu Jai, 19

which, as in most apartments I'd visited, suffers from lack of space, as if cooking were not an important activity in an urban home. Three lacquered bookcases, a sofa, and an easy chair fill the sitting room. On top of the television, a collection of stuffed dogs is displayed. A live dog, a long-haired dust-mop type, barked upon our arrival, and followed us from room to room during our visit. Each room held another collection of the professor's books, carefully arranged on shelves and tables.

YUHUI Eighty-year-old grandmother Geng Yuhui moved with difficulty and had to be assisted to sit on the sofa beside me. She was dressed in traditional Chinese style: her gray pants, blouse, and satin vest matched the color of her thinning hair.

Her parents, she explained, had raised seven children. She herself had four daughters and a son. And now, she declared with disdain, each of her children has but one child. Born in Tiejin, she completed six years of primary schooling and six years at the Provincial Girls Teacher Training College. Her cheerful satisfaction with her life was tempered only by her experiences during the Cultural Revolution.

"My father owned a tea shop and mother was a housewife. Father was a modern man; it was he who most influenced me. In our family boys and girls were treated the same. All had the same opportunities to study. Such ideas were rare then.

"My mother had bound feet. She was unable to walk like people with normal feet; it was very painful. Her toes were like rubber. She could only stay home and do housework. My father wanted her to take the wrapping off her feet, to liberate them, but my mother was very influenced by the grandmothers. She thought bound feet were a thing of beauty and wanted us to bind ours as well. My father wouldn't permit it.

"I met my husband at the Teachers Training College; we became friends and I took him home to meet my parents. He was a good man, a scholar, and very able. We had a very happy married life. I taught from 1935 on. When I gave birth to this son, I stopped teaching. In the early sixties I moved to Beijing and began teaching again. I taught up until the Cultural Revolution. It's very painful to recall those days; we were treated as outcasts. When it was all over I was invited back to teach.

"In my mother's time, most women were housewives, but in my generation, many women worked and now they get their pensions. This is a very positive change for women. You see, we women have abilities and by working we have money in our own hands. That means equality, that we are treated well. I have my pension; I can be independent. Sometimes my son gives me money, but I really don't need it. He cannot ask me to do this or that, because I am economically independent. That said, he's very good to me. My pension is not very high, so at the end of the month he always asks, 'Mother, do you need money?' And he gives me some. My daughter-in-law is also very good. We get along very well.

"Now my granddaughter is nearly twenty! There's so much difference between the generations. The policy of one child per family makes for spoiling. I had five children and none of them were spoiled because I had so many. But my granddaughter? She wants everything—always the very best. And everything she wants, she gets, including pocket money. She is very spoiled because she is an only child. Sometimes she says the food at the university is not good enough for her, so she announces, 'Today I went to a restaurant with a schoolmate,' and she tells how much money she spent. Most children grow up well behaved but an only child—it's very difficult. They are always spoiled."◆

XIAOXUAN The professor's wife, Yu Xiaoxuan, forty-four, is a handsome woman, calm and elegant. During our talk, however, she appeared shy and far less confident than her mother-in-law. She was wearing a blue satin Chinese jacket, gray pants, and dangling enamel earrings. Her nails were painted pink, and she wore her hair in a bun at the nape of her neck. She works part-time selling tickets in a cinema.

Her parents were of peasant origin, but her father had joined the army during the Japanese occupation. Thereafter, the family moved often. During the Cultural Revolution, Xiaoxuan spent six years working on a farm in Inner Mongolia.

"We had only one child, because at the time we earned very little and could not have supported another child. I used an IUD as contraceptive. We are better off now, of course. There are no real problems in our family. My only worry is a future job for my daughter. I hope she will study well and have the opportunity to go abroad. I want her to develop her career elsewhere. If she can complete her studies abroad, I hope she will find a job there, because in China, when allocating jobs, they still prefer to hire a man rather than a woman."◆

JIA Nineteen-year-old daughter Jia was not dressed in Chinese attire. Like thousands of other university students, she was wearing blue jeans and a sweater. Her shiny black hair was shoulder length, with a wisp of bangs across the forehead. She was an attractive, self-assured young woman and she spoke openly of her generation's concerns about the future.

"I'm in my second year of university, studying economics. Since our country is focusing on the market economy, what we learned before may be useless in the future. That's why we want to study the commodity economy, like stocks, investments, and so on. Of course, I don't know what kind of work I'm going to do; it will depend on the development of our economy and on the opportunities I'll have. I'd like to have own my own business in a few years.

"The older generation has very traditional concepts and they are the current managers of Chinese society. We must wait our turn. But when our generation takes over, society will see major changes. We follow what's happening in and outside the country very closely. We have a library with newspapers from all over the country. The reading room is always crowded with students who seek information. Also, there's a very strong work ethic at the university. It's because 80 percent of our students come from rural areas and they hope that if they study hard, they will be able to move to the city and become an urban person. That's the great hope: to leave the peasant life behind.

"Among my classmates, most of the boys come from the countryside, while the girls come from the city. The teachers don't necessarily favor the boys, so the boys don't play the male superiority game.

"I'd like to work a few years after graduation and then consider marriage, somewhere between twenty-five to thirty years old. The minimum legal age is twenty for girls, twenty-two for boys. For a husband, I want qualities like tolerance and understanding. A husband and wife should understand each other well, because they face all sorts of problems in daily life. Another thing is ambition. A boy should have ambition, not be satisfied with the present, always try to pursue the better—the best—situation.

"Our generation is going to have to cope with the results of the single-child policy. It's starting to show up in schools. It makes relationships more difficult, especially when both boy and girl are only children. They are used to being spoiled and like to have the last word."

With a mischievous look and a smile, Jia added, "And that goes for me."◆

GENGSHANG Professor Liu was casually dressed in a shirt and beige cardigan. He is not a large man, and his body seems dominated by his professorial head. He is a scholar of history, and his views on the current trends in the Chinese family added perspective to his description of his own family's relationships. He is a forceful speaker, enthusiastic and animated throughout our conversation—so much so that I wondered throughout our conversation if the translation fully relected his strong feelings.

"There have been big changes in Chinese society in my time. One, of course, is the breakup of the large family into nuclear units. It has become impossible to maintain a large family today. Because we are deeply influenced by Confucian philosophy, children owe fealty to their parents, and this maintained big families for generations. The elders were the main authority in the family. It is a very feudalistic custom. People considered happiness to be a big family. But actually, in those big families there were many shortcomings, many conflicts. So as we move from the past to this modern world, there is a breakup of the extended family. This is a problem for all mankind."

The professor stopped as if to ponder his last sentence. When he continued it was to say hurriedly, "The pace of life itself has changed. We devote more time to our work and have less time to spend with the family." Then, with a wink and a smile, he added, "We even have less time to spend on disagreements between mother-in-law and daughter-in-law, and among generations.

"The gains in women's emancipation made in the past forty years is another influence that has brought about change—for my generation as well as for my daughter's. My wife works, earns her own money, buys what she wants with it—mostly food, as it turns out. She's an independent person. Where she works they have a social club and recently they began offering dancing lessons. My wife joined the class to learn to dance. I liked the idea, but my mother? She is strictly opposed to it. Also, women want to dress nicely, want to look prettier, more beautiful, now. It's not just the young, but the middle-aged and older women as well. My mother is strictly opposed to such things. It's difficult for her to keep up with the changes. I have to become a mediator. My mother loves my daughter very much. She wants to know everywhere she goes, everything she does. Her greatest wish is to keep her granddaughter under her guidance. But my daughter? The only thing she wants is to be free of her grandmother. This is a very typical situation.

"My mother likes living with us, and we get along together, but my wife and I agree that no matter what kind of son-in-law my daughter marries, they should live by themselves. We don't want to live with them, because we work and have no time to address the contradictions of a family—between mother-in-law and daughter-in-law, father-in-law and son-in-law. So we will live separately.

"There is such a difference among the generations, and I believe the influence of the mass media has deepened the gap. For example, my mother lived through eight years of war, the occupation, and she hates the Japanese. My generation doesn't hate the Japanese; we did not experience that period. My daughter's generation admires the Japanese. They like their modern economic development, their lifestyle. They see it all on television.

"There are so many questions this younger generation will have to face, whether they are university graduates, workers, or merchants. The economy is in transition. After graduation, students will have to find jobs, and salaries are very low. Only those working in private enterprises get higher pay. As traditional concepts fade, contradictions between the generations will increase. It's happening faster than we realize.

"As for my daughter, I want only one thing: that she study well. As a student of economics, she should also learn foreign languages. She wants to go abroad after university and I support that. If she does have that opportunity, I hope she will come back and serve our motherland. Her economic studies will be very useful for the future of our country. Another wish I have is that she will find a good husband, one who will strive for progress all the time. To see her married happily is my wish."◆

Like the Lung family in Thailand, Professor Liu and his family hope their daughter will prosper and live happily. Although the professor's mother benefited from a very progressive childhood herself, she has trouble adjusting to her granddaughter's world and expectations. Intergenerational conflicts have always existed, to be sure, but change was not as radical or as swift in the past. Women were not permitted as much autonomy, and individuals were not so sure of their rights or independence as are the youth of today—nor were they as impatient with those who didn't keep up with the times.

AMMAN, JORDAN

The young Jordanian student interviewed in chapter 6 in her grandmother's elegant home had very strong feelings about intergeneration conflict and about the emerging independence of women. At twenty-one, Dalia is a sociology student at Amman University **Dalia El Sherif, 20** and has lived in Egypt and England for short periods of time. The daughter of affluent professional parents who are far from being strict, Dalia sees reason for revolt against a society that restricts her choices.

"There is a basic contradiction in our lives. Our families raise us to achieve. They want us to study, to be able to think for ourselves. But then what? If you want to marry someone, you don't have the right. You want to be treated like the males in the family, but you aren't. Why? Because you are female. Why can't I drive a truck? I want to learn, but nobody will teach me. Just because I'm a woman.

"Women have the right to work outside the home but can't do whatever work they choose—like being an electrical engineer, for example. Some have the freedom to choose a husband, but he still has to meet all sort of familial criteria, socially and financially. The husband controls everything in the marriage because he's the one who has money, he's the one who is going to pay, to provide a house, everything. These days girls have few rights. Oh yes, they can say yes or no to the marriage, but they don't really have the right to choose.

"In a husband I want someone who will share his life, our life, not compartmentalize his and mine. I want us to be on the same level. Each of us will be different, but we must be complementary to each other. Some men say that they want that, but when they go back home, I see the way they treat their mothers—so I have to wonder."

Dalia smiled while shaking her head in mock wonderment. "I have plans for my future. I'd like to continue my studies abroad. I want to go abroad, understand other cultures, and someday, I want to work. I'm lucky; my parents are pretty modern. I think they understand."◆

Dalia and her Chinese peer, Jia, are impatient young women who refuse to be held back by gender discrimination. Like many of the girls interviewed, they speak of rights and freedoms unknown to earlier generations of women. Yet parents may not be well prepared to meet the needs of such ambitious young women. Constant encouragement and guidance are necessary if an adolescent girl is to develop wise judgment and a secure sense of self. When these supports are lacking, the girls are diminished and, more often than not, never fully attain the self-esteem they need to manage their lives in the most productive—and safe—manner. This is a significant dilemma for today's youth—both boys and girls: knowing that one has more rights or autonomy in society than one's parents had is one thing; knowing what to do with those rights is quite another.

KAMPALA, UGANDA

Mary Kasozi Kaya, the longtime volunteer trainer for the Ugandan YWCA whom we met in chapter 6, has vast knowledge of the issues facing Uganda's youth—especially its young women—based on years of counseling young people. Like many who work with adolescents, she laments the absence of parents' involvement in preparing girls for a world where more independence and mobility combine with sexually explicit media to confuse, or mislead, young people. As Mary Kaya explains, "At the YWCA, we have many school dropouts. Because school fees are so high, parents can't afford to keep all their children in school—especially girls. When you've got a girl and a boy, you want your boy to be better off than the girls; the result is that many girls have to give up their schooling. Girls who want to attend secondary school but can't pay the fees are easy prey for older men who, in the era of HIV/AIDS, seek virgins for their sexual pleasure. The girls have little knowledge of their anatomy, of sexual practices or contraception. Tragedy awaits them. 'Sugar daddies' take few precautions to protect girls from pregnancy or STDs."

Another Ugandan woman, a schoolteacher in Kabarole District, has witnessed the consequences of such situations. Mrs. Alice Turyahikayo, head mistress of the Kivambi Secondary School for Girls, was widowed three years ago by a car accident. In her late thirties, she is the mother of three daughters and contributes to the support of her parents as well. She is an attractive young woman, with a shy smile that belies her position of authority. We met in the headmistress's house, which is in the parklike setting of the schoolgrounds.

She has the responsibility, she says, "of leading girls to womanhood in the times of HIV." She continued, "Our job here is to prepare these girls for their future, prepare them for life. The essential goal, mainly, is to make them honest citizens who treat one another well. We also try to prepare them to be self-reliant; we emphasize practical education, subjects that can enable them to support themselves and, eventually, their dependents.

"Girls are beginning to realize that women can contribute something worthwhile to society. The more they are aware of their talents and capabilities, the more attitudes change. They know that they are different from men, but they can do what men do and contribute to national development as much as men. This question of equality of men and women is not part of the curriculum, but we expose them to various lectures or we get visiting lecturers to talk about women's potential.

"My greatest fear for these girls, the most difficult problems they will face, is the killing disease. You see, in school there is no real sex education, no talk about relationships between men and women, but we do give such information through the career counseling department. The biggest problem is that we don't have very many women in the teaching profession. For instance, this is purely a girls school, but the majority of the teachers are men. We need more trained women.

"We teach the girls about the dangers of HIV. Some take it seriously, but you have to repeat it over and over again. For instance, we talked about the dangers of having sex outside of marriage and of pregnancy. We talked and talked, and when it came to their physical examination we found two girls pregnant. So you have to wonder if what you told them really mattered.

"I have cases here of girls who have lost their parents. Mainly it's the fathers, but I have one who has lost her mother. I have a case of a father who has just discovered that he is HIV-positive. All he wants to do is see his children through school before he dies.

"The girls are aware of the HIV situation; they are aware, but of course, human nature is human nature."

The lack of sex education for the young is a blatant failure of our families and schools. To protect adolescents from the dangers of exploitation, pregnancy, ill health, and even death, attitudes to early sex education must change. Understanding how relationships, sexuality, and family life are successfully managed is a critical element of a child's education, one that profoundly shapes his or her future. Conversations with scores of parents in a dozen countries reveal just how few among them have given, or are willing to provide, information on sexual relationships to their youngsters. Some hide behind the fear that "knowing leads to doing," while others keep children ignorant due to religious beliefs. Most are simply unwilling to broach a "delicate subject" with their children. Many parents—and schools—look the other way when sex education is suggested. These attitudes sacrifice young people needlessly. There is no better argument for sex education than the facts: countries with early, and continuous, sex education in school are those with the lowest rates of teenage pregnancy and the lowest rates of abortion. The Netherlands and Sweden, for example, are at the forefront of sex education at early ages in the school system and have the lowest teenage pregnancy and abortion rates.[1]

When talking with young men throughout my travels, I found that most had not only thought carefully about marriage, but also formed precise ideas about the type of woman they would want as a life partner. They also recognize that there has been significant change is women's position in society, and women's aspirations, since their own mothers' youths.

Attitudes to family are clear among the young; without exception they speak of wanting smaller families than those in which they grew up. Most adolescent girls aspire to more than motherhood, and the boys view large families as a financial burden, a barrier to providing well for their wives and children.

SAN SALVADOR, EL SALVADOR

In a modest neighborhood of El Salvador's capital, Luis Mauricio Benavides Sosa lives with his mother and nine-year-old half-brother in a cement-brick house of which they are visibly proud. His mother, Rosa Vilma Sosa, interviewed in chapter 4, makes a living buying fish from wholesalers and

Luis Mauricio Benavides Sosa, 20   selling it at the market, where she has a stall.

She sells fish every day, including Sundays, when Luis Mauricio takes his turn doing the housekeeping and preparing the meals. He is an outgoing young man with a ready smile and joking manner. His father works for the Water and Sewer Authority and lives elsewhere with another woman, yet father and son maintain an amicable relationship. Luis's younger brother has a different father.

"I work as a car mechanic here in the neighborhood. I have only two years of high school, but I learned my trade through an organization that offers a six-month course in automobile mechanics.

"My mother and I used to live on a farm in a very dangerous area. It was a lonely place with deep gorges and fast rivers. When we visit our relatives now, we see how different it is. During the [civil] war we lived through a lot of shootings; we had to dive on the floor with mattresses to protect us. There were planes and even tanks in the street.

"On my father's side I have a lot of relatives who were either in the armed services or the police. I was even taken into the army once, but they kicked me out because I was only fourteen years old. You are supposed to be eighteen years old to be recruited. The soldiers rounded me up with many other children one day. We were forced at gunpoint to go to the barracks. My uncle is a lieutenant in the army, so he intervened. Many had to stay because they were the right age and height requirements.

"My mother has guided me well; she has always been with me. We seldom see the other relatives. When my great-grandmother died, they all took off in different directions. We don't communicate with them because their lives are unstable; they live with this woman or that one. We never know who the current mate is at any given time. My father has influenced me some, but my uncles always talked to me about staying straight and not doing things I will regret later on.

"No, I'm not married, and please, no, I don't have children. I have a girlfriend, but I don't see her very often. I can't think about marriage at this point. Life is too hard to even consider it. You have to have a good, steady job, and feel that you've accomplished something. But the way my moth-

er and I earn our living, marriage is
out of the question for now. I can't
continue my studies, because what I
earn is just not sufficient to pay for
it. I have to work long hours, so
there's no time for anything else. I can
do one thing well, but not two. I'll have
to remain a mechanic.

"Having a wife, or just living with
a girl, would take much more than I
can offer. An older, more mature
man, at least thirty, has a better
chance to make a relationship last
longer. It's a shame to see husbands
and wives who are separated. My
brother's father has never helped
my mother. She tried to get help
through the courts, but that didn't

Luis Mauricio Benavides Sosa in front of
San Salvador home with his mother, Rosa
Vilma Sosa, and half-brother William
Enrique

work. He hasn't been around in nine years. My brother doesn't know who
his father is. Young people are trying to change that. And they believe in
smaller families, too. There is too much overpopulation in the world.

"I want my wife to be a simple person, not a party girl. There are so many
girls around who dress in miniskirts and like dancing. This is not wrong,
but it shouldn't be the only thing they like. A girl should have some
Christian principles and have her priorities straight. I want my wife to be
more like me. I like to be by myself; I'm not interested in going out with friends
or joining a gang. And I want to be a good father.

"That means advising children on the right ways to act. It also means not
being an alcoholic like so many men who arrive home late at night all drunk.
If this is common in a home the children will think it's the way to behave.
The parents fight, or the father hits the mother or the children. The children lose respect for them, and that's how they live."◆

Luis's comments on fatherhood were echoed by several of the young men
interviewed. It may be that the current generation has witnessed too many
divorces, too many single-parent families, too many desertions by fathers.
When these young men speak of parenting, their words express a concern
for responsible parenthood and a will to be caring husbands and fathers.

SENOU, MALI

About half an hour's drive outside of Bamako is a series of villages known
as Senou. Most homes are made of the traditional banco bricks with

thatched roofs. Among the houses stand the cylindrical granaries where the year's harvest is stored. Upon arrival, we were greeted by an elder who led

Gaossou Coulibaly, 24   us to the village center, where a great shade tree provided relief from the withering sun.

Once settled in the shade, we were formally presented to the village chief, sixty-five-year-old Alou Coulibaly. It was early afternoon. Children of all ages gathered to watch us, standing at a distance, in awe of a significant event. Chief Coulibaly spoke of the many changes he had seen in past years, mentioning specifically the deterioration of the natural environment and the transformation to a cash-based local economy. He lamented the migration of young men to the coastal countries of West Africa, a traditional practice for generations past, he said, but one which has today become a worrisome necessity.

"If you are to marry and provide for your children, you have to exile yourself. Some even stay away altogether." Indeed, two of the chief's sons live and work in Abidjan, in the Ivory Coast. One is a mechanic, the other a driver.

The chief's youngest son, Gaossou, is the only son who remains to help his father in the fields. A tall young man, he seemed self-confident and relaxed, although his hands, roughened by fieldwork, constantly twisted together as we spoke. He was wearing dark pink pants and a matching shirt, a colorful combination on a bright afternoon. Asked why he hadn't married, he explained proudly that since Senou is so close to the city, they have picked up urban ways, like marrying later. In rural villages, he said, they marry at fourteen or fifteen.

"I have a fiancée here in the village. We know each other and she likes me. We'd like to get married this year, but I don't know if it will be possible. I've waited, because taking a wife is a responsibility. You have to provide for her, to give her what she needs.

"In my father's time, nothing lacked in the village; there was plenty of water, and we raised good crops. That's no longer the case. The lack of water, the change in climate, are causing many problems. God has to bring us help. In the dry season, there's no work. And there are many more people here as well. The population of Senou has grown too much; people have too many children. That is why life is becoming more difficult. I'd like to find work, but there is little to do here. The opportunities are few unless you go far away. But I must stay and help my father.

"To provide for my children, I'm going to plant fruit trees. That way if the crops fail at least I will have fruit to sell to provide for my family." Pointing off to the west, Gaossou, said, "I've started planting over there. Some trees are already bearing fruit."

"My fiancée and I have already discussed the number of children we will have, only four or five. After that she will use family planning. You get it at the hospital.

"I want my children to go to school. That's the only way to succeed, to know how to read and write. We will discipline them well. We have to show them the right way of life. I'll also make them help me, so they know about difficulties in life. While I'm alive I will provide for them, but afterward, they must know how to get along in life. They might say, 'My father has this and that,' and not work hard themselves. I don't want my children to be lazy like that. And I don't want them to run off just because they can earn money in the city.

"Here in the village, with my friends, we play cards, soccer. Sometimes we organize dances. If one of us earns some money we'd like to build a soccer field or a place to hold dances, so that we can have some entertainment in the evenings. During the dry season, there is no work, nothing to occupy us. Young people have nothing to do but hang around." ◆

As we have heard from each of the young people interviewed, marriage is a major preoccupation. Yet for many, we also hear, it is a dream that must be deferred. Gassou Coulibaly wants to succeed, to be able to support a wife; so does Derren Mangum. Gassou must stay with an aging father and will plant fruit trees to provide for his wife. Derren, living on his own, is waiting until his business provides a secure livelihood. Each has an egalitarian marriage in mind. Whether it be an educated youth from a financially secure background, or a young man from a semiliterate peasant family, many young people find that the costs of providing for a family in today's world are simply beyond their means.

BARAIPARA, BANGLADESH

I had spent the day with Rokya Buli, a community development agent who works in a series of villages not far from Bogra. In each of the families we visited, the main concern of parents was how to provide dowries for their daughters. Without sufficient dowry there was no hope of marriage, and their daughters, who ranged in age from fourteen to seventeen, would soon be "too old" to find husbands.

Rupali and Fanci, ages sixteen and fifteen, are the daughters of landless farmers. Frail and willowy, both girls have dark skin, black eyes, and flashing smiles that would easily capture a young man's heart. Rupali spoke eloquently of her hopes. "I want my husband to be tall and well-educated. He should have been to school and be intelligent."

Her friend, Fanci, had other ideas. She had wanted to go to school, but it was out of the question. "I have five sisters; we are six girls and a boy. My

Village girls Fanci Chanmia and friend
Rupali Abdur Rouf in Baraipara,
Bangladesh

parents are very poor." The girl reached out and took my hand, saying, "If you will take me with you, I could go to school; it would make me happy. There is nothing here for me. Not even a marriage with a poor man."

Later in the day, Rokya and I had a discussion with a group of young male volunteers who work in her community development project. I asked them about the issue of dowry, saying how unfortunate it is that girls cannot marry because their parents can't afford sufficient dowries. Almost angrily, one young man replied, "We don't care about dowry! We would willingly marry without it—but we can't marry because we have no jobs. We have no way to support a wife."

My thoughts returned to the Bengali boy on the plane: Is that what the young must do? Leave the family in order to, one day, have a family?

The search for an adequate livelihood is only one of many daunting challenges facing today's youth. A yearning for education, responsibility to parents, communications among generations, and fears of illness or drugs are issues common to youth on all continents. Although, inevitably, actions sometimes fall short of aspirations, the words of young people themselves are encouraging. Based on the interviews here, it seems that regardless of origins—rural or urban, educated or semiliterate—young people have begun to grasp the notion of their individual worth and, further, the equal worth of women and men. They speak of marriages that operate as partnerships, and of smaller families that will allow them to better provide for their children and to give them adequate education and guidance. They themselves, however, will need to find their way with comparatively little guidance from their elders. Despite their parents' best intentions, the rapid pace of change means that the only life-maps today's youth may find are the ones they draw themselves.

Part Three

Facing the Challenges

Eight | Nature's Families, Peoples' Needs

The people who are living in urban areas with noise and all . . .
I wonder what would happen to them once they get into a very silent
place.

—Sumio Saito, Tokyo, Japan

Thirty years ago, a visit to Yemen took me to the port of Hodeidah, where moisture from the Red Sea stifles any breeze that might provide relief from the ovenlike heat. Caught between the desert and oil-stained beaches, the scraggly port town offers those who gather there little more than a glimpse of a horizon different from the country's arid, mountain-bound interior.

The White Fathers, an order of priests who choose to serve in desert settings, built a boys' orphanage there years ago. Their aim is to give a home, food, skills, and affection to a few of the hundreds of children whose families can't provide for them. Winding through the narrow alleys of town, we came upon a massive fortresslike structure. The "children's home" has twelve-foot-high, unpainted, sun-baked walls; no color, trees, or joy flourish there. Straddling its only entrance, in a chair propped against the door frame, a formidable, bearded guard grumbled a greeting. He was the boys' keeper; his duty was to keep them from escaping. In fact, most of the day he was the sole companion to the sixty boys housed there: funds for employees were limited. Early each morning an elderly woman arrived to cook two daily meals, and twice a week a carpenter taught elementary woodworking. During the remainder of the days—and weeks, and months—the children were left to do as best they could on their own.

As we entered the sandy compound, in which two cement-block buildings suffered the sun's torment, a mob of giggling boys rushed toward us. Ranging in age from seven to thirteen, the boys were like boys everywhere: front teeth lost and not yet found, scabby knees, and puppylike bodies. What made them different was their desperate need for what the priests couldn't provide—affection. To be able to touch an adult, a woman, to have her look into your eyes, smile, and touch the top of your head, was a joy each sought.

At one point, a tiny hand slipped into mine. The face of a small boy smiled up at me. His hand tugged mine gently; his silent message: "Follow me."

The spindly child guided me out into the sun, around the building, to the far side of the empty compound. The heat leadened our movements. Then, slowing his pace even more, as if we were nearing something secret, he pulled me to the edge of the building, to a shaded corner, where he knelt to the sand. There, alone and slightly withered, a tiny green plant, barely six inches high, emerged from the barren soil. Ever so gently, the child's hands stroked the sand around it, rearranging and caressing the earth as if it would then better nourish his only possession.

Little do we comprehend our dependence upon the natural world, or how very much our physical, emotional, and spiritual health is intertwined with the health of nature. The Yemeni child knew and was well aware of nature's vulnerability.

Only in the past few decades has the international community begun to consider the global consequences of overuse and abuse of the planet's natural systems. A century of industrialization, urbanization, population expansion, and the plunder of natural resources has left us with an irreparable loss of species, with infertile lands and polluted air and water. As the twenty-first century began, millions of families, in all regions of the world, suffered the consequences of environmental degradation and poor management of the human habitat.

Soils and minerals; grasslands and forests; and rivers, lakes, and oceans— these are the foundation on which we create our livelihoods. And all have deteriorated dramatically since the mid-1900s. This is not "someone else's" problem. Climate change bedevils all regions; air pollution clouds cities; foul slum quarters menace public health; chemical residues in water poison wildlife and, yes, people, in all nations. In the past decades we have seen an increasing number of "natural" disasters and environmental "accidents," and refugees who flee these events or the long-term degradation that results.[1] These trends are even more worrisome when we recognize that, although population growth rates are decreasing, the actual number of inhabitants of our world continues to rise, creating even more pressure on our natural environment.

The quality of that environment has become a global concern with ramifications for families' health, livelihood, and, ultimately, long-term well-being. This became quite clear from interviews with families in all the countries we visited. In this chapter, we hear families speak about the environment in which they live, its past bounty and its current vulnerability.

GOUNDAKA, MALI

My arrival in Mali coincided with the end of the annual Ramadan festivities, during which Malians dress in their best finery. Bamako's streets overflowed with colorful *boubous*—long cotton dress—and turbans, and children of all ages were smiling with pride in their new dresses or stylish shirts and pants.

Malian sociologist Tieman Diarra, a researcher at Bamako's Institut des Sciences Humaines, was to be my guide and interpreter. He is a quiet man of medium height, slow of speech, and totally unflappable. He had suggested we travel north to the region of Mopti, a trading center on the banks of the Niger. There we could meet families yet untouched by the influence of city life: nomads, pastoralists, farmers, and the river's fishermen.

It was early April, and temperatures on the fringe of the Sahara desert were insufferably high. So it was in Mopti, a city unlike any I've seen before or since. Perched on the Niger River and its seasonal inlets, Mopti's markets attract all sizes of pirogues—long, canoelike boats—that come and go, trading in food, wood for fuel, cooking pots, and surprising luxuries. The riverbanks are crowded with people fishing, bathing, or washing their laundry, and with their goats or prized sheep. The Niger is wide enough to give a distant peaceful appearance to the villages on the other side, too wide to clearly reveal their poverty. Our destination was Goundaka, a village half an hour's drive from Mopti on a barely discernable dirt road.

Goundaka, meaning "secret" in the Peul language, should be kept that way—a secret village. Its setting is beautiful, a gift of nature in an otherwise hostile Sahel. At the base of a slate rock formation, Goundaka benefits from rainwater that rolls down the hillside to create a natural—and reliable—pond. Its waters have dried up only once in living memory.

One reaches the village through a Sahel-style forest—large, old trees, placed too far from one another to provide much relief from the sun. At the village center stands a stunning example of the region's pinnacled mosques. In the adobe-fenced compounds that branch out from it reside more than one hundred families. Approaching the village from the other side, one walks through market gardens surrounding the pond. A small mango grove, tall, thick, and richly green, serves as the village gate. Goundaka is blessed with a dependable water source, good soils, shade trees, and a population of both farmers and herders. Close to Mopti, it has a ready-made market for its produce.

Mamadou Diab, 95

Dika Dabo, 55

Dicko Diarra, 35

Hawra Sow, 35

Brema Toure, 39

Moussa Ouri Barry, 70+

As Tieman Diarra and I walked into the village, dozens of children appeared from nowhere. They examined us carefully; some, to demonstrate their bravery to one another, dared to take our hands. When we asked that they lead us to the village chief, they guided us through people's yards and into alleys left and right until we arrived at a small, cement-brick building. Professor Diarra stood by the side of the door and, without entering, requested permission to meet with the chief. A voice called out, telling us to enter and to sit on the floor facing him.

It was cool and dark inside; the only light filtered through a small window and the open door. A single chair was propped against the wall in a corner, and woven mats covered the earthen floor. Sitting on the mat beside the chief, ninety-five-year-old Mamadou Diab, were three of his counselors. One of them, a nephew named Brema Traore, was to be our host for the next two days.

MAMADOU   The chief was happy to announce that he was born in 1900. He is blind and unable to walk well, but singularly articulate. While emphasizing his great age, he reached out to pat my hand, to make sure I listened carefully to his stories. He wore an embroidered skullcap and a long gray robe, and his white goatee was neatly barbered. During the ensuing hours, he puffed constantly on a small, handheld pipe, entertained by those who came by to pay their respects with jokes and village news. As village chief, he is arbiter, decision maker, giver of counsel, and source of village lore and history.

Mamadou himself is something of a legend. One of the few of his generation able to attend school, he was later inducted into the French army while Mali was still a colony. His education and experience beyond the village contribute to his reputation as a learned, respected man. Twice a widower, he had, two weeks prior to our visit, taken a new wife, a fifty-year-old widow named Kadiatou Kasambara. His need for a wife resides in the constant surveillance that his frailty and blindness demand. Several times, while we talked, he lit his pipe and tossed the match absentmindedly onto the dry reed mat between us.

As we sat introducing ourselves, Kadiatou and the chief's daughter, Dika, appeared in the doorway. They brought portions of rice-and-millet porridge for all present. Served in individual gourd dishes, it was to be eaten by rolling it with the fingers into mouthful-sized portions. A large bowl of water was first passed among us for the purpose of rinsing our hands.

In Goundaka, as elsewhere in Mali's innumerable villages, no serious business can be commenced before sharing a meal. I couldn't help feel this was an elegant custom, rooted in knowledge of travelers' appetites. I ate the sugared porridge with gratitude and sensed that our host was told that I had enjoyed his food, for his manner changed to one of relaxed complicity as he talked about his village.

"Goundaka is a good village, on a good site. I became the chief a long time ago—about forty years or so. Those of us who went to school were taken into the French army. By the time I returned my father was getting old; it was time for me to become chief. I had to learn all the village history, the names of all the ancestors, who is married to whom and who is the son or daugh-

Visiting Goundaka's village chief, Mamadou Diab (*center*), with Brema
Toure (*right*) and unidentified villager

ter of whom. Few of us know these details, so we have to pass them on to
someone younger.

"I had twelve children with one wife and three with a second. Of the first
twelve only four are still living; seven died as infants, another at age six. With
the second wife, just one child remains; two died young, and so did the wife.
These days there are fewer deaths among children, because we give vaccinations.

"The village is getting bigger; every year people come and ask if they can
settle here. We send someone to their village to find out if they are honest
and good workers, if they will help us develop our village. If so, we let them
come. We want the village to grow. The only problems we have result from
the competition between farmers and herders. The pasturelands here are very
good, but there is no longer enough land for everyone. Farmers want to cultivate the pasture areas. That creates problems with the herders, of course.
And then there is the problem of water.

"When I first became chief there was so much water, so much rain, that
I had to crush three eggs, one at each end of the village, one in the center,
to protect us from floods. You see, the river runs nearby, and in those days
it overflowed from too much rain. That was a long time ago, I think the last
time was 1963. Since then the rains have diminished little by little. There
are still specific places in the river where you find water during the dry season, but they are few.

"Now, when the rainy season is due we are obliged to plead with God to
send us rain. I have to pray to a marabou [saintly man]. He cites verses in
the Koran asking for rain. That was never necessary before. And crop
yields were better as well. We had enough food for everyone. Now the mil-

let crop doesn't suffice to feed us; we are obliged to grow and sell vegetables in order to buy our millet. With water from the pond we irrigate small
gardens and raise eggplant, onions, potatoes.

"In 1973 to 1974 and then again in 1984 to 1985 we had terrible
droughts. Nothing grew—nothing. Everyone had to leave the village. They
traveled to the borders of the Ivory Coast and Burkina Faso, looking for food.
But in Burkina there was drought as well. Only the elders stayed behind.
We were too old to go off." The old chief remained quiet for a time, content
to draw on his pipe and listen to others speak of the great droughts.◆

DIKA   The chief's daughter Dika, fifty-five, a stockily built woman, was dressed
in a flowing green *boubou;* she wore rings on the middle toe of each foot.
Joking with her father, she told him he couldn't hoard the guests. She insisted that we come visit her then and there. Her family compound consists of
a series of woven-grass huts; as we walked there the midmorning sun
baked everything in sight, including us. Under the only tree in her yard, a
lonely donkey stood statue-still, unwilling to move in the intense heat.

In the shade of a lean-to kitchen, relatives of various ages gathered around.
The children were barefoot, and all wore a T-shirts from faraway places. The
babies, passed from one adult to the other, wore only beaded string belts around
their midriffs. A tiny girl crawled into Dika's lap to sleep as she told the story
of her childlessness.

"I married at thirteen. I had one child, but it was born dead. I had gone
to the hospital in Mopti when I was seven months pregnant; I knew something was wrong, but it didn't help. I had to have a cesarean to get him out;
after that I couldn't conceive.

"There are other cases like mine here. The mother of that child over there
was my sister. She died giving birth. That man sitting there, his wife died
of a sixth pregnancy. She had a brother whose wife also died in childbirth.
That's three in one family. It's frequent here. Because I had no children of
my own, I raised my younger brother's children.

"The women here are tired by all the work they do—tired out by the lack
of water and poverty. There is a water pump, but to use it you have to pay
five francs. That's why women fetch their water at the pond. The husbands
try to dig wells for the compounds, but the water is too far down.

"We also have to go out looking for wood to cook with. In the dry season we have to go far because the herders cut trees so their animals can eat
the leaves. They do it clandestinely because it is forbidden. We pick up the
branches left behind and use them for kitchen fuel.

"When I was young this was a village surrounded by trees. You could barely see it. There were dangerous animals in the forest. But now that so many
people have come and cut the trees, everything is different. Before we

were happy; we didn't have to buy anything. Now we are obliged to buy many things, even wood in the dry season. And to buy things, we need to sell our vegetables. We hire a pushcart and take our crops to the Mopti market two or three times a week. That's the way we earn money to provide what our children need."

While we talked, a young girl arrived with a small pail, filled with a yogurt-like cream. Sweetened with sugar, it was better than any ice cream. One of Dika's adoptive children, a two-year-old girl, climbed into my lap to have a taste. She fidgeted with my skirt and blinked incessantly to prevent insistent flies from getting into her eyes, one of which was infected.◆

DICKO AND HAWRA   Next, Brema Toure, the chief's thirty-nine-year-old nephew, wanted to show us his home and introduce us to his two wives. He had not told them of his plans, and they were surprised by this sudden visit. Each presented her home with pride, especially delighted to show that the couple owned a wooden bed: they didn't sleep on the ground, as did most villagers.

Dicko Diarra, thirty-five, Brema's first wife, is also his first cousin. She is a tall, slender mother of four children. She told us that she'd had two miscarriages after her first child, but went for treatment and was cured. "I was born here in Goundaka. My mother is Brema's father's sister. The family arranged our marriage when we were small. The wedding took place when I was sixteen and my husband was twenty."

Dicko had a serene, contented demeanor. She was proud of her home and children. The interior of her house was neat and arranged tastefully. The

A gathering at Brema Toure's home: Brema (*right front*) holding his son and (*back row, second and third from left*) cowives Hawra Sow and Dicko Diarra

bed was high and wide, covered with a white bedspread. Pots hung from the ceiling, carefully arranged by size.

Brema's second wife, Hawra Sow, is not from Goundaka. She is a divorced woman from a village called Kowyareri, in another county. Also thirty-five, she was dressed in a bright yellow *boubou*, with her hair braided and a yellow scarf tied cockily around her head. Her home was but a few meters from Dicko's and was equally neat and attractive. Close by, corrals for sheep and goats were carefully shaded by straw roofs.

"I raise the animals for sale. With the revenue I buy clothes and extra food. I had two children by my first husband, but they both died of malaria. I haven't had any children with this husband. I get along well here; my cowife is nice, and I help her with her children sometimes. This husband is good to me, not like the first one." Hawra paused a moment, then added, shyly, "We are a love-match."

BREMA Brema beamed with pride throughout our tour of his domain. He is a handsome fellow of medium height with a constant wide smile. His distinguishing feature was a bright yellow, woolen ski cap, which he wore continuously during our days in Goundaka. He told how his happiness was founded on the fact that his two wives got along well.

"It is not always that way," he admitted. "But the first wife is a cousin and is well adjusted. The second one I met at market and I liked her a lot. We talked often and realized we liked each other. When she agreed, I went to her father and asked to marry her.

"A wife must respect her husband and his family. Any wife who doesn't is a bad influence on the children. A child follows in the footsteps of its parents. For me, for example, the qualities of a wife are important in educating my children. The same thing is true for my behavior. Both parents are examples for children. If I observe parents who are not in agreement, I wouldn't let my daughter marry into that family.

"The example of my parents was very important to me. They are both dead now, but their influence set me on the right path. My father died before I was born, so his brother became my father. As is our custom, he married his brother's widow, my mother. He is the one who educated me, who sent me to the Koranic school. I went to the village school during the day and to the Koranic school at night. He also taught me all I know about farming.

"I attended school for six years, and then I went *en exode* [a self-imposed exile] to find work. Many young people do it. It's a custom that exists since the time of my father."

Brema appeared ill-at-ease when speaking about his time abroad. In the Sahel it is expected that young men go off to find work in neighboring countries, especially during the pre-harvest season when food is less abundant.

Fewer mouths to feed helps the villagers survive, and if he is lucky, the young man returns with enough money to take a bride.

"In all," Brema continued, "I stayed away for ten years, in the Ivory Coast. The first time I only lasted six months. That was 1972. I wasn't yet married. I traveled around looking for work. I carried things on my head, I swept, cleaned—anything to earn a bit of money. I returned to Goundaka with a little money and clothes for everyone in the family. It is a way of helping our parents.

"After marrying I went off again. I left my wife and children here but I never stayed away more than seven months. The second time I got a real job; I was an accountant in a small shop. Sometimes I was able to come back with lots of money, other times not so much—but always enough to pay my parents' taxes and buy clothes for the children and my wife. I stayed three years but I came back every seven months to the village to help out with the harvest.

"Most young men here go off like that. There are people who arrange everything for you—transportation, identity card, vaccination, everything. In recent years, with the ongoing droughts and changing climate, more and more young people leave. Too many, I think. They hope to be able to send back money to buy food. It's no longer a question of clothes and taxes, now it is food itself. In fact, they go all over the world, to France, to Germany, to Libya—even to America.

"You know, I've lost half the children we had. I only have four now. The first died at two months, the second died of malaria, the third was born with a defect, and the fourth died suddenly—we don't know why. My eldest is an eleven-year-old daughter and the youngest is a little over a year. My daughter still goes to school. I don't know where that will lead but I want her to go to school as long as she studies well. It is important she know how to read properly; there are so few people who read in this village.

"Of course, there are children who think that because they have gone to school they are better than others. Just because they have gone to school they think our traditions are old-fashioned. They can speak French so they think they are no longer African. When asked a question by the elders, they reply in French. The elders get very upset. I tell my children to always speak in our language, at least to our elders."

When we took our leave of Brema's wives and children, he suggested he show us his fields. He pointed out the different crops, and at the pond, he showed us the pumps that had been bought with money contributed by each farmer. Powered by gasoline, the pumps pull water from the pond and spread it over the tomato beds. Brema is somewhat aware of the threats to Goundaka's environment; he, like many men of the village, has worked in neighboring countries and has gained perspective on the limits of the land.

Herder and farmer Moussa Ouri Barry

By now I had become an admirer of this man. Knowing it was unlikely that we would meet again, my throat tightened as I said adieu. I spoke of what a lucky man he was, of what a fine village he lived in, of his beautiful family. The huge smile under the yellow ski cap disappeared for a moment. He looked off at the dust-enveloped horizon, saying, "I only hope I won't have to go *en exode* again soon—or ever, for that matter."◆

MOUSSA Before taking leave of Goundaka, we visited the home of another villager, an elderly herder, Moussa Ouri Barry. He was a tall, energetic man. He wasn't sure of his age, but thought he was in his mid-seventies. As he told of the changes he had witnessed, he corroborated the story of Goundaka's environmental problems from a herder's perspective.

"My father came to settle here a long time ago, just after I was born. We could raise a lot more cattle then because there was more grass. There was a lot of wildlife as well—too much, even. When I was a boy there were lions, hyenas, panthers—all the animals that attack cattle. There were deer and wildebeest. Now they're gone. They died or went to the south. There's nothing left—nothing.

"Now there are too many cattle and there's not enough pasturage for them. In the past the herds were big but they were vulnerable to illness. Since we began vaccinating the cattle, there are too many. People are not careful. There is just so much grass, and if there are too many cattle, they should limit their number. This is a vast pasture region and there are many sources of water, but more and more people have come to live here. And that means more families who own cattle.

"I have eight children, and four others died. Some are farmers, others herders. Even in the old days, my father and grandfather did both—herding and farming. They never went far from here, only to other villages, not other countries."◆

As we walked back through the mango grove, the thought crossed my mind that Goundaka, the secret village, is a metaphor for our world. Once plentiful and productive, its resources are now depleted and vulnerable. Where there was once sufficient rain there is now too little. The once limitless land is now coveted by more and more people, causing disputes among the different groups that seek their livelihoods from it. With the lack of rain and shortage of farmland and forests, farmers are forced to create market gardens to earn what is necessary to buy staple foods, and Goundaka's women must go further and further from the village to find wood for fuel. Hunting is futile, for the wild animals are gone. Drought, unstable food supplies, and population growth among both humans and herds, force Goundaka's young to find work elsewhere.

These changes have imperceptibly, but surely, diminished the quality of life of Goundaka's inhabitants. The chief has, in his own long lifetime, witnessed the changes, and he is aware of the pressures his village faces. Yet, believing in the tradition of hospitality and the virtues of growth, he welcomes new settlers as long as they are "honest and good workers."

Throughout my travels, what distressed me most in talking with the older generation was how quickly environmental degradation and loss is occurring.

NEAR BUSHENYI, UGANDA

The drive out to visit Azaliya Rwabulinbale on the Bushenyi road provided a vision of plenty. Everywhere, rich soils sprouted vegetable and banana plantations. Our companion, John Rwabulinbale, a field-worker from the local YWCA, had suggested that we visit his parents, who could tell us about generations past. We turned off the main highway and headed south for a half hour or so. As we drove through seemingly endless hills covered with tall grasses, I asked if this area had always been grasslands. "Oh, yes," was his immediate, definitive, reply.

Azaliya Rwabulinbale, 82

The Rwabulinbale farm sits on a hilltop overlooking the green hills that stretch as far as the eye could see. Surrounded by a few trees, the house is a two-room cottage made of adobe bricks and topped by a tin roof. In front of the door, three wooden chairs faced westward, well-placed to capture the afternoon sun.

The elderly Azaliya, a small man in height and build, was seated in one of the chairs. He doesn't walk much anymore, he explained, because "the knees are too painful." The whites of his eyes were dotted with black and red age spots that lent intensity to his gaze. Being hard of hearing, Azaliya

Azaliya Rwabulinbale (*center*), wife Edianne Kengeye by his side (*on left*), and their grandchildren and neighbors

speaks loudly but confidently: he is the patriarch, adept at making decisions and giving orders. Azaliya began by saying he was born not far from his hill-top home.

"I came here in 1947. There was just one other person. It was a forest—a real forest, with big trees, small ones, thick ones. Wild animals were every-where: lions, buffalos, hyenas. We had to kill them. We got poison from the Roman Catholic missionaries because the beasts were eating our goats and sheep. We'd just drop the poison with leftover pieces of goats or sheep—that's how we got rid of them.

"When I was young, there weren't many schools or churches. Now there is a church and a priest at every corner. And we were not many people, either. Now we are too many. It's a big change. My parents dressed in goats' skins. Now we dress in textiles and have fashions. Back then we had one style for women and one for men, so fashion is a very big change. And our people speak languages we didn't have before, like English and Swahili. Some of us don't know them because we lack education. A good change is the standard of living in our homes. Before we didn't sit in chairs; we just sat on the ground.

"Now there are people all over the place. I don't even know half of them. They've cut down all the forest. Families want to build homes, and here we build with wood. Also, to expand our gardens, we cut down the trees. First I planted bananas as our table food; then I extended the garden and planted coffee as a cash crop. The trees that we didn't cut dried up, but most were cut by the settlers. Luckily, we have a protected spring near the house. It's had water ever since I came here. Lots of changes have taken place, but the water is still running."◆

While listening to Azaliya's description of his land, I recalled that his son had not known that the area had once been forested and filled with wild animals. For him, one generation later, it had always been grassland. From one generation to the next, we are unaware of our impact on our natural environment—or the impact this environment, in turn, has on our lives, our health, and our long-term well-being. Sometimes it is the elders alone who realize how much has been lost.

CACOAL, BRAZIL

The nation of Brazil is endowed with the largest natural forest remaining on the planet. In the 1960s and 1970s the Brazilian government began building roads into regions of the Amazon river basin in an effort to open up land for an increasing number of landless farmers from the poorer regions of Brazil. As in many regions of the world today, the need for land preempts the exercise of environmental safeguards and long-term planning. And in the case of Brazil, it has had a devastating consequence on its indigenous peoples, who, to maintain their ways of life, retreat further into the forest or attempt to adapt to unfamiliar ways.

Emile Witt, 82

Marguerita Borchache Witt, 78

In the preceding chapter, we heard about the childhood of Monica Witt Braga, the young mother in Cacoal, a large town deep in the Amazon state of Rondônia. Monica's parents and grandparents were among the settlers who came to cut the forest and farm the land over twenty years ago. The story of their

Amazon settlers Marguerita Borchache Witt and Emile Witt in front of their home in Cacoal

struggle to make a living in the virgin forest is one that continues today, as more settlers seek a livelihood in one of nature's great wonders.

The elder Witt couple, Emile and Marguerita, are both of German origin and were born in the arid southern region of Brazil. Their home is a small cement structure on an unpaved, potholed street. It has both indoor and outdoor kitchens. Near the house are an outside bread oven, a well, and a garden with corn, cassava, and orange trees. When the elderly couple escorted us around their neighborhood, pointing with pride to friends' homes or their church, they were playful and happy together.

MARGUERITA Marguerita is a solidly built woman who seemed to radiate energy. Her clear, blue-gray eyes sparkled and cried alternately during her story. She is proud of her life as daughter, wife, mother to many, and now, in her later years, grandmother and great-grandmother. Her childhood was marked by poverty, an alcoholic father, and her mother's early suicide by poison. As the elder daughter, Marguerita was put in charge of raising her younger siblings, twelve in all. School was out of the question.

"A man, a widower with four children, needed a wife, and people told him how much I liked children and was good with them. So he came to ask me to marry him. I raised his children like my own, and we had two more together. We were married twenty-four years when he died of leukemia. Emile, my current husband, is his brother. He had been widowed with ten children. Everyone thought we should get married, so I asked him and he said, 'Fine.'

"When we came here there was nothing, only a dense forest. We liked it. I had never seen a forest because where we lived, in Espirito Santo, there was none left.

"We came because of our children. They wanted to come because there was little land for them in Espirito Santo, no opportunity for a better life. My son came first, three months ahead of us. He kept writing to say, 'Please come, Mum.' So we got a truck together with my sister and we all came.

"There was nothing here—nothing, just the forest. Then trucks started coming in. One person told another and the word spread. Thirty trucks a day would come, bringing the families who just put up their tarpaulins. Some set up shops, all in tents. It was very difficult. Many people failed. There was a lot of sickness, especially malaria. It was a tremendous struggle.

"When we bought our land, a part of it had already been cleared. We had to cut the rest of the trees. Every year we'd cut a bit more. We planted rice and corn to sell. We were poor, but we managed to get by. We lived there in the country almost five years and then bought this piece of land here in town. It was very far to go to church. We were getting old, and you have to go on foot. Now we are closer. When we had the first church service here, we prayed that everyone would have land to live on.

"I would like Cacoal to become very big. But we need a decent mayor. The one we have isn't doing anything. He isn't making roads, and we have terrible trouble with electricity. The government sends money, but our governor eats it and doesn't send it here.

"My mother's life was very hard. She suffered a lot because of my father's drunkenness, raising thirteen children out in the sticks, having to work so hard. My life is much easier: I have a good house and I live surrounded by my children—more than thirty grandchildren, and four great-grandchildren! We have a very united family. Luckily I married the two brothers. If God takes my husband first, I will be alone for the rest of my life. I will look after my grandchildren. God will stay with me all the way."◆

EMILE Emile, who was soon to celebrate his eighty-second birthday, was a fragile-looking man with a head of pure white hair. He was a bit hard of hearing but loved to talk and describe the Amazon settlers' life. Neither grandparent could read, and they'd had to rely on their son to protect them from the "land-grabbers," who took advantage of farmers who cleared the land only to find out it wasn't legally theirs.

Emile was wearing shorts, and when we went on tour of the neighborhood he donned a fedora and carried an umbrella. He is very active, still gardens, and constantly teases his wife.

"We were ten brothers and sisters. We are scattered around the world now. My wife and I had ten children. In Espirito Santo I worked as a stonemason. When my wife died, I stayed a widower for three years, until I met Marguerita. It was the will of God. He wanted it, so it worked.

"In Bahia there are too many people, in Ceará, too. People go hungry. You plant, but there is nothing to harvest. That's why people are coming here. When we first came it was dense jungle; there were many wild animals. We used to keep pigs and they were eaten by wild animals. There were monkeys, deer, pacu. There was a beautiful vine with grapes. It was a lovely place. But we had to cut the forest to survive. I cut several acres—big trees, two meters in diameter. I gave some wood to build the church. I burned the rest and then planted.

"When they opened the road, bad people came in. They were only after the timber. They didn't want settlers to come, because they wanted to take all the good wood out first.

"Once a policeman came and told me to leave our land. We had rice and manioc already planted—rice, corn, chickens. I felt like killing him. I took my hunting gun and waited for him. He said, 'You shouldn't be here. You should be in the forest.' And I said, 'No, sir. This is my land to feed my wife and children.' He wanted me to go further into the forest. I said, 'This is my land; I've invested in it.' He calmed down and left. I got the surveyor to come measure the land and put it in my name.

"When it was forest it was the most beautiful thing in the world. We used to hunt for food—wild pigs, big ratlike things. There were so many different animals. They are far away now.

"There were Indians here also. We didn't have problems with them. They lived very close. It was beautiful then; not like now."◆

At the commencement of the third millennium, we are barely beginning to understand the damaging burdens we have placed on the natural systems that sustain us—and the long-term consequences of this damage. One concern currently under study is the perceived increase in what we call natural disasters. To be sure, no one would argue that natural disasters are a new phenomenon. But at the end of the twentieth century there was increasing evidence that humankind's pressure on natural systems and climate may be increasing the intensity and frequency of these so-called natural disasters.[2] We know, for example, that deforestation results in erosion, the silting of riverbeds, the overflowing of riverbanks and widespread flooding. At the same time, as the planet's atmosphere traps heat close to the earth's surface, the resultant warming of that atmosphere may contribute to the intensity of storms.

BARAIPURA, BANGLADESH

Bangladesh is a low-lying delta nation, created by the watershed of the Himalayas, caught between the land mass of India and the Burmese-Thai peninsula. Flooding is a natural phenomenon and has for centuries created fertile land (not unlike the Nile Valley, where, until the construction of the Aswan High Dam, annual flooding replenished soils). In the past century, however, the Himalayan watershed, the mountains of Nepal and India, have been substantially deforested as more people seek livelihoods from the mountain environment. Erosion of mountainsides fills the river systems with silt, which accumulates along their journey through Bangladesh to the Bay of Bengal. The riverbeds grow shallower, and can no longer contain their waters in periods of high rainfall.

Mohammed Abul Kashem, 50
Kazal Abul Kaham, 75
Rigia Begum, 49
Samsumahar Abul Kasham, 17

Our journey took us first to Bogra by four-wheel-drive vehicle and numerous river ferries. Much of the route was built on causeway-type roads, built four to five meters above rice fields for protection against floods. One could easily see why: low-lying fields were half-submerged, and sunken boat hulls emerged here and there from the water.

The following day we left Bogra for the drive to Baraipura village, where our community development worker guide, Rokya Buli, was to introduce us to several farming families. Again, we took a ferry, a small one this time. Between the ferry and the village, along the causeway, we drove on temporary bypasses to avoid a series of broken bridges, toppled by the last floods.

The fields were small in size and farmers had scooped up the earth and built retaining walls for the plots at varying levels. Men with shoulder sticks holding bundles of harvested rice on each end moved along with a swift, hip-swinging gait. Others prepared the fields for new plantings. In Bangladesh, every season is both a planting and harvest season—luckily so, for that is the only way the country is able to feed itself. Nowhere in our ride through rural areas did we see women—only an occasion girl carrying a small burden. Most women are enclosed in purdah, virtual nonparticipants in activities outside the home.

The Abul Kashem family consists of six individuals of three generations. Each generation had witnessed its land "taken by the river." The grandmother saw her father's land disappear under the river in the 1970s; her husband's land was taken in the early 1980s, and a decade later, her son's property disappeared when the river changed its course once again. Each time the family began anew. Miraculously, all had survived the floods; only possessions were lost.

The Kashem home is built of reeds and wooden beams with an earthen floor. It is neatly organized, with a large bed, another small bed in a corner, a huge carved trunk which held the family linens and valuables (an antique for which they apologized, saying it was "too old"). The small garden in back of the house was planted with flowers and it is there, well hidden from neighbors, that the Kashem women thrash their rice.

Mohammed Abul Kashem planting rice on his riverside plot

MOHAMMED Mohammed Abul Kashem is a tall, handsome man, appearing self-confident and reflective. He seemed a bit skeptical about my visit until I began to talk about potato farming in my home state of Maine. The subject caught his interest and soon he wanted to talk at length.

"I was born nearby, within the same jurisdiction. The house we lost to the river is very close—half a mile. I grew rice, chili, and jute on the land there. It was good land; I made a good living.

"I owned my land and did everything I could to protect it. I raised the ground by excavating earth, bringing it from other places. Nature and I made the land; I made it much higher. It was a lot of work but it wasn't enough. Floods are a thing of God, God-given. The river broke its banks; the water became turbulent; waves lashed at the ground and took everything in the house. I had to hire a boat. We carried all we could with us by boat, everything that could be saved, even the poles for the house.

"We came here to find a place to settle and I built this house. We are still suffering. It's terrible to know that all you own is under the river. The river changed its course against us. It is still in the same place, covering our land. What I have now is less than half of what I had before. Farmers in our country are like farmers elsewhere; they try to cope with erosion of land and floods. There will be more floods. My grandfather said there will be floods. Even his grandfather said the same thing. There will always be the rains and the flood season. There's no country that can stop that. But if some efforts could be made to control the river, it would be good.

"When the flooding occurs it washes away the soil. Sometimes sand is left behind. In other places, it leaves behind very fertile soil that helps double the crop. That's a gift from the flood. But it does not always happen that way."◆

KAZAL Mohammed's mother wore a dark violet sari, frayed and worn. Her posture and quick walk denoted strength and pride. Indeed, she told me she was pleased that a stranger would come and pay attention to her story, her life. Before beginning our conversation, she wanted me to see where the family land had once been. She sent me off with her son for a walk to the riverbank. There before us stretched the wide Jamuna, a branch of the Brahmaputra. About a mile across, land began again as islands, and then beyond that, the opposite bank. Beneath the river lay the fields and livelihood of thousands of families. When I returned to the house Kazal was pleased I had seen the river, saying simply, "Floods are God-given, yes, but they are the origin of our misery."

In the quiet of her courtyard, Kazal began her story. "I was born in a place called Dighapara. I don't know my age, but maybe more than seventy-five. My son is not yet fifty. I was married when I was just an immature little girl.

Seventeen-year-old Samsumahar Abul Kashem working in the courtyard with her grandmother, Kazal

I bore three children. Two daughters and one son. I had those three children,
no others. So, God blessed me. All of them are married. After I married, my
husband's land was taken away. When I was a girl we didn't see such
things. In my whole childhood I never saw a flood like that.

"My father grew jute and rice, but his land was all taken by the river. Some
people were hurt and all our cattle drowned. When my husband's land was
taken by the river, no cattle or people were killed. We were just in a kind
of terrible suffering.

"When my son lost his land to the river, no cattle died, only one man was
killed. The river took our clothes, our rice, cooking material and pots. We
suffered terribly. Allah knows. Many corpses floated by. The river water was
polluted so we couldn't drink it. The deputy commissioner of Bogra brought
us food, rice and wheat. We survived by eating those things. The army gave
us clothes.

"And that is our life. You settle somewhere and then waves take your life
away. It is sad to see this so many times in one lifetime. But you have come
here and are not neglecting me. That makes me happy. Old people should
be accepted, they should be heard."◆

RIGIA Kazal's daughter-in-law Rigia is in her late forties. The end of her
faded salmon-colored sari was draped over shoulder and head, and she kept
her eyes lowered at all times, as women are taught to do. When she
described her experience with the floods she seemed to connect everything to the situation of her daughter, who, because of the poverty imposed
by loss of land and possessions, is not able to marry. There is no money for
a proper dowry.

"I was twenty-three when I married. Then my father died, the floods came, and my life of sorrow began. What could we do? The rains came, there was water all around. We took the children to the embankment and made them stay there. Misfortune never comes alone. The first flood took our land; a few years later a second flood took our house."

Rigia hesitated a moment and then, looking directly at me, asked, "Why do you want to hear these stories of my life? For me, it is very difficult. It makes me very sad.

"Now I am trying to save money for my daughter to marry. If the crops are good, there may be a chance that a suitable young man might accept her. This is my only worry, to give a life to my daughter."◆

SAMSUMAHAR   Rigia's daughter was extremely shy. Barely sixteen, she appeared far older. A tall young woman, she had the demeanor of one who wants to please but doesn't quite know how. When I asked what qualities she would like to find in a husband, her reluctance seemed due less to shyness than shame. She explained that she can't marry because the family is too poor to afford a dowry.

"I was eleven years old when the floods came. It was a terrible, frightful thing for me. We are still afraid the floods will come again. Each year we live in fear.

"I used to go school and read until class nine, age fourteen. But I couldn't go any further because of money problems. Now because of lack of money I can't get married. Someday I hope to have a husband who is educated. He should have been to school and be intelligent. And he will not beat his wife. Every girl wants these qualities in a man—a man who will not beat his wife, who will not verbally abuse her. I hope he won't beat me so I don't suffer."◆

Our hosts insisted we eat lunch with them. The meal consisted of rice, a spicy leaf sauce, and a hard-boiled egg. It was a tasty meal, and served in the most gracious of ways in the cool shade of their home. For a while we talked about my travels and stories of other families. Everyone had many questions about families elsewhere, about their crops, their children. Were there floods elsewhere? What did other people do about them?

At one point, Rokya Bali leaned over to me and confided that she had found a young man for Samsumahar, whose family would not ask for a large dowry. She was to arrange for the families to meet. If the young people liked each other, a marriage might be in the offing. Nature's havoc could take possessions, yes, but at least in this family it would not take a girl's future.

HARTSBURG, MISSOURI

Six months after my visit to Bangladesh, I left Washington, D.C., to travel to Missouri to talk to families who were recovering from the summer floods of 1993, some of the worst in living memory. From the plane window, one could observe the winding river patterns, small farms surrounded by wintergreens, clumps of trees, occasional ponds that sparkled in the afternoon sun. I could see the juncture of the Mississippi and Missouri rivers. The rivers and their tributaries are the lifeline of America's heartland and huge commercial barges, sometimes as many as ten clamped together, could be seen on the dark brown rivers. Since 1944, a series of dams and levies has regulated irrigation and flooding on the Missouri and the branches of the Mississippi. But in 1993, rains came in such abundance as to breach the levees spanning nearly 10,000 kilometers, flooding homes, businesses, and farmland; all told, the financial losses were estimated at $1.9 billion.[3]

Alfred Beckmeyer, 82
Orion Beckmeyer, 54
Barbara Beckmeyer, 51

The town of Hartsburg sits on the edge of a vast plain that has seen its share of flooding. Yet, according to the older generation, the floods have become increasingly destructive. Indeed, according to the *New York Times*, the Soil Conservation Service estimated that almost half of the nearly one million acres of the Missouri River floodplain were damaged by sand and erosion in the summer's floods.[4] Some farmers I met said it was because "we've tampered too much with nature" with all the construction—highways, factories, shopping malls, parking lots—along the banks of the intricate river system that makes up the Mississippi valley.

The Beckmeyer family has farmed the land around Hartsburg for three generations, and each of the generations was there to greet us: grandparents, parents, and two children with their spouses. Their three farmhouses were on the same hill, barely a quarter of a mile apart along a winding road. Their lands, however, were not adjacent to their homes. Most were down in the "bottoms," the name given to the floodplain seen in the distance.

ALFRED Eighty-two-year-old Alfred Beckmeyer sat in the front parlor in his armchair with a blanket around his arthritic legs. He said his father's family had been farmers in Illinois. His bright blue eyes squinted when he told of losing his parents when barely eight years old, of working in a shoe factory as a teenager, and then, prodded by an uncle, of attending university, where he earned a degree in agriculture.

"I can't remember when I didn't want to farm. When I visited my grandmother, she'd always say, 'Alfred, whatever you do, don't become a farmer.' But I wanted to be a farmer. I graduated in 1935. I met my wife at church and eventually, her father helped me find a farm I could take over. Now both my sons are farmers right nearby."

When I asked about the recent floods, the elder shook his head, as if in disbelief. "There were the floods of 1944, '47, '51. Then there was 1973, '86, '93. We built a house down in the bottoms, with a bathroom water cistern, electricity all installed, then the big one came along in '44 and it was too dangerous to stay down there. We moved to this house in '44. The house down in the flats is still standing, but nobody's lived there since. Then there were the floods of 1973; they were bad and they spurred the building of the levees. We thought all that would help. But this time—I don't know. We had twenty inches of rain. My son Orion has four feet of sand on half his acreage. The land is lost. I think the climate is definitely changing."•

ORION   A few hundred yards down the road, I visited the home of fifty-four-year-old Orion, a tall, lanky man who was wearing cowboy boots, jeans, and a denim shirt. We sat at the kitchen table as he explained that he had fifty beef cattle and grows corn, soybeans, and wheat. Until a few months before, he had farmed 950 acres; now, the problem is sand.

"There's a quarter million acres in Missouri covered with two feet of sand. In some places it is five feet deep. It's impossible to remove. It would take very special deep plows to try to turn the sand under.

"Farmers who don't raise cattle have lost everything. The force of the floodwater was such that it swirled around my grain bins in whirlpools. They now sit in fifteen-foot holes, toppled over in a heap.

"We've fooled around too much with nature. Now it's fooling with us."♦

BARBARA   Later that afternoon, Orion's wife, Barbara, took me on a tour of Hartsburg and the "bottoms." We drove by fields of sand, a beach hundreds of miles from the ocean. What we saw was a beautiful waterlogged floodplain scattered with abandoned farm buildings—mud everywhere. Barbara said that she and her husband were not too worried about the financial consequences of the flood, explaining, "During the seventies and eighties we were lucky. The crops were good and we were able to put away savings. And we have a good retirement plan. Other farmers, those that go year by year, are suffering."

Suddenly, pointing she said, "That's my mother-in-law's childhood home over there, with the porch ripped off. See, the watermark is just under the roof. Hartsburg may well be abandoned this time. Even the town cafe is for sale."♦

Whether it be a lack of renewable water in Goundaka or uncontrollable rivers in Bangladesh and the American Midwest, the impact of human activity on the natural environment can have serious consequences, affecting millions of families throughout the world. As these examples demonstrate, water alone—too little, or too much—can transform countless human lives.

Drinking water sources are particularly vulnerable and becoming more scarce. Population Action International points out that in 2000, 505 million people were living in water-scarce or water-stressed conditions; by 2025, that figure could well rise to between 2.4 and 3.2 billion people.[4] In coastal areas, saltwater is seeping into freshwater supplies; irrigation farming is vulnerable to water table depletion and salinization.

The demand for water, land, fuel, and housing expands daily. So, too, do urban settlements. The human-made environment—cities, towns, and the transportation systems that connect them—weigh heavily on the natural world.

BANGKOK, THAILAND

In the Klong Toey slums of Bangkok, three generations of the Singtoh family share a self-built wooden structure that has developed haphazardly into a two-story, five-room home. It has access to running water and electricity, but no sewerage. Household and human wastes flowed under the wooden "patio" on which we sat, its stench rising to remind us. The drainage ditch beneath us was home, no doubt, to the mosquitoes that hummed about. That said, the main pollution problem the family faces is noise. The house sits within ten feet of the railroad tracks. Trains pass every five minutes or so in a deafening, cadenced roar. Despite the home's shortcomings, the Singtoh family fears for their precious dwelling. They are squatters and fear eviction at any moment, at the whim of city officials.

Like millions of slum-dwelling families the world over, the Singtohs fled rural poverty to find work in a city. The fifty-six-year-old father, a farmer from Thailand's harsh northeast, explained simply, "On the farm, you can get money only once a year. Here you can get a salary every month, and I have to support seven people."

In talking with Mr. Singtoh's daughter, a woman who sells noodles on the neighboring streets, I learned that city life, its crowding and insecurity, has taken its toll. "I'm better off than my mother; she worked in the fields and didn't have a house, just a hut. But city life is very difficult. My husband is a day laborer, but his earnings are not enough to keep us. Everyday he asks me for money—in the morning, then again in the evening. I am married to a man who likes to drink. Many drink and quarrel. There is much violence in families. It's not a good life."

The Thai family interviewed in chapter 2, live in a more prosperous neighborhood of Bangkok. Businessman Thada Loca-apichai told us about his experience of urban life.

"The pollution in Bangkok is very bad. At the outset, Bangkok had no urban planning. Then it was too late. Now the pollution is inescapable. I know several people who are having health problems because of it—the motorcycles, the tuk-tuk drivers, and the buses. You can't help smell the fumes. On a motorcycle, no matter how fast you go, you still have to breathe. There was a big campaign on unleaded gas and poisonous air, but we also have too much dust. Bangkok is probably the most dust-tainted city in the world because of construction. The authorities must act. Municipal departments should be more strict. There are many health problems in the making. People are sneezing, have runny noses and flu symptoms. They just don't realize they are allergic to pollution. And if you can't stand that kind of life, you have to live far away, at least a two-hour drive."

Overly rapid urbanization, resulting in its slums, pollution, competition for livelihoods, and social discord, is a festering social issue that demonstrates the importance of how we conceive and build viable communities. Urban planning often comes too late, as people move to urban areas faster than local authorities can offer services or housing to receive them.

WADI MOUSSA, JORDAN

In the Hui Autonomous Region of China, as described in chapter 6, I visited nicely appointed homes carved out of a hillside. There, the inhabitants were resisting government efforts to move them into newly built homes on a windswept plain where they could be better served and organized into work teams. In Jordan, I found families who had been enticed out of their traditional—and splendid—cave homes in the ancient city of Petra. There were mixed reactions to the new arrangement, and many spoke of the social problems that came with the move.

We arrived just as the sun fell behind the bizarre rock formations inside of which lies the ancient Nabataean city of Petra. An Arab people, the Nabataeans carved their capital into the stone of a series of deep, narrow canyons on the caravan routes between Gaza, the Red Sea, and the Persian Gulf. Wadi Moussa is the contemporary gateway to Petra; a word meaning "city of rock" in Greek. From the fourth century B.C.E., a remarkable example of humans' marriage with nature's beauty had flourished here—an entire city of administrative buildings, banks, elegant homes, commercial establishments, all carved with ornate columns and frescoes into the deep red stone of the canyon. Conquered by the Romans in 106 C.E., Petra is today a tourist marvel where the ancient carved buildings' doors stand sentinel-like in elegant streets reached by horseback through a narrow canyon entrance.

The people of contemporary Petra belong to the Bdoul tribe. As far back as anyone can remember, they lived in the canyon city. Without running water or electricity, about two thousand people lived in Petra's caves, in harmony with one another, their herds, and the lands they farmed. By 1986, they began to be viewed as a nuisance by the developing tourist industry. The government approached them, saying they would be much better off if they moved out of Petra, to Wadi Moussa, where they would be near schools, health facilities, and government services. The government promised to move them into nice houses; government agents even showed them architects' sketches of the traditional-style homes they would be given. Little by little, the families were persuaded to move to Wadi Moussa. They now find themselves in boxlike cement homes built too close to one another, deprived of the space, privacy, and beauty of Petra's caves.

In Wadi Moussa, we met first with the head of the Village Council, who emphasized the social disruption that came with the move and with the development of the tourist industry. He spoke of crowded living conditions and of disputes among families, of alcohol abuse, and even drugs. Adjustment to the new situation, he explained, depends on how families are able to organize their resources as a family unit and mitigate the intergenerational conflicts that result from the radical change in living conditions. He offered to introduce us to a family who had been relatively successful in so doing.

Dokhlalla Salem, 50
Rakheih Salem, 40

The Salem family had moved from their caves ten years earlier. We met on the terrace of their home, a drab building they have enlarged at their own expense.

The grandfather, Goblan Salem, a tall, impressive man whose demeanor spoke of his authority, had never resided anywhere but in the caves. He admitted he would never adjust to living in a house that is to him "more like a prison." The elder admitted, wistfully, "Sometimes we take our donkeys and go back down to visit our homes."

Dokhlalla Salem in front of his Wadi Moussa home with wife, Rakheih, Spanish-born daughter-in-law, Laila, and son, Haroun

DOKHLALLA   Goblan's son Dokhlalla, who we learned is the more active authority in the family, explained, "Down in Petra the living space was much greater; you could have three caves equal to ten rooms this size. I had two caves, one was the kitchen and the other was for living and sleeping.

"We lived in neighborhoods or quarters, each quarter belonging to a family. Each man had at least three or four caves. You would choose the largest cave as the living room. They measured something like seven by seven meters, with high ceilings and good windows. We painted the interiors. A smaller cave would be a bedroom and another cave would be for keeping your sheep. Some people chose to be next to each other. In some cases, the houses were big enough for three generations. When a boy and a girl got married, they just moved out and settled in a new cave. If there was no cave available they would stay with his parents until one came free. It was just like any other town or city.

"When we moved here we really felt uncomfortable due to the small, crowded rooms. We are twelve family members; that means we're supposed to get a complete unit, not this half-unit they gave us. They did not ask us, and they did not listen to us. When the children started nagging, 'What's going to happen to us?' I had to build an extension. If my son decides to come we will build again. A family of nine got a house like this. The families that were six now have become nine, and they don't have space for them. And, these houses belong to the government; we have no idea what will happen next. We don't know what our legal status is.

"There are no benefits at all for having moved. Nothing has improved. Despite the hardships, Petra was much better. At least you were on your own: you didn't have to mix with people. Since we were far away from one another, if we visited someone, they treated us regally, as if we were guests. Here you are just a nuisance. You fight every day with your neighbors. In the very beginning there were many problems. The children were the cause of most of them. The closeness to one another caused friction and conflicts. Basically, we had to learn to live in a community for the first time.

"We didn't have electricity in Petra, so we didn't watch television. Now we have it. But what they show us is nothing. I'm not interested in women's bodies, so I don't watch." He turned to nod at those listening, adding, "Even if they give us radars, we don't want them.

"I'm not going to say anything bad about the government. I have to be fair. We have all the services: we have a health center, we have a preparatory school, we have a mosque, we have electricity and water. We send girls and boys to school.

"The problem is with our work. When they made us move out we thought we would continue working our land in one season and working in the tourist industry in the other. We all work selling things to tourists. And there are more tourists than before, truly. The problem is all the regulations: the government refuses to let us sell whatever we want. Every day they come up with new regulations. The tourism industry is seasonal: two to three months of tourists, and then for five months we have no work. What money we get from those two to three months must last for the rest of the year. Our people have become poor and have to get assistance from the National Aid Fund. It is shameful for us.

"And there is the problem of our land. We want our own farms. But it all belongs to the government. We used to have vineyards and gardens with tomatoes; there were twenty vegetable markets and shops in the caves. We had contracts for our vegetables; our refrigerators ran on gasoline, and we would keep food. Now they say only one-third of the land will be given to the original owner. We don't have land and we are not allowed to work as before in Petra. People are adrift and afraid for the future of their children. Some have left, others have begun to drink and take drugs. Our community is suffering the consequences.

"I am lucky. My children are close to me and work with me. I have three married sons and the fourth is getting married next month. We live next to one another, we eat together. My father lives next to me. If he is sick, I look after him; if I am sick, he looks after me. This is our way of life. The older people love Petra more than we do. They spent their lives there. They love it. My generation was able to adapt, but the younger generation is now used to having electricity and water; living in Petra means nothing to them.

"We used to fetch water on donkeys, but since we were happy it did not matter to us. Here it comes through tap. The women are quite happy with all these services. They don't want to go back."◆

RAKHEIH At this point everyone began laughing at his observation that life in Wadi Moussa was easier for their women. And indeed it is, according to his wife, Rakheih. Now just forty, Rakheih has given birth to ten children, the first at age fifteen. In Petra she gave birth assisted only by neighbors. Now she can easily find health care nearby.

When I asked about the elders, she replied, "Most of them didn't like to move up here. At least down there, when they felt cold they could build a fire inside the caves and get warm. Here they aren't able to get warm. But the younger generation likes it here. We have very good neighbors. All my life I have never had a fight with anybody. We are happy here."◆

As we took our leave of the Salem family, Dokhlala began joking about their situation, making light of the family's difficulties. "One thing good about the tourist industry is that you meet many people. I have made friends with many foreigners through my work in Petra. And my son even found a wife.

A Spanish student, studying Arabic, came to visit Petra. They met and now she is our wonderful daughter-in-law. We get along well; she lives like us."

Changing habitat and new customs are issues confronting the Bdoul and millions of other families in a rapidly urbanizing world. On every continent, one hears talk of the "village-ization of cities" that results when rural people bring rural customs and needs to urban settings: they build homes with only elementary notions of construction or safety standards and shape neighborhoods into tiny villages, with vegetable gardens between buildings and farm animals kept in any possible space. In contrast, the move from Petra was well planned, yet the traditional ways of the Bdoul were not always considered and their families have suffered the consequences.

Safe and healthy living quarters are a minimum requirement for a life of dignity. As world population swells another 2 to 3 billion people in the next half-century, the need for safe and appropriate housing will expand beyond any hope of governments' ability to provide it.

Overpopulation and environmental degradation also contribute to a lack of safe and healthy working conditions. In preceding chapters, several families alluded to dangerous, even toxic, conditions they endure in the workplace. In chapter 6 we met Helosa Peireira Schuenck, the Brazilian widow in Nuevo Friburgo, who retired early from her factory job for environmental health reasons. "I worked as a monitor, to see that everything was ship-shape. I got special treatment because I worked in a polluted environment, I was able to retire after twenty-five years. Normally it is thirty years."

The Bangladeshi garment worker, Shahida Begum, whom we met in chapter 4, told us of her pride in her home, which, she announced, was "safe." But when she introduced us to her thirteen-year-old son, a slender, almost frail boy, he appeared to be near exhaustion, with dark circles under his eyes. Shahida announced proudly, "This is my eldest. He's the one who works in the tannery. Show us your hands."

The boy, Nasum, looked embarrassed but obeyed his mother without question. The adolescent hands he extended toward me were deeply reddened and, in spots, gray and caked with dried, hardened skin or scablike formations. They looked like the diseased hands of an old man. "I work with chemicals in the factory," he said shyly. "We asked if they could give us gloves, but they said no. All my skin falls off. I'd like to leave the tannery, to find work abroad."

In Shanghai, factory worker Chi Wenmei, interviewed in chapter 6, told how her parents came from the countryside to work in the city's factories, and of how her mother died of liver problems soon after retiring from her job in a chemical factory. Wenmei operates a loom at a textile factory, where, she says, the shifts change continuously and dust and noise are a constant problem. The resulting fatigue, she claims, diminishes the time she can spend with her husband and child. "I am always tired, and thus my family duties suffer."

The Tanaka family of Japanese miners, introduced in chapter 5, added a different dimension to questions involving pollution and livelihood. Kunihiro, fifty-one, is a miner like his father, Umematsu, now seventy-seven. Both men are proud of their profession and both consider themselves fortunate, for neither has been involved in a mining accident. As we sat in their home, Kunihiro described his work. "The main work in the coal mining industry is to dig tunnels to reach coal veins; my job is to support those who prepare and reinforce the tunnels, sometimes at 500 meters depth. From the entrance to the mine, the galleries measure roughly 15,000 meters. There used to be three mines. But China can produce coal more cheaply. Also, many nations are beginning to stop mining because of the pollution caused by coal. That is why I didn't encourage my son to be a miner."

Although it threatens the livelihood that has sustained his family for generations, Kunhiro recognizes the need for environmental protection. "In Omuta City there has always been pollution caused by the shipbuilders and aluminum manufacturers. The area that surrounds the factories gets contaminated from the company's waste. There is PCB contamination of our rice. Our soil is affected. I worry about the underground water in this area. So far it is drinkable and it is not used for industries. We have to be responsible about all this, even if it means reducing coal mining and losing jobs."

To the environmental hazards caused by pollution, resource depletion, and unplanned urbanization, we must add those caused by armed conflict. The wars of the twentieth century significantly damaged the long-term viability of entire regions of our planet. Land mines, bomb craters, chemically poisoned soils and water, burned forests, and abandoned war machines are but a few of the remnants of those conflicts.

GUARJILA, EL SALVADOR

A prime example of the environmental impact of warfare can be found in El Salvador. An estimated 25 percent of the nation's natural environment was severely damaged by the long civil war. The flight of the civilian population from rural areas left entire regions depopulated and unproductive. Most fled to urban areas, where 50 percent of housing is substandard. Safe drinking water became a serious problem, and 60 percent of child deaths were attributed to diarrhea.[6]

Environmentalists Manuel Benitez Arias and Melay Machado, of the San Salvador branch of the World Conservation Union (IUCN), spoke of the demise of El Salvador's original forests: only 1 percent remain, and even these are endangered or disappearing. National parks are being settled by people seeking land, and the National Park Service lacks the personnel to control overexploitation.

In the cities, rapid urbanization has exacerbated the problem of waste disposal. Many streets and squares are filled with heaps of trash. Despite widespread emigration to Mexico and North America, El Salvador remains one of the most densely populated and poorest countries of the region.

Guarjila is a refugee resettlement village in a forlorn, hilly region of Chalatenango. It was pouring rain when we arrived in the dreary village, where pigs, chicken, donkeys, and cattle, mixed with mud and children in the town's few streets. It was a town where people and shacks looked as if they had been scattered from the sky, without plan or intent.

Maria Amparo, 37

We met thirty-seven-year-old Maria Amparo at her workplace, a woodworking factory that is part of the cooperative network of the community. The resettlement "village" is organized cooperative-style: each family must contribute labor and assistance to others. One-third of the families are headed by women, mostly widowed by the war while they waited in refugee camps.

Maria Amparo is a stocky, strong-looking young woman. Her years as a guerrilla—years of hiding, fighting, and fear—had aged her, she admitted. She is a war widow and mother of a child born while she was a guerrilla radio operator; she showed us shrapnel scars on her arms and legs.

"I didn't spend all the war years with the guerrillas because I was wounded. They sent me to a refugee camp, where I healed before returning to fight. In the Mesa Grande camp we lived in tents, one close to another. The camp was enclosed with barbed wire; there was no space for the children to play. There was no privacy for the adults. The place was like a prison. The older people were all right, but the children were constantly fighting and then the parents would get angry and start arguing. Soon they would be at each other's throats.

"The greatest problem here is land. The owners don't want to sell it. Yet we want to build houses and have better living conditions for our people; we want to get them out of the mud." Maria looked up, hesitating a moment. Then, with a shake of her head, she smiled for the first time. "In fact it is so muddy I'm not even sure it is safe to build houses on it.

"Once we went back to where our house used to be before the war. But, to tell the truth, we couldn't tell if there had ever been a house there or not."

Maria Amparo's childhood home may well be another metaphor for the earth we inhabit. Whether it be in El Salvador, Vietnam, or Kosovo, precious agricultural lands have been severely damaged by the folly of warfare. Yet as population increases in the next century, the need for agricultural land will increase. Population Action International estimates that the minimum amount of land needed to supply a vegetarian diet for one person without any use of artificial chemical inputs or loss of soil is slightly less than a quarter of an acre. An estimated 420 million people already live today in countries that have less than that amount of acreage per person. This number will increase substantially between now and 2025.

Protecting our natural systems—soils, water, forests—is becoming a survival issue for millions. And, as we have learned from the families interviewed, there is no time to lose.

Our planetary and individual health is dependent on striking a balance between our numbers, our consumption of resources, and our enlightened care of the earth. Families throughout the world are struggling for livelihoods in endangered environments, bereft of safe and healthy working and living conditions. Whether it be in Mali, Missouri, or Brazil, we are asking too much of our natural bounty and placing future generations at risk.

Nine | Family Health, Personal Risks

My husband was a bicycle maker. He died of jaundice seven years
ago. We couldn't afford to send him to a doctor or buy the medicines.
He died because of that.

—Esharm Khatoom, Dhaka, Bangladesh

The road, outfitted with deep ruts and occasional boulders, led us to a road
sign with a hand-painted arrow indicating the turn off to Peaceville. The
dusty hamlet so named was a collection of simple one-room wooden cottages,
twenty-odd kilometers from Accra, Ghana. The town was named for its most
respected inhabitant, a seventy-year-old nurse and midwife named Peace
Acolatse. Children, chickens, and dogs gathered quickly, and noisily,
around our car to help her greet us.

Dressed in the white, starched uniform of her profession, Peace Acolatse
welcomed us warmly and we followed her into her home, to a small room
which served as sitting room, bedroom, and dining area. The second room
housed her nursing clinic. As she described the health issues of her town,
she motioned to the far corner, where, quiet and unnoticed, a woman lay
on a small cot. "She is quite ill and needed somewhere to stay," explained
our hostess. "Because of our economic situation there is no transportation.
Funds are always lacking. I had to give up my car. It was too expensive, the
petrol and all. It's a shame, because now there's no transportation to the hospital. Sometimes I send a child running to find a car. There are times when
they find no one to help."

Improvements in individual health and well-being resulted in a marked increase
in longevity in the twentieth century. Infant and maternal mortality declined
rapidly as vaccinations, antibiotics, and improvements in public sanitation
and health services became available. We heard evidence of this repeatedly in the preceding chapters, when elders told of siblings or children who died
young—sometimes as many as half or two-thirds of the children in a family. Ma Yuzhen, the eighty-four-year-old Hui peasant grandmother in
Tongxin, China, who was quoted in chapter 3, lamented, "I was married at
fifteen and, in all, I had thirteen children. Only five survived. Some died right

after birth, others lasted a few days. My husband died of tuberculosis thirty-three years ago. It was a miserable life then. We suffered from hunger and many diseases. Nowadays, young people even complain about food, saying steamed bread isn't good enough!"

Indeed, improvements in nutrition and advances in medicine and medical technologies have prolonged lives to a point where we live, on a global average, more than twenty years longer than those born at the turn of the twentieth century.[1] Food is more plentiful and more varied. New medicines subdue infection and prevent illness. In 1977, the World Health Organization was able to announce the eradication of smallpox, and there is justified hope that polio will soon follow. Put simply, we don't die as much as before. As a result, we have witnessed a quadrupling of the world's population in the span of a century. From 1.5 billion inhabitants in 1900, we passed the 6 billion mark just before the turn of the millennium.[2]

But, as Peace Acolatse's example so graphically illustrates, good health and the benefits of health care remain elusive to many. In some nations, public health facilities are more than adequate and serve the needs of all citizens; in others, only the rich or those in urban areas have access to quality health care. The HIV/AIDS pandemic is a good example of the ramifications of this two-tiered health care situation. In December 2000, UNAIDS estimated there were 36.1 million people infected by the HIV virus.[3] According to the same report, there were 5.4 million new infections in 1999 alone, creating a never-ending drain on health care resources and families' well-being. For the poorer nations, medications for the treatment of AIDS are far too expensive to provide to all, while in the wealthier nations, survival rates have been increased through access to improved medications.

Then, too, good health is more than the absence of disease. Everywhere, in wealthy or poor communities, practices abound that poison bodies, psyches, and family relationships. These social diseases can only be controlled if there is the will to do so. Drug, tobacco, and alcohol abuse are on the rise in many nations. Domestic violence wounds bodies and spirits. Unwanted pregnancies result from a lack of access to contraceptives or a partner's refusal to permit their use. Traditional nutritional beliefs, social customs, and rites of passage lead to poor health for millions of women and children.

In the preceding chapter, some families spoke of the pressing issues of environmental health. We know that since 1945, over 75,000 new chemicals have been introduced into our environment, with known and unknown consequences for human health. The range of family health issues is far too vast to be covered here. This chapter will focus on the health concerns raised most frequently in the family interviews—namely, alcohol and substance abuse, women's reproductive health and sex education, domestic violence, HIV/AIDS, and

mental health. The first, alcohol and substance abuse, is a veritable afflic-
tion in family life worldwide.

High in the clouds on a mountainside coffee plantation in El Savador, I
heard once again the story of a family's struggle with alcohol and its near
tragic consequences.

RURAL EL SALVADOR

The road led us high into the mountains, where coffee plants cover steep slopes
in one of the loveliest settings imaginable. The plantation became a cooperative following El Salvador's land reform of 1980. Two hundred thirty asso-

Rafael Antonio Sibrion, 77

Martir Sibrion, 35

ciates and their families live on roughly 850
hectares, the homes scattered in family compounds
here and there along the access road. The road would
be impassable in a rainstorm, already eroded and gullied to a nearly imprac-
ticable point. The inaccessibility of the plantation has isolated these families from much of the bustle of modern life. If a good road were ever built,
a way of life would quickly disappear.

RAFAEL   Rafael Antonio Sibrion, seventy-seven, was one of thirteen children who then had thirteen of his own. He has worked on coffee plantations
his entire life. His home is an abandoned brick warehouse where bags of coffee were once stored. The fact that he has become a cooperative associate,
a partial owner of the plantation, gives the elder a sense of reward and justice for a lifetime of hard labor.

Rafael stood straight and confident, his blue eyes looking out over the hills,
as he began explaining the family's situation. "All the people here admire my
wife and me because we have a happy life and we have stayed together so long.
The truth is that we have nothing—no material things. We have only enough
resources for the current day. But the best blessing of all is that my children
are intelligent and have studied some—not much, but some of them have completed a first or second year in high school. I feel this is a blessing.

"When I came here I didn't know anyone and no one knew me. We would
talk to the children and say that God would be watching us all the time. I have
raised my children with a firm but careful hand. At least once or twice a year
we would see the priest. There were feasts and parties. We were always
together as a family—not like today's children who want to get away from their
parents. I have given my children a good example, and they are doing well.

"The poverty here has chased many people away. I have a brother and
a son-in-law in the United States. The son-in-law left four years ago and
hasn't returned to visit. His wife and the three children live with me." His
eyes clouded for a moment, caught in sadness. "He left her because of his
economic situation, but he sends money for the children from time to

time. Since I have nothing to leave my children or grandchildren, the only thing we can try to do is to make good men and women out of them. Give them some education and a good upbringing. If they have some schooling they will not be fooled like we were in the past."◆

MARTIR   Rafael's thirty-five-year-old son, Martir, is tall in comparison to his father. He smiles easily and has a proud, distinguished bearing. Martir is a reformed alcoholic; he takes pride in having rejected the illness and in raising himself from field laborer to his office job, where he sits regally tabulating workers' hours and pay.

"I am the second of my parents' thirteen children. We are six boys and seven girls. All but one live around here. My father taught us to work the land. It was his whole life, and he taught us the love of the land. My parents brought us up to be good people. "But at thirteen I was already an alcoholic. It started when my older brother and I learned how to make chaparra. It's like whiskey. My parents drank it every mealtime. It was cheaper to make it ourselves, so I helped my brother make it. As the 'cooks,' we had to taste it, to know when it had reached the right stage. The result is that I became hooked. At first it was small amounts, but it increased. We did all that in order to help with the family finances.

"We all drank, my parents and we two older boys; the girls were not allowed. At first it was innocent, but when we realized what we were doing, we were horrified. It was too late. It was a tragedy to be an alcoholic. "When I was thinking of getting married, I had to stop drinking for a while because I wanted to impress my girl. She said that if I didn't stop we would not get married. This was only a lapse of about one and a half years. After that I started

Rafael Antonio Sibrion (*in straw hat*), Martir Sibrion (*to his right*), and a gathering of family at the cooperative coffee plantation

drinking again and I was soon at the point of separating from my wife.

"When I was the warehouse manager, some mornings I would arrive drunk. I had to drink. Sometimes my supervisor would reject my work. My mind was all messed up, and the work reflected my lack of clear thinking. I had to have a bottle in my desk drawer, and I looked forward to lunchtime, when my colleagues and I got together to drink. At four in the afternoon I would come back home. Near my house I would stop at the cantina and drink some more. It's a sickness, but many people do not understand.

"I was very lucky because my boss was a member of AA. He put up with my behavior and tried to give me the AA message. He is a good man, and something in him made me listen. At that point, only a miracle could have made me stop, because there was not a day without a drink.

"The alcohol problem exists in part because of our idea of machismo. As a consequence, we don't want to admit that we are sick. We find excuses for our behavior. It will soon be six years since I realized I was an alcoholic. My life has taken a better turn, and now I realize how lucky I am, starting with my wife, who is a real treasure, my children, and the respect of my parents.

"In the past our family was very traditional: the man is the boss, the king, and wants to arrive only to give orders, to impose his will on those he rules— the wife and children. In my case, thank God, things are different. My wife and I are of one mind. I try to help her whenever I can. After work, I sweep and clean." Martir laughed aloud, adding, "Maybe I don't make tortillas or wash dishes, but most everything else I do.

"For my children, setting a good example for them is very important, because children imitate the actions of adults. I raise the boys and girls the same. They are still young, a girl thirteen, boys twelve and eight, and the last, a girl four years old. I tell them that education is important, that they must treat their neighbors well. I want to prepare them for earning a living, so that they have a better life than we have. I can't stop thanking god for so many blessings—they are all part of my happiness. I thank god for giving me the will to react and begin the change in my life."◆

Alcoholism, as described by Martir Sibrion, knows no boundaries of class, nation, or education. It is found is in families around the world of all economic and educational backgrounds. In San Salvador, a visit to the Alcoholics Anonymous office revealed that there were 450 AA groups in the capital city alone. Nationwide 35,000 people are AA members; 43 percent of the population say they drink regularly.

But alcohol is just one element of the substance abuse crisis, as is illustrated by the story of a wealthy Salvadoran businessman and philanthropist, Jaime Hill. An eloquent and candid man, Jaime Hill is a well-known figure in El Salvador, Miami, and even Washington, D.C. Our time together

was spent discussing how he had become an activist in the fight against substance abuse, and why he had created a foundation, Fundacion Antidrogas
de El Salvador (FundaSalva), for that purpose. His willingness to recount his personal experience with addiction in
Jamie Hill, 58
order to call attention to the dangers of alcoholism and drugs in all social classes provides a powerful statement to his fellow Salvadorans and all who
encounter him.

We met in his vast, sun-filled office at the foundation, on the outskirts
of San Salvador. Jaime Hill is an energetic man with an easy smile. His hands
constantly punctuated his story, which he tells without hesitation.

His grandfather, he explained, left Manchester, England, at age twenty-
three with a few bales of wool and a desire to seek his fortune in Central America.
He was very successful in so doing. His marriage to the daughter of a coffee grower led him to develop the local "black gold" by industrializing coffee production and marketing it abroad.

"He had seven children and, around 1912, he sent them to study in California. Maybe coming from England, he felt that the education here was
poor and wanted to send his children elsewhere. One among them was my
father, then eleven years old. He didn't come home until he was twenty-three,
when he and his two brothers returned to the Santa Ana area and bought
land for more coffee plantations. They built a mill to increase coffee
exports to the United States and Germany. After World War II, when the coffee business took off, our family's wealth began. Subsequently they went into
the banking and insurance businesses and into diverse industries.

"My father was an extremely good man, but he had difficulty commu-
nicating and was very authoritarian. He arranged my life for me without ever
asking me what I wanted. I had hoped to become an agricultural engineer,
but when I was seventeen my father announced, 'I don't want you to study
agriculture. You are going to the University of Pennsylvania. Everything has
been arranged; just sign the application.'

"All I wanted was to wear blue jeans and boots and work on the land. Instead
I found myself at the Wharton School with people who wanted to learn how
to make money. It didn't occur to me to ask, in a humble way, 'Are you thinking of my feelings?' That's how families were run at that time.

"When I graduated in 1960, my father sent me to Europe for a month
and then, without consulting me, arranged an internship with the First National
City Bank in New York. He told me, 'You are going to learn about banking.'
I never thought of saying anything. When I was twenty-six years old, he said,
'That girl you are going out with, she's very nice, from a nice family. Why
don't you think of getting married?' So I did. And so my life went, built on
someone else's wishes.

"The turning point came in 1979, during the civil war. I was kidnapped for ransom. I spent four months in captivity. I was forty-two years old. For the first time in my life I was alone. I was forced to recognize that my life had been planned by my father, that I was not happy, that money wasn't everything, that I didn't know what I wanted. I had made no major choices about my life at all at that point. I had to ask myself: 'Who is Jaime Hill? If they kill me because the ransom is not paid, am I satisfied with my life?'

"When I was freed I started drinking like hell. I used to drink socially before that, maybe three or four scotches in an evening. But I began drinking heavily. I was a hell of an alcoholic but I never showed it. When I was drunk I was very polite, more talkative, more charming. I was so insecure, I didn't know what was going on. There was a big pain inside of me. I was confused. I was nobody! Of course I knew I was Jaime Hill—I was a friend of presidents, I played polo, I was a businessman, I owned a Mercedes. But what did that mean to me? In fact, they had done me a favor when they kidnapped me. It wasn't until much later that I discovered, through the foundation, that I was actually suffering from post-traumatic stress syndrome (PTSS).

"Meanwhile, one of my daughters had her own problem. She had attended a junior college in Washington, D.C., but quit after her first year to become a bilingual secretary. She didn't like that, so she went back to school. She attended Boston University and graduated cum laude in political science. At her graduation she admitted that she had been 'wild' in college and believed she was a borderline high-risk substance abuser. She told me she wasn't sure what she wanted to do in life but she would like to do something for our country. We discussed her fears of addiction and that led to the idea of becoming involved in the alcohol and drug treatment field, since there was nothing of the sort here. We then decided she should go to a treatment center to help her get her act together and, at the same time, to obtain training in the field of substance abuse.

"Our experiences—hers and mine—are at the origin of the foundation, which is primarily aimed at educating people and preventing substance abuse. But for those who are already addicted we have a rehabilitation program for both alcohol and drugs. Wherever we go to do prevention, we find substance abuse—in schools, slums, or businesses. That 's why we developed the rehabilitation program.

"We have a staff of forty-eight people and, of course, many volunteers. In rehabilitation, they work with AA patients in self-esteem classes. Those classes are wonderful. If you don't have self-esteem, you hate yourself; and if you hate yourself, you cannot live with yourself; and if you cannot live with yourself, the only way you can live is to drink. After two drinks you don't give a damn what happens.

"We go to areas where we know there is alcoholism and talk to people.

That's how we discovered this sickness called post-traumatic stress syndrome. In response, we created the rehabilitation program. We offer PTSS counseling. We teach people about it: how to recognize the symptoms and how to deal with it. It's so common after a war. Suppose you were in the war and someone started shooting. You were running with three, four friends. They fall down and you just keep running. You save your life. You are a hero because you came out alive. But all of a sudden the war is over; you remember what happened. You remember you didn't stop and help.

"We found a thirteen-year-old boy in Cerro de Huazapa who didn't speak, looked very angry; he seemed to hate everybody. After we worked with him for a time, he told us what had happened. He was with the guerrillas. The army was approaching, so they hid in some abandoned huts. He had a little brother, about a year old. The baby started crying and someone said, 'Don't let him cry, because they will discover us.' He had to suffocate the child to prevent discovery. He was one of the worst cases of PTSS I've seen. He is working with us now and has become a leader in Cerro Huazapa. He relies on his prayers. When there is a lot of suffering, I believe you have more love to give afterward.

"Until we do something about curing the minds of the people, it's all for nothing. For example, there has been an increase in suicides here, but I don't know if it is due to the consumption of drugs or the post traumatic stress, or both. I do know that 80 percent of the crimes committed here are drug related. It's quite a price—people being killed, people doing things they would never do unless somehow drugged.

"Alcoholism breaks down the whole family system because alcohol causes violence. Not necessarily physical violence, but, for example, violence in the way I address you, in the way I talk to myself. When violence is inside a home, the family is destroyed. And if the family is destroyed, the whole society is destroyed. To me alcohol is the most harmful drug we have in Central America.

"It's a national habit to consume alcohol here. People don't realize the harm they are doing to society. Alcohol kills all spiritual feelings, and respect or love for other people. It makes you become a very material person. When you are under the influence of alcohol you know that you are suffering inside. You see power through material things: money, political power, and so on. This is what is ruling the society today. People want to become powerful through money. They don't respect laws; they don't respect their family; they don't respect their neighbors. They just maneuver to obtain power. That's the only thing that makes them feel good because they are alcoholics. Like me. You see, I'm not talking about street drunks, but about alcoholics like me, people who drink so as not to suffer.

"The most common drugs are the legal ones: antidepressants, sleeping pills, Valium. They are sold over the counter at the drug store. Marijuana is consumed by the lower classes; it comes through El Salvador and is consumed here in small amounts. And then there is cocaine.

"There was an epidemiological study on cocaine in this country over a year ago, and the results were amazing. When they started tracking where it was being used they found that the main users came from Colonia San Benito and other wealthy neighborhoods. Youths who are fortunate enough to have rich parents who send them to study abroad become users. And this is crucial to El Salvador's future, because these young people will be the future leaders of this country. The situation is very dangerous. We have to change our whole way of life if we are going to save El Salvador.

"Right now I am one of the happiest men who has ever existed. I am at peace with myself and feel that I am helping to do something for the people of El Salvador, to allow them to be happy."◆

It will be a long time before Salvadoran society fully recovers from the devastation of the violent civil war that ended in 1992. Over 70,000 Salvadorans lost their lives and thousands of homes were destroyed. The family dislocation, emigration, and overly rapid urbanization that resulted from the war had unpredictable consequences on the social fabric of Salvador. As Jaime Hill explains, among those consequences is a high incidence of substance abuse ranging from alcohol to heroin and cocaine to glue sniffing among street children.

As the 1997 *World Drug Report* notes, illicit drug consumption has increased throughout the world in recent years, becoming one of the most daunting problems of our time—a growing scourge that ruins million of lives and reaps vast profits used for corruption, intimidation, and destabilization of governments. One of the prevalent myths is that substance abuse is mainly a disease of poverty and social dysfunction—a false assumption indeed. No social class—and thus, no family—is free from the threat of substance abuse. There may be reasons why a particular society has a higher rate of substance abuse than another, but on the whole, substance abuse strikes all social classes and all ages.[4] And the health, behavioral, and economic consequences fall first upon the family of the addict: money spent on alcohol or drugs is not spent on family food, and those under the influence of drugs often commit verbal and physical violence on family members.

In chapter 6 we met Dorothy Mangum, who grew up in Harlem. She described how her childhood neighborhood had changed and how drugs were a contributing factor to that change. "We used to take the children to Central Park to see the sailboats on the lake and just sit there. When it was real hot at night, we slept in the park, because it was too hot in the apartments. Now you don't even want to walk there. What has happened? I can only say that the drug people may need a quick fix; they need money. When I was young, women would go out to the movies with their friends and they would go home, say, at one o'clock, but now, no matter where they live, they are afraid in their homes as well."

In the United States, the economic costs of alcohol and drug abuse surpass the budgets of many nations. If one factors the costs of special alcohol and drug services, medical costs, lost earnings due to illness or premature death, maintenance of prisons and the court system, and the cost to crime victims, plus the cost of car crashes and fires, the estimated total in 1995 came to between $276 and $375 billion.[5]

When speaking of the costs of health care and disease prevention—and the lack of them—it is important to consider the availability of health care in remote areas or in regions of the world, where health care professionals are scarce, or, in the case of a Jordanian family, not readily accepted by the community. Here, the case for access to reproductive health care is dramatically clear.

BANI HAMIDA, JORDAN

The farm of elderly widower Abdel Karim Larman is perched on a mountain in the Bani Hamida region of Jordan, high above the Dead Sea. A sheepherder who had saved his earnings for many years to buy his land, Abdel was proud to tell us that the three hundred olive trees he planted ten years ago now produce twenty tanks of olive oil per year.

Abdel Karim Larman, 75
Jazia Larman, 38

ABDEL   Born in 1920, Abdel said that his parents died when he was very young and he was raised by his brothers. "I married when I was eighteen. My wife and I lived together for forty years. She gave me four boys and four girls. She died three years ago and now I want another one!" he said with a wink. "I bought this land myself. This area was completely isolated, but god gave me the power to buy a little land and build. We even have a well. This is the best of times, because I'm able to rest. And there is more food than before. We even raise rabbits for food. The four sons will inherit the land. One lives with me and is a seasonal worker—one day he works, one day he doesn't. I will take you to meet his wife."◆

The elderly farmer led us up the hillside to where his home, which he shares with a son and the son's family, was couched on the flank of a sun-baked mountain. It was an oblong structure consisting of three rooms. Each room was entered from the outside. When we followed him inside, it took a few moments to adjust to the darkness, for there was but one small window to give light. There were no furnishings, just cooking and storage pots and a couple of trunks lined up against the walls.

A tall woman rose from the mat spread in one corner to greet us. "This is the daughter-in-law," explained our host. And, as custom warranted, he did not remain long in his son's wife's home. He turned and left.

JAZIA   The statuesque woman was extremely shy. We sat together on the floor mats with our backs against the wall. She answered questions diligently, not quite understanding why I was interested in what she called her "miserable life." She was, she said, born to a family of six sisters and two brothers. Her father was a farmer who died two years after she married. Both her mother and grandmother are still living. Jazia had attended two years of school, but was then kept at home, because, she said, "It's our way of life.

"I married at eighteen. My husband is a day laborer. Sometimes he helps in harvesting, sometimes he does construction work. He also goes to the lake to fish and sells what he catches.

"I am thirty-eight years old. I have seven children here with me and two daughters who are married. They married young: one was fifteen, the other one seventeen. So I have nine children in all. The oldest boy still goes to school. That is what I would like for all my children, that they become educated, that they avoid this life of poverty."

As we discussed Jazia's family situation, I suddenly realized there was an infant close to us, in a wooden box on the floor next to her. The box was covered with netting and, until then, I hadn't realized it held a living being. Jazia noticed my surprise and said, "That is my latest daughter, she is just a month old."

Barely had she uttered the words when she burst into tears, and then sobs. Her distress shook her entire body. I leaned forward to put my arm around her shoulders. Then, quickly, as if she feared being interrupted, she told the story of her beloved eldest daughter. At seventeen, Jazia's husband had given the girl in marriage to a forty-five-year-old blind man, without consulting either Jazia or the daughter. Subsequently they learned that the marriage had been arranged so that Jazia's husband could marry the blind man's eighteen-year-old daughter. The "swap" had sacrificed two teenaged girls. The second wife lived in the room next door and had already borne a child.

Slowly, between sobs, Jazia told me that she didn't want any more children, that life was too difficult, but that her husband wanted more and more children.

I asked if she had been to see a doctor for her pregnancies. Again, the woman began to cry, answering, "There is a doctor, a woman doctor, but it is far away. My husband has never allowed me to go there or to see any doctor." Jazia pulled at my hands as if to make me listen more closely, adding, "Even though my husband has a new wife, a young woman who can give children, he still wants me to have more. Can you imagine—more children in this poverty?"◆

Jazia's plight is not uncommon. I often encountered mothers who wanted to limit the number of children they bore. Many simply wanted to plan their pregnancies so as to rest between them; others said they wanted only the number of children they could easily feed, clothe, and send to school. But the gap between their view of children's needs and welfare and their husbands' understanding of the same is sometimes unbridgeable. They point out that some men see proof of their manhood in the birth of children, rather than in the way he provides for those children. For many years, family planning efforts were focused only on women, ignoring the fact that many women are unable to use contraceptives without their husbands' approval. Fortunately, the UN Population Fund (UNFPA) and a host of family planning organizations now recognize the importance of involving men and boys in family planning education programs.

The Brazilian father, Walter Araujo, quoted in chapter 6, gives credence to the need to reach men in family planning efforts. He laughed at his past ignorance, saying, "Do you think I would have had these seven children if I had known about birth control?"

Health education, ranging from notions of nutrition and child care to reproductive health and birth spacing, is a priority for family health. Women, particularly, are prone to suffer in silence, believing that problems in the reproductive system are but part and parcel of women's lot. Lack of education concerning their anatomy and health, as well as traditonal modesty, prevent them from seeking counsel and reaching out to other women for information.[6]

There is no better illustration of the importance of gender-centered health education or service delivery than the international effort to eradicate the practice of female genital mutilation (FGM). The practice is often referred to as female circumcision and is a cultural practice that, with time, has become confused with religious practice, particularly in Islam.

FGM has untold consequences for girl children and grown women. Infection is common due to the unsterile razors or knives used to excise the clitoris and, in some regions, the labia as well; complications arise during sexual relations, including pain and tears in the peritoneum; and severe complications often occur at childbirth. In Mali, Uganda, and Egypt, countries where families were interviewed for this book, the percentage of women and girls who have undergone FGM is 90 percent, 5 percent, and 97 percent respectively.[7] Attempts to outlaw the practice have met with little success; yet indigenous women-to-women education programs have made significant inroads in the last decade. By disassociating the practice from religion, and educating women on the health consequences for their daughters, these programs have facilitated a serious dialogue among women, health practitioners, and religious leaders.

Networks of women's health educators are essential to meet a broad range of family health issues. So, too, are governments' investments to improve public health, health education, and health care service delivery, especially in rural or slum areas, where they are sorely lacking. In 1999, the World Health Organization reported that government expenditures on public health, health education, and health care services ranges from 2 percent of GDP in the poorest nations to more than 9 percent in France, Germany, and Switzerland. Governments' capacity to invest in public health varies, as does their commitment to its equitable distribution.

In chapter five we met a migrant worker named Mohammed Abdur Rouf in a small village in northwestern Bangladesh. His wife, Belli, told us of his emigration and return to their village and of how she had managed to fend for her family during his absence. When I asked about her family's health, she told the following story.

"It's been three years since I lost a son. My womb was dried up. His neck got caught in the uterus. There was no one to help me with the birth. I was alone. I had been bleeding constantly for three days. Of course, I went to the hospital. I went there every week. It was Saturday when I suddenly had pain. The child arrived at 11 A.M. on Sunday. The condition of hospitals and the behavior of doctors are very bad. The nurses are also careless. They ask for money. Sometimes we could borrow money for the hospital, but not for the kind of assistance I needed. Sometimes we give money and nothing

Belli Abdur Rouf at her home in Bairapura village

happens; the doctors don't even stay. They just leave everything behind and go away. The nurses don't care about the patient, either. They don't provide medicine at the hospital. I went there several times but they didn't give any medicine. They demand money, oil, soap. If you can't provide those things, they don't come.

"I lost both a son and a daughter while giving birth. So I am left with just the three daughters. That is the reason my husband gives for beating me: that I have no son. But that is probably not true, because all the women in our village are beaten by their husbands."

Belli's reference to domestic violence was, alas, repeated in interviews with families across cultures and across social and economic circumstances. As we learn more about domestic abuse, we discover a pervasive "silent epidemic" that spans our world and its families. In every country I visited, people spoke of the violence they had endured as children or, for many women, at the hands of husbands.

In Susaka City, Japan, the eighty-six-year-old grandmother interviewed in chapter 1, Setsu Nakasawa, told of the dire poverty of her childhood and, quite unexpectedly, admitted to the tragedy that her first husband's violence brought to her life. "I was twenty-three when it was arranged that I marry a man in Tokyo. I didn't get along well with my husband, so I returned to my family. But my husband's relatives thought I was a very good wife, so they wanted me back. I returned to him for a while and gave birth to a daughter, but I still couldn't get along with him, so we got a divorce. It was because of the beatings. When his work didn't go well, he beat me. I always thought I shouldn't resist, so I didn't do anything against him. I just got beaten. But I left because I was afraid to die."

For years, social and health activists have been saying that domestic violence is one of the most urgent public health challenges—but few listen. National laws, based on custom and tradition, are slow to change. In the United States, according to the National Violence Against Women Survey, 1.5 million women are raped and/or physically assaulted by an intimate partner annually.[8] More than 52 percent of those women are younger than twenty-five.

The Missouri farmwife Geneal Young, interviewed in chapter 1, spoke of her work with a women's organization that assists battered women and undertakes public education programs to publicize the dimensions of the problem. The difference among countries is not so much in the incidence of domestic abuse but in the degree to which public officials take the problem seriously enough to change laws, protect victims, and undertake preventative education.

SAN SALVADOR, EL SAVADOR

At the Jose Simeon Canas University in San Salvador, sociologist Zola de Innocenti spoke angrily of the epidemic of domestic violence there. When I asked about the trends most influencing family structure and well-being, her answer was blunt and simple: "The socialization of patriarchal culture that runs throughout society and has consequences for everything: economy, health, education, and extreme violence. Violence toward the weakest and poorest family member is all-pervasive throughout Salvadoran society: women, children, the elderly. Hospital statistics on battered children reveal that children fear their fathers and turn to the streets for peace and security.

"Of course, a high percentage of violence is alcohol-driven, but the macho mentality legitimizes violence. It is considered the right of a man to beat his wife; women believe it also. People don't get involved in others' violence; it is a private domain, a tradition of violence of fathers to daughters, of husbands to wives and children. Women call in the police only when the child is nearly dead."

At the Salvadoran Human Rights Commission—the Procuraduria Derechos Humanos—lawyer Anita Calderon de Buitrago told of the efforts to reform the penal code so as to protect women more readily from abuse.

"We are developing new laws on domestic violence. But culture makes it difficult for judges to uphold women's rights. We have to retrain our lawyers and judges as well. Usually there are no witnesses to the violence or they are minors, or frightened. Bruises are not enough; law demands proof of who did it. Women are afraid and often drop charges."

Albertina, the Salvadoran midwife who we met in chapter 4, spoke of the violence she endured and continues to witness. "When my husband would arrive home drunk he would beat me. It went on for years until I finally left. Now I see the hospital full of battered and hurt women. They lie to the doctors, who don't know how to treat them if they don't tell the truth—why they are hurt, how it happened. Bruised and purple, they tell the doctor they fell off the bed. We see babies born bruised because the men actually kick pregnant women in the stomach. Still, the women say nothing, even when it is possible the baby will die. We must teach them to tell the truth. Self-esteem is to love ourselves.

Albertina went on to mention another dimension to the domestic violence epidemic, which she believes is a public health issue that must be addressed. "The truth is that many girls get their first sexual experiences at home, raped by their uncles, their brothers, or other males in the family. Or perhaps it happens in the streets; it is very commonplace. Once it happens, they feel so low, think very little of themselves. I try to advise them to go to the medical center to be checked by a doctor. This raping happens very often, frequently at home. But parents don't talk to their daughters; these things are not discussed."

Albertina's plea for educating the young about their bodies and their sexuality is a serious one. Knowledge of human anatomy and sexuality is sorely lacking in families themselves and in the education systems of many nations. Even in the twenty-first century, the subject is often considered taboo.

Missourian Geneal Young, fifty-eight, told of her bewilderment as a mother when it came to the sexual education of her son and daughter. "I'm a lot more liberal with my children than my mother was. My mother never told me about married life or sexuality—nothing at all. With my children, every time I wanted to bring up the subject, they seemed to already know about it, and they didn't want to discuss it. Maybe I was hesitant or didn't feel I knew much myself, not having had any teaching experience from my own parents. Sex was almost like a dirty word back then. So I've fallen into my mother's footsteps and haven't said an awful lot. I know my daughter is on the pill. They seem to know everything already, even about AIDS. I hope they are being careful."

In 1933, one of the pioneers of the family planning movement, Norwegian-born Elise Ottesen-Jensen, denounced ignorance about their own reproductive systems as the primary cause of illness and misery among the women she served. Her life's work was to provide sex education to all—women, men, and children—in an effort to improve family health. Ottesen-Jensen was indeed a visionary; since then, experience has demonstrated clearly that sex education from an early age onward gives individuals the knowledge needed to safely manage their sexuality and fertility, which in turn has a positive impact on health. The Netherlands, for example, has long been a leader in sexuality education in schools from a very young age, and, as of 2000, had the lowest teenage pregnancy rate and the lowest teenage abortion rate of any country. Figures show that in 1992, the United States had a teenage birth rate of 61 births per 1,000 girls, while during the same year the Netherands had 6 per 1,000—ten times fewer than in the United States, where sex education in the schools remains a controversial issue.[9] But the goals of sex education go far beyond the prevention of unwanted pregnancies and sexually transmitted diseases. Improving adolescents' knowledge of and attitudes towards sexual matters also affirms a healthy sexuality, free of abuse and coercion.

In China, thirty-year-old Zhang Yanfeng, who is the deputy manager of joint venture business in a village near Shanghai, commented: "Most families don't teach their children about sex because it is a very private subject. The young are very curious, but it is very difficult to talk about that between the parents and the child. In school they teach a course, so the children have hygienic knowledge. But they teach about anatomy, not about the reproductive cycle and sex education. Children try to find books about sex. In families this is something to talk about in person with our children."

One of the few instances when a mother told me she had no qualms about speaking of sexuality with her children took place in Susaka City, Japan, where thirty-eight-year-old Shigeko Nakasawa, the well-educated farmer's wife and mother of three preadolescent children, stated, quite simply, "It is my responsibility, mine and my husband's, to teach our children all they need to know to have a good life. In today's world they need to know about the world, about other people, about their bodies and their sexuality. I will tell them about all these things."

As we learned in preceding chapters, too many young people have little knowledge of their bodies and how they function, or of how the reproductive cycle works. This ignorance can lead to unwanted pregnancies and deadly diseases. Also, such knowledge—or lack thereof—profoundly influences an individual's life. An understanding of relationships, sexuality, and family life is essential for creating one's own family. A lack of understanding in these areas can cause untold physical and psychological harm.

Premarital sex is on the rise, as is the incidence of pregnancy among unmarried teens. Yet, as Monica Braga, the young Brazilian mother quoted in chapter 8, points out, many parents resist addressing their children's entry into adolescence, and thus avoid teaching them about responsible sexuality. Some hide behind the fear that "knowing leads to doing," others keep children ignorant due to religious beliefs. But most are simply unprepared to broach a delicate subject with their children. Monica added, "Young girls are afraid and ashamed to buy contraceptives. Mothers should talk to their daughters so they don't have to have abortions. Fathers are important, but the most imporant educator is the mother."

The World Health Organization estimates that worldwide, 20 million non-medical (illegal) abortions are performed each year. Of them, an estimated 80,000 result in the woman's death and hundreds of thousands of women suffer from long- or short-term disabilities. This is due to governments' prohibition on legal abortion or to social constraints that condemn them. Beyond this needless human tragedy, we also know that spacing one's pregnancies improves considerably the health of both mother and child. According to UNICEF, a child's risk of death increases by about 50 percent if the period since the previous birth is less than two years.[10] At the same time, planned maternity substantially reduces demands on health services and saves innumerable lives.

One underestimated advantage of sex education is that it improves the ability of women and girls to negotiate when and how they have sexual relations. This is a crucial element in the prevention of HIV infection. Protecting oneself from sexually transmitted diseases is impossible if one doesn't know how, or if one doesn't dare, to demand protection.

In every country I visited, HIV/AIDS haunted families' conversations, a subject of fear and worry. Like the Namsai family in Mesai, Thailand, whose daughter returned home from Bangkok infected with HIV, millions of families face the scourge of the invisible infection. As Brazilian mother Ircema Passos commented, with a shrug of her shoulders, "Only the young are dying these days. The cemeteries are full of the young who die from AIDS."

The December 2000 UNAIDS Report stated that the total number of people living with HIV/AIDS globally is estimated at 36.1 million. Twenty-one million have died since the beginning of an epidemic that continues to take its toll unabated: an estimated 15,000 people are infected every day.[11] Current infection rates are tragically high in Africa and in regions of Asia and Latin America. In 2000, South Africa became the nation with the highest rate of infection.

Beyond the economic and medical consequences of the AIDS pandemic, including the drain on health care delivery systems, the social consequences are daunting. In many countries, an entire generation of young professionals who were destined to become the nation's leaders has succumbed to the disease. In addition, UNAIDS estimates that 13.2 million children have been orphaned by AIDS, a figure that is difficult to fathom, and demands immediate responses from public and private institutions. A grandmother in a small town in northwestern Uganda, who told us of her family tragedy, is but one among millions who fend for their AIDS-orphaned grandchildren.

BUSHENYI, UGANDA

In this remote market town on Uganda's western slopes, I met Vanice Bremena, a small, slight woman who began our conversation by saying, "People are wondering why I'm losing all my children. They say there is something wrong in my family because I've lost almost all my children to the killing disease [as HIV/AIDS is known in local parlance]. Others are losing children also, but they wonder why it is so serious in my case. I don't know why

Vanice Bremena, 59   it is so for me."

We had found her home by walking down the path from the town's petrol station to a small clearing. Her house was a one-room, mud-and-stick structure with a palm frond roof badly in need of repair. It was close to neighboring houses, so there was no land on which to grow food. At fifty-nine, Vanice was destitute and discouraged. She kept her eyes lowered as she told her story. She is the daughter of a chief who had seven wives and did not educate his daughters. Her duty now, she explained, is to see to it that her grandchildren continue in school.

"I married when I was eighteen. My husband divorced me after twenty years. I had nine children with him. When my husband got a new wife, the oppression started. I was no longer recognized in the home as a wife, mother, or responsible person. My husband tried his best to see that I was tortured, physically, mentally, and spiritually, so that I would leave the house. I finally did, but I couldn't take the children with me. I worked as a ward maid in one of the hospitals to pay the children's school fees. Their father didn't pay even though they lived with him. I worked there for twelve years and then retired because of age. I started to sell food at the market, to trade. Then, in 1982, the killing disease started taking my children. Seven are now dead. Sitting in front of you are the orphans—fatherless, motherless children. Ten of them. And there are six more who are not here.

"My husband, their grandfather, lives just twenty kilometers from here. He is perfectly able to help out, but he refuses. When our children died he was informed, but he won't take any responsibility for the grandchildren. Can you believe this? We think this problem is a curse on Ugandan women—all these men who don't take responsibility for their families, for the grandchildren of their dead sons and daughters. The same is true for the in-laws: instead of taking the children of their sons themselves, and caring for then, the in-laws brought the children here, to me. Many grandparents say, 'Since my own son or daughter died of the disease, why should we bother to look after these children? They are going to die also.' This is the mentality they have.

"I live here with my sister and my grandchildren. Caring for them began to eat up the capital I used for trading. I have nothing left. My children didn't leave anything worth saving, neither a plot, nor land, nor a building—nothing. They were too young, not well-established. They were just collecting children, as people seem to do nowadays. Seven children, gone. The latest is the mother of this little girl; she passed away two months ago. I have no means of support, no income at all. I can't grow food because I have no land.In the morning I take the children to the forest and we collect firewood. I sell it,

Vanice Bremena (*back row, smiling*) surrounded by her AIDS-orphaned grandchildren and her sister

a bundle at a time, and that's how I make my living. It is the only income I can depend on.

"I wanted to keep the children together as a family, but it is not possible. The volunteers have taken some, but these here I must care for. If there is anyone who wants one of these children, I would give them.

"That girl beside you, Harriet, is thirteen, but she is not the oldest. There are others who are older who are not here. We live by god's mercy and grace."◆

The only time Vanice smiled or laughed during the hours I spent with her was as I was getting ready to leave and asked her grandchildren to sing into my tape recorder. They sang willingly, swaying and rocking, delighted that I could replay their voices. Even the hymns were boisterous occasions, and we all laughed together. In all I counted twelve children among us; three others had been "placed" with a relative, and three more were absent on errands.

In Uganda's capital, Kampala, I asked to meet with the Honorable Dr. Speciosa Wandira Kazibwe, then minister of women in development, culture, and youth and now vice president of Uganada. Dr. Speciosa, as she is affectionately known, welcomed my questions about the AIDS epidemic's impact on the family, commenting, "The extended family is part and parcel of our society, but it is now disrupted. The economy has uprooted people from villages, and if one is working in town they are supposed to support those in the village. Alas, that is not the case. The burden is being carried more and more by women in rural areas.

"Now we have the HIV deaths and the high death rate of women between twenty-five and thirty-five years. That means they were infected eight to ten years earlier at fifteen or sixteen. They die as young mothers. Who is there to take care of the orphans? Who supports the grandparents? It is this we must solve. We are discouraging the notion of orphanages; we want to keep children in families whenever possible."

Her words came back to me that afternoon, when, in a public garden near my hotel, I began talking with two young boys who were idling near a small fountain. After a few minutes they asked me if I could give them some food. I replied by asking where their parents were. The answer was awkwardly phrased but very clear: "They are died."

The following day I visited the offices of the AIDS Support Organization (TASO), a nonprofit AIDS education and service organization that has done remarkable work with AIDS patients and their families since the epidemic overwhelmed the health services of Uganda in the 1980s. I was greeted by the assistant director, Anne Kaddumakasa, an attractive woman in her late thirties, who was herself widowed by AIDS. Since all the offices were occupied by counseling sessions, Anne and I sat at a table in the shaded garden. Anne, a soft-spoken and gracious woman, had only recently been promoted to her job as assistant director. In the following days, she introduced me to her parents, her children, and the orphans of her sister Beti, who died of AIDS at age thirty-eight. Beti had been separated from her husband because he married another woman. Now both are dead, and Beti's children live with Anne's parents, Benedict and Anne Kiyimba, whom we met in chapter 3.

"TASO was begun in 1987 by fifteen volunteers," Anne told me, "some HIV positive, others not. TASO provides food assistance, free medicines, counseling for both patient and family. At present there are 30,000 patients, seven centers in hospitals throughout the country. We have nearly one hundred patients per counselor because of limited funds. We train counselors and we encourage community efforts to respond to the epidemic. We have medical services that work with patients and their families and we promote positive attitudes about infected people through public testimonies in schools and neighborhood meetings. We use songs and theater to entertain and educate."

Prior to assuming her present position, Anne had been an AIDS counselor and, she admitted, "It is very difficult to be a counselor for long. Sometimes you go to a patient's home and find them dead. You need time to recover, but we have no time. TASO sometimes organizes an outing for all the counselors; we play games, talk together for a few days. It is very helpful for our mental well-being, but there is not enough money to do it very often."

A few days later we drove to Anne's home, about eight miles from Kampala. Six of her seven children were waiting for us. The eldest showed **Anne Kaddumakasa, 38** me the two pigs he raises and plans to sell to pay for his schooling. The house was small and pleasant, with a well-tended flower garden and a vegetable plot that provides a significant amount of their food.

Anne explained that it is less expensive to send her children to boarding school than to public school, "If you add up food and daily transportation for each. My children range in age from four to sixteen years. The sixteen year old has to travel to school every day; I pay for his transportation. The others go to boarding school. It is expensive, but the quality of education is better. The nearby schools have poor standards. Education is critical, and it is the best thing I can do for my children."

Anne's husband was an agronomist and the manager of a cooperative farm. He also owned a farm 150 kilometers from Kampala. His brother has taken it over and gives none of its income to Anne and the children.

"The disadvantage of my husband not having a will," Anne explained, "is that the culture took over. My brother-in-law has taken our land. If my husband had had a will, the children and I would have gotten the land, thus the income from it. In Uganda, if the husband leaves a will there is a law

AIDS worker Anne Kaddumakasa, widowed by the disease, in front of her home with six of her seven children

that gives 15 percent of his property to the widow and 75 percent to the children. The rest goes to other dependents of the deceased, the close relatives.

"I encouraged my husband to write a will. In fact, he deceived me, saying that he had done so. When he died and I approached the lawyers, they admitted they knew him and that he was planning to make a will, but he hadn't done so. It was too late to do anything.

"In rural areas it is quite common that widows are expelled from their homes by their husbands' families. But in urban families or in circumstances where the widow has a bit of education, they normally know where to go for guidance. There are, for example, Legal Aid Project lawyers who provide free legal services. But in rural areas it is common practice that widows are chased from their homes. They may be aware of their rights, but the clan still has a big influence on what happens to property. When women are cheated they fear going to court because they may be threatened, even killed."

Anne grew wistful at one point, saying that her mother often chides her about her work with HIV/AIDS education. "People keep asking, 'Why are you doing this, talking about this, promoting promiscuity with condoms,' and so on. They still don't understand. They are ignorant about the disease and how it is transmitted. We have a long way to go to educate them."◆

The HIV/AIDS pandemic is a human tragedy of unfathomable proportions, for individuals, families, and nations. The crisis in health care emanating from HIV/AIDS must be examined in light of the already weak health infrastructure in the poorer communities of all nations. Given the increasing demands on existing services, education becomes essential as a means of preventing infections that drain overburdened health care facilities. The AIDS crisis also requires attention to the legal issues of inheritance, survivors' rights, and orphan care.

Looking at the challenges to family health at the turn of the twenty-first century, the variety of needs is daunting, indeed. One concern mentioned in several interviews was mental illness, and how depression is increasingly recognized as a major public health issue.

Some suggest that as the population ages in the coming decades, we may see a marked increase in depression. Elders face not only physical decline and the prospect of death, but also the feeling that they are no longer useful or productive. Some elders feel they are a burden on their families, or believe they are not welcome in them.

Takeo Takano, eighty, a retired businessman in Tokyo, pointed out that after retirement, "people don't know what to do. They should have hobbies and we have to think of that now in the big companies."

His daughter, Emmy Saito, joined in, saying, "What is interesting is that my mother got depressed, not my father. She was very proud of the fact that my father was a manager of Mitsui Corporation. When he retired she felt empty. Her identity was caught up in her husband's position. She began to have mental problems."

Emmy's mother lives in a care facility that would be totally unaffordable to the average family. As the proportion of older citizens expands in the next decade, mental as well as physical health care for elders will be one of the priorities of public health services. In the United States, for example, the highest rate of suicide is among eighty to eighty-four years olds.[12]

The families who speak here address a a range of health and health care issues: alcoholism and substance abuse, public and private violence, reproductive health and sex education, mental health, and the HIV/AIDS tragedy. In all cases, the need is for more education and delivery of high-quality health services. If we are to improve family health and well-being, considerable investments in education, public health infrastructures, and legal initiatives are needed in all societies. In addition, policies that promote good health must include stricter environmental laws to reduce toxins and their effects on human health.

We are at the point where we know how to prevent or cure most diseases. To a great degree, what we need now is to alter the practices or behaviors that lead to disease and dysfunction,and the equitable distribution of care to those who suffer from them. It has become largely a question of will, the will to invest, to educate, to provide services—and to speak out.

Ten | Faltering Households, Families Rebuilt

We knew lots of nice people in the streets. We were all equal to each other. It was a big family.
　　　　　　　—Beth de Oliveira Maia, Rio de Janiero, Brazil

My visit to Hacer des Ninyo, the street boys' home, was joyously chaotic. Visitors are rare, and more rare still are huge chocolate cakes like the one I brought with me. Eighteen excited boys greeted me. They live in the "home" on a quiet street in San Salvador. The building has no distinguishing features. It is perfect for housing teenage boys: nothing in its construction can bend or break except, of course, its windows.

One boy, who had just turned fourteen, insisted on being interviewed. I was told by the teachers that he had fled a violent home where he had been repeatedly physically abused. He was slim and his small size made him appear much younger than his years.

"My name is Javier Alexander Calles. I used to sing in buses. I just roamed around the city, begging, trying to make some money. Many people hit me, or cursed at me. One day a woman came up to me and said if I wanted to go to a nice place she could arrange it. That's when a man brought me here. A teacher gave me clothes to wear. They had good food and treated me nicely. I stayed one day, then another, and then—I'm still here. The teachers tell me what is good and what is bad. I have learned that one has to be responsible, not to bother others, they also have rights. I want to be free of poverty. My dream is to have a job, a house, and an institution to help children, so they are not so lost."

The value of the family unit is perhaps most cherished by those who have been deprived of one. Sometimes, society may deny certain people a traditional family situation, but that does not mean that the people involved care little about family life or that they should be judged negatively by others. During my travels, I kept hearing, "The family should be . . ." or, "A true family is. . . ." It seemed to me that an uninformed arrogance had invaded social discourse to proclaim harsh judgments on families that did not conform to a so-called norm. Indeed, significant variations in family size and form are well documented. These variously sized families are also variously configured. According to UN estimates, in 1999, average family size ranged from 7.0 persons in Algeria to 2.1 in Sweden.[1] Where is the norm, then? In addition to setting up false standards of normalcy, critics tend to cast blame on the vulnerable families themselves, while ignoring society's capacity to wound family groups.

The stories that follow are those of families wrenched apart by forces far beyond their control—forces ranging from cultural dislocation, to war, emigration, political exploitation, natural disaster, illness, and domestic violence. Their attempts to return to the haven of family or to create another, more caring group tell us that the bonds of family are far from weak, and are not disappearing. On the contrary, the people who speak in this chapter testify to the power of family.

In the mountains of California, family members tell how they hold on to one another even when there is a conscious attempt to destroy their culture.

BISHOP, CALIFORNIA

Of Bishop's five thousand inhabitants, approximately one thousand live on the Paiute Native American Reservation on the outskirts of the town. They are the ancestors of the nomadic Paiute tribe that once roamed the fertile Owens Valley. Bound by mountains to both east and west, the valley is a vast depression in the earth's crust that has been drained of its mountain source water for the benefit of faraway Los Angeles. Today, Bishop is best known as a place to buy fuel for your car on your way to somewhere else.

In chapter 5 we met Chief Alvin Bowman and his son-in-law, Bob Mora, who live on the reservation. I also interviewed the women of the family, Chief

Bob and Barbara Mora near their home in Bishop, California

Bowman's daughters and granddaughter, and spoke more with his son-in-law.

I had met the Bowmans through a woman who worked at the reservation's medical center, whom I had asked to help me find a family willing to participate in the family interviews. A week before I was to interview the Bowmans, I learned that the grandmother, Pauline Harrison Bowman, had passed away. Since I doubted the family would still want to participate in the interviews, I called and left a message with Pauline's granddaughter, Amanda, saying I would, of course, respect the family's wishes. When I called the second time, Amanda simply said, "Come over this evening."

Rena C. Brown, 36
Barbara J. Mora, 47
Bob Mora, 42

Amanda Narcomey, twenty-six, is a beautiful young woman with dark hair and eyes, who manages the computerized health records at the Indian Health Center. Her house sits along a road that crosses the reservation, just off CA 395. Amanda, her ten-year-old daughter, Jan, and an active kitten greeted me. As I explained the interview project, two aunts joined us—first Barbara, then Rena.

In this gathering of women, the conversation turned quickly to the woman who had been their mother and grandmother: her ways, her love for them, and her death. Apparently, just a few weeks before she died, she had voiced a wish to "write things down," telling her story so that the grandchildren could learn about the family. She hadn't had time to do it, but the daughters believed she would have approved of their participation in the family interviews. My arrival, they said, was like a sign: their mother had sent me as a vehicle for their stories and her story. One by one, each woman wept as she spoke of Pauline Bowman. Their grief was for her, yes, but also for the sadness that had dogged their lives—for the years of separation, of loneliness as children, of violence and untimely death.

RENA AND BARBARA   Sisters Rena and Barbara took turns speaking, adding details or anecdotes to one another's stories as they built the story of the family they shared. It was Rena who began the story, saying, "My parents had eleven children, but two died as infants. We were nine adults, but two of them have since died. My eldest sister, Amanda's mother, was killed by her husband in a fit of rage, and a younger brother died of alcohol poisoning.

"My mother's people went through a lot of trauma. We don't know exactly what happened, but we do know that they were herded from one place to another by the government: 'Get out of here'; 'go over there'; 'try to make a life for yourselves.' This is what they endured, trying always to make a life together. When mother was very small, her dad used to put her in front of him on his horse and take her to Mammoth Lakes. It would take three days or so because he would stop to fish, or meet with other Indians and hold healing ceremonies. Her mother was not a very fair parent; there wasn't any closeness; she had no ability to show emotion for her children. Back then women knew their roles and rarely escaped them. If a man came along and wanted you for his wife, he would approach your father and the decision would be made. You were simply told, 'This is where you are going now.' That was it.

"Our mother tried to be as fair as she could with us kids. But she was a product of her own parenting and she had suffered a lot. Maybe our parents' decisions were not always the best, but they didn't have today's comforts of parental counseling, teachers, or PTA.

"We were all sent off to the government's Indian school, one by one. The poverty at home was too much. Oftentimes Dad couldn't find work and they didn't have the money to raise so many kids, or even to feed us at times. They thought we would be better off and get an education at the Indian schools. But the whole purpose of the school was to strip us of our Indian heritage, our language and customs."

Barbara, the elder sister, interrupted suddenly, adding, "I remember my arrival at the school so clearly. We were gathered in this big auditorium, fresh off the bus from the reservation. The first thing the man said was, 'You are no longer Indians.' The school did everything to keep us from bonding to our parents or siblings. I had a sister who was there, but they wouldn't let me talk to her. This happened to all the Indian kids of my generation.

"When we told my parents what happened in school they would cry; it really hurt them. You know how close Indian families are. This is the worst thing that could happen—an absolute nightmare—and for it to be sanctioned by the government!

"If you did anything wrong they would cut off your hair. Things like dressing, speaking, or acting like Indians of your own tribe was forbidden. They didn't allow Indian clubs; they didn't allow Indian anything. I was so mixed up from that school. I finally ran away when I was sixteen. I was just tired of keeping the confusion inside me.

"Two years later, the FBI went to the school and found kids chained to their beds; they had been beaten. There were massive abuses. The school was closed down."

Rena returned to her story, saying, "I was sent there at the age of five. It was too young. When Dad left me I cried and cried. They babied me for two or three days and then threw me in with all the other kids. It was like having a lot of little sisters, and we clung together finding safety in numbers. They controlled your whole day. We couldn't dress Indian and weren't allowed to talk with our real sisters. I would see them from afar and wave.

"We didn't think of complaining because they were in control of everything and could do anything they wanted with us. It was in the middle of nowhere in Oklahoma. They paid the farmers around the school if they found an Indian child who tried to run away. We all had escape plans, but the trails were watched and some kids died trying to get away. There were stories of children before us who killed themselves rather than stay in the school. Children were taken from the plains, from their tribes, shorn of their hair, and thrown in these schools until they did what they were supposed to do. It was horrible."

Barbara concurred by saying, "The worst you can say about a Navajo is that he acts as if he doesn't have a family. And that's what they were trying to do to us. Cut us off from our families. Make us into white people."

Rena continued, "At times Mom would drink with my Dad. She was torn between being with Dad, who wanted to forget his misery, and taking care of the children. Without the drinking Dad was a very attentive father. They both did the best they could. We were the envy of the community here because we went on vacations together. My Dad was a rodeo bronco rider, and he took us with him. My parents didn't encourage us to mix with other kids because we were busy doing family things. And even to this day, people say, 'You people are always together, you do everything together.' They taught us to take care of each other, the sense of family responsibility. I always saw my mother and father together. I saw my friend's parents splitting up, marrying different people, but my Mom and Dad have always been together. Dad doesn't have children from another woman and Mom didn't go with other men; they were always together, all lovey-dovey.

"I think Mom and Dad really suffered when one of us was suffering. Recently one of the sisters had a real bad marriage and the son-in-law treated the whole family really badly, just disrespectful and insulting. Even though they suffered emotionally, my parents never turned their back on my sister or said anything harsh or hurtful to her. When she needs to come home Dad treats her normally, like nothing has changed.

"Dad is seventy-six now and in good health. He still drives and chops wood and has two dogs and does things. He visits Mom at the cemetery every day. As a Navajo he believes that everyone has a purpose and that you are told what your purpose in life is. That way you are a whole person. If you don't know who you are or who your clan is, you are incomplete. Children are raised to know this. But for us, sent away to school as we were, we lost that feeling.

"My brother, Alvin Jr., won't even speak about boarding school. At eighteen, he went to Vietnam, as did most of his friends. He learned to speak Vietnamese and had a Vietnamese girlfriend. He wrote and told us about his girlfriend, but at the end, they couldn't come home together because they weren't yet legally married. It was a traumatic event in his life. Now he talks only about his friends who were killed. He saw too much over there.

"He used to write beautiful letters on stationery with the Marine emblem. The words were beautiful, but up in the corner of the paper he would sketch pictures of people running and shooting. What really struck me as odd, even as young as I was, was that he would write those lovely letters, telling about his dreams, his plans for when he returned, how he was going to take care of Mom and Dad, and there in the margins were those horrible battlefield scenes.

"When he came home he was traumatized like so many Vietnam vets, in shock, with tons of problems he didn't begin to understand. He would go off on a tangent, maybe because of going through withdrawal from LSD and marijuana. Yet he never received any help from the VA hospital.

"The army brainwashed the soldiers so they would do as they were told. Alvin faithfully served his country. He went over there and gave his mind. Now he is here, but he isn't living a life. He's in seclusion. He is an artist and a very giving person. But he is just a recluse. Like my mother, he has diabetes, but he is not taking care of himself. He has given up. The only thing he has is his artwork. He paints with oils and does beautiful work.

"My other brother, Gary, is in his thirties and lives in Seattle. He, too, had a drinking problem but he's a real happy-go-lucky type, always joking. I recently visited him and met his girlfriend. He is not drinking anymore so I think he will have a good life.

"The younger brother, Ernie, passed away two years ago. He had been away from the family for two years, ever since he and my mother had an argument. They were very close. He was her baby, a very beautiful baby, and his personality was outgoing like Gary's. He knew that he could get his way with my mother. So my mother made sure he got what he wanted. The day came when Ernie raised his hand to my Mom and struck her. It broke her heart.

"It broke his heart too. They could no longer face each other. They never spoke again. He was living in the San Francisco area when we learned that he had died of alcohol poisoning. If you drink a high concentration, your body gets so saturated that it shuts down, and that's it."

Rena continued, "Alcoholism is a big problem in this community. Indian school, separation, poverty—all that contributes to lack of self-esteem, and people take refuge in drink. My husband used to get drunk and go to high school at the same time. That was just what you did here in Bishop. After school they'd go down to the river, drink, and come home drunk. Since we got together, he stopped. It was a hard struggle, but he did it for our marriage and our children. In the end it was really for himself."

Barbara joined in, "As women we went through phases of drinking as well. All through my marriage, I didn't drink at all, but after my marriage I started drinking. After thirteen years of marriage I thought it was a failure and I wasn't used to failure. When my sister was killed I became the eldest. It was a scary thing for me.

"In Native American families you are groomed early in life for a leadership position within the family. People look up to you. It has taken a long time for me to say I can do the job. My husband and I work with young Indians all over the area now. We organize pow-wows, dances, all sorts of meetings so that the young learn about their heritage and take pride in it."

BOB AND BARBARA   The next evening, the conversation continued in Barbara's home, a mobile unit placed at the end of an unpaved driveway. Firewood was stacked high outside the house, ready for winter. As I parked the car, Barbara and Bob Mora came out to welcome me. Inside, a fire crackled in an iron stove and a small black mongrel dog lay on the sofa, which was covered with a machine woven Navajo blanket.

Bob Mora, whom we first met in chapter 5, joined the navy at age eighteen. After two stints in the navy, he returned to Bishop and now works in electrical maintenance at the local supermarket. When I asked how he and Barbara had met, Bob began, saying, "We met in a bar; I used to play pool and the bar was one of my hangouts. I was drinking at the time. I realized that Barbara was having problems with alcohol, too. Her first marriage was rough and she was living in fear of her husband. The only way she could deal with it was with drinking and drugs. Her son was nine or ten at the time and he needed help, too. So I just stepped in and helped her—and myself. We don't drink anymore. We may have a few glasses with dinner, but that's the limit. We both know we don't want to go back to drinking. We have seen a lot of couples who drink and it's not good. The children suffer so much. Amanda and her sister, Star, have had pretty tragic childhoods, and we felt that we could be role models for them."

Barbara continued her own story by telling about fleeing the Indian school as a teenager and meeting an Englishman on the bus. He was, she said, "a real gentleman, a lot older than I." He invited her to go with him to Hawaii and he took care of her until she was seventeen. Then they married. His family was well off and the couple traveled the world. They lived in France, England, and Puerto Rico. But soon after they married he took Barbara's passport and refused to give her spending money. He began beating his young wife and refusing to give her food, saying that he wanted a slender wife. After years of abuse, Barbara finally fled the marriage and returned to Bishop with her young son.

"When I came back, I was very depressed. My son was almost six. I hadn't told my parents about my situation, but when I learned that my sister was in an abusive relationship and my Mom said, 'Leave it alone, she will be fine,' I said, 'No! She will not be fine. I lived through it. I know.' I told her everything that had happened. I had hoped that someone would help me, but there were no women's shelters. I went to the police once and they took me right back to him. In foreign countries, the woman is like property.

"There was a lot of mental torture with my husband. He would keep me awake at night telling me the philosophy he believed in and making me repeat exactly what he said. When we moved to England he attempted suicide, and the doctors diagnosed him as schizophrenic. But we just went on. He threatened me constantly. He told me that if I left him, he would kill me. Seventeen years of this.

"When I finally left, I was terrified. He wrote a letter saying he was going to kill me. I took it to my lawyer and he got me the divorce. I didn't want anything from him—just my freedom. I was so frightened I used to sleep under the bed. I drank and used drugs. For nearly five years this went on. I had been such a healthy person before but I couldn't function because I was so terrified. At this low point, I remember praying and saying, 'I need help.'

"My son was really bright in school. He did well here. But at about seventeen he began to change. He got into trouble often and began failing in school, a boy previously so bright. I know all the counselors in Bishop as well as the police because we had to find all sorts of help for him. Then I learned that schizophrenia is inherited in some cases and will manifest itself at adolescence. He has to be in an institution now. It is one of the biggest heartbreaks of my whole life. He can call ten times a day and not remember what he said the time before. He tells me all sorts of weird things that, of course, are not true. Had I known the schizophrenia was inherited, I would not have put him through this.

"Now I've gone on to obtain a degree in education. I teach traditional dance and ceremonies to children and they come to me with their problems. All these kids—they love me and I love them.

"Culturally I have gone 'back to the blanket.' I really value what was taken from me. I don't trust bureaucracies, boarding schools, institutions. I am like a Holocaust survivor. I am happy for each day, that I've made it this far. I am really happy. I have my family now.

"Mom and Dad were like a pool of water. When you went out and got thirsty you could come back and take a drink and you would be refreshed. If ever you needed to come back you knew where the spring was. Dad would always say, 'Never say 'good-bye' or 'see you later.' In our family we have always come back."

I was shaken by the stories of the Bowman/Mora family, which expressed the grief of land usurped and culture denied; of children sent away to abusive schools and life-destroying wars; of domestic violence and alcoholism. Yet despite it all, the strength of family bonds called them to "return to the spring."

Intentional cultural extinctions proceed even today, and have inspired the creation of watchdog groups such as Survival International, which attempt to monitor the practices that destroy entire cultures. The Surui people of the

Brazilian Amazon here tell a story that is repeated in many remote areas of our planet.

CACOAL, BRAZIL

The Amazonian town of Cacoal, Rondônia, was created by settlers when roads were built into the Amazon forests in the 1970s. In Cacoal, the subject of the indigenous peoples, and the way they have been "contacted," is a controversial one. The Brazilian Bureau of Indian Affairs, FUNAI, is charged with protecting the indigenous tribes from avaricious land-grabbers, rubber tappers, foresters—all of whom ignore the Indian's rights and unwittingly bring disease. But FUNAI has not always been successful, unable, perhaps, to work quickly enough when new tribes are discovered.

Maria Barcelos, a woman of Indian, Portuguese, and African descent who founded a local children's rehabilitation center, told us of the nearby Surui tribe which, when first "found" by outsiders, numbered four thousand. With ensuing disease, their number plummeted to three hundred, and twenty-five years later is barely up to six hundred. Maria suggested we visit one of their settlements, a village of one hundred people with several resident missionaries.

In the tiny settlement, wooden cabins with tin roofs and no doors served as the Surui's homes. The roofs make the interiors so hot that no one remains inside during the day. Cooking is done in traditional fashion, in the open air. The cabins are set on foot-high stilts so the Amazonian rains can flow underneath the house when necessary. Inside, the furnishings were few: tin pots, a chair or two, a table. Our host's wife proudly showed us her platform bed and mattress, but, somewhat embarrassed, she explained the hammock that hung beside it: "It's my husband. He still prefers a hammock." Gun, bows, and arrows hung on the bedroom wall.

Napitojan, 34

There were six cabins in view, separated from one another by one hundred meters or so. In front of each cabin a fire smoked between three large stones. By one of these fires, we sat and discussed the changing life of the Surui. Those who gathered around to listen were all, men and women alike, dressed in T-shirts. The men wore shorts with them, but the tiny women wore the shirts as dresses. The older Surui were tattooed, with huge circles that crossed on their faces. Most women were nursing an infant or toddler. A vivid blue-green pet parrakeet with clipped wings pecked at the cooking pots beside us. Children crowded around, giggling and teasing.

Our host was Napitojan, thirty-four years old. He was not tattooed. His mother sat with us, her small hands busy making baskets. His father, who sat without speaking, had been the clan's chief when they lived in the forest. But when the whites came in the mid 1970s and so many of their people died, he asked someone else to take over. Napitojan added, sadly, "He lost his courage and strength.

"I have five children," he continued. "The youngest is taking medicine for tuberculosis. That is why I say it isn't very good today. My oldest child is thirteen. He is studying here in the village. He likes it. He is in the fourth year.

"We used to live further into the forest. We hunted and ate things from the forest. Then, in 1972, we met white people. They were cutting the forest and started shooting us. We killed two white men and ran into the forest. The elders called us together and said: 'The whites are going to come into conflict with us. They will come again and upset us. The whites will not leave. You will see, we will end up using clothes like they do. It will be the end of us. Those of us that survive will turn into whites.' So the boys said: 'Let's go and kill the whites.' The elders said: 'No, we don't kill them. If you kill them it will be the end of us. We won't die because they shoot us; we will die because we will get sick.' The boys didn't believe the elders. I didn't believe either.

"I was ten years old, already quite big, big enough to shoot birds. They elders held meetings, saying over and over, 'We won't be Indians any longer, we will use clothes from now on.' The young men didn't believe it. About fifteen days later, a plane appeared. All the men went; three hundred Indians went to see what was happening. That was when Francisco Meireles from FUNAI came and brought lots of presents, and the Indians approached him. They exchanged arrows for machetes. Francisco put the objects very close to his shack, where he could look out and see the Indians. He shouted: 'Come here, I won't kill you now. I have no arms, no rifle.' And the Indians started to come close, take the knives and go away. He said: 'Nobody is going to kill anybody, take the machete. If you want to kill me, kill me. I'm from FUNAI.' He said that. 'I am not the rubber tapper who wants to kill you.' But we didn't understand very well; he spoke Portuguese and we didn't understand.

"The Indians were behind him with the arrows pointing. Then they got used to him. He didn't say why he wanted to be friends with the Surui. Even today he has never told us why. [In fact, his primary purpose was to vaccinate the Indians and prevent disease.]

"The Indians went back to the *maloca* [a special meeting house] and spoke to the elders, who called us together and said, 'This is the end of us, because we will get sick. White men will give us sickness, and we will die.'

"The elders were right. They told the truth. Ten days later the sickness came and attacked us. Many people died. I thought no one would live. It was measles, diarrhea, influenza. I thought my father was going to die, too. Raimundinho's father died. My father's brother died. All the women died, and almost all the children. And there was no one left to bury them.

"First we moved to the place where they hung up the presents. They marked off our territory. Then the land-grabbers came. So we moved here, where we could claim our land so that white people couldn't take it. That was in 1976.

"Life is not right now. It's not good for us to live among the whites. My father thinks the life of the young is very strange. It makes him sad. This morning he spoke to us and said: 'Don't forget our way of life.' Every morning he sings and tells us stories.

"In the old days, we lived on hunting. We'd spend a week in the forest and then come back and drink. We used to have two or three women. Now we have to stay with one. We have forgotten the old ways. We're not drinking any more. We used to spend ten days in the forest hunting, staying in the *maloca*. We'd get fat there. We'd come back strong and not get attacked by sickness. Now if we spend even three days in the forest, we get sick and have to come back.

"There are some animals left but they are far away—pigs and monkeys. We didn't used to hunt deer, but now we are doing that. In the old days, you used to be able to get a tapir and eat it the same day. Only adults eat it, not children. We also ate cara, potatoes, manioc, and papaya. Now we drink coffee and like sugar, too. We used to use honey from bees. We drank *chicha* [corn wine]. We eat differently now—rice, beans, salt, oil. We get lots of pimples. We drink soft drinks, rum, and spirits.

"When the children grow up, sometimes they want to study. That's why our life isn't very good. This boy here, his mother wants him close to home, but he wants to go off to study. In the old days, the family used to stay together.

"Nobody yet has found a job. We go away to study, but we don't like it so we come back."

At Maria Barcelos's home that evening, an elder Surui appeared in the sitting room, tattooed and dressed with a feathered necklace and shorts. He sat watching me. Maria explained that he had lost his wife and children to measles twenty years earlier. She had taken him in, and although he still prefers his nomadic life, he reappears from time to time to spend a few days with her family.

He asked if I was a 'believer.' I asked in return why he wanted to know. He replied that in the year 2000, a fire would consume the forest and everyone who was not a believer would die. "Only the believers will go to heaven to meet Jesus."

Maria shook her head in dismay. She explained that some Indians were selling their land rights because they were taught that "the End is coming"—that the land would soon burn and be useless.

Cultural destruction or exploitation is an ongoing phenomenon. The indigenous activists and the international human and cultural rights groups that have emerged in past decades to defend vulnerable populations have much work ahead. So, too, do those who work with another vulnerable group: street children. UNICEF estimates that worldwide there are 100 million children, ranging in age from three to eighteen years of age, who live by their wits on the streets of the cities. Most are not orphans but simply children who flee household poverty or violence, desperate enough to believe they can live better on their own. They struggle to find food, shelter, and, if lucky, the means to take some money home from time to time. They also develop family support systems among themselves.

RIO DE JANEIRO, BRAZIL

One of the world's most beautiful cities, Rio de Janeiro, is fraught with disparities of income, education, and hope among its 10.6 million inhabitants. Rio's magnificent beaches may be famous, but so too are its *favelas*, or slums, notorious for their danger and violence. For some, Rio's main streets are even worse than its slums. In July 1993, the brazen massacre of street children

Elizabeth Cristina Borges de Oliveira Maia, 17

Rogerio, 17

who were sleeping on the steps of the Candelaria Church in central Rio shocked the world community. Were poor children becoming society's disposable people, an annoyance to be eliminated on city streets? Off-duty military police, known for their hostility to the thousands of children who live on Rio's streets, were suspected of being the murderers who opened fire on the sleeping youngsters; five were killed outright, and another two were taken away and later found executed. For the estimated 10 million children who live on Brazil's city streets, life now had an added dimension: fear of execution.[2]

It was a hot, dusty April afternoon when, accompanied by a social worker from an organization known to the Rio street children, I went to meet teenagers Beth and Rogerio on the steps of Rio's Opera House. Beth is a survivor of the Candelaria incident. Our conversation was made difficult by the noisy city traffic and by the fact that the couple's attention was often focused on who was coming and going around us. They live frightened, alert to danger in whatever form. From time to time, however, they relaxed enough to be simply two teenagers in love; jostling and teasing each other as we talked.

BETH Seventeen-year-old Beth was obviously pregnant. Her dark, freckled face still had the round, chubby form of adolescence. Wearing elastic jogging shorts, a T-shirt, and new sneakers, she chewed gum noisily and appeared surprisingly self-assured.

Beth said she had attended school until age eleven. "After that there was no point. The kids just used to hang around together and play. Even at school, they would be having it off with each other, boys and girls. There was smoking and drugs. I wasn't like that; neither was Rogerio.

"I was born here in Rio. I never knew my father. I had a brother and a sister. The sister died young. My mother lived with my grandmother and worked as a housemaid. She died when I was twelve.

"My granny lived in a house belonging to the government. It wasn't very nice. There was nothing there for me. My granny is good, but she is very old; she didn't understand me. I think she is my mother's mother, but I'm not sure. She takes in lots of children, so people and the church give her food for them. There are some days when she doesn't get a mouthful to eat. She has too many so-called grandchildren. So I left there to live on the street.

"I knew lots of nice people in the street. It was like a big family. We lived by the Candelaria and asked people for food. We got leftovers from restaurants. We were all equal to each other. Everybody helped everyone else. We had a good time. We used to laugh and dance together. We also used to fight and get beaten up. We were a real family, and I was treated with a lot of love. But many of my street family have been killed. We were about sixty. Eight were killed at Candelaria. The oldest was twenty-one, the youngest six. I went back to live with my granny because I was afraid to stay on the street after that. We all were. I didn't have any family left. What was I going to do there? Even before the Candelaria, the police used to beat us up. If we're on the streets at night and no one is around, even if we aren't doing anything, they'll beat us up. If a policeman finds you alone, he will kill you.

"If I had a younger sister, I wouldn't want her to live on the streets. It was difficult being a girl, but we behaved just like boys. When I first went to the street, I was very badly treated. There are people who beat the children and rape them. There was one person, a twenty-two-year-old boy who was part of the group, and he would try to rape the girls. He was very ugly. He looked like King Kong. Very ugly! There was a big group of homosexuals, too; they had their own family.

"I took the pill for a while, but it made me sick. You see, the street kids know about family planning and how to avoid pregnancy. They know about HIV, too. The doctor came every month and examined us. They taught us about HIV; we even did theater about it. It's the rich people who have AIDS, not us street people. It's the artists and the rich. There's a fellow, a friend of Rogerio, who is rich; he owns two shops. He used to be very handsome. Now his hair is falling out. The social workers used to come and give us condoms, but we didn't always use them. The girls like being pregnant.

"And then there are the drugs, mostly glue. People sniff glue if there is nothing to eat. Sometimes we are very hungry. We have to eat the food from the garbage. The glue stops the hungry feelings. I've never sniffed. Rogerio did; he sniffed so much he didn't have his head screwed on right."

Beth looked up for a moment and, for the first time, smiled. "I met Rogerio soon after I went to live on the streets. We've been together for a year and a half. Now we're having a baby."◆

ROGERIO With this introduction, Rogerio pushed at Beth's shoulder, jokingly. Also seventeen years old, he is a dark-complexioned youth of slight build and looks somewhat smaller than Beth. His black eyes, dotted with thick lashes, darted in all directions, as if he were the prey of some invisible force. He said he had been kicked out of three schools, explaining, "The last time was when a teacher pulled me by the ear, so I hit her." When I asked about the small crosses cut into his right cheek, he said they were from street fights. I wondered. This seemed an illogical explanation for such neatly sculptured scars.

"Yes, I had a family before. My grandparents are dead, but I have a mother and father. They're separated. They live in Vigario Geral, one of the slums. I have three sisters. No brothers—only one who died. The police killed him. He went to buy bread at the bakery and the police came and killed him along with several others. He was thirteen.

"I left home because my stepmother was very mean to me. And my mother's new husband beats her. He used to beat me as well. I haven't seen my family since I was eleven. Beth is my family now. Street families stick together; they move from place to place together. We are always the same families, but we have different homes.

"We're going to have a child, so I'm going to find a job. I worked as a mechanic once. And I'm trying to find a place for us to live. Somehow I will do it." The youth hesitated, and then with a shrug continued, "A father is a father. A mother is a mother. I don't know what a father is. If anyone comes and beats up your child, the father comes and beats the shit out of them. To bring up a son, put him in school. I'll teach my child. The school can teach, but I will, too. It's the only thing I can think of at the moment. The mother has responsibility for everything. The mother of a child has total responsibility—but I have total responsibility also. We both made this child, so we can divide it in half. I'm happy I'll be a father. I don't have any expectations at the moment. I am just expecting a baby! I'll do anything. I'll sweep the streets, clean the floor."◆

BETH Beth joined in to finish the conversation, saying, "I don't intend to live with my grandmother when the baby is born. There's no room there, and there are a lot of rats. When you lie down, the rats run all over you. They suggested rat poison, but she doesn't have money to buy it. We're trying to find a room. We'll leave the streets and live together.

"It's good to have a child and look after it. It's nice to be a mother. A real mother is the kind of mother that I had, someone who looks after her child and loves her for always. It is perpetual love. And even more responsibility than love. Much more. I'll be ready when the times comes."

Beth laughed, then added a bit wistfully, "You don't get anywhere in the street, no matter how hard you try. It has nothing to do with violence. It's just that street children are never anything. Yet, I admit, the first time I really felt a sense of family was in the Candelaria."◆

We left the young parents-to-be on the steps of the Opera House. Turning to see them for a last time, I marveled at their resilience and optimism. I wondered if the course of their lives could possibly be altered, as they hoped.

This phenomenon of runaway or cast-off children bedevils all societies, less advantaged and wealthy. In the United States, for example the National Runaway Switchboard estimates that 1.3 million youngsters, under the age of eighteen, run away from their homes each year.[3] Family conflict, violence, sexual or psychological abuse, and poverty are the reasons most often cited for children's flight from their original families. They are found in groups, in networks they sometimes call families, in large and small cities throughout the world.

BANGKOK, THAILAND

In the urban turmoil of Bangkok, UNICEF supports an attempt to respond to the growing number of street children. The project recruits and trains young teachers to work with street children and their special needs. Among those needs are literacy, skills training, health care and AIDS prevention, and assistance in recovering from the practice of sniffing glue or paint thinner or addiction to heavier drugs.

One of the UNICEF-sponsored teachers, twenty-two-year-old Amar, is a recent graduate with a degree in physical education. He offered to take us to meet his charges and then guided us to the intersection of two wide avenues. There, three boys waited for the traffic lights to change, ready to rush out to the cars and wash the windows of reluctant motorists. Normally seven boys share the corner, but four had been arrested that morning for sniffing glue. Amar admitted that this happens quite regularly, "Glue is a cheap high for them."

Pok, 14
Taweesak, 14
Toi, 13

The boys were gangly adolescents, puppylike, dressed in a dusty version of the teenager uniform: T-shirts, pants, and sneakers. When we asked if they would talk with us over lunch at a nearby sidewalk restaurant, they agreed. We ordered a simple rice, vegetable, and chicken meal. The vegetables and chicken remained untouched, too unusual a taste for these youngsters.

Social worker and teacher Amar (*second from right*) with Toi, Pok, and
Taweesak in Bangkok

Although they shared a liking of Chinese kung-fu movies, the three
boys were as different as three could be. Taweesak was the tallest, a nice-
looking fourteen year old with deep-set eyes, the one who had most to fear
from sex traders who prey on street children. Pok seemed to be more hardened, almost frightening in his rough demeanor, yet when I asked the
younger boy, Toi, what he wanted to study, Pok advised him, "Go to school
and learn everything you can."

Toi, a recent recruit to the group, had two large scars on his face, the result,
he explained, of being hit by a car in the streets of Bangkok. As he sat in
his chair, he twisted his T-shirt and twisted his body—slumped, then sat
straight—alternately frightened, reassured, and insecure. Like the others,
he told of responsibility as a family breadwinner.

"My family comes from the north. My mother lives with a new husband,
so I'm not staying with her. I live my aunt. Both my mother and my aunt
are deaf and mute. I stay with my aunt because she's alone, nobody is taking care of her. I've been with her since I was small. I had two sisters. One
died, and the other got married. So I'm left alone to take care of my aunt.
My father left when I was little. I never met him.

"I get about 100 baht a day [approximately US $4 at the time of the inter-
vew] wiping car windows, but if the police come, I earn less. I give it all to
my aunt; she waits every afternoon on the sidewalk for me to give her the
money. If I'm lucky I make maybe 200 baht and I give 150 to my aunt. If
I earn more I'll spend the rest for me. I go to play snooker or to the movies.

"I'd like to be able to repair electrical appliances, mending things; there
are courses for street children I could take, but I have to work instead. My

aunt doesn't want me go to school at all. She just wants me to wipe windows to make a living for her."

Amar joined in, saying, "That's right. His mother and aunt don't want me to take him to school because there is no one else to take care of them. He is their only family."

When we walked past the intersection after lunch we found Toi's mother and aunt sitting propped against a building. The women appeared old and fragile; the mother had few teeth remaining. They had come to wait for the boy's precious earnings. When we greeted them, their looks remained suspicious. Amar shook his head as we walked on, saying, "For the paltry sum these boys earn, 100 to 150 baht per day, they could be free of responsibility and go to school. I'm certain the mothers would let the kids go to school as long as they had the 150 baht a day. It means subsidizing the mother so the child has a chance. You can't just help the kids—you have to help the mothers, the family."

Three youngsters, on the other side of the globe from Beth and Rogerio, yet facing the same necessity of fending for themselves in hostile surroundings. These youngsters might have a chance for a better life if they did not carry family responsibilities at such a young age. Toi provides for a deaf-mute mother and aunt. His responsibility to his family makes of him a poor and, to some, detested street child.

Elsewhere, in countries where war has raged, countless children have lost contact with their families or have been orphaned. In Uganda and El Salvador, I met children who had been persuaded to leave the streets and live in rehabilitation centers. Depending upon their age and how long they have been on their own, they are more or less able to make the adjustement and stay off the streets permanently.

KAMAPALA, UGANDA

The Reverend Dr. Kefa Sempangi is the founder and director of the Africa Foundation, an organization that seeks to find, house, and educate children who have become separated from their families. At the time of my visit, he had several houses in Kampala and a compound outside the city where he housed and schooled children of different ages and needs.

"Due to the civil war and HIV deaths," he explained, "families have been dislocated. Children are sent to a relative in the city to be less of a burden on the home. Others flee their homes due to abuse and violence. In Kampala, they live inside the city dump, where they burrow into the refuse because the process of fermentation creates warmth. They eat only what they can scavenge; when we give them clean, warm food, they have terrible digestive problems.

Members of Reverend Sempangi's "family" with the author in
Kampala

"Sometimes I ask myself, 'What constitutes a family?' There are family ties that go beyond the visible blood-link. The Africa Foundation is not
an organization; it is a family. We are registered, we have a postal box, we
fulfill all the obligations of an institution, but as far as we are concerned,
we are just a family, an extended family. We are providing things that are
not available to these children.

"One of our boys has now grown up and married. He comes to show us his
wife and child, just as you do in a normal family situation. These children in
my care are my children, even though I know they must have a mother or a
father somewhere. They are happy here; they call each other brothers and sisters. They can't marry each other. It is an African taboo. You can't marry someone from the same clan or family. And we are a real family."

Rev. Sempangi has found a way to give vulnerable children a new, caring support group, and many do call it their family. As these stories suggest,
people form alternative families when life's events deprive them of more conventional family units. A woman in Bangladesh gives us another example
of this family formation among strangers.

NARAYANGUNJ, BANGLADESH

Naripokkho, meaning For Women, is the name of a women's service organization created by activist women in Dhaka, Bangladesh. When I met with
Naripokkho's leaders to discuss family issues, I learned that their work on
a range of women's welfare issues had led them to become advocates for women
trapped in the world's so-called oldest trade. The task is not an easy one,
and it can be dangerous work in societies like Bangladesh's where militant

religious groups seek to deprive women of voice, representation, and public life.

My meeting with Naripokkho workers resulted in their suggestion that I meet with women who had formed a family of sorts, out of necessity, in the country's brothels. For the Naripokkho workers, the prostitutes' lives are an example of the extent to which people will go to re-form families when the biological family fails them.

It was arranged that one of their volunteers would take me to Narayangunj, a town on the outskirts of Dhaka, where "one of the biggest and oldest brothels" is located. Well over a thousand women live and work in the complex of brothels that are housed in seventeen buildings, each with about sixty rooms. We were to meet several prostitutes who are involved in protesting an attempt to evict the women from several buildings—the only homes they have. (The Narayangunj brothels, Tanbazar and Nimtoli, were closed in the summer of 1999.) Their leader at that time was an attractive women in her early forties, a prostitute known as Rita. She became their leader by daring to lead a street demonstration of prostitutes to oppose eviction.

The ancient taxi rattled on for half an hour to reach our destination. It was another busy town, crowded with people and vehicles of all sorts—some mechanized, others pulled by animals, still others pulled by wiry-bodied men. We asked the taxi to drop us off in the central market, near an alley that led to the brothel where Rita lives and works. The narrow alley was filled with shops, men, and children; all were obviously curious about the two strange visitors.

The brothel's entrance was cluttered with pails in which dishes soaked, several small children at play, and a surly old man who was hawking his wares. Inside, the corridors were crowded with cooking utensils, smoking charcoal stoves, and, again, playing children. As we entered, sari-clad women appeared in several doorways opening onto the corridor, curious to see who had come.

Rita, about 35

Miloni, 40

The brothel rooms were quite small. Those I visited each contained a large bed, a standing closet, a chair. There was not room for much else: no water nor room to bathe or cook. Meals were prepared in the corridors or outside in a back courtyard. The atmosphere was one of a busy apartment house, where children played and women busied themselves with domestic chores, albeit while waiting for a client and a few minutes behind closed doors.

RITA Rita's room was on the third floor, up a dark, narrow staircase that smelled of the curry of past meals. She welcomed us with confidence and a businesslike demeanor. She was dressed in a bright red sari and had decorated herself with dozens of gold bangles, visible symbols of her success.

We sat on either side of her, on her bed, to learn about her situation. Her story was similar to that of others with whom we met later: she had come to the brothel to find safety, protection, and moral support—and a liveli-hood—because all else had failed. The sex workers help each other, she explained. "We care for each others' children, and when someone is sick, we help pay her expenses." We learned that Rita's commitment to the group of women and children she considers her family is total. Rita told us the story of how she had come to be part of this alternative family.

"I was two-and-a-half years old when my mother died. My father remar-ried and my stepmother brought me up. When I was seventeen and in the last class of secondary school, my father died. He left no money for us. My exams were imminent, but I had no means to pay for the exam forms. I sold my mother's jewelry to do so.

"I passed the exams and wanted to continue studying, but my stepmother was getting many marriage proposals for me. She realized that if I was to be married, she would have to spend a lot on wedding expenses. She did-n't want that, so she behaved very cruelly to me; she neither let me go out, nor allowed me to stay in our house. I was helpless financially.

"I tried to find work; I went to factories to ask for work, but no one hired me. Finally I became a maidservant in somebody's house. While I was there, my employer raped me. He raped a maidservant in his own house! I report-ed it to the police and the story was published in newspaper—with my name. Thereafter the process continued. I was raped again and again. I was never safe because men knew my story.

"I had read in a magazine about a brothel in Jessore so I decided to go there. I knew that there, at least you are protected and safe. While I was there I fell in love with a client and married. But I did not know his character. I gave him money so he could start a business. But he was ruined and took all my money. We had a child, and I had saved 5,000 takas for my daugh-ter so she wouldn't have to face the same fate as I had. My husband demanded my savings and I refused. He divorced me, but wouldn't let me take my child. He wouldn't even let me see her. She died three months later. I suspect it was because she didn't get my breast milk. It was then that I came to Narayangunj.

"Here, we each have our own room. My room is a shop, really. I am sell-ing a ware. And anybody can come if the door is open. But there is absolute control of privacy for everybody. No one can enter without permission. If I tell a client that he cannot use me today, he must respect that.

"We pay 30 taka per day [US $0.75] for our rooms, although it varies with the size. There are some at 40, and some at 20 taka. This one is 30. That is all we have to pay to stay here. There are no pimps, but if someone brings in a client who pays 500 taka [approxmately US $11], then of our own volition, we gladly give the pimp 50 to 100 taka. There's nothing fixed about it. When I was more active in the business I would earn anywhere from 10,000 up to 15,000 taka a month [US $230 to $345].

"Now I am paid 200 taka a day by the landlord for my organizing work here. I am to manage the establishment, to ensure that no prostitute is victimized or physically abused. No one should intimidate them or terrorize them. There are over a thousand prostitutes in this area, Women from all over the country. They have no one to assist them.

"And they have children, of course. There are some four hundred to five hundred children in the brothels. Many women come here with their children. Others, who want a kind of motherhood, get pregnant here. Since they know that they have no chance of marriage, they sometimes ask the customers to make them pregnant. They want to be mothers. That's why I'm involved in trying to avoid these evictions. Whole families would be on the street. Some politicians are trying to oust all the prostitutes from the area. So I've raised money and tried to help them.

"Because I am literate, I can represent these women to the authorities. I have more courage than those who have no education. For example, religious leaders want donations from us all the time. I said, 'Stop! No, we don't give donations to them every time they ask!' There are too many groups who say they are Islamic, but they are competing with each other and they don't tell us honestly; they just want our money. Our children can't even go to school in the area because the mosques and schools don't want them.

"Women have to manage to send their children to school at their own expense. But no one must know they are the children of prostitutes. If people identified the child as a prostitute's child, it would make it difficult for the child in later life. Those who can afford it send their children out of the area, to boarding schools. The others grow up the way the environment demands and the society dictates. Some boys become shopkeepers. They live here and get customers for the women. If the child is a girl—most are married off to outsiders. We collect money for the girls' dowries and they are married outside this area. Only one out of ten girls becomes a prostitute.

"In the meantime, the children can't go out; only once in a while they play in the alley or on the verandas. We have a strong support system here. We collect money for each others' needs. We aren't obliged to make contributions, but when there is a death, for example, and someone can't afford the costs, we raise money for it. If a girl of a poor family needs money for her marriage, we pay from our funds.

"We look out for each other. If somebody wants to leave the brothel, we counsel her. If, for example, a man wants to take her away and promises to train her in some profession, we give our fullest cooperation. We say, 'No matter where you go or what you do, do not lose your self-respect. Think well in advance before you opt for the other life. If you should find out that you are seduced because of your money or your jewelry, that the man's attraction is only for those things, don't stay with him. He will exploit you.'

"There's this solidarity among us. If somebody is in trouble or a customer beats up a woman, we all get in there and throw that person out. One thing we know for sure: at least we get a square meal here every day. No one wants to live with her hunger out on the street.

"This aside, these women should have a future. They should not have to live in a dark alley for the rest of their lives. Whatever I can do for them, I'll do it—through organizing some kind of cottage industry for them to survive in the world outside or some other means. I have approached the government and other organizations about it, but we need cooperation from the government. I am being subsidized to talk with the law enforcement agencies about the rights of the prostitutes, about their desire to get out of their profession into some other work, handcrafts and cottage industries. We must build up public support for the prostitutes. I go out and talk about these things. I became famous when I spoke up at a press conference about evicting the prostitutes. Now they are using me as their spokesperson. We have a thirteen-member executive committee. We believe we can achieve something by our efforts. Out of about one thousand women, there are roughly eight hundred who are willing to come out and do something.

"We also organize about health issues. Most of our women know about AIDS, for example, but they are not so conscious about it. We use condoms mostly to avoid pregnancy. They are available from the betel leaf shop. Everyone buys her own supply and keeps it in her room. We explain its use to our clients in a variety of ways: 'Listen, brother, you don't know if I have a disease. Similarly, I don't know what disease you are carrying. I may transmit my disease to you if I have any. So, this [condom] is good for both of us.'

"They don't refuse often. But if the man does not accept it, what else can we do? Every weekend we have a medical check. I think AIDS has already arrived in Bangladesh—but not here yet."◆

MILONI   While we discussed the problem of condom use, another woman entered Rita's room. Rita smiled and announced, "This is Miloni, a friend who lives here." Rita explained our visit to the older woman, who then commented on the efforts to rehabilitate prostitutes.

"It is fine to set up cottage industries to employ prostitutes, but it has to be done well. I tried to leave here and went back home with my children. I worked for cottage industries for a time, but the earnings weren't enough to care for my three children. So I returned because of need. I had hopes of rehabilitating myself but it was not possible. With what I earn here I've married my daughters to good men and my son is an apprentice carpenter. I am

Miloni, mother and sex worker, in her quarters in Narayangunj

proud of what I've done for my children. On the outside a woman can't do that."◆

As Rita accompanied us down the stairs, a small boy of about seven walked close by her, his hand barely touching her skirts. She laughed aloud at him, saying, "This is Johag; he is like a husband to me. He was Parul's child, but she has gone and left him with me. He is very possessive. I have one customer who is very regular. Everybody calls him my husband because he comes every day. In fact, we live like husband and wife. Every time he comes, Johag gets very jealous. The reason I am so very fond of him is because of my lost daughter. He is almost the same age as my daughter would be. I love him very much."

We left Rita on the doorsill of her home. Once a refugee from violence, she has found a family of sorts. The orphaned seventeen year old is now a woman surrounded by those who admire and support her, and she in turn is determined to support them. She has an adopted son, and a host of sisters, and a devoted man friend who provides a steady source of income. She feels she has found safety in her home; yet those who work with her in the efforts to promote prostitutes' rights fear for her safety.

Safety is a basic requirement of all life. Alas, for many it is an elusive goal. The twentieth century, despite its great achievements, was a time of violent conflicts in which millions lost their lives. Millions more were made refugees, forced to seek security far from ancestral lands and families. The United Nations Development Programme (UNDP) states that in the 1990s alone, war and internal conflicts forced 50 million people to flee their homes. From the Armenians in the early century, to the European Jews and then the Palestinians at mid-century, to the Kosovars and Chechens in its final months, the world community has witnessed untold suffering and displacement of civilian populations. UNDP also states that there are currently more than 10 million refugees and 5 million displaced persons.[4] Added to the flight from conflict, we are witnessing, increasingly, an exodus from degraded lands or other environmental disruptions. Whatever the cause of their flight, families are uprooted, their members often scattered and family unity destroyed. Most refugees harbor the hope of returning one day to their homes and livelihoods; in the meantime, keeping the family together is their primary goal.

BAQ'A REFUGEE CAMP, JORDAN

Some of the oldest functioning refugee camps in today's world are those of the Palestinians in Israel, Jordan, and Lebanon. With the creation of the State of Israel in 1948 and the resulting internal violence, hundreds of thousands of Palestinians fled their ancestral lands. Half a century later, nearly 4 million Palestinians are still considered refugees. Two generations have been born and raised in "transitory" camps; their parents continue to hope they will return to their land one day. One such camp is not far from Amman, the capital of Jordan, and is known as Baq'a camp. Over 120,000 Palestinians,

Sheikh Salem al-Aidi, 58

Hossein Kassem, 33

stranded in refugee status, reside there. The camp is in fact a large town, with shops, markets, narrow streets, and a bustling street life. Its status as refugee camp means it depends on outside financing and its inhabitants are temporary guests of the Jordanian government.

Sheikh Salem al-Aidi is the head of a refugee family that has lived in the

Longtime refugee Abu Faisal at home in Baq'a camp, Jordan

crowded Baq'a camp since 1967. His home is indisinguishable from the hundreds that crowd together in a villagelike style. Homes are built with large cement bricks painted in muted colors. Inside, each has a courtyard for hanging laundry and children's play. We sat in the sitting room, leaning back against the comfortable pillows that line the walls.

ABU FAISAL   Abu Faisal, as he is known to his friends and neighbors, is an informal camp leader. As we talked in his home, several residents came to seek his advice or assistance. He listened to each patiently and then gave instructions on whom to see and what to do.

A tall, heavyset man, Abu Faisal has a friendly smile and a fondness for teasing and jokes. The political nature of his family's story brought out little rancor; he related the facts of his exile as they came, without apparent bitterness.

"Actually, our journey began in 1948. We owned land in an area called Bast al Falegh, just one kilometer from the sea. People lived in harmony with the each other; there was no animosity between us and the Jews. When the war started we were among the first to encounter the Jewish gangs, Argon and Agella, because we were near the sea and they arrived by ship. The gangs killed five people in our area. Baadieh Shoubacki, an engineer, was one of the first to graduate from Cairo University. They killed his whole family—father, mother, children. The rest of us, out of fear of the gangs, fled the village and went to Toulkarem. Before we left, we asked our Jewish neighbor, a man named Moulki, to keep our belongings and cattle for us. I had a poodle called Rick, and Moulki kept him for me. He was a good friend and cried because we were leaving. He said, 'Don't worry, everything—including the dog—will be safe until you come back.'"

Abu Faisal hesitated a moment, smiling at the memory, then returned to his story. "Our village had six or seven clans; they all left together and scattered across a wide area. We moved several times, first to Toulkarem, then El Jedida, and in 1950 to a camp called al Karrea. We came here after the 1967 war.

"In these camps, people gather according to their village of origin; they attempt to re-create the neighborhoods and relationships they left behind. This adversity draws us closer together. If you ask people in this camp, they will tell you they are from Jerusalem, Haifa, or Toulkarem; they will never say they are from Baq'a camp. They have not forgotten. We send our young away to school, abroad, to have a chance in life, but they come back. This is their identity, their family.

"I keep telling our children and grandchildren that they have a country called Palestine and lands in Bast el Falegh, that they should struggle all their lives to go back to that land."

Abu Faisal reflected on his words for a moment, then added with a smile,

"I am still asking Israel to return the dog because he was my friend. When Moulki took him in his car, he barked like crazy!"◆

HOSSEIN Abu Faisal's nephew, Hossein Kassem, is a dental technician and, like his uncle, very active in the organization of camp life. He studied dentistry in Hungary and, at thirty-three, is married and the father of one child.

"My generation is involved with working in voluntary organizations, supporting needy families in the camp. Sometimes we help elderly people who have no family or we clean the streets. We organize social evenings, cultural events, sport events, to educate the new generation. The impact of camp life is heavy psychologically. The high population density has a negative impact, for sure. There is little privacy or space for kids to play. They have to stay inside. That brings them together but it also creates problems. It's like a ghetto.

"Also, it is difficult to contemplate making improvements or additions to one's house; everything is transitory, thus improvements are unnecessary. This is all due to our refugee status."◆

Being suspended in time and in unfamiliar, temporary space year after year has untold consequences for refugee families. As the number of refugees has increased, so has our knowledge of the pathologies of camp life. Whether the camps are in Central America, Africa, Europe, or Asia, family life inside them is put to the test of deprivation, lack of dignity, and loss of hope. For women, security is a major concern; too often they are victimized, harassed, or exploited within the camps. In the camps for Cambodian refugees in Thailand, a social worker spoke of the troubles she witnesses.

ARANYA PHATET, THAILAND

At the height of the refugee exodus from the Cambodian civil war in 1979–80, over 360,000 Cambodians fled into Thailand. The border town of Aranya Phatet became one of the centers for their support as camps were hastily built nearby to accommodate the fleeing famililes. Between March 1992 and May 1993, the repatriation effort was successful in emptying most camps under the auspices of the UN High Commissioner for Refugees. The remaining refugees with whom I talked were waiting for resettlement in areas not yet deemed secure, or waiting for family members who had yet to join them for the return.

The camps were well-organized groupings of bamboo-and-thatch houses. Dust flew as dozens of children played ball and bicycles came and went through the camp. A senior social worker, Wilai Sangnoi, who works with the Khmer Women's Association, welcomed us and spoke of her concerns before we met with several refugee families.

"There are many women alone, because the husbands either died in the fighting or have gone back to Cambodia. The women have nothing; they are poor, alone, depressed. Some of them have no families to go back to in Cambodia. A big problem is suicide: If a woman doesn't have any support or is beaten by a man, nobody is there to care for her. She feels alone, so she wants to die. Also, it is very dangerous when women go outside the camp. They are threatened by men who want their money or who use them.

"We see alcohol problems, depression, and psychotic people. All are very common. Alcohol is a big problem with the men. Many have suffered trauma, and when you ask them why they like drinking alcohol, they say, 'If I drink it makes me calm down. I can sleep easily.' Many are violent when they drink: they hit the wife or the children. So the wife comes to us for help. When I lived in Cambodia I never saw these problems. We had good family education, men never beat women. They respected them. But the Khmer Rouge regime made people despair. Violence became a way of life."

Phen Yuk, 65
Prem Thuon, 57
Y Rom, 45

For those families who have been able to stay together, the problems of dislocation seem less traumatic. The family of a former soldier is an example: three generations live together, planning their return and the children's future.

The home of Phen Yuk and and Prem Thuon and their family of nine is tucked away in a quiet alley of the camp, a haven from the sun and its relentless heat. Everything inside is made of bamboo: chairs, table, shelves. We sat outside under an overhanging roof; far-off children's voices were carried to us by an afternoon breeze.

Cambodians Phen Yuk and Y Rom (*standing*) with wives, children, and grandchildren in their refugee camp home in Thailand

PHEN YUK   Phen Yuk is a quiet, thoughtful man, proud that he and the family were making do with their meager means until such time it would be safe to return to Cambodia. There, he hoped to find land to farm.

"I was born to a farming family, but when I married, I became a soldier in the French army. In those days the army built the railroads. That is what I did. When the French left I stayed in the national army until the Khmer took over. We fled the Khmer in 1986. I'm waiting for my name to be called so I can return and start a new life. I will be a farmer again, and my grandchildren will go to school. I don't see any future for my grandchildren except for those who can go to school. My son-in-law will help me farm."◆

Y ROM   Y Rom, the son-in-law, is a bicycle repairman. He earns extra money using his bicycle as a transportation service back and forth across the Thai-Cambodian border. Given the number of land mines in the region, this is perilous work.

"We go back and forth. It is dangerous, but since we need income, I do it. I go and buy milk and things for the children. There is food assistance in the camp, but it is irregular. I am taking care of this family. Since I married their daughter in 1979, I've been making all the family arrangements and most of the income. They are my responsibility. When we go back to Cambodia there will be land to farm and I will also be able to do motorcycle repairs."◆

When I turned to say good-bye to Prem Thuon, she said, "I am looking forward to going back. We have two sons who live in Cambodia who can help with farming and I will look after their children. We will support each other, lean on each other, to make our living."

"Leaning on each other" is the common lot of displaced families. Even more than other families, their survival depends upon family solidarity. Environmental refugees are often as vulnerable as those who flee conflict. On the limits of the Sahara Desert in central Mali, hundreds of families displaced by the great Sahelian drought of 1984–85 remain in a state of limbo, despite the efforts of international organizations and the Malian government to assist them.[5] Most that remain are households headed by women who wait for their men's return, or for the money those men send home from abroad.

MISSIRA, MALI

The settlement at Missira, a half-hour drive from the trading center of Mopti, began with eighty-six displaced Tuareg families who had barely escaped starvation and had lost their principle livelihood, their cattle and camels. A decade later, eighty families remain, of which forty-four are headed by women, most of whom are widows. For the men of Missira, the only means of earning cash is a disaster for the fragile environment. They were given pushcarts, in hopes they would use them for trading, but the only trade they found was that of fuel wood. They cut the few remaining trees of the region and sell wood by the roadside. For women, the making of leather trinkets—key chains, pillow covers, or bracelets—is the only source of income.

Grandmother Elhasba sat in a worn Tuareg tent, smoking a small pipe. She was quite deaf and was often shaken by a bad cough. Her daughter, Djedi, told us she suffers from fever and chronic back pain. Djedi was a constant smiling host. As we talked she worked on yet another of the braided bracelets she sells to provide the women's only income. She showed us a basket she made that sells for 600 CFA [approximately US $1]; it takes her five days to weave such a basket. As she explained, "We are just waiting for the men to return."

Elhasba Netthouomahana, 80
Djedi Minthhamdouss
Gamoudiouworkoy, 35

ELHASBA The grandmother told of the Tuareg way of life and of her nine childen, of whom only five remain. "As far back as we can recall, we followed our animals and engaged in the salt trade with our camel caravans. That is how we lived; we traded salt for whatever we needed and we sold milk. We also did leather work for sale in the towns. My grandfather had all sorts of animals: cows, sheep, and goats. He had a favorite place he called his own, but in reality we were always moving. We lost all that in the first drought of 1973. Slowly we rebuilt the herds and stayed in the Timbuktu area, but then the next drought came, and we lost everything again. Even the camels died, and that meant we couldn't engage in the salt trade

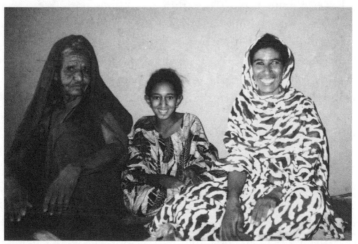

Tuareg refugee women in Mali: Elhasba and her daughter Djedi with neighbor's daughter

anymore. Many turned to begging. We women sold things here in the Mopti area, but we weren't wanted, welcome.

"Here we had to adjust to new foods, to rely on strangers to teach us how to cultivate certain foods, to rely on the honesty of those who distribute food and who might 'overlook' two women without male support."◆

DJEDI Djedi said that her father had died in 1980, and that since then there were only a few times when men of the family were actually present. "I married my cousin in 1982. We had two children but both died, one as an infant and the other at one year. The child you see here was given to us by my brother. I will raise him since I have no children of my own. He is mine now.

"My husband left to find work eight years ago. I think he is in Libya. Many went off, to Burkina, to Mauritania. There are few men here at all. I don't know when he will return.

"I have had word about my husband when people come back occasionally, I write him letters to send back to him. Apparently he is in good health, but work is difficult to find. In the meantime we survive by making these bracelets and key chains to sell. Luckily one of my brothers sends money from time to time.

"What is difficult is being without men. Ours is a very private culture. Women stayed secluded for the most part, at home. Without men, we must do everything ourselves and we lack the knowledge. We have little revenue, so we rarely eat enough."◆

The two women, waiting in the desert heat for return of their relatives, represent well the essential needs of families: support of its members, counsel and livelihood skills for the benefit of the group. Yet the reality of today's world is that economic disparities within and among nations forces millions of people to leave their families in order to offer that support and livelihood. The International Labor Organization estimates that 120 million men and women are economic exiles, seeking work in wealthier nations.[6] The pressure on family relationships, the psychological costs to both children and adults, is inestimable. Many poor mothers, for example, leave their children with others in order to find work caring for the children of wealthier women. Such is the case of a young Salvadoran mother.

WASHINGTON, D.C., AND SOYAPANGO, EL SALVADOR

The capital of the United States of America is a multicultural, multilingual city. Its inhabitants come from all over the country—and the world—to work in government agencies or the burgeoning service and infotech industries. The city's African American population has been the backbone of Washington for many generations and accounts for 61.4 percent of its population.[7] In recent decades, the city has seen an influx of Central American immigrants, who find work in its affluent suburbs and in mostly low-wage jobs in the city itself.

The family of Marina Pleitez Meija is divided between Washington and El Salvador. Her story is increasingly typical of the stories of many recent U.S. immigrants, in which the middle gener- **Marina Pleitez Meija , 34**
ation seeks work as servants in the wealth- **Mercedes Pleitez, 53**
ier nations, their meager incomes **Jessica Xiomara Meija Henriques, 11**
supporting both children and parents back in their homelands.

Marina is a housemaid in suburban Washington. She was one of seven children whose father abandoned the family when Marina was eight years old. Five years ago she left her children with her mother-in-law in El Salvador to find work in the United States. Once she found employment, she sent money to her husband so that he, too, could make the journey north. They now have legal resident alien status in the United States, and send money to the mother-in-law each month for the upkeep of the family.

MARINA   Marina is just over five feet tall. She has a girlish demeanor that belies the fact that she is the mother of three children, ages eight, ten, and fourteen. Her story of exile is not uncommon; it is one filled with risk, fear, and hope. We sat in my home in Washington as she told of her circumstances and her journey north.

"I lived with my mother and my grandparents in the small hamlet of San Antonio Silva. My mother worked seasonally harvesting coffee while my grandmother took care of us. My grandparents were like my parents. When my father left with another woman, our life was thrown into turmoil and sadness. Nothing can compare to that moment. As children, being abandoned was an unbelievable feeling. We were just thrown away like so much trash. My mother worked on a coffee farm each year until around November, then she would take in laundry to wash and iron. She was never able to afford schooling for us.

"My worklife began when I was eleven years old. I worked in a textiles factory. I didn't do much; I was too young. I helped with the cleaning and swept the floor. My oldest sister had been working there for about five years. I went to join her in San Salvador and was so proud to be helping our family. We would send money to my grandmother to help support my younger brothers. When I was fourteen I started working in a plastics factory, and I worked there until I left El Salvador.

"While working there, I had a child, my oldest son, but I didn't want to marry the man. Then I met my husband. He liked my boy and since then we have had two children of our own.

"I had no plans to leave El Salvador while my children were so young. But one of my sisters, who was already here, sent word to me saying that if I would like to come, she could help me. I still hesitated. The following year we had an increase in prices; El Salvador was going through very difficult times. I began to think there was no other solution. My sister kept writing, saying, 'Think about it seriously because this is a wonderful opportunity for you. What we didn't have when we were young is now possible for our children here.'

"I decided to come. I contacted a guide and paid for the false documents and trip. We went by bus all the way to Tijuana, via Guatemala. I was pretending to be a Mexican woman. The Mexican police stopped us and asked for our papers; they took my passport and visa. We spent one night in jail. I didn't know what was going on. The guide paid some money and they let us go.The following day, they told us that sixteen of us would be going in a trailer. It was like a moving van. It had canvas on top and cubicles under a false floor where they hid us. They lined us up, one with the feet one way, the next with the feet the other way. I was scared to death. Everything was locked up; we couldn't see what was going on. There were two little holes so we could breath. I think we went through several checkpoints, because the police would poke the truck with long sticks to see what was being transported. Once we arrived in Los Angeles, we got out of the truck; everyone was dizzy, not knowing where we were. I couldn't believe that we had made it without the police catching us.

"For the first twenty-two days I couldn't find work. I didn't know any English at all. I felt lost and I said to myself, 'Oh my God, what am I doing here!' My cousin placed a call to El Salvador and I had a chance to talk to the children. My husband said, 'Come back to El Salvador. We are suffering without you here, the children need you, get back here.'

"Luckily I found a job, first in a dry cleaners and then with an American woman who speaks a little Spanish. I feel comfortable with her and I love her children.

"It is still difficult to accept being outside my country, far from home, being away from my children. I would come home tired and think and think. I couldn't sleep in the beginning. It is difficult to accept the fact that my children are there and I am here.

"After nine months, my husband was able to come. He came with a woman guide. He suffered a great deal; he had to walk and walk, hundreds of miles. He was forced to hide many times. When they were in Tapachula, on the border between Guatemala and Mexico, they had no food and were terribly hungry. He had some money in the hem of his pants and was able to buy something to eat. By the time they got to Mexico, they didn't even have shoes; they had worn them out by walking so much. The guide did nothing to remedy the situation in spite of the fact that they had paid her a large amount of money.

"In Mexico City, they mutinied and went straight to a police station to try to return home. They had no more money, no food, no shoes. That's when a man called me wanting $250 to let my husband out of jail. What a racket! Of course I had to send it. When he was freed, he and his two friends went on by themselves. He had been on the road three months when they finally walked across the river into the United States. When he arrived here I couldn't recognize him. He was very thin and ill. But he was happy to be here.

"But now I have problems with him because he drinks so much. We haven't been living together for about a year. He says he drinks because he is alone and I tell him he should go back to El Salvador. It might be easier for me to think that he is there. About a year ago I tried to get him to go to a group that gives therapy for drinking. I made the arrangements and had the money for it. I waited and waited in front of the place but he didn't show up. He said he was afraid to go to the appointment. I told him he should be more afraid of going drunk in the street. I told him to go away. I am fed up. It's a useless battle.

"By now I have accepted my fate a little more. I miss my children very much but I know that they will understand as they get older. I think it's the hardest for children when parents leave. As soon as I get my papers straightened out I will go to see them and bring them here. My mother-in-law says she will suffer if I take them away. They have grown up with her. It's a mess, any way you look at it.

"The idea of coming here was to acquire something to leave our children; even if one is illiterate one can work hard and achieve a better life. All I can

In San Salvador, Erick, Jessica, and Wilfredo, the children of expatriate worker Marina Pleitez Meija, await her return

ask God is that when they come to this country, they'll be more ready to adapt. I keep asking my mother-in-law to take them to church because that is bound to help them."◆

A few months later, in a populous suburb of San Salvador, I found the house that Marina so missed. It is part of a long cement-block building, divided into eight individual homes, where each family and its belongings are crowded into three small rooms. Arriving with photographs of Marina and her husband made me a welcome guest, of course. The children, a bit shy at first, began slowly to ask about their parents. Jessica, the eleven-year-old daughter, asked several times, "My father is very tall, isn't he?" Five years had increased his height considerably in her young memory.

MERCEDES The children's grandmother and Marina's mother-in-law, Mercedes Pleitez, looked much older than her fifty-three years. She had been raised in Soyapango, which, she explained, had once been open farmland. The only daughter of poor farmers, she had learned to be a seamstress but can no longer "even thread the needle" due to poor eyesight. She had five children, whose father left with another woman soon after the last was born. That son, Jose Antonio, had recently attempted to enter the United States illegally. He was arrested in Texas and sent back. Mercedes does not want him to try again.

"It's enough that my first son is there. He went because of Marina, and he suffered because of it. The change has caused him to be very unhappy. Being there is very difficult, but they went because they're looking for a better life. When my son and Marina worked in the factory here, their earnings were never enough. The terrible political and economic situation in this country forced them to leave. There was no other way.

"Having the children here with me is no problem. Marina has always told me they will send for them one day. I love them as if they were my own children. They have everything they need because the parents work for it. We have money to pay for school, for food. There is never a shortage of milk or of things like vitamins.

"But the children need their parents. The older boy has problems that need their attention. He has kind of a rebelliousness inside him, like resentment. He wants to pick fights and he has a very bad temper. I've taken him to the doctor because it's getting pretty bad. The doctor prescribed tranquilizers. There is too much anger inside him. The girl doesn't have these problems; she is just very stubborn and doesn't want to do what she is supposed to do.

"It's been five years, and the children don't ask too much about the parents.

It makes me very sad when I think how long it has been since they left. And it might be a lot longer. Sometimes the sadness overcomes me."◆

It is a contradiction of today's world that to ensure a family's welfare, one must sometimes leave the family behind. Marina's children are among many whose parents chose economic exile over poverty. For both children and adults, for those left behind and for those who struggle in a strange land, the consequences are distressing. Marina's husband is maladapted to his new land, and her faraway eleven-year-old daughter says, "My mother sends me nice clothes and toys but I would rather have my mother."

The families who speak in this chapter are not necessarily traditional family groups, but they have found, or created, the relationships of caring and support that they believe constitute a family unit. The Bowman family, torn apart by Indian schools, war, and illness, has found their roots and returned to one another. The young couple living on Rio's streets believe they will create a family to make up for those they did not have. The street boys of Kampala and Bangkok have found support from one another and guidance from teachers and social workers who often become substitute parents. Rita, the prostitute and advocate for the rights of other prostitutes and their children, is in reality a head-of-household. Refugees Abu Faisal and Phen Yuk have managed to hold their refugee families together, and keep their hope of return to their homelands alive, despite the trauma of dislocation and death. And Marina, the young Salvadoran mother who dared venture to another land without even knowledge of the language to aid her, is able to provide education and well-being for her faraway children.

Swept this way and that by life, these individuals have managed to find support and caring among relatives or strangers. The families they have formed may not meet the test of the "norm," but they are nonetheless caring groups that support and honor their members. The courage they have shown as they struggle to hold families together or to create new families for themselves warrants our admiration. It also warrants the support of enlightened public policy.

Conclusion | Private Lives and Public Policies

Are we being good ancestors?

—Jones Salk

In her work-worn dress and rundown shoes, Brazilian elder Ella Borges carries herself with grace and the utmost dignity. As we sat on her bed in a ramshackle hut adjacent to a deserted villa in a busy neighborhood of Rio de Janeiro, she spoke eloquently of her childhood. Ella, who is of Afro-Brazilian descent, was born in a faraway rural area, but when she turned ten years old, she was sent to the city. "My mother was ashamed of me," she admitted, "because my skin was so dark, much darker than hers or that of my sisters and brothers. She didn't want me around. I was sent to Rio to become a maid in a wealthy and distinguished family."

Ella took pride in the fact that her employers treated her well. They sent her to school and gave her all the advantages of a real daughter. When it came time for Ella to marry, they provided the young couple with a fine wedding and the furnishings for their home. "But I married a weak man," Ella explained. "He was swindled and lost all our money. He ran away in shame; I never heard of him again." Ella had to sell all her belongings to pay his debts. They had no children, and Ella never remarried.

Now, in her late sixties, Ella lives in an abandoned, rat-infested house. Here she is able to take in "anyone who needs a place to sleep": street children, battered women, or transient laborers. She gathers donations of food and clothes from local churches and manages somehow to provide for her guests. "Over the years," she said with a measure of pride and sadness, "I've raised sixteen children. They all call me Mother and come back from time to time to see me."

An impoverished, childless woman nearing seventy, Ella Borges gathers the needy around her and nurtures youngsters nobody else wants. Sixteen unrelated people call her Mother, and there is little doubt that her family will continue to expand.

Ella Borges offers security, support, and solace to needy people. In return she feels part of a caring group. Is this not a kind of family— a group of individuals who support and care for one another, bound by empathy and a sense of mutual responsibility? To be sure, each family is different. Families come in all sizes and combinations of old and young, male and female members. We witnessed that diversity in the preceding chapters. Permitted to look behind the curtain of family privacy, we found admirable families of all kinds, but also learned that the family is not always the secure place we wish it to be. When successful, families respect their individual members and nourish them physically, emotionally, and spiritually. At their worst they exploit, abuse, or abandon their own.

We have heard scores of family stories. From them arise suggestions for easing the multiple pressures on families in this period of profound transition. These pressures will not go away; they are here to stay, or to be replaced by others, perhaps even more daunting.

What can we learn from these families? How did or do they cope with the forces of change? And what is the role of public policy in managing the context in which families must function? What can we do, individually and as citizens, to require family-friendly public policies? And how do we hold our decision-makers accountable to the coming generations?

From our elders we heard about the profound changes they have witnessed. As relationships among generations and strict gender roles are transformed, shifts in authority and family decision-making reshape family interaction.

New egalitarian relationships within the family sometimes confuse elders, and they fret that the young are not as responsible as they once were. They worry about the quality of their late life: about health care, leisure, companionship. That worry is justified in a time when extended families are more and more rare, and when family work obligations leave no one to care for the elderly within the home. The question of society's role in providing elder-friendly communities is becoming paramount as longevity increases.

As the twenty-first century began, women's participation in democratic discourse within the home and society cut across all cultures and classes. The concept of women's equality to men transformed women's perception of themselves and their place in the community, nation, and world. Reaching from bourgeois mansions to nomadic tents, it is one of the most dynamic social forces of our time. Nearly everywhere, the status of today's women is far better than that of their foremothers a century or half-century ago. Access to education and opportunities for salaried work, the capacity to plan pregnancies, and improvements in legal status concerning inheritance, property rights, marriage, divorce, and domestic violence have totally reshaped women's lives.

The United Nations played a significant role in women's advancement: the International Women's Year (1975) and the UN Decade for Women

(1976–1985) that followed raised awareness about the unequal status of women and gave women the opportunity to participate in international forums where their rights were formulated. Governments were urged to examine laws and customs concerning women and to rescind or discourage those that barred women and girls from full participation in society. These gains have altered our way of life, to be sure, but much more remains to be done: millions of women remain voiceless and vulnerable due to legal inequality, traditions, or, in the extreme case of the Taliban in Afghanistan and to a lesser degree other religious institutions, to religious obscurantism. Today access to reproductive health care and family planning is part and parcel of women's human rights, yet some patriarchal forces will go to dangerous lengths to control women's bodies: the Vatican, for example, continues to condemn modern contraception and "has repeatedly maintained that its complete prohibition of condoms for the prevention of HIV/AIDS transmission—even among married couples—will not be lifted in the future and that only abstinence and fidelity in marriage will be the panacea of the pandemic."[1] Margaret Sanger, the American pioneer in family planning, once noted that "if women were not allowed the knowledge to control their own bodies, they would never be free." Indeed. The resistance to reproductive choice and to women's right to control their bodies represents the last gasp of patriarchal control.

Investments in accessible health care and family planning services, in girls' education, and in women's economic opportunities are necessary if all women are to live more healthy and productive lives. This may not happen, however, until such time as far more women are in the seats of power, members of the legislatures where laws are fashioned and the agencies where policies are implemented.

The economic and social transformation that has resulted in a shift in gender roles within the family and society at large is a cross-cultural reality. As women's lives are reshaped by more access to education and public life, so, too, are those of men. The adjustment to these emerging roles is an ongoing process. There appears, for example, to be a shift in attitudes—and more than a little confusion—about the responsibilities and expectations that come with manhood. Many men retain a lingering ambivalence about women working outside the home, perceiving it as a threat to their authority. Some say it is a contributing factor to divorce and family breakdown. Others see it as an important contribution to family well-being and their wives' personal enrichment. In any case, women's participation in, and contribution to, the world economy is a reality and is clearly here to stay.

What is most disturbing is evidence that significant numbers of men—husbands and fathers—are walking away from family responsibilities. The fact that over 25 percent of the world's households are headed by women speaks clearly to this assumption, as do several of the interviews in this book. There appears to be little data on the factors resulting in these women-led households—on, say, the percentage of women who are widowed, divorced, abandoned, or left alone by men forced to seek work abroad. But the interviews herein too often testify to men's failure to take responsibility for children and families. As we attempt to formulate more family-friendly policies, it is imperative that we study not only the reasons for men's absence from the family but also the forces that undermine men's commitment to it. At the same time we must acknowledge the reality of single-parent, women-headed families, and support rather than punish them.

On a brighter note, it appears that increasingly, men—and especially younger men—see the opportunity for more egalitarian relationships between men and women as a boon, a fortunate trend that may allow them to become more involved in family life and less beholden to strict and restrictive gender roles. These men decry the competition of the workplace and long working hours, which deprive them of a life balanced with family, leisure, and work.

Raising children in a complex, changing world is no easy task, and becomes even more complicated in families in which both parents are employed outside the home. From the interviews we learned that when a mother works, the father is becoming more willing to pitch in and share child care duties. Many fathers see this as an opportunity their own fathers didn't have. Indeed, there is recognition that the connotation of *fathering* is becoming more than the dictionary definition of "begetting" or "siring" a child. The meaning of *fathering* is becoming parallel to that of *mothering*—to nurture and to nourish.

Government and business should join families in embracing this new partnership, and restructure labor policies to provide a more family-friendly work environment for parents, with flexible work hours, subsidized child care, and paid family leave. At the community level, intergenerational initiatives such as after-school programs that provide interaction between the elders and the young benefit both age groups and support families in general. Most of all, we must be clear about one thing: if our primary concern is children's well-being, then supporting the adults who love and care for them is the priority, regardless of the marital status, gender, sexual orientation, or biological relationship of those caregivers. Secure parents raise secure children.

Today's youth live in a confusing time, no matter where they reside. They are besieged by drugs, violence, pornographic images, and rampant materialism, and they often wonder where they will fit in a world where education is too costly, employment opportunities are few, and "making good" almost always means leaving the haven of the family far behind. For the youth of less advantaged families, affordable educational opportunities and skills training programs are essential, and are too often sorely lacking.

The young also need guidance in family life skills, especially in the era of HIV/AIDs. The more one learns about local practices, the more it seems that talking to children about sexuality is almost universally avoided. Even the simplest facts of menstruation and hormonal development are often left shrouded in silence, resulting in fear and anxiety among adolescents or, worse, undesired pregnancies or illness. Although the family context is preferable for learning about the challenges of adulthood, considering the realities, schools must also provide basic family life education. The argument, put forth by conservative leaders, that sex education causes teens to initiate sex is simply false. Researchers in the United States, for example, have found that adolescents participating in several programs that combine discussions of abstinence with information about contraception have tended to delay having sex.[2]

It was truly remarkable to hear the young—both boys and girls—articulate their hopes for a life partner with the same education level and with whom they may "share everything," including household tasks. Another profound change is many youths' desired family size of two or three children, much smaller than the families in which they were raised.

For young people from poorer families, alas, there is a disturbing family dilemma: the lack of employment opportunities prevents them from starting families of their own. Their inability to marry and have children due to economic reasons has profound consequences for society. Adulthood denied may lead to disillusionment and anger.

The change in the natural environment described by the elders confirms that environmental degradation is proceeding at a swift pace, and that this destruction has a profound impact on family life. The Arctic ice cap has thinned by 40 percent; global warming threatens the world's coastlines and the lives of billions of people; and thousands of chemicals are in our waters, soils, and air, and in the food we eat.[3] Another century of careless exploitation of our natural environment will leave us bereft of untold species, life-giving forests, and sufficient potable water.

Initiatives to reduce pollution, conserve natural resources, and protect all fragile ecosystems and species must be undertaken now, at all levels—in schools, communities, nations, regions, and international bodies. Unfortunately, many leaders who profess to be concerned about "the family" permit and promote unfettered exploitation of the environment, ignoring the fact that family security is dependent upon long-term ecological security.

Just as environmental well-being is a global family concern, so, too, is human health. The diseases that stalk the earth travel from one continent to another and can be prevented only by international initiatives. HIV/AIDS, substance abuse, and public and private violence are all issues that require concerted action by nations working cooperatively. In the case of HIV/AIDS, for example, the wealthier countries must ensure that funds and drugs are made available to combat the wrenching crisis in Africa; failure to do so would be both morally reprehensible and pragmatically unwise. And as a world community, we cannot turn out backs on the millions of children orphaned by AIDS; a generation of young must be cared for and schooled, and this, too, will require focused multinational efforts. At national levels, investments in rural medical facilities, affordable urban clinics, and reproductive health care and education are already in demand, and that demand will only increase in the years ahead.

At the same time that information technology began to bring us together in a vast global family, it also began to separate us one from another within our families. It is no longer necessary to talk, listen, or be entertained as a family group. Human interaction is replaced by private entertainment, from Walkmen and portable telephones to home video and the Internet. Families of all backgrounds refer to the impact of these communications technologies on family communications, on the way families spend time together, and thus on family traditions and behavior.[4] Seventy-nine-year-old Erna Beckmeyer of Hartsburg, Missouri, noted plaintively, "We don't face each other anymore when we talk. We're always facing the television."

Where once information and values were passed down by family elders, today they often come from afar, from totally different cultures, via mass media. Families everywhere expressed concern about the content of these media and voiced their fear of cultural homogenization and Westernization. A Jordanian grandfather complained, "Now we have TV as a third parent. It shows ugly things, violence and excessive liberty." In the absence of competing images, media have the potential to warp the young's fledgling value system. Public financial support for quality, educational media and for indigenous cultural institutions could help balance the picture they receive.

"Our responsibility," Jonas Salk often said, "is to anticipate the future." Being part of our global village requires a broadening of our sense of family, a commitment to a larger community. It demands solidarity with future generations everywhere, and a long-range view of our common well-being. Many interviewees expressed their concern that in this time of transition, it seems that our rights have run ahead of our sense of duty and responsibility to others. Teaching the next generation their rights and responsibilities, their obligations to community and society, must begin in the family.

Just as we ask families to be responsible for their own, we must ask our leaders to be responsible for the needs of future generations. That often means making unpopular decisions that may not be in the short-term interests of material gain for individuals or corporations. Good stewardship requires making decisions through the prism of many generations hence—not that of the next election.

Far too rare are genuinely open, informed, and creative public debates on housing, employment policies, health care, child and elder care policies, equitable family law, environmental sustainability, and corporate responsibility for the health and well-being of the global community. Rather than bemoaning the demise of the family, we should be raising these issues in our houses of worship, our schools, associations, universities, and parliaments. We must hold our leaders accountable for the decisions that shape tomorrow's world. It is our responsibility.

As readers have observed, upon arriving in each country to conduct these family conversations, I sought assistance in identifying individuals—community activists, religious leaders, academics, or government officials—whose work enables them to pinpoint the trends affecting families. Almost without exception, I was sent to consult with—women. The common response was: "You are interested in our families? Oh, yes, I know a woman who . . ."

That family policy is considered a women's issue, and thus often relegated to the policy sidelines, is troubling on many levels. It is also harmful—to family security, to children, and to women and men alike. Until we begin to look at families as partnerships among the generations and between both members of a couple, we will once again be playing the separatist game. Remember, it took twenty or more years to get policy makers to consider women in their development policies and to consider the critical role of men in the promotion of family planning. Those years of ignoring *who does what* and *who decides what* were wasted opportunities. Let us focus efforts not on mothers but on parents, not on women but on the couple, not on the individual but on the family group.

Our families have changed far more than the institutions or policies that serve them. Employment policies, school schedules, and community services, for example, were designed for a time when generations of families lived in proximity and women remained in or close to the home. Now outdated, they create a conflict between work and family responsibilities. If they remain outdated, it represents an abdication of our social responsibility.

The United Nations has served us well. It has provided the forum and often the impetus for research and action on a host of issues critical to the world's families. The UN's efforts on behalf of children, women, the elderly, refugees, the disabled, indigenous peoples, the environment, HIV/AIDS and other public health issues, family planning, labor issues, and of course, at its core, human rights, has brought untold benefit to billions of people.

Those who attack the United Nations are often the same people who, while espousing democratic principles and "family values," would deny equal rights to women, oppose family planning, and resist adherence to global conventions on the major transnational problems of our times.[5] A farmer I met in rural Uganda remarked, "It worries me that people are not serious about changing the situation we are in. I was hoping that things would change—but the people we put our confidence in are not looking down at the grassroots needs." Or, I would add, ahead to the future.

These family stories are not meant to be exhaustive or even representative. They serve only as sample testimony on the trends besetting families in a time of epochal change. From them we learn that global forces are shaping local realities as never before, that only a combination of global and local policies will meet the challenges now before the world community. Perhaps, also, this inquiry will expand our perception of others' lives and clarify, thus, our responsibilities for the common good.

The changes today's families are experiencing are the result of many trends, not all of them bad. The most important trend may well be the infusion of democratic and egalitarian ideals into family relationships and decision-making. The lament over lost family values is essentially a desire to return to a different time, when family and societal structures were rigid and clear. This is neither possible nor desirable.

The past century and its technological revolution have altered every facet of everyone's life—including the way families live, work, define themselves, make decisions, and spend time together. Families are smaller, more mobile, better educated, and, as a result, are exploring new roles for generations and the genders. This is not a change that can be reversed.

In the days before movies, radio, television, and the Internet, few people knew that alternatives existed to the way they lived or what they had. Before cars and trains, trucks and jets, they could not get to places where people lived differently, nor could new products get to them. Relatively few people had heard of the concept of individuals' rights; they were part of a family or clan and did what was expected of them. The concept of democracy, if not its total fulfillment, has now spread worldwide. Governments everywhere are being pressured by their citizens to yield to it. So, too, are families. This is not a change that can be reversed.

In the past, men ruled. Women helped. They did what they were allowed to do, or forced to do. Few women dared think they might aspire to more than marriage, frequent motherhood, and work in the home and on the land. Although some traditional societies afforded women a measure of power and respect within these roles, the roles were rigidly defined. Then came the idea that women could aspire to full participation in society at all levels and in many forms. If that were not enough, the advent of modern contraception provided women with the means to decide if and when to bear children. This option, hitherto unknown in the human experience, changed forever the relationship between women and men. This is not a change that can be reversed.

The democratization of the family has had far-reaching effects. The young no longer accept elders' opinions without question. Children, who once worked and were brought up to fill their parents' shoes and take care of the elders in their turn, now attend school and come home with wide-ranging ideas and surprising goals. Many women have ambitions for themselves, beyond the goals of their menfolks and beyond the achievement of their children. A growing number of men are also declining prescribed gender roles by forming partnerships with their spouses and opting for more active participation in childrearing. More and more same-sex couples feel able to live openly and proudly. These are not changes that will be reversed.

These aspirations are not just disconcerting—they are revolutionary. The traditional patriarchal family is being transformed, and what's more, the traditional outcasts from the patriarchal family, such as single parents, childless adults, orphans, homosexuals, and even street children and prostitutes—all these people are finding that they can form new alliances that feel to them like families, and thus *are* families. They no longer need to win acceptance in a patriarchal setting—and that, to the patriarchs, may be the most disturbing change of all.

As tradition collides with democratization and globalization, all social institutions are undergoing profound reform; the family is no exception. The redefining of family relationships is a universal phenomenon. This situation may look like breakdown to those facing backward, but it looks like renovation to those facing the future. And if policymakers wish to support families, they must turn to face the future as well.

The concept of "family values" may have become corrupted and misused, but the value of families is beyond doubt. Across cultures and nationalities, throughout all social classes and degrees of education, these families' message is clear: We are all struggling with disruptive trends—some beneficial, some destructive—but the family group remains the undisputed and coveted foundation of human society.

Notes

Introduction

1. Global life expectancy rose from forty-six to sixty-six years in the past half century. UN Population Division, *World Population Prospects: The 2000 Revision* (New York: UN Department of Economic and Social Affairs, 2001).
2. Thomas W. Wilson Jr., "A Bedrock Consensus of Human Rights," in *Human Dignity* (New York: The Aspen Institute for Humanistic Studies, 1979), 47.
3. UN Population Division, *World Urbanization Prospects: The 1999 Revision, Data Tables and Highlights* (New York: UN Department of Economic and Social Affairs, 2000).
4. International Labor Organization (ILO), *World Labour Report 2000* (Geneva: ILO, 2000), 267.
5. International Labor Organization (ILO), "Nature and Extent of International Migration Labor," in *Protecting the Most Vulnerable of Today's Workers* (Geneva: ILO, 1997); (www.ilo.org/public/english/protection/migrant/papers/protvul/ch2.htm).
6. Women-headed households range from less than 20 percent in South Asia to 31 percent in Western Europe and almost 50 percent in some African countries. UN Department of Economic and Social Affairs, Statistics Division, *The World's Women 2000: Trends and Statistics* (New York: UN, 2000). For a discussion regarding the global percentage of female-headed households see Alain Marcoux, *The Feminization of Poverty: Facts, Hypotheses and the Art of Advocacy* (UN Food and Agriculture Organization, October 1997) [cited 11 March 2001]; (www.fao.org/sd/WPdirect/WPan0015.htm). For limited urban and rural date see UN Population Division, *Living Arrangements of Women and Their Children in Developing Countries: A Demographic Profile* (New York: UN, 1995).
7. UN, *UN Declaration on the Elimination of Violence Against Women* (Vienna, 1993) [cited 16 March 2001]; (www.un.org/documents/ga/res/48/a48r104.htm).
8. Religious restrictions are also a factor. At a November 30–December 1 conference on AIDS, Vatican officials stated categorically that condoms could never be morally allowed. See John Norton, "Vatican Officials Say AIDS Problem Involves More Than Condoms," *Catholic News Service*, 30 November 2000.

9. UN, *1998 Demographic Yearbook* (New York: UN, 2000).

10. United States' child support payment statistics available in Timothy Grall, *Child Support Payments for Custodial Mothers and Fathers: 1997*, Current Population Reports, P60-212 (U.S. Census Bureau, October 2000), 4. According to news reports child support payment is not well-enforced in Japan; see "A Weakening of the Ties that Bind," *US News & World Report*, 12 June 1995.

11. UN Population Division, *World Urbanization Prospects: The 1999 Revision* (New York: UN Department of Economic and Social Affairs, 2000).

12. World Resources Institute, *World Resources: 2000–2001* (Washington, D.C.: World Resources Institute, 2000), 64.

13. UNAIDS, *AIDS Epidemic Update: December 2000* (Geneva: UNAIDS, 2000), 3.

14. Statistics in all of the country boxes were taken from the following sources: UN Population Division, *World Population Prospects: The 2000 Revision*; UN Statistical Division, *The World's Women 2000* (New York: UN, 2000); UN Development Programme (UNDP), *The Human Development Report 2000* (New York: UNDP, 2000).

15. *New York Times*, 12 November 1993.

16. Statistics Bureau & Statistics Center of Japan, *Monthly Report on Current Population Estimates* (Japan: Statistics Bureau & Statistics Center, October 2000) [cited 12 March 2001]; (www.stat.go.jp/english/15k2.htm#15k2-1).

17. UN Population Division, *World Population Prospects: The 1998 Revision* (New York: UN Department of Economic and Social Affairs, 1999).

18. Statistics Bureau & Statistics Center of Japan, "Population 15 Years Old and Over by Labour Force Status, Employed Persons by Industry," in *Labor Force Survey: Average Annual Results* (Japan: Statistics Bureau & Statistics Center of Japan, January 2001) [cited 12 March 2001]; (www.stat.go.jp/english/154b.htm).

19. Donna M. Hughes, and Laura Joy Sporcic, Nadine Z. Mendelsohn, Vanessa Chirgwin, "Factbook on Global Sexual Exploitation" and "Trafficking in Women and Prostitution in the Asia Pacific," Coalition Against Trafficking in Women (CATW) and CATW-Asia Pacific www.uni.edu/wms/hughes/catw/asiapr15.htm. Also see Gwen Robinson, "Tribunal Will Hear Secrets of Sex Trade," *The Daily Telegraph*, 7 March 1994.

20. World Bank, *World Development Report: 2000/2001: Attacking Poverty* (New York: Oxford University Press, 2000).

21. "News of Population and Birth Control," *IPPF Newsletter*, (April 1952).

22. Amara Pongsapich, *Changing Family Patterns in Thailand* (Bangkok: Social Research Institute, Chulalongkorn University), 353.

23. Divorce rate statistics available from the Thai National Institute of Development Administration. For a discussion of family cohesion being threatened by mistresses and second wives see "Women Forced to Suffer in Silence," *Bangkok Post*, 4 June 2000. And for a discussion of sexual behavior and divorce see "Thailand Tops List of 15 Countries on Use of Condoms in Casual Sex—Thai Men Do It 80 Times a Year," *Bangkok Post*, 4 June 2000.

24. Donna M. Hughes, and Laura Joy Sporcic, Nadine Z. Mendelsohn, Vanessa Chirgwin, "Factbook on Global Sexual Exploitation" and "Trafficking in Women and Prostitution in the Asia Pacific," Coalition Against Trafficking in Women (CATW) and CATW-Asia Pacific www.uni.edu/wms/hughes/catw/asiapr15.htm.

25. World Health Organization (WHO) and UNAIDS, *Epidemiological Fact Sheet on HIV/AIDS and Sexually Transmitted Infections: Update 2000* (Geneva: WHO, 2000).

26. Vitit Muntarbhan, "A Scourge in Our Midst," *Bangkok Post*, 13 November 1992.

27. World Resources Institute, *World Resources 2000–2001* (Washington, D.C.: WRI, 2000).

28. G. Heilig, *Can China Feed Itself* (Laxenburg: IIASA, 1999) [cited 18 March 2001]; (www.iiasa.ac.at/Research/LUC/ChinaFood/inex_s.htm).

29. UN Population Division, *World Population Prospects: The 2000 Revision*.

30. Robert Engelman, Richard P. Cincotta, Bonnie Dye, Tom Gardner-Outlaw, Jennifer Wisnewski, *People in the Balance: Population and Natural Resources at the Turn of the Millennium* (Washington, D.C.: Population Action International, 2000), 22, 28.

31. UN Development Programme (UNDP), *Human Development Report* (New York: UNDP, 2000).

32. Population Action International, *The PAI Report Card 2001: A World of Difference, Sexual and Reproductive Health & Risks* (Washington, D.C.: Population Action International, 2001).

33. UN Statistical Division, *The World's Women: 2000*.

34 *Uganda: Epidemiological Factsheet on HIV/AIDS and Sexually Transmitted Infections, 2000 Update* (Geneva: UNAIDS, 2000).

35 Irene Ovonji Odida, "Land Law Reform: Challenges and Opportunities for Securing Women's Land Rights in Uganda," presented at a delegate workshop on Land Tenure Policy in African Nations, February 16^19, 1999. Available at *http://bdsn.parallelweb.net/land/Ugirene.htm#FTNT1*.

36 Interview with Mahfouz El Ansari, editor of *El Goumeria*.

37. UN Population Division, *World Population Prospects: The 2000 Revision*.

38. For a discussion of the economic impacts on the Gulf War in Jordan, see Fairouz M. Masoud, "Impact of Gulf War on Long-Term Physical Development Plan for Jordan," presented at GIS/GPS Conference 1997, Qatar.

39. Engelman, et al., *People in the Balance*, 24, 28.

40. World Bank, *Jordan Water Resources Sector Study*, Report 7099-JD (Washington, D.C.: World Bank, June 1988).

41. "Kin in U.S. Keep Salvador Afloat in Cash," *Miami Herald*, 23 January 1992.

42. UNICEF, *Children and War: Report on the Psychological Impact of Violence on Children in Central America* (Costa Rica: UNICEF, March 1990).

43. UNICEF, *State of the World's Children 1997* (New York: Oxford University Press, 1997).

44. UN Development *Programme, Human Development Report for Brazil: 1996* (Brazil: UNDP/IPEA, 1996) [cited 17 March 2001]; (www.undp.org.br/hdr/Hdr96/rdhbin.htm).

45. For a discussion of regional economic disparity in Brazil see Atila P. Roque, Joao Sucupira, Sonia Correa, and Jorge Eduardo Durao, *Poverty Again at the Center of the Debate* (Social Watch Instistute, 1996) [cited 18 March 2001]; (www.socwatch.org.uy/). Data also taken from UN Development Programme, *Human Development Report for Brazil: 1996.*

46. See the UN Population Division, *World Population Prospects*, 1998 and 2000 revisions.

47. U.S. Census Bureau [cited 18 March 2001]; (www.census.gov/Press-Release/www/1999/cb99-238.html).

48. AFL-CIO, *Facts About Working Women* (Washington, D.C.: AFL-CIO); (www.afl-cio.org/women/wwfacs.htm).

49. For estimates of the homeless population in the United States see Urban Institute, *America's Homeless II: Populations and Services* (Washington, D.C.: Urban Institute, February 2001) [cited 18 March 2001]; (www.urban.org/housing/homeless/numbers/index.htm). For estimates of children living in poverty see Joseph Dalaker and Bernadette Proctor, *Poverty in the United States* (Washington, D.C.: U.S. Census Bureau, September 2001), v.

50. Greater Washington Research Center, *Single-Parent Families: A First Look Based on 1990 Census Data* (Washington, D.C.: Greater Washington Research Center, 1992).

51. Bureau of Justice Statistics, *National Crime Victimization Survey* (Washington, D.C.: U.S. Department of Justice, July 2000). A summary of the 1998–1999 findings is available at www.ojp.usdoj.gov/bjs/cvictgen.htm. A summary of homicide trends (1976–1999) in the United States is available at www.ojp.usdoj.gov/bjs/homicide/gender.htm. For more information about violence against women see the Rape Abuse and Incest National Network (RAINN) Web site: www.rainn.org/stats.html.

52. Lester R. Brown, Michael Renner, and Brian Halwell, *Worldwatch Institute Vital Signs 2000* (New York: Norton, 2000), 150–51.

53. Peter D. Hart Research Associates, "Americans See the Drug Problem as Bad and Getting Worse" (Washington, D.C.: Peter D. Hart Research Associates, 1994).

Chapter One

1 For population statistics refer to *Historial Estimates of World Population*, (US Census Bureau: Washington,DC) available at www.census.gov/ ipc/ww/worldhis.html.

Chapter Two

1 United Nations Statistical Division, *The World's Women 2000*, (New York: United Nations, 2000).

2 "Separate and Unequal," *Far Eastern Economic Review* (April 14, 1994) 22.

Chapter Three

1. UN, *UN AIDS Report 2000*, (Geneva, 2000). The UN Population Fund notes that in twenty- nine African countries, life expectancy at birth is currently seven years less than it would have been without AIDS *(State of World Population 1999)*.

2. UN, Secretariat, Population Division, Department of Economic and Social Affairs, October 1999.

3. UN Division for Social Policy and Development.

4. Report of the Expert Group Meeting in Care Giving and Older Persons, Gender Dimension, 1997; (www.un.org/esa/socdev/agemalta.htm).

5. State Family Commission of China, *Basic Views and Policies Regarding Population and Development*, November 1999; (www.sfpc.gov.cn/epopindex.html).

6. For statistics on elderly abuse in the United States see *The National Elder Abuse Incidence Study: Final Report* (Washington, DC: U.S. Department of Health and Human Services, September 1998). For a discussion of elderly abuse in other countries see L. Tornstam, "Abuse of Elderly in Denmark and Sweden. Results

from a Population Study," in *Journal of Elder Abuse & Neglect*, vol 1:35–44, 1989; Elizabeth Podnieks et al., *National Survey on Abuse of the Elderly in Canada* (Toronto: Ryerson Polytechnical Institute, 1990); and Claudine McCreadie, Elder Abuse: Update on Research, (London: ACIOG, 1996).

7. Expert Group Meeting on Older Persons: Gender Dimension (Malta, 1997); (www.un.org/esa/socdev/agemalta.htm).

8. Cited in Administration on Aging, *Grandparents Raising Grandchildren*; (www.aoa.dhhs.gov/factsheets/ageism).

9. UNAIDS, *AIDS Epidemic Update: December 2000* (Geneva: UNAIDS, 2000).

10 Ken Bryson and Lynne Casper. *Coresident Grandparents and Grandchildren* (Washington, DC: U.S. Census Bureau, May 1999).

11. Cited in Administration on Aging, *Age Discrimination: A Pervasive and Damaging Influence*; (www.aoa.dhhs.gov/factsheets/ageism).

12. UN Population Division, *Demographic Trends 2000–2050* (New York, 1999).

13. UN Division for Social Policy and Development, *UN Principles for Older Persons* (New York, 1991).

Chapter Four

1. UN, Secretariat and International Labor Office, Statistics Division (Geneva, 1999).

2. Salma Chaudhuri and Pratima Paul Majumder, *The Conditions of Garment Workers in Bangladesh- -An Appraisal* (Dhaka: Bangladesh Institute for Development Studies, October 1991).

3. Hossain Sillur Rahman and Mahabub Hossain, *Rethinking Rural Poverty, A Case for Bangladesh* (Dhaka: Bangladesh Intitute for Development Studies, 1992).

4 United Nations Statistical Division, The World's Women 2000 (New York: United Nations, 2000). Also see United Nations Population Division, Living Arrangements of Women and Their Children in Developing Countries: A Demographic Profile (New York: United Nations, 1995).

Chapter Five

1. International Labor Organization (ILO), "Report of the Tripartite Meeting of Experts on Future ILO Activities in the Field of Migration," in *Protecting the Most Vulnerable of Today's Workers* (Geneva: ILO, 1997); (www.ilo.org/public/english/protection/migrant/papers/protvul.htm).

2. Tim Johnson, "Kin in U.S. Keep Salvador Afloat in Cash," *Miami Herald*, 28 January 1993.

3. Hossain Zillur Rahman and Mahabub Hossain, *Rethinking Rural Poverty, A case for Bangladesh* (Dhaka: Bangladesh Institute for Development Studies: 1992).

4. Poverty level data from World Bank, *World Development Report: 2000/2001: Attacking Poverty* (New York: Oxford University Press, 2000). Family size data from UN Department of Economic and Social Affairs, Population Division, *Population Prospects: The 2000 Revision* (New York: UN, 2001).

5. Alain Marcoux, *The Feminization of Poverty: Facts, Hypotheses and the Art of Advocacy* (UN Food and Agriculture Organization, October 1997) [cited 11 March 2001]; (www.fao.org/sd/WPdirect/WPan0015.htm).

Chapter Six

1. Alain Marcoux, *The Feminization of Poverty: Facts, Hypotheses and the Art of Advocacy* (UN Food and Agriculture Organization, October 1997) [cited 11 March 2001]; (www.fao.org/sd/WPdirect/WPan0015.htm).

Chapter Seven

1. UN Department of Economic and Social Affairs, Population Division, *Population Prospects: The 1998 Revision* (New York: UN, 1999).
2. Thousands of people living in the Nile delta suffer from renal failure and liver disease caused by pesticides and fertilizers that have leached in to the river. A majority of villages have access to clean water drinking water, but most households still lack indoor plumbing, and residents must use their canals, fed by polluted Nile water, for bathing and washing of clothes. See Peter Theroux, *The Imperiled Nile Delta*, National Geographic, January 1997.
3. Researchers with the National Institute on Drug Abuse find that thought there are wide fluctuations in the use of different types of drugs, the number of teenaged drug abusers overall has remained relatively stable since studies began in 1975, despite a large increase in prevention campaigns. Today over half (54 percent) of teenagers have tried an illicit drug at least once. See Lloyd Johnson, Patrick O'Malley, and Jerald Bachman, *Monitoring the Future: National Findings on Adolescent Drug Use—Key Findings, 2000* (Bethesda: National Institute on Drug Abuse, National Institutes of Health, 2001).

Chapter Eight

1. Janet N. Abramovitz, "Averting Unnatural Disasters," in *State of the World 2001*, ed. Lester R. Brown, Christopher Flavin, and Hilary French (New York: Worldwatch Institute Books/Norton, 2001), 123–124.
2. Ibid., 123.
3. Keith Schneider, "Legacy of the '93 Flood: Sand, Sand and More Sand," New York Times, 9 June 1994, A1.
4. Robert Engelman, et al., *People in the Balance: Population and Natural Resources at the Turn of the Millennium* (Washington, D.C.: Population Action International, 2000).
5. UNICEF, *Children and War: Report on the Psychological Impact of Violence on Children in Central America* (Costa Rica, 1990).

Chapter Nine

1. UN Population Division, *World Population Prospects: The 2000 Revision* (New York: UN Department of Economic and Social Affairs, 2001).
2. UN Population Fund, *The World at Six Billion* (New York: UN, 1999).
3. UNAIDS, *Report on the Global HIV/AIDS Epidemic: December 2000* (Geneva: Oxford University Press: 1997).
4. UN Office for Drug Control and Crime Prevention, *World Drug Report* (Vienna: Oxford University Press, 1997).
5. The National Institute on Drug Abuse and the National Institute on Alcohol and Alcoholism,

The Economic Costs of Alcohol and Drug Abuse in the United States (Bethesda: NIH, 1995).

6. Hind A. S. Khattab, *The Silent Endurance, Social Conditions of Women's Reproductive Health in Rural Egypt.* (Amman, Jordan: UNICEF and The Population Council, 1992).

7. Amnesty International, 2000; (www.amnesty.org/ailib/intcam/femgem/fgm9.htm). Also see *Female Genital Mutilation: A Call for World Mobilization* (New York, RAINBO: 1995).

8. P. Tjaden and N. Thoennes, "Prevalence, Incidence and Consequences of Violence Against Women: Findings from the National Violence Against Women Survey," *Research in Brief* (Washington, D.C.: National Institute of Justice, U.S. Department of Justice, November 1988).

9. Campaign for Our Children, from Child Trends, Inc.; (www.cfoc.org/freqmis.html). Also see Planned Parenthood Federation of America, *Fact Sheet*, February 2000; (www.plannedparenthood.org/library/TEEN-PREGNANCY/REDUCING.HTML).

10. UNICEF, "Facts for Life—Timing Births," January 1999; (www.unicef.org/statis/).

11. UNAIDS, *Report on the Global HIV/AIDS Epidemic: December 2000* (Geneva, 2000).

12. National Center for Health Statistics, U.S. Bureau of Health and Human Services, *Vital Statistics of the U.S.* (Washington, D.C.: USGPO, 1991).

Chapter Ten

1. *United Nations Statistical Division, The World's Women 2000* (New York: United Nations, 2000).

2. See www.foundation.novartis.com/brazilian_street-children.htm "Street Children in Brazil" Novartis Foundation for Sustainable Development, 2000.

3. Statistics and research on runaway youth in the United States can be found at http://207.142.102.10/news.asp, web site for the National Runaway Switchboard.

4. *United Nations Development Programme (UNDP), Human Development Report* (New York: UNDP, 2000), 136.

5. International Labour Organization (ILO), "Report of the Tripartite Meeting of Experts on Future ILO Activities in the Field of Migration," in *Protecting the Most Vulnerable of Today's Workers* (Geneva, ILO, April 1997). Available from http://www.ilo.org/public/english/protection/migrant/papers/protvul.htm.

6. International Labour Organization (ILO), "Nature and Extent of International Migration Labor," in *Protecting the Most Vulnerable of Today's Workers.*

7. *Population Estimates Program, Population Division, U.S. Census Bureau,* Washington, D.C., 1999.

Conclusion

1. "Vatican Reiterates Hardline Stance on Condoms for HIV Prevention," *Conscience, Winter 2000/2001.*

2. Douglas Kirby, *No Easy Answers: Research Findings on Programs to Reduce Teen Pregnancy* (Washington, D.C.: National Campaign to Prevent Teen Pregnancy, 1997).

3. Christopher Flavin, "Rich Planet, Poor Planet," in *State of the World 2001* (New York: Worldwatch Institute, 2001), 10.

4. According to a report by *TV-Free America*, "Parents spend 38.5 minutes per week

in meaningful conversation with their children, while children spend 1,680 minutes per week watching TV." Quoted in Pati Doten, "Tuning In and Tuning Out," *Boston Globe*, April 6, 1995, 5.

5. For an example of an attack on the UN from a right-wing think tank, see Patrick F. Fagan, *How UN Conventions on Women's and Children's Rights Undermine Family, Religion, and Sovereignty, Backgrounder No. 1407* (Washington, D.C.: The Heritage Foundation, February 2001). www.heritage.org/library/backgrounder/bg1407es.html.